Authorized Self-Study Guide

Implementing Cisco Unified Communications Manager, Part 2 (CIPT2)

Chris Olsen, CCSI, CCVP

Cisco Press

800 East 96th Street
Indianapolis, IN 46240 USA

Implementing Cisco Unified Communications Manager, Part 2 (CIPT2)

Chris Olsen

Copyright © 2009 Cisco Systems, Inc.

Published by:
Cisco Press
800 East 96th Street
Indianapolis, IN 46240 USA

Printed in the United States of America

First Printing October 2008

Library of Congress Control Number: 2008014863

ISBN-13: 978-1-58705-561-4

ISBN-10: 1-58705-561-9

Warning and Disclaimer

This book is designed to provide information about Cisco Unified Communications administration and to provide test preparation for the CIPT Part 2 exam, which is part of the CCVP certification. Every effort has been made to make this book as complete and accurate as possible, but no warranty or fitness is implied.

The information is provided on an "as is" basis. The author, Cisco Press, and Cisco Systems, Inc. shall have neither liability nor responsibility to any person or entity with respect to any loss or damages arising from the information contained in this book or from the use of the discs or programs that may accompany it.

The opinions expressed in this book belong to the author and are not necessarily those of Cisco Systems, Inc.

Trademark Acknowledgments

All terms mentioned in this book that are known to be trademarks or service marks have been appropriately capitalized. Cisco Press or Cisco Systems, Inc., cannot attest to the accuracy of this information. Use of a term in this book should not be regarded as affecting the validity of any trademark or service mark.

Corporate and Government Sales

The publisher offers excellent discounts on this book when ordered in quantity for bulk purchases or special sales, which may include electronic versions and/or custom covers and content particular to your business, training goals, marketing focus, and branding interests. For more information, please contact: **U.S. Corporate and Government Sales** 1-800-382-3419   corpsales@pearsontechgroup.com

For sales outside the United States, please contact: **International Sales**   international@pearsoned.com

Feedback Information

At Cisco Press, our goal is to create in-depth technical books of the highest quality and value. Each book is crafted with care and precision, undergoing rigorous development that involves the unique expertise of members from the professional technical community.

Readers' feedback is a natural continuation of this process. If you have any comments regarding how we could improve the quality of this book, or otherwise alter it to better suit your needs, you can contact us through e-mail at feedback@ciscopress.com. Please make sure to include the book title and ISBN in your message.

We greatly appreciate your assistance.

Publisher: Paul Boger

Associate Publisher: Dave Dusthimer

Cisco Representative: Anthony Wolfenden

Cisco Press Program Manager: Jeff Brady

Executive Editor: Brett Bartow

Managing Editor: Patrick Kanouse

Development Editor: Kimberley Debus

Project Editor: Seth Kerney

Copy Editor: Gayle Johnson

Technical Editors: James McInvaille, Joseph Parlas

Editorial Assistant: Vanessa Evans

Book Designer: Louisa Adair

Composition: Octal Publishing, Inc.

Indexer: Brad Herriman

Proofreader: Paula Lowell

Americas Headquarters
Cisco Systems, Inc.
170 West Tasman Drive
San Jose, CA 95134-1706
USA
www.cisco.com
Tel: 408 526-4000
800 553-NETS (6387)
Fax: 408 527-0883

Asia Pacific Headquarters
Cisco Systems, Inc.
168 Robinson Road
#28-01 Capital Tower
Singapore 068912
www.cisco.com
Tel: +65 6317 7777
Fax: +65 6317 7799

Europe Headquarters
Cisco Systems International BV
Haarlerbergpark
Haarlerbergweg 13-19
1101 CH Amsterdam
The Netherlands
www-europe.cisco.com
Tel: +31 0 800 020 0791
Fax: +31 0 20 357 1100

Cisco has more than 200 offices worldwide. Addresses, phone numbers, and fax numbers are listed on the Cisco Website at **www.cisco.com/go/offices**.

About the Author

Chris Olsen, CCSI and CCVP, has been an IT and telephony consultant for 12 years and has been a technical trainer for more than 17 years. He has taught more than 60 different courses in Cisco, Microsoft, and Novell and for the last four years has specialized in Cisco Unified Communications. Chris and his wife, Antonia, live in Chicago and Mapleton, Illinois. He can be reached at chrisolsen@earthlink.net.

About the Technical Reviewers

James McInvaille, CCSI No. 21904, is a Certified Cisco Systems Instructor for Cisco Learning Partner Global Knowledge Network, Inc., as well as a contract consultant. As an instructor, he is responsible for training students worldwide and consulting in the deployment of routing, switching, and IP telephony solutions. Previously, Mr. McInvaille was a Solutions Engineer for EDS for the Bank of America voice transformation project. Prior to EDS, Mr. McInvaille was a Senior Network Engineer for iPath Technologies, based in Reston, Virginia. In this role, he provided technical training and professional services to Service Providers and Enterprise users of Juniper Networks routing and security product line. During this time, Mr. McInvaille earned his Juniper Networks Certified Internet Professional (JNCIP #297) certification. Prior to iPath, Mr. McInvaille was the Lead Technical Consultant (LTC) for the Carolina's region of Dimension Data, NA. As an LTC, his responsibilities included the support and guidance of five engineers and technicians involved in the consultation, implementation, delivery, and training of VoIP and IP telephony solutions, as well as high-level routing and switching designs. In his spare time, Mr. McInvaille and his beautiful wife Lupe enjoy riding their Harley Davidson near their home in Kershaw, South Carolina.

Joe Parlas, CCSI No. 21904, has been an instructor for more than eight years, concentrating specifically on Cisco Voice technologies. He has consulted for numerous Fortune 500 and Fortune 1000 companies, such as Sweetheart Cup, Inc., Black and Decker, and McCormick Spice. He has also acted as a senior consultant with Symphony Health Services, Inc. in various capacities. Joe holds the CCNP, CCNA, A+, and MCSE: Messaging 2003 industry certifications and primarily teaches for Global Knowledge Network, Inc. as a contract instructor. Joe recently relocated his company, Parlas Enterprises, to the San Diego area, where he lives with his wife Parvin Shaybany.

Dedication

This book is dedicated to my beautiful wife, Antonia. Her unending support, love, and compassion are always a driving force in my life.

Acknowledgments

I would like to thank the entire team at Global Knowledge for their excellent support and creation of a high-quality learning environment. Thanks also to the staff at Cisco Press for their excellent support and advice.

Contents at a Glance

Contents

Icons Used in This Book

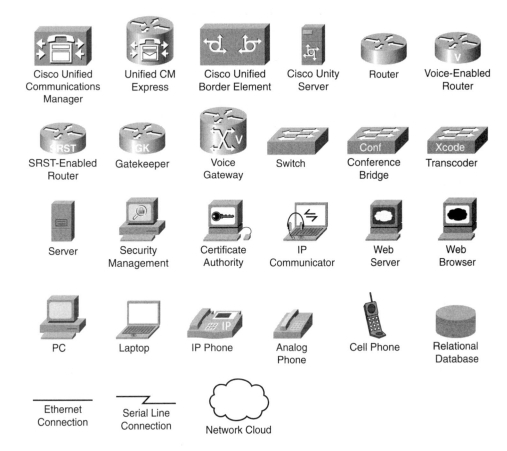

Cisco Unified Communications Manager

Unified CM Express

Cisco Unified Border Element

Cisco Unity Server

Router

Voice-Enabled Router

SRST-Enabled Router

Gatekeeper

Voice Gateway

Switch

Conference Bridge

Transcoder

Server

Security Management

Certificate Authority

IP Communicator

Web Server

Web Browser

PC

Laptop

IP Phone

Analog Phone

Cell Phone

Relational Database

Ethernet Connection

Serial Line Connection

Network Cloud

Command Syntax Conventions

The conventions used to present command syntax in this book are the same conventions used in the IOS Command Reference. The Command Reference describes these conventions as follows:

- **Boldface** indicates commands and keywords that are entered literally as shown. In actual configuration examples and output (not general command syntax), boldface indicates commands that are manually input by the user (such as a **show** command).

- *Italic* indicates arguments for which you supply actual values.

- Vertical bars (|) separate alternative, mutually exclusive elements.

- Square brackets ([ ]) indicate an optional element.

- Braces ({ }) indicate a required choice.

- Braces within brackets ([{ }]) indicate a required choice within an optional element.

Foreword

Cisco certification self-study guides are excellent self-study resources for networking professionals to maintain and increase their internetworking skills and to prepare for Cisco Career Certification exams. Cisco Career Certifications are recognized worldwide and provide valuable, measurable rewards to networking professionals and their employers.

Cisco Press exam certification guides and preparation materials offer exceptional—and flexible—access to the knowledge and information required to stay current in one's field of expertise, or to gain new skills. Whether used to increase internetworking skills or as a supplement to a formal certification preparation course, these materials offer networking professionals the information and knowledge they need to perform on-the-job tasks proficiently.

Developed in conjunction with the Cisco certifications and training team, Cisco Press books are the only self-study books authorized by Cisco. They offer students a series of exam practice tools and resource materials to help ensure that learners fully grasp the concepts and information presented.

Additional authorized Cisco instructor-led courses, e-learning, labs, and simulations are available exclusively from Cisco Learning Solutions Partners worldwide. To learn more, visit http://www.cisco.com/go/training.

I hope you will find this guide to be an essential part of your exam preparation and professional development, as well as a valuable addition to your personal library.

Drew Rosen
Manager, Learning and Development
Learning@Cisco
September 2008

Introduction

Professional certifications have been an important part of the computing industry for many years and will continue to become more important. Many reasons exist for these certifications, but the most popularly cited reason is that of credibility. All other considerations held equal, a certified employee/consultant/job candidate is considered more valuable than one who is not.

Goals and Methods

The most important goal of this book is to provide you with knowledge and skills in Unified Communications, deploying the Cisco Unified Communications Manager product. Another goal of this book is to help you with the Cisco IP Telephony (CIPT) Part 2 exam, which is part of the Cisco Certified Voice Professional (CCVP) certification. The methods used in this book are designed to be helpful in both your job and the CCVP Cisco IP Telephony exam. This book provides questions at the end of each chapter to reinforce the chapter content. Additional test preparation software from companies such as http://www.selftestsoftware.com will give you additional test preparation questions to arm you for exam success.

The organization of this book will help you discover the exam topics that you need to review in more depth, help you fully understand and remember those details, and help you test the knowledge you have retained on those topics. This book does not try to help you pass by memorization, but helps you truly learn and understand the topics. The Cisco IP Telephony Part 2 exam is one of the foundation topics in the CCVP certification. The knowledge contained in this book is vitally important for you to consider yourself a truly skilled Unified Communications (UC) engineer. The book aims to help you pass the Cisco IP Telephony exam by using the following methods:

- Helping you discover which test topics you have not mastered

- Providing explanations and information to fill in your knowledge gaps

- Providing practice exercises on the topics and the testing process via test questions at the end of each chapter

Who Should Read This Book?

This book is designed to be both a general Cisco Unified Communications Manager book and a certification preparation book. This book is intended to provide you with the knowledge required to pass the CCVP Cisco IP Telephony exam for CIPT Part 2.

Why should you want to pass the CCVP Cisco IP Telephony exam? The second CIPT test is one of the milestones toward getting the CCVP certification. The CCVP could mean a raise, promotion, new job, challenge, success, or recognition, but ultimately you determine what it means to you. Certifications demonstrate that you are serious about continuing the learning process and professional development. In technology, it is impossible to stay at the same level when the technology all around you is advancing. Engineers must continually retrain themselves, or they find themselves with out-of-date commodity-based skill sets.

Strategies for Exam Preparation

The strategy you use for exam preparation might be different than strategies used by others. It will be based on skills, knowledge, experience, and finding the recipe that works best for you. If you have attended the CIPT course, you might take a different approach than someone who learned Cisco Unified Communications Manager on the job. Regardless of the strategy you use or your background, this book is designed to help you get to the point where you can pass the exam. Cisco exams are quite thorough, so don't skip any chapters.

How This Book Is Organized

The book covers the following topics:

- **Chapter 1, "Identifying Issues in a Multisite Deployment,"** sets the stage for this book by identifying all the relevant challenges in multisite deployments requiring Unified Communications solutions.

- **Chapter 2, "Identifying Multisite Deployment Solutions,"** is an overview of the solutions to the challenges identified in Chapter 1 that are described in this book.

- **Chapter 3, "Implementing Multisite Connections,"** provides the steps to configure Media Gateway Control Protocol (MGCP) and H.323 gateways as well as Session Initiation Protocol (SIP) and intercluster trunks to function with Cisco Unified Communications Manager (CUCM).

- **Chapter 4, "Implementing a Dial Plan for Multisite Deployments,"** provides a dial plan solution and addresses toll bypass, tail-end hop-off (TEHO), and digit manipulation techniques in a multisite CUCM deployment.

- **Chapter 5, "Examining Remote-Site Redundancy Options,"** provides the foundation for maintaining redundancy at a remote site in the event of an IP WAN failure by exploring the options for implementing Survivable Remote Site Telephony (SRST) and MGCP fallback.

- **Chapter 6, "Implementing Cisco Unified SRST and MGCP Fallback,"** presents the configurations to implement SRST and MGCP fallback, along with implementing a gateway dial plan and voice features in the SRST router.

- **Chapter 7, "Implementing Cisco Unified Communications Manager Express in SRST Mode,"** discusses the configuration approaches of Cisco Unified Communications Manager Express (CUCME) to support SRST fallback.

- **Chapter 8, "Implementing Bandwidth Management,"** shows you how to implement bandwidth management with Call Admission Control (CAC) to ensure a high level of audio quality for voice calls over IP WAN links by preventing oversubscription.

- **Chapter 9, "Implementing Call Admission Control,"** describes the methods of implementing CAC in gatekeepers and CUCM and explores the benefits of Resource Reservation Protocol (RSVP) and Automated Alternate Routing (AAR) in CUCM.

- **Chapter 10, "Implementing Call Applications on Cisco IOS Gateways,"** describes Toolkit Command Language (Tcl) and VoiceXML to implement call applications on gateways.

- **Chapter 11, "Implementing Device Mobility,"** describes challenges for users traveling between sites and provides the solution of mobility.

- **Chapter 12, "Implementing Extension Mobility,"** describes the concept of Extension Mobility and gives the procedure for implementing Extension Mobility for users traveling to different sites.

- **Chapter 13, "Implementing Cisco Unified Mobility,"** gives the procedure for implementing both Mobile Connect and Mobile Voice Application of Unified Mobility in CUCM and a gateway.

- **Chapter 14, "Understanding Cryptographic Fundamentals and PKI,"** describes the required fundamental principles and concepts of cryptography that are relevant to implementing secure voice implementations in a Cisco Unified Communications installation.

- **Chapter 15, "Understanding Native CUCM Security Features and CUCM PKI,"** helps you understand the security protocols of IPsec, Transport Layer Security (TLS), SRTP, and SIP digest and the methods to implement secure voice in a CUCM installation.

- **Chapter 16, "Implementing Security in CUCM,"** demonstrates how to further implement security in a CUCM installation by securing IP Phones for their configurations, signaling, and secure media for audio and conference calls.

CHAPTER 1

Identifying Issues in a Multisite Deployment

Deploying Cisco Unified Communications Manager in a multisite environment has considerations that pertain only to multisite deployments. Deploying Cisco Unified Communications solutions between multiple sites requires an appropriate dial plan, enough bandwidth between the sites, implementing quality of service (QoS), and a design that can survive IP WAN failures. This chapter identifies the issues that can arise in a multisite Cisco Unified Communications Manager deployment.

Chapter Objectives

Upon completing this chapter, you will be able to explain issues pertaining to multisite deployment and relate those issues to multisite connection options. You will be able to meet these objectives:

- Describe issues pertaining to multisite deployments

- Describe quality issues in multisite deployments

- Describe issues with bandwidth in multisite deployments

- Describe availability issues in multisite deployments

- Describe dial plan issues in multisite deployments

- Describe Network Address Translation (NAT) and security issues in multisite deployments

Multisite Deployment Challenge Overview

In a multisite deployment, some of the challenges that can arise include the following:

- **Quality issues:** Real-time communications of voice and video must be prioritized over a packet-switching network. All traffic is treated equally by default in routers and switches. Voice and video are delay-sensitive packets that need to be given priority to avoid delay and jitter (variable delay), which would result in decreased voice quality.

■ **Bandwidth issues:** Cisco Unified Communications (Cisco UC) can include voice and video streams, signaling traffic, management traffic, and application traffic such as rich media conferencing. The additional bandwidth that is required when deploying a Cisco Unified Communications solution has to be calculated and provisioned for to ensure that data applications and Cisco Unified Communications applications do not overload the available bandwidth. Bandwidth reservations can be made to applications through QoS deployment.

■ **Availability issues:** When deploying Cisco Unified Communications Manager (CUCM) with centralized call processing, IP Phones register with CUCM over the IP LAN and potentially over the WAN. If gateways in remote sites are using Media Gateway Control Protocol (MGCP) as a signaling protocol, they also depend on the availability of CUCM acting as an MGCP call agent. It is important to implement fallback solutions for IP Phones and gateways in scenarios in which the connection to the CUCM servers is broken because of IP WAN failure. Fallback solutions also apply to H.323 gateways but are already created with H.323 dial peers in a proper H.323 gateway configuration.

NOTE   Cisco Unified Communications Manager (CUCM) used to be called Cisco CallManager (CCM) .

■ **Dial plan issues:** Directory numbers (DN) can overlap across multiple sites. Overlapping dial plans and nonconsecutive numbers can be solved by designing a robust multisite dial plan. Avoid overlapping numbers across sites whenever possible for an easier design.

■ **NAT and security issues:** The use of private IP addresses within an enterprise IP network is very common. Internet Telephony Service Providers (ITSP) require unique public IP addresses to route IP Phone calls. The private IP addresses within the enterprise have to be translated into public IP addresses. Public IP addresses make the IP Phones visible from the Internet and therefore subject to attacks.

NOTE   The challenge of NAT and security is *not limited to multisite deployments*. For example, for Cisco Attendant Console (AC), the line-state and call-forwarding status of the primary line of each user is presented with each record entry. When you use CUCM and Attendant Console across Network Address Translation (NAT) interfaces, or when a firewall is between them, TCP traffic works correctly with the NAT transversal. Therefore, most of the AC functionality works. However, the problem is with the Attendant Console line status, which uses User Datagram Protocol (UDP). Also, the UDP traffic from the CUCM servers cannot pass through the NAT interfaces. Therefore, the needed UDP ports must be opened through the firewall.

Quality Challenges

IP networks were not originally designed to carry real-time traffic; instead, they were designed for resiliency and fault tolerance. Each packet is processed separately in an IP network, sometimes causing different packets in a communications stream to take different paths to the destination. The different paths in the network may have a different amount of packet loss, delay, and delay variation (jitter) because of bandwidth, distance, and congestion differences. The destination must be able to receive packets out of order and resequence these packets. This challenge is solved by the use of Real-Time Transport Protocol (RTP) sequence numbers and traffic resequencing. When possible, it is best to not rely solely on these RTP mechanisms. Proper network design, using Cisco router Cisco Express Forwarding (CEF) switch cache technology, performs per-destination load sharing by default. Per-destination load sharing is not a perfect load-balancing paradigm, but it ensures that each IP flow (voice call) takes the same path.

Bandwidth is shared by multiple users and applications, whereas the amount of bandwidth required for an individual IP flow varies significantly during short lapses of time. Most data applications are very bursty, whereas Cisco real-time audio communications with RTP use the same continuous-bandwidth stream. The bandwidth available for any application, including CUCM and voice-bearer traffic, is unpredictable. During peak periods, packets need to be buffered in queues waiting to be processed because of network congestion. Queuing is a term that anyone who has ever experienced air flight is familiar with. When you arrive at the airport, you must get in a line (queue), because the number of ticket agents (bandwidth) available to check you in is less than the flow of traffic arriving at the ticket counters (incoming IP traffic). If congestion occurs for too long, the queue (packet buffers) gets filled up, and passengers are annoyed (packets are dropped). Higher queuing delays and packet drops are more likely on highly loaded, slow-speed links such as WAN links used between sites in a multisite environment. Quality challenges are common on these types of links, and you need to handle them by implementing QoS. Without the use of QoS, voice packets experience delay, jitter, and packet loss, impacting voice quality. It is critical to properly configure Cisco QoS mechanisms end to end throughout the network for proper audio and video performance.

During peak periods, packets cannot be sent immediately because of interface congestion. Instead, the packets are temporarily stored in a queue, waiting to be processed. The amount of time the packet waits in the queue, called the queuing delay, can vary greatly based on network conditions and traffic arrival rates. If the queue is full, newly received packets cannot be buffered anymore and get dropped (tail drop). Figure 1-1 illustrates tail drop. Packets are processed on a first in, first out (FIFO) model in the hardware queue of all router interfaces. Voice conversations are predictable and constant (sampling is every 20 milliseconds by default), but data applications are bursty and greedy. Voice therefore is subject to degradation of quality because of delay, jitter, and packet loss.

Figure 1-1   *Tail Drop*

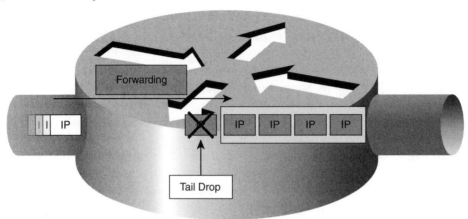

"IP" refers to any type of Internet Protocol (IP) packet
in the output queue for an interface.

Bandwidth Challenges

Each site in a multisite deployment usually is interconnected by an IP WAN, or occasionally
by a metropolitan-area network (MAN) such as Metro Ethernet. Bandwidth on WAN links
is limited and relatively expensive. The goal is to use the available bandwidth as efficiently
as possible. Unnecessary traffic should be removed from the IP WAN links through content
filtering, firewalls, and access control lists (ACL). IP WAN acceleration methods for
bandwidth optimization should be considered as well. Any period of congestion could
result in service degradation unless QoS is deployed throughout the network.

Voice streams are constant and predictable for Cisco audio packets. Typically, the G.729
codec is used across the WAN to best use bandwidth. As a comparison, the G.711 audio
codec requires 64 kbps, whereas packetizing the G.711 voice sample in an IP/UDP/RTP
header every 20 ms requires 16 kbps plus the Layer 2 header overhead.

Voice is sampled every 20 ms, resulting in 50 packets per second (pps). The IP header is
20 bytes, whereas the UDP header is 8 bytes, and the RTP header is 12 bytes. The 40 bytes
of header information must be converted to bits to figure out the packet rate of the overhead.
Because a byte has 8 bits, 40 bytes * 8 bits in a byte = 320 bits. The 320 bits are sent
50 times per second based on the 20-ms rate (1 millisecond is 1/1000 of a second, and
20/1000 = .02). So:

.02 * 50 = 1 second
320 bits * 50 = 16,000 bits/sec, or 16 kbps

> **NOTE**   This calculation does not take Layer 2 encapsulation into consideration. You can
> find more information by reading the QoS Solution Reference Network Design (SRND)
> (http://www.cisco.com/go/srnd) or *Cisco QOS Exam Certification Guide*, Second
> Edition (Cisco Press, 2004).

Voice packets are benign compared to the bandwidth consumed by data applications. Data
applications can fill the entire maximum transmission unit (MTU) of an Ethernet frame
(1518 bytes or 9216 bytes if jumbo Ethernet frames have been enabled). In comparison to
data application packets, voice packets are very small (60 bytes for G.729 and 200 bytes for
G.711 with the default 20-ms sampling rate).

In Figure 1-2, a conference bridge has been deployed at the main site. No conference bridge
exists at the remote site. If three IP Phones at a remote site join a conference, their RTP
streams are sent across the WAN to the conference bridge. The conference bridge, whether
using software or hardware resources, mixes the received audio streams and then sends
back three unique unicast audio streams to the IP Phones over the IP WAN. The conference
bridge removes the receiver's voice from his or her unique RTP stream so that the user does
not experience echo because of the delay of traversing the WAN link and mixing RTP audio
streams in the conference bridge.

Figure 1-2   *Resource Challenges*

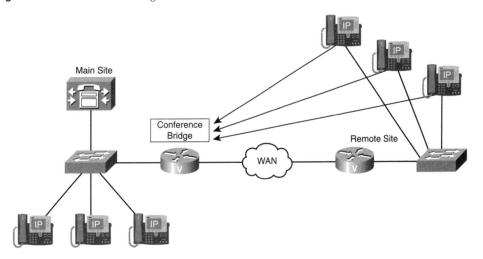

Centralized conference resources cause bandwidth, delay, and capacity challenges in the
voice network. Each G.711 RTP stream requires 80 kbps (plus the Layer 2 overhead),
resulting in 240 kbps of IP WAN bandwidth consumption by this voice conference. If the
conference bridge were not located on the other side of the IP WAN, this traffic would not

need to traverse the WAN link, resulting in less delay and bandwidth consumption. If the remote site had a CUCM region configuration that resulted in calls with the G.729 codec back to the main site, the software conferencing resources of CUCM would not be able to mix the audio conversations. Hardware conferencing or hardware transcoder media resources in a voice gateway are required to accommodate G.729 audio conferencing. Local hardware conference resources would remove this need. All centrally located media resources (Music On Hold [MOH], annunciator, conference bridges, videoconferencing, and media termination points) suffer similar bandwidth, delay, and resource exhaustion challenges.

Availability Challenges

When deploying CUCM in multisite environments, centralized CUCM-based services are accessed over the IP WAN. Affected services include the following:

- **Signaling in CUCM multisite deployments with centralized call processing:** Remote Cisco IP Phones register with a centralized CUCM server. Remote MGCP gateways are controlled by a centralized CUCM server that acts as an MGCP call agent.

- **Signaling in CUCM multisite deployments with distributed call processing:** In such environments, sites are connected via H.323 (non-gatekeeper-controlled, gatekeeper-controlled, or H.225) or Session Initiation Protocol (SIP) trunks.

- **Media exchange:** RTP streams between endpoints located at different sites.

- **Other services:** These include Cisco IP Phone Extensible Markup Language (XML) services and access to applications such as attendant console, CUCM Assistant, and others.

Figure 1-3 shows a Unified Communications network in which the main site is connected to a remote site through a centralized call-processing environment. The main site is also connected to a remote cluster through an intercluster trunk (ICT) representing a distributed call processing environment. The combination of both centralized and distributed call processing represents a hybrid call-processing model in which small sites use the CUCM resources of the main site, but large remote offices have their own CUCM cluster. On the bottom left of Figure 1-3 is a SIP trunk, typically over a Metro Ethernet connection to an Internet Telephony Service Provider (ITSP). The benefit of the SIP trunk is that the ITSP provides the gateways to the PSTN instead of your providing gateways at the main site.

Figure 1-3 *Availability Challenges*

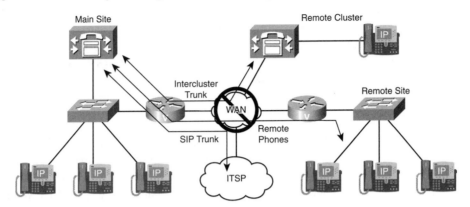

An IP WAN outage in Figure 1-3 will cause an outage of call-processing services for the remote site connected in a centralized fashion. The remote cluster will not suffer a call-processing outage, but the remote cluster will not be able to dial the main site over the IP WAN during the outage. Mission-critical voice applications (voice mail, interactive voice response [IVR], and so on) located at the main site will be unavailable to any of the other sites during the WAN outage.

If the ITSP is using the same links that allow IP WAN connectivity, all calls to and from the public switched telephone network (PSTN) will also be unavailable.

> **NOTE**   A deployment like the one shown in Figure 1-3 is considered badly designed because of the lack of IP WAN and PSTN backup.

Dial Plan Challenges

In a multisite deployment, with a single or multiple CUCM clusters, dial plan design requires the consideration of several issues that do not exist in single-site deployments:

- **Overlapping numbers:** Users located at different sites can have the same directory numbers assigned. Because directory numbers usually are unique only within a site, a multisite deployment requires a solution for overlapping numbers.

■ **Nonconsecutive numbers:** Contiguous ranges of numbers are important to summarize call-routing information, analogous to contiguous IP address ranges for route summarization. Such blocks can be represented by one or a few entries in a call-routing table, such as route patterns, dial peer destination patterns, and voice translation rules, which keep the routing table short and simple. If each endpoint requires its own entry in the call-routing table, the table gets too big, lots of memory is required, and lookups take more time. Therefore, nonconsecutive numbers at any site are not optimal for efficient call routing.

■ **Variable-length numbering:** Some countries, such as the U.S. and Canada, have fixed-length numbering plans for PSTN numbers. Others, such as Mexico and England, have variable-length numbering plans. A problem with variable-length numbers is that the complete length of the number dialed can be determined only by the CUCM route plan by waiting for the interdigit timeout. Waiting for the interdigit timeout, known as the T.302 timer, adds to the post-dial delay, which may annoy users.

■ **Direct inward dialing (DID) ranges and E.164 addressing:** When considering integration with the PSTN, internally used directory numbers have to be related to external PSTN numbers (E.164 addressing). Depending on the numbering plan (fixed or variable) and services provided by the PSTN, the following solutions are common:

—**Each internal directory number relates to a fixed-length PSTN number:** In this case, each internal directory number has its own dedicated PSTN number. The directory number can, but does not have to, match the least-significant digits of the PSTN number. In countries with a fixed numbering plan, such as the North American Numbering Plan (NANP), this usually means that the four-digit office codes are used as internal directory numbers. If these are not unique, digits of office codes or administratively assigned site codes might be added, resulting in five or more digits being used for internal directory numbers.

Another solution is to not reuse any digits of the PSTN number but to simply map each internally used directory number to any PSTN number assigned to the company. In this case, the internal and external numbers do not have anything in common. If the internally used directory number matches the least-significant digits of its corresponding PSTN number, significant digits can be set at the gateway or trunk. Also, general external phone number masks, transformation masks, or prefixes can be configured. This is true because all internal directory numbers are changed to fully qualified PSTN numbers in the same way. Another example is if the internal directory number is composed of parts of the PSTN number and administratively assigned digits such as site codes plus PSTN station codes, or different ranges, such as PSTN station codes 4100 to 4180 that map to directory numbers 1100 to 1180, or totally independent mappings of internal directory numbers to PSTN numbers. In that case, one or more translation rules have to be used for incoming calls, and one or more calling party transformation rules, transformation masks, external phone number masks, or prefixes have to be configured.

—**No DID support in fixed-length numbering plans:** To avoid the requirement of one PSTN number per internal directory number when using a fixed-length numbering plan, it is common to disallow DID to an extension. Instead, the PSTN trunk has a single number, and all PSTN calls routed to that number are sent to an attendant, auto-attendant, receptionist, or secretary. From there, the calls are *transferred* to the appropriate internal extension.

—**Internal directory numbers are part of a variable-length number:** In countries with variable-length numbering plans, a typically shorter "subscriber" number is assigned to the PSTN trunk, but the PSTN routes all calls *starting* with this number to the trunk. The caller can add digits to identify the extension. There is no fixed number of additional digits or total digits. However, there is a maximum, usually 32 digits, which provides the freedom to select the length of directory numbers. This maximum length can be less. For example, in E.164 the maximum number is 15 digits, not including the country code. A caller simply adds the appropriate extension to the company's (short) PSTN number when placing a call to a specific user. If only the short PSTN number without an extension is dialed, the call is routed to an attendant within the company. Residential PSTN numbers are usually longer and do not allow additional digits to be added; the feature just described is available only on trunks.

■ **Type of Number (TON) in ISDN**: The calling number (the Automatic Number Identification [ANI]) of calls being received from the PSTN can be represented in different ways:

—As a seven-digit subscriber number

—As a ten-digit number, including the area code

—In international format with the country code in front of the area code

To standardize the ANI for all calls, the format that is used must be known, and the number has to be transformed accordingly.

■ **Optimized call routing**: Having an IP WAN between sites with PSTN access at all sites allows PSTN toll bypass by sending calls between sites over the IP WAN instead of using the PSTN. In such scenarios, the PSTN should be used as a backup path only in case of WAN failure. Another solution, which extends the idea of toll bypass and can potentially reduce toll charges, is to also use the IP WAN for PSTN calls. With tail-end hop-off (TEHO), the IP WAN is used as much as possible, and the gateway that is closest to the dialed PSTN destination is used for the PSTN breakout.

NOTE   Any two-way phone call has two phone numbers: the calling number, or Automatic Number Identification (ANI), and the called number, or Dialed Number Identification Service (DNIS). Any two-way call goes from the ANI to the DNIS. Digit manipulation is the process of changing the ANI and/or the DNIS to any other number.

Overlapping and Nonconsecutive Numbers

In Figure 1-4, Cisco IP Phones at the main site use directory numbers 1001 to 1099, 2000 to 2157, and 2365 to 2999. At the remote site, 1001 to 1099 and 2158 to 2364 are used. These directory numbers have two issues. First, 1001 to 1099 overlap; these directory numbers exist at both sites, so they are not unique throughout the complete deployment. This causes a problem: If a user in the remote site dialed only the four digits 1001, which phone would ring? This issue of overlapping dial plans needs to be addressed by digit manipulation. In addition, the nonconsecutive use of the range 2000 to 2999 (with some duplicate numbers at the two sites) would require a significant number of additional entries in call-routing tables because the ranges can hardly be summarized by one (or a few) entries.

Figure 1-4   *Dial Plan Challenges: Overlapping and Nonconsecutive Numbers*

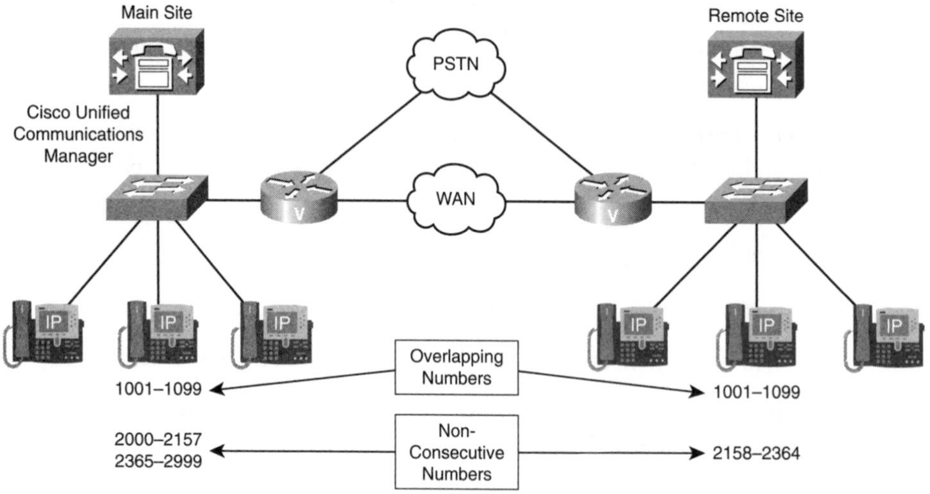

NOTE   The solutions to the problems listed in this chapter are discussed in more detail in the next chapter.

Fixed Versus Variable-Length Numbering Plans

A fixed numbering plan features fixed-length area codes and local numbers. An open numbering plan features variance in length of area code or local number, or both, within the country.

Table 1-1 contrasts the NANP and a variable-length numbering plan—Germany's numbering plan in this example.

Table 1-1   *Fixed Versus Variable-Length Numbering Plans*

Component	Description	Fixed Numbering Plan (NANP)	Variable-Length Numbering Plan (Germany)
Country code	A code of one to three digits is used to reach the particular telephone system for each nation or special service. Obtain the E.164 standard from http://itu.org to see all international country codes.	1	49
Area code	Used within many nations to route calls to a particular city, region, or special service. Depending on the nation or region, it may also be called a numbering plan area, sub-scriber trunk dialing code, national destination code, or routing code.	Three digits	Three to five digits
Subscriber number	Represents the specific telephone number to be dialed, but it does not include the country code, area code (if applicable), international prefix, or trunk prefix.	Three-digit exchange code plus a four-digit station code	Three or more digits

continues

Table 1-1 *Fixed Versus Variable-Length Numbering Plans (Continued)*

Component	Description	Fixed Numbering Plan (NANP)	Variable-Length Numbering Plan (Germany)
Trunk prefix	The initial digits to be dialed in a domestic call, before the area code and the subscriber number.	1	0
Access code	A number that is traditionally dialed first "to get out to the PSTN," used in PBXs and VoIP systems.	9	0
International prefix	The code dialed before an international number (country code, area code if any, and then subscriber number).	011	00 or + (+ is used by cell phones)

Examples:

- **Within the U.S.**: 9-1-408-555-1234 or 1-555-1234 (within the same area code)

- **U.S. to Germany**: 9-011-49-404-132670

- **Within Germany**: 0-0-404-132670 or 0-132670 (within the same area code)

- **Germany to the U.S.**: 0-00-1-408-555-1234 (Note: the 1 in 00-1-408 is the U.S. country code, not the trunk prefix.)

The NANP PSTN number is 408-555-1234, DID is not used, and all calls placed to the main site are handled by an attendant. There is a remote site in Germany with the E.164 PSTN number +49 404 13267. Four-digit extensions are used at the German location, and DID is allowed because digits can be added to the PSTN number. When calling the German office attendant (not knowing a specific extension), U.S. users would dial 9-011-49-404-13267. Note how the + is replaced by the international prefix 011 and the access code 9. If the phone with extension 1001 should be called directly, 9-011-49-404-13267-1001 has to be dialed.

NOTE In the examples shown following Table 1-1, dialing out from the U.S. illustrates the common practice of dialing 9 first as an access code to dial out. This use is common but optional in a dial plan. However, if the access code is used, the 9 must be stripped before reaching the PSTN, whereas the other dialed prefixes must be sent to the PSTN for proper call routing.

Variable-Length Numbering, E.164 Addressing, and DID

Figure 1-5 illustrates an example in which the main site with CUCM resides in the U.S. and a remote site without CUCM resides in Germany. The NANP PSTN number in the U.S. is 408-555-1234. Note that DID is not used, because all calls placed to the main site are handled by an attendant. A remote site in Germany has PSTN number +49 404 13267. Four-digit extensions are used at the German location, and DID is allowed because digits can be added to the PSTN number. When calling the German office attendant (not knowing a specific extension), U.S. users would dial 9-011-49-404-13267. If the phone with extension 1001 should be called directly, 9-011-49-404-13267-1001 has to be dialed.

Figure 1-5   *Variable-Length Numbering, E.164 Addressing, and DID*

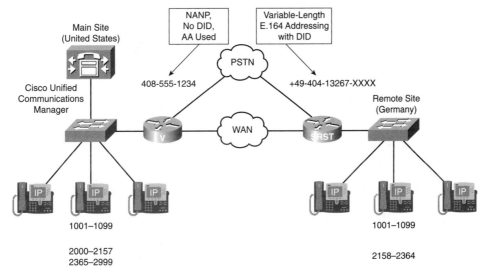

The logic of routing calls by CUCM over the WAN or through the PSTN is appropriately transparent to the phone user.

Optimized Call Routing and PSTN Backup

There are two ways to save costs for PSTN calls in a multisite deployment:

- **Toll bypass:** Calls between sites within an organization that use the IP WAN instead of the PSTN. The PSTN is used for intersite calls only if calls over the IP WAN are not possible—either because of a WAN failure or because the call is not admitted by Call Admission Control (CAC).

■   **Tail-end hop-off (TEHO):** Extends the concept of toll bypass by also using the IP
    WAN for calls to the remote destinations in the PSTN. With TEHO, the IP WAN is used
    as much as possible, and PSTN breakout occurs at the gateway that is located closest
    to the dialed PSTN destination. Local PSTN breakout is used as a backup in case of IP
    WAN or CAC.

CAUTION   Some countries do not allow the use of TEHO or toll bypass because it is
illegal to bypass their international tariff collections, which would deprive their operators
of international inbound revenues. When implementing either, ensure that the deployment
complies with legal requirements of that country.

In the example shown in Figure 1-6, a call from Chicago to San Jose would be routed
as follows:

1.   The Chicago CUCM Express user dials 9-1-408-555-6666, a PSTN phone located
     in San Jose.

2.   The call is routed from Chicago CUCM Express Router to the San Jose CUCM cluster
     over the IP WAN with either SIP or H.323.

3.   The San Jose CUCM routes the call to the San Jose gateway, which breaks out to the
     PSTN with what now becomes a local inexpensive call to the San Jose PSTN.

4.   The San Jose PSTN Central Office routes the call, and the phone rings.

Figure 1-6   *Tail-End Hop-Off (TEHO) Example*

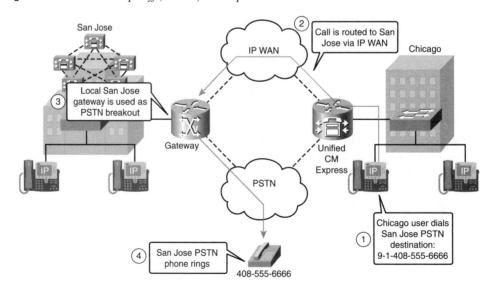

If the WAN were unavailable for any reason before the call, the Chicago Gateway would have to be properly configured to route the call with the appropriate digit manipulation through the PSTN at a potentially higher toll cost to the San Jose PSTN phone.

NAT and Security Issues

In single-site deployments, CUCM servers and IP Phones usually use private IP addresses because there is no need to communicate with the outside IP world. NAT is not configured for the phone subnets, and attacks from the outside are impossible.

In multisite deployments, however, IP Security (IPsec) virtual private network (VPN) tunnels can be used between sites. The VPN tunnels allow only intersite communication; access to the protected internal networks is not possible from the outside—only from the other site through the tunnel. Therefore, attacks from the outside are blocked at the gateway. To configure IPsec VPNs, the VPN tunnel must be configured to terminate on the two gateways in the different sites. Sometimes this is not possible; for instance, the two sites may be under different administration, or perhaps security policies do not allow the configuration of IPsec VPNs.

In such a case, or when connecting to a public service such as an ITSP, NAT has to be configured for CUCM servers and IP Phones. Cisco calls this Hosted NAT Traversal for Session Border Controllers.

In Figure 1-7, Company A and Company B both use IP network 10.0.0.0/8 internally. To communicate over the Internet, the private addresses are translated into public IP addresses. Company A uses public IP network A, and Company B uses public IP network B. All CUCM servers and IP Phones can be reached from the Internet and communicate with each other.

As soon as CUCM servers and IP Phones can be reached with public IP addresses, they are subject to attacks from the outside world, introducing potential security issues.

Figure 1-7   *NAT and Security Issues*

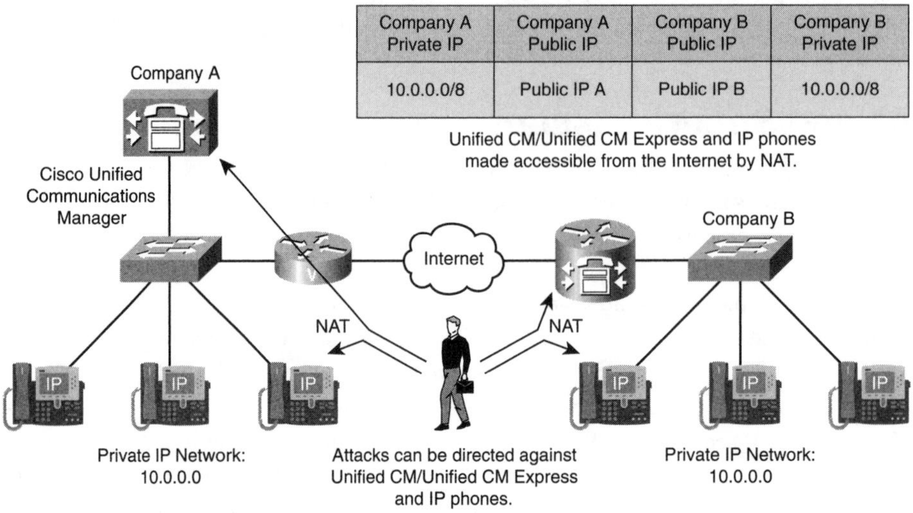

Company A Private IP	Company A Public IP	Company B Public IP	Company B Private IP
10.0.0.0/8	Public IP A	Public IP B	10.0.0.0/8

Unified CM/Unified CM Express and IP phones
made accessible from the Internet by NAT.

Company A

Cisco Unified
Communications
Manager

Internet

Company B

NAT   NAT

Private IP Network:
10.0.0.0

Attacks can be directed against
Unified CM/Unified CM Express
and IP phones.

Private IP Network:
10.0.0.0

Chapter Summary

The following key points were discussed in this chapter:

- Multisite deployment introduces issues of quality, bandwidth, availability, dial plan, and NAT and security.

- During congestion, packets have to be buffered, or they can get dropped.

- Bandwidth in the IP WAN is limited and should be used as efficiently as possible.

- A multisite deployment has several services that depend on the availability of the IP WAN.

- A multisite dial plan has to address overlapping and nonconsecutive numbers, variable-length numbering plans, DID ranges, and ISDN TON and should minimize PSTN costs.

- When CUCM servers and IP Phones need to be exposed to the outside, they can be subject to attacks from the Internet.

References

For additional information, refer to these resources:

- Cisco Unified Communications Solution Reference Network Design (SRND) based on CUCM release 6.x, June 2007

- CUCM Administration Guide, release 6.0 (1)

Review Questions

Use these questions to review what you've learned in this chapter. The answers appear in Appendix A, "Answers to Chapter Review Questions."

1. Which of the following best describes DID?

    a. E.164 international dialing

    b. External dialing from an IP Phone to the PSTN

    c. VoIP security for phone dialing

    d. The ability of an outside user to directly dial into an internal phone

2. Which of the following statements is the least accurate about IP networks?

    a. IP packets can be delivered in the incorrect order.

    b. Buffering results in variable delays.

    c. Tail drops result in constant delays.

    d. Bandwidth is shared by multiple streams.

3. Which statement most accurately describes overhead for packetized voice?

    a. VoIP packets are large compared to data packets and are sent at a high rate.

    b. The Layer 3 overhead of a voice packet is insignificant and can be ignored in payload calculations.

    c. Voice packets have a small payload size and are sent at high packet rates.

    d. Packetized voice has the same overhead as circuit-switching voice technologies.

4. In a multisite deployment, both IP Phone _____ and _____ packets are affected by WAN failures.

    a. Data, video

    b. Signaling, data

    c. Data, media

    d. Signaling, media

5. Which two of the following are dial plan issues requiring a CUCM solution in multisite deployments?

    a. Overlapping directory numbers

    b. Overlapping E.164 numbers

    c. Variable-length addressing

    d. Centralized call processing

    e. Centralized phone configuration

6. What is a requirement for performing NAT for Cisco IP Phones?

    a. Use DHCP instead of fixed IP addresses

    b. Exchange RTP media streams with the outside world

    c. Use DNS instead of hostnames in CUCM

    d. Exchange signaling information with the outside world

7. Which is the most accurate description of E.164?

    a. An international standard for phone numbers including country codes and area codes

    b. An international standard for local phone numbers

    c. An international standard for dialing only local numbers to the PSTN

    d. An international standard for phone numbers for DID

8. Which of the following is the most accurate description of TEHO?

    a. Using the PSTN for cost reduction

    b. Using the IP WAN link for cost reduction

    c. Using the IP WAN link for cost reduction with remote routing over the WAN, and then transferring into a local PSTN call at the remote gateway

    d. Using the PSTN for cost reduction with minimal IP WAN usage

9. What is the greatest benefit of toll bypass?

    a. It increases the security of VoIP.

    b. It creates an effective implementation of Unified Communications.

    c. It reduces operating costs by routing internal calls over WAN links as opposed to the PSTN.

    d. It implements NAT to allow variable-length numbering.

CHAPTER 2

Identifying Multisite Deployment Solutions

A multisite deployment introduces several issues that do not apply to single-site deployments. When implementing CUCM in a multisite environment, you must address these issues. This chapter shows you how to solve issues that arise in multisite deployments.

Chapter Objectives

Upon completing this chapter, you will be able to describe solutions to issues that occur in CUCM multisite deployments. You will be able to meet these objectives:

■ Describe how quality of service (QoS) solves quality issues in multisite deployments

■ Describe solutions to bandwidth limitations in multisite deployments

■ Describe survivability and availability features in multisite deployments

■ Describe solutions for dial plan issues in multisite deployments

■ Describe how Cisco Mobility and Extension Mobility resolves issues for mobile users

■ Describe how a Cisco Unified Border Element (CUBE) can solve NAT and security solutions in multisite deployments

Multisite Deployment Solution Overview

Figure 2-1 illustrates a typical multisite deployment.

Figure 2-1 *Multisite Deployment Solutions*

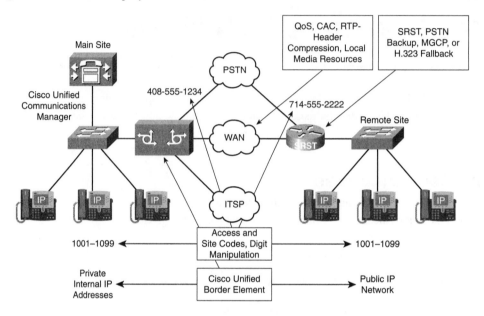

This deployment incorporates the following solutions to multisite deployment issues:

- Availability issues are solved by Cisco Unified Survivable Remote Site Telephony (SRST), which may include Media Gateway Control Protocol (MGCP) fallback or H.323, both using dial peers.

- Quality and bandwidth issues are solved by quality of service (QoS), call admission control (CAC), Real-Time Transport Protocol (RTP) header compression, and local media resources.

- Dial plan solutions include access and site codes, as well as digit manipulation.

- Network Address Translation (NAT) and security issues are solved by the deployment of a Cisco Unified Border Element.

Quality of Service

QoS refers to the capability of a network to provide better service to selected network traffic at the direct expense of other traffic. The primary goal of QoS is to provide better service—including dedicated bandwidth, controlled jitter and latency (required by some real-time and interactive traffic), and improved loss characteristics—by giving priority to certain communication flows. QoS can be thought of as "managed unfairness," because whenever one type of traffic is given a higher priority, another is implicitly given a lower priority. The QoS designer must assess the level of each type of traffic and prioritize them best to suit the business needs of each organization.

Fundamentally, QoS enables you to provide better service to certain flows. This is done by either raising the priority of a flow or limiting the priority of another flow. When using congestion-management tools, you try to raise the priority of a flow by queuing and servicing queues in different ways. The queue-management tool used for congestion avoidance raises priority by dropping lower-priority flows before higher-priority flows. Policing and shaping provide priority to a flow by limiting the throughput of other flows. Link efficiency tools prevent large flows (such as file transfers) from severely degrading small flows such as voice.

When implementing QoS, you must do the following:

- Identify traffic, such as voice, signaling, and data.

- Divide traffic into classes such as real-time traffic, mission-critical traffic, and any less-important traffic where QoS policy is implemented.

- Apply QoS policy per class, usually on a router interface, specifying how to serve each class.

QoS Advantages

QoS can improve the quality of voice calls when bandwidth utilization is high by giving priority to Real-Time Transport Protocol (RTP) packets. Figure 2-2 demonstrates how voice (audio) traffic is given absolute priority over all other traffic with Low-Latency Queuing (LLQ). This reduces jitter, which is caused by variable queuing delays, and lost voice packets, which are caused by tail drops that occur when buffers are full. To avoid the complete blocking of other traffic, voice bandwidth should be limited by defining the bandwidth used by the maximum number of calls with the priority command within the LLQ configuration. The number of voice calls should also be limited by a CAC mechanism. Therefore, additional calls will not try to further saturate the WAN link, and ideally they will be configured with Automated Alternate Routing (AAR) to route the additional calls through the public switched telephone network (PSTN).

Figure 2-2 *QoS Advantages*

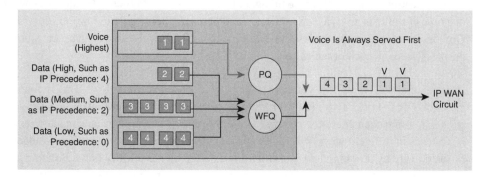

As an analogy, QoS builds a car-pool lane for prioritized drivers with LLQ. CAC is the mechanism that limits the maximum number of cars that can be in the car-pool lane at once.

> **NOTE** Video frames containing visual images are also sent over RTP and should also be configured with their own priority queue in LLQ. The Cisco best practice is that the priority queue should not exceed 33% of the interface bandwidth.

Finally, to ensure proper service for voice calls, you should configure QoS to guarantee a certain bandwidth for signaling traffic such as Session Initiation Protocol (SIP) or Skinny Client Control Protocol (SCCP) with class-based weighted fair queuing (CBWFQ). Otherwise, despite the fact that the quality of active calls may be okay, calls cannot be torn down, and new calls cannot be established.

> **NOTE** QoS is not discussed further in this book. For more information, refer to the Cisco Quality of Service or Optimizing Converged Cisco Networks courses.

Solutions to Bandwidth Limitations

Bandwidth on the IP WAN can be conserved using the following methods:

- **Using low-bandwidth codecs:** If you use low-bandwidth (compression) codecs, such as G.729, the required bandwidth for digitized voice is 8 kbps, or approximately 26 kbps in RTP, compared to the 64 kbps, or approximately 87 kbps in RTP, that is required by G.711. These bandwidth calculations are based on using a PPP or Frame Relay header of 6 bytes. The numbers would change if a different Layer 2 header were used.

■ **Using RTP-header compression:** When you use RTP-header compression (compressed RTP [cRTP]), the IP, User Datagram Protocol (UDP), and RTP header can be compressed to 2 or 4 bytes, compared to the 40 bytes that is required by these headers if cRTP is not used. cRTP is enabled per link on both ends of a point-to-point WAN link. It should be selectively used on a slow WAN link, typically less than 768 kbps. It does not need to be enabled end-to-end across all faster WAN links.

■ **Deploying local annunciators or disabling remote annunciators:** If spoken announcements are not required, the use of annunciators can be disabled for Cisco IP Phones that do not have a local annunciator. Otherwise, local annunciators could be deployed. CUCM supports annunciators running only on CUCM servers for media provided by the IP Voice Streaming Application service. Therefore, local annunciators can be implemented only if a local CUCM cluster is deployed or if clustering over the IP WAN is being used.

■ **Deploying local conference bridges:** If local conference bridges are deployed, the IP WAN is not used if all conference members are at the same site as the conference bridge.

■ **Deploying local Media Termination Points (MTP):** If MTPs are required, they can be locally deployed at each site to avoid the need to cross the IP WAN when using MTP services.

■ **Deploying transcoders or mixed conference bridges:** If low-bandwidth codecs are not supported by all endpoints, transcoders can be used so that low-bandwidth codecs can be used across the IP WAN. Then have the voice stream transcoded from G.729 to G.711. For conferences with local members using G.711 and remote members using low-bandwidth codecs, mixed conference bridges with digital system processor (DSP) hardware in a gateway can be deployed that support conference members with different codecs.

NOTE CUCM can perform conference calls with a software conference bridge only with the G.711 codec.

■ **Deploying local Music On Hold (MOH) servers (requires a local CUCM server) or using multicast MOH from branch router flash:** Deploying local MOH servers means that CUCM servers have to be present at each site. In centralized call-processing models in which CUCM servers are not present at remote sites, it is recommended that you use multicast MOH from branch router flash. This eliminates the need to stream MOH over the IP WAN. If this is not an option, you should use multicast MOH instead of unicast MOH to reduce the number of MOH streams that have to traverse the IP WAN. Multicast MOH requires multicast routing to be enabled in the routed IP network.

■ **Limiting the number of voice calls using CAC:** Use CAC with CUCM or a gatekeeper to avoid oversubscription of WAN bandwidth from too many voice calls.

Low-Bandwidth Codecs and RTP-Header Compression

In Figure 2-3, a voice packet for a call with the G.711 codec and a 20-ms packetization period is being passed along a Frame Relay WAN link. The RTP frame has a total size of 206 bytes, composed of 6 bytes of Frame Relay header, 20 bytes of IP header, 8 of bytes UDP header, 12 bytes of RTP header, and a 160-byte payload of digitized voice. The packet rate is 50 packets per second (pps), resulting in a bandwidth need of 82.4 kbps. Note that when compressed RTP (cRTP) is used, the bandwidth is considerably reduced to 11.2 or 12 kbps.

Figure 2-3 *Low-Bandwidth Codecs and RTP-Header Compression*

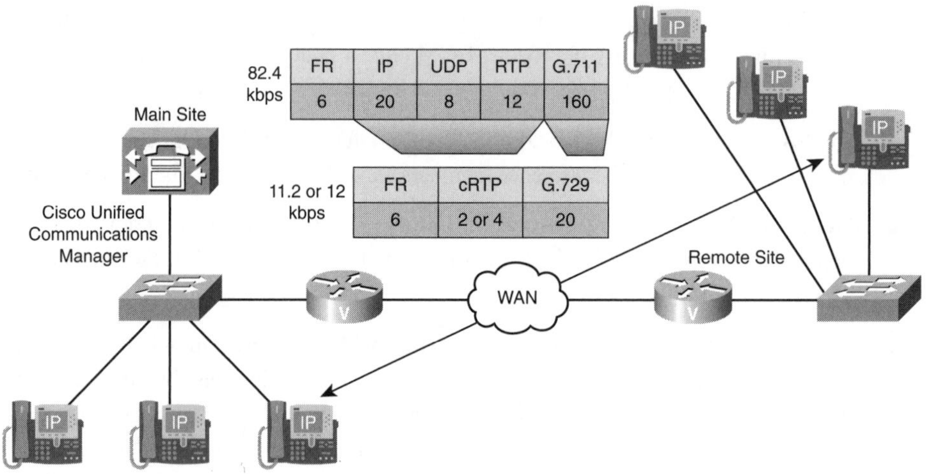

NOTE   The default codec with CUCM is G.711, with a 160-byte sample size and a 20-ms packet interval.

When you use cRTP and change the codec to G.729 with CUCM regions, the required bandwidth changes as follows: The frame now has a total size of 28 or 30 bytes per frame, composed of 6 bytes of Frame Relay header, 2 or 4 bytes of cRTP header (depending on whether the UDP checksum is preserved), and a 20-byte payload of digitized, compressed voice. The packet rate is still 50 pps (because the packetization period was not changed), resulting in bandwidth needs of 11.2 or 12 kbps.

Seven G.729 calls with cRTP enabled require less bandwidth than one G.711 call without cRTP (assuming that cRTP is used without preserving the UDP checksum).

Codec Configuration in CUCM

The codec that is used for a call is determined by the region configuration in CUCM. Each region in CUCM is configured with the codec that has the highest permitted bandwidth requirements:

■ Within the configured region

■ Toward a specific other region (manually configured)

■ Toward all other regions (not manually configured)

Regions are assigned to device pools (one region per device pool), and a device pool is assigned to each device, such as a Cisco IP Phone. The codec actually used depends on the capabilities of the two devices that are involved in the call. The assigned codec is the one that is supported by both devices; it does not exceed the bandwidth requirements of the codec permitted in region configuration. If devices cannot agree on a codec, a transcoder is invoked. But if a transcoder is unavailable, audio would fail.

Disabled Annunciator

Figure 2-4 shows how bandwidth can be conserved on the IP WAN by simply disabling annunciator RTP streams to remote phones.

Figure 2-4 *Disabled Annunciator*

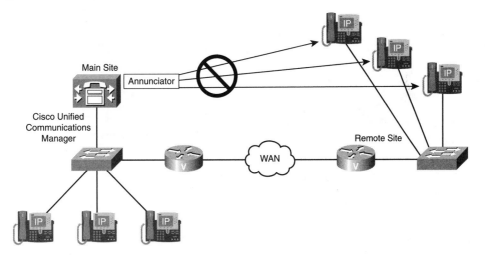

The annunciator is a CUCM feature that sends one-way audio of prerecorded messages over RTP to IP Phones. An example is the replacement to the fast busy reorder tone with the recorded message "Your call cannot be completed as dialed; please . . ." If announcements should not be sent over a saturated IP WAN link, Media Resource Group Lists (MRGL) can be used so that remote phones do not have access to the annunciator media resource, as shown in Figure 2-4.

> **NOTE**   Because not every call requires annunciator messages, and because the messages usually are rather short, the bandwidth that may be preserved by disabling the annunciator is minimal.

Local Versus Remote Conference Bridges

As shown in Figure 2-5, if a local conference bridge is deployed at the remote site with the remote site gateway DSPs, it keeps voice streams off the IP WAN for conferences in which all members are physically located at the remote site. The same solution can be implemented for MTPs. MRGLs specify which conference bridge (or MTP) should be used and by which IP Phone.

Figure 2-5   *Local Versus Remote Conference Bridges*

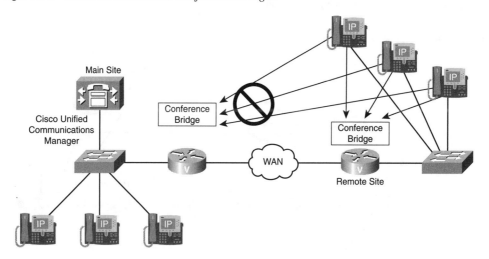

Mixed Conference Bridge

As illustrated in Figure 2-6, a hardware conference bridge is deployed at the main site gateway. The hardware conference bridge is configured to support mixed conferences, in which members use different codecs. Headquarters IP Phones that join the conference can use G.711, whereas remote IP Phones can join the conference using a low-bandwidth codec. The end result is a minimum WAN utilization with relatively high voice quality.

Figure 2-6 *Mixed Conference Bridge*

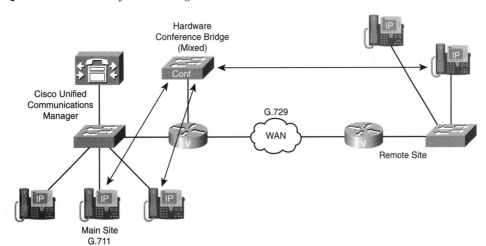

Transcoders

As shown in Figure 2-7, a voice-mail system that supports only G.711 is deployed at the main site. For example, Cisco Unity Express (CUE) is a branch office voice-mail system that supports only G.711. One CUCM server is providing a software conference bridge that also supports G.711 only. If remote Cisco IP Phones are configured to use G.729 over the IP WAN with CUCM Regions to conserve WAN bandwidth, they would not be able to join conferences or access the voice-mail system. To allow these IP Phones to use G.729 and to access the G.711-only services, a hardware transcoder is deployed at the main site in the gateway using DSP resources.

Remote Cisco IP Phones now send G.729 voice streams to the transcoder over the IP WAN, which saves bandwidth. The transcoder changes the stream to G.711 and passes it on to the conference bridge or voice-mail system, allowing the audio connection to work.

Guidelines for Transcoder Configuration

When implementing transcoders to allow G.711-only devices to communicate with remote IP Phones using G.729, consider the following guidelines.

The first step is to implement the transcoding media resource. Because CUCM does not support software transcoding resources, the only option is to use a hardware transcoding resource by first configuring the transcoder at the Cisco IOS router and then adding the transcoder to CUCM.

Figure 2-7   *Transcoders*

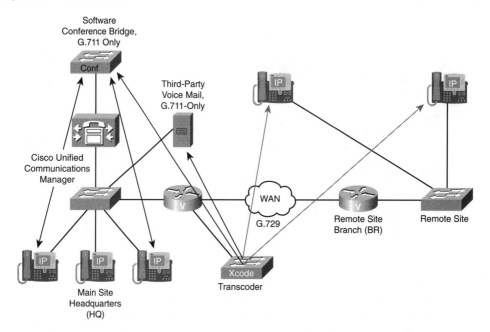

The second step is to implement regions such that only G.729 is permitted on the IP WAN, and the transcoder can be used, if required. To do so, all IP Phones and G.711-only devices, such as third-party voice-mail systems or software conference bridges that are located in the headquarters, are placed in a region (such as headquarters). Remote IP Phones are placed in another region (such as BR). The transcoding resource is put into a third region (such as XCODER).

Now the maximum codec for calls within and between regions must be specified:

■ **Within BR—G.711:** This allows local calls between remote IP Phones to use G.711.

■ **Within HQ—G.711:** This allows local calls within headquarters to use G.711. These calls are not limited to calls between IP Phones. This also includes calls to the G.711-only third-party voice-mail system or calls that use the G.711-only software conference bridge.

■ **Within XCODER—G.711:** Because this region includes only the transcoder media resource, this setting is irrelevant, because there are no calls *within* this region.

■ **Between BR and HQ—G.729:** This ensures that calls between remote IP Phones and headquarters devices such as IP Phones, software conference bridges, and voice-mail systems do not use the G.711 codec for calls that traverse the IP WAN.

> **NOTE**   Calls between IP Phones at headquarters and remote IP Phones do not require a transcoder. They simply use the best allowed codec that is supported on both ends from the CUCM region settings—ideally, G.729.
>
> A transcoder is invoked only when the two endpoints of a call cannot find a common codec that is permitted by region configuration. This is the case in this example. The remote IP Phones (which support G.711 and G.729) are not allowed to use G.711 over the IP WAN, and the headquarters voice-mail system and software conference bridge do not support G.729. CUCM detects this problem based on its region configurations, and the capability negotiation performed during call setup signaling identifies the need for a transcoder.

- **Between BR and XCODER—G.729:** This ensures that the RTP streams between remote IP Phones and the transcoder, which are sent over the IP WAN, do not use G.711.

- **Between HQ and XCODER—G.711:** This is required for the G.711-only devices at headquarters to be allowed to send G.711 to the transcoder.

Multicast MOH from the Branch Router Flash

Multicast MOH from the branch router flash is a feature for multisite deployments that use centralized call processing.

The feature works only with multicast MOH and is based on MOH capabilities of Cisco Unified SRST. The Cisco IOS SRST gateway is configured for multicast MOH and continuously sends a MOH stream, regardless of its SRST mode (standby or fallback mode).

In fact, neither CUCM nor the remote IP Phones are aware that the SRST gateway is involved. To them it appears as though a multicast MOH stream has been generated by the CUCM MOH server and received by the remote IP Phones.

Therefore, the remote Cisco IP Phones are configured to use the centralized CUCM MOH server as their MOH source. The CUCM MOH server is configured for multicast MOH (mandatory), and the max-hops value in the MOH server configuration is set to 1 for the affected audio sources. The max-hops parameter specifies the Time to Live (TTL) value that is used in the IP header of the RTP packets. The CUCM MOH server and the Cisco IOS SRST gateway located at the remote site have to use the same multicast address and port number for their streams. This way, MOH packets generated by the CUCM MOH server at the central site are dropped by the central-site router because the TTL has been exceeded. As a consequence, the MOH packets do not cross the IP WAN. The SRST gateway permanently generates a multicast MOH stream with an identical multicast IP address and port number so that the Cisco IP Phones simply listen to this stream as it appears to be coming from the CUCM MOH server.

Instead of setting the max-hops parameter for MOH packets to 1, you can use one of the following methods:

■ **Configure an access control list (ACL) on the WAN interface at the central site:** This prevents packets that are destined for the multicast group address or addresses from being sent out the interface.

■ **Disable multicast routing on the WAN interface:** Do not configure multicast routing on the WAN interface to ensure that multicast streams are not forwarded into the WAN.

NOTE Depending on the configuration of MOH in CUCM, a separate MOH stream for each enabled codec is sent for each multicast MOH audio source. The streams are incremented either based on IP addresses or based on port numbers (the recommendation is per IP address). Assuming that one multicast MOH audio source and G.711 a-law, G.711 mu-law, G.729, and the wideband codec are enabled, there will be four multicast streams. Make sure that all of them are included in the ACL to prevent MOH packets from being sent to the IP WAN.

When using multicast MOH from branch router flash, G.711 has to be enabled between the CUCM MOH server and the remote Cisco IP Phones. This is necessary because the branch SRST MOH feature supports only G.711. Therefore, the stream that is set up by CUCM in the signaling messages also has to be G.711. Because the packets are not sent across the WAN, configuring the high-bandwidth G.711 codec is no problem as long as it is enabled only for MOH. All other audio streams (such as calls between phones) that are sent over the WAN should use the low-bandwidth G.729 codec.

An Example of Multicast MOH from the Branch Router Flash

As illustrated in Figure 2-8, the CUCM MOH server is configured for multicast MOH with a destination Class D multicast group address of 239.1.1, a destination port 16384, and a max-hops TTL value of 1. Cisco recommends using an IP address in the range reserved for administratively controlled applications on private networks of 239.0.0.0 to 239.255.255.255.

Figure 2-8 *Multicast MOH from Branch Router Flash*

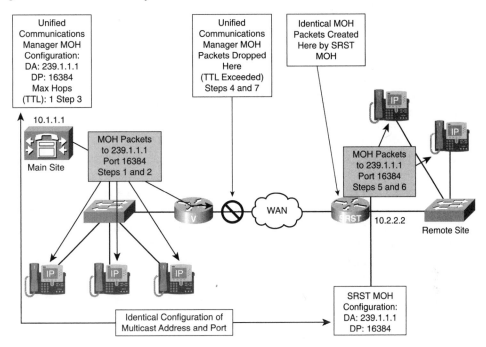

The SRST gateway located at the remote site is configured with the same destination IP address and port number as the CUCM MOH server.

When a remote phone is put on hold, the following happens:

1. According to the MRGL of the remote phone, the CUCM MOH server is used as the media resource for MOH.

2. CUCM signals the IP Phone to receive MOH on IP address 239.1.1.1, port 16384.

3. The CUCM MOH server sends multicast MOH packets to IP address 239.1.1.1, port 16384, with a TTL value of 1.

4. The router located at the central site drops the multicast MOH packet sent by the CUCM MOH server because TTL has been exceeded.

5. The router at the remote site is configured as an SRST gateway. In its Cisco Unified SRST configuration, multicast MOH is enabled with destination address 239.1.1.1 and port 16384. The SRST gateway streams MOH all the time, even if it's not in fallback mode.

6.   The IP Phones listen to the multicast MOH stream that was sent from the SRST gateway to IP address 239.1.1.1, port 16384, and play the received MOH stream.

7.   Whether or not the remote gateway is in SRST mode, MOH packets never cross the IP WAN.

> **NOTE**   If an MOH file is used in router flash, only a single MOH file can be configured to play at a time. This is unlike CUCM, where many different MOH files can be configured.

An Example of Multicast MOH from the Branch Router Flash Cisco IOS Configuration

As shown in Figure 2-9, the name of the audio file on the branch router flash is moh-file.au, and the configured multicast address and port number are 239.1.1.1 and 16384, respectively. The optional **route** command can be used to specify a source interface address for the multicast stream. If no route option is specified, the multicast stream is sourced from the configured Cisco Unified SRST default address. This is specified by the **ip source-address** command under the Cisco Unified SRST configuration (10.2.2.2 in this example). Note that you can stream only a single audio file from flash and that you can use only a single multicast address and port number per router.

Figure 2-9   *Multicast MOH from the Branch Router Flash Cisco IOS Configuration*

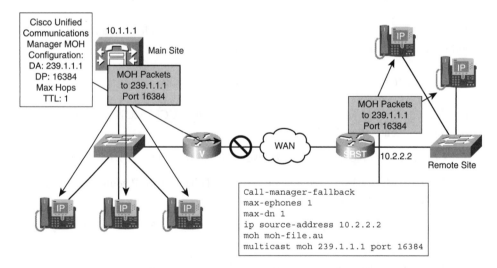

A Cisco Unified SRST license is required regardless of whether the SRST functionality will actually be used. The license is required because the configuration for streaming multicast MOH from branch router flash is done in SRST configuration mode. Also, even if SRST functionality will not be used, at least one **max-ephones** for every Cisco IP Phone supported and at least one **max-dn** for every directory number (dn) on all phones must be configured.

Alternatives to Multicast MOH from Branch Router Flash

Sometimes multicast MOH from branch router flash cannot be used. For instance, perhaps the branch router does not support the feature or does not have a Cisco Unified SRST feature license. In that case, you can consider the following alternatives:

■ **Using multicast MOH:** When you use multicast MOH over the IP WAN, the number of required MOH streams can be significantly reduced. Thus, less bandwidth is required compared to multiple unicast MOH streams. The IP network, however, has to support multicast routing for the path from the MOH server to the remote IP Phones.

■ **Using G.729 for MOH to remote sites:** If multicast MOH is not an option (for instance, because multicast routing cannot be enabled in the network), you may still be able to reduce the bandwidth consumed by MOH. If you change the codec that is used for the MOH streams to G.729 and potentially enable cRTP on the IP WAN, each individual MOH stream requires less bandwidth and hence reduces the load on the WAN link. The bandwidth savings are identical to those that are achieved when using G.729 and cRTP for standard audio streams, which was discussed earlier. To use G.729 for MOH streams, the MOH server and the remote IP Phones have to be put into different regions, and the audio codec between these two regions must be limited to G.729.

Availability

You can address availability issues in multisite deployments in several ways:

■ **PSTN backup:** Use the PSTN as a backup for on-net intersite calls.

■ **MGCP fallback:** Configure an MGCP gateway to fall back, and use the locally configured plain old telephone service (POTS), H.323, or session initiation protocol (SIP) dial peers when the connection to its call agent is lost. This effectively makes the gateway use a locally configured dial plan, which is ignored when the gateway is in MGCP mode. If H.323 is deployed, the dial peers have the same functionality in or out of SRST mode.

■ **Fallback for IP Phones with SRST:** Cisco IP Phones using either SIP or SCCP must register to a call-processing device for the phones to work. IP Phones that register over the IP WAN can have a local Cisco IOS SRST gateway configured as a backup to a CUCM server in their CUCM group configuration. When the connection to the primary CUCM server is lost, they can reregister with the local SRST gateway. Alternatively, CUCM Express can be used in SRST mode, which provides more features than standard Cisco Unified SRST.

- **Call Forward Unregistered (CFUR):** This is a call-forwarding configuration of IP Phones that becomes effective when the IP Phone is not registered.

NOTE   CFUR was introduced in CallManager version 4.2, and it appeared again in CUCM version 6.

- **Automated Alternate Routing (AAR) and Call Forward on No Bandwidth (CFNB):** AAR allows calls to be rerouted over the PSTN when calls over the IP WAN are not admitted by CAC. CFNB is a call-forwarding configuration of IP Phones, which becomes effective when AAR is used.

NOTE   AAR is configured for calls to and from IP Phones within the same cluster. Calls to a different cluster over a SIP or H.323 trunk do not use AAR. They are configured to fail over to the PSTN with CAC by configuring route groups and route lists with path selection within the route pattern.

- **Mobility solutions:** When users or devices roam between sites, they can lose features or have suboptimal configuration because of a change in their actual physical location. CUCM Extension Mobility and the Device Mobility feature of CUCM can solve such issues. In addition, Cisco Unified Mobility allows integration of cell phones and home office phones by enabling reachability on any device via a single (office) number.

PSTN Backup

As shown in Figure 2-10, calls to the remote site within the same cluster are configured with AAR to use the IP WAN first, and then they use the PSTN as a backup option. The end result is reduced operating cost with toll bypass over the WAN, and successful delivery of the same calls over the PSTN but potentially at a higher operating cost if the WAN fails.

Figure 2-10   *PSTN Backup*

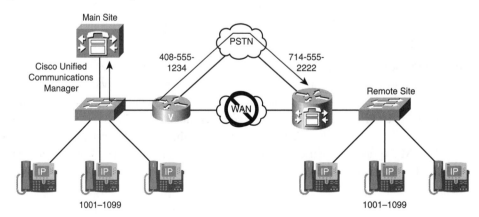

MGCP Fallback

MGCP gateway fallback is a feature that improves the availability of remote MGCP gateways.

A WAN link connects the MGCP gateway at a remote site to the CUCM at a central site, which is the MGCP call agent. If the WAN link fails, the fallback feature keeps the gateway working as an H.323 or SIP gateway and rehomes to the MGCP call agent when the WAN link becomes active again.

Figure 2-11 shows how MGCP fallback improves availability in a multisite environment.

Figure 2-11 *MGCP Fallback: Normal Operation*

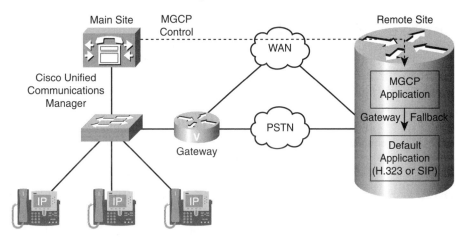

The figure illustrates normal operation of MGCP fallback while the connectivity to the call agent (CUCM) is functional:

■ The MGCP gateway is registered with CUCM over the IP WAN.

■ CUCM is the call agent of the MGCP gateway that is controlling its interfaces. The gateway does not have (or does not use) a local dial plan because all call-routing intelligence is at the call agent. MGCP functions in a client/server model, with CUCM as the server and the gateway as the client.

When the MGCP gateway loses the connection to its call agent, as shown in Figure 2-12, it falls back to its default call-control application (POTS, H.323, or SIP). The gateway now uses a local dial plan configuration, such as dial peers, voice translation profiles, and so on. Hence, it can operate independently of its MGCP call agent. Without MGCP fallback, the MGCP gateway would be unable to process calls when the connection to its call agent is lost.

Figure 2-12 *MGCP Fallback: Fallback Mode*

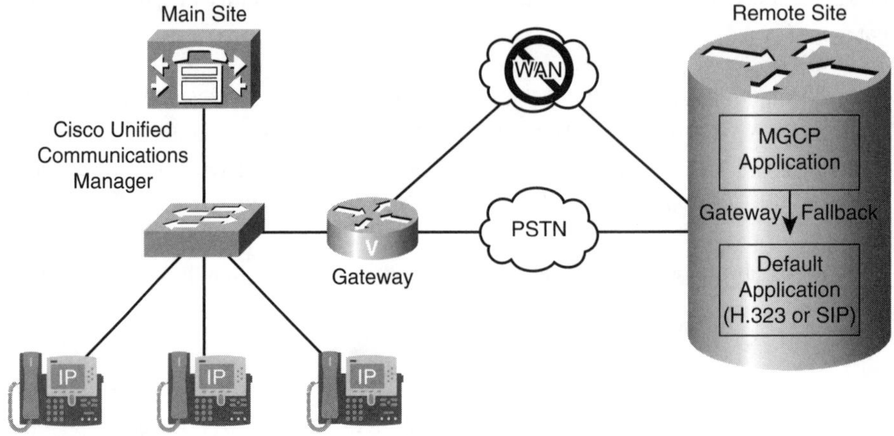

Fallback for IP Phones

Fallback for IP Phones is provided by the SRST Cisco IOS feature and improves the availability of remote IP Phones.

A WAN link connects IP Phones at a remote site to the Cisco Communications Manager at a central site, which is the call-processing device. If the WAN link fails, Cisco Unified SRST enables the gateway to provide call-processing services for IP Phones. IP Phones register with the gateway (which is listed as a backup CUCM server in the server's group configuration of the IP Phones). The Cisco Unified SRST obtains the configuration of the IP Phones from the phones themselves and can route calls between the IP Phones or out to the PSTN.

> **NOTE**   When a Cisco IP Phone is in SRST mode, the configuration on the phone should never be erased, because the phone will not function until the connection to CUCM is restored.

Figure 2-13 shows how fallback for IP Phones improves availability in a multisite deployment with centralized call processing.

This figure illustrates normal operation of Cisco Unified SRST while the connectivity between IP Phones and their primary server (CUCM) is functional:

■   Remote IP Phones are registered with CUCM over the IP WAN.

■   CUCM handles call processing for IP Phones.

Figure 2-13   *Fallback for IP Phones: Normal Operation*

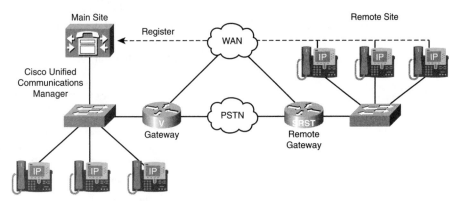

When Cisco IP Phones lose contact with CUCM, as shown in Figure 2-14, they register with the local Cisco Unified SRST router to sustain the call-processing capability necessary to place and receive calls.

Figure 2-14   *Fallback for IP Phones: Fallback Mode*

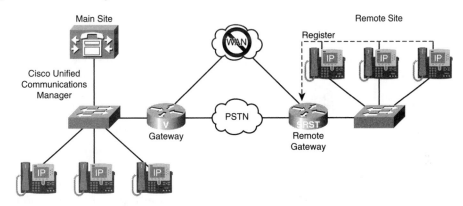

The Cisco Unified SRST gateway automatically detects a failure, queries IP Phones for configuration, and autoconfigures itself. The Cisco Unified SRST gateway uses Simple Network-Enabled Auto-Provision (SNAP) technology to autoconfigure the branch office router to provide call processing for Cisco IP Phones that are registered with the router.

CUCM Express in SRST mode can be used instead of standard Cisco Unified SRST functionality. In this case, IP Phones register with CUCM Express when they lose connection to their primary CUCM server. CUCM Express in SRST mode provides more features than standard Cisco Unified SRST.

Using CFUR During WAN Failure

As discussed, IP Phones located at remote locations can use an SRST gateway as a backup for CUCM in case of IP WAN failure. The gateway can use its local dial plan to route calls destined for the IP Phones in the main site over the PSTN. But how should intersite calls be routed from the main to the remote site while the IP WAN is down?

The problem in this case is that CUCM does not consider any other entries in its dial plan if a dialed number matches a *configured* but *unregistered* directory number. Therefore, if users at the main site dial internal extensions during the IP WAN outage, their calls fail (or go to voice mail). To allow remote IP Phones to be reached from the IP Phones at the main site, configure CFUR for the remote-site phones, as shown in Figure 2-15. CFUR should be configured with the PSTN number of the remote-site gateway so that internal calls for remote IP Phones get forwarded to the appropriate PSTN number.

Figure 2-15   *Using CFUR to Reach Remote-Site IP Phones Over the PSTN During WAN Failure*

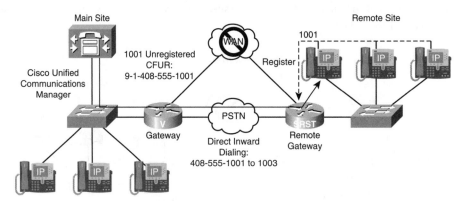

Using CFUR to Reach Users on Cell Phones

If a mobile user has a laptop with a softphone (for instance, Cisco IP Communicator) and the user shuts down the laptop, CFUR can be used to forward calls placed to the softphone to the user's cell phone, as illustrated in Figure 2-16. The user does not have to set up Call Forward All (CFA) manually before closing the softphone application. However, if the softphone is not registered, calls are forwarded to the user's cell phone. This is another application of the CFUR feature that improves availability in CUCM deployments.

Figure 2-16   *Using CFUR to Reach Users of Unregistered Software IP Phones on
Their Cell Phones*

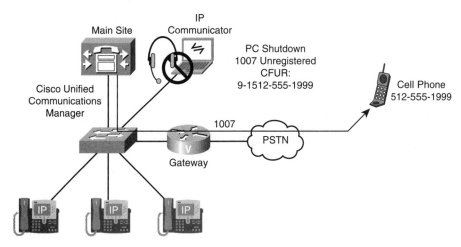

AAR and CFNB

If a call over the IP WAN to another IP Phone in the same cluster is not admitted by CAC,
the call can be rerouted over the PSTN using AAR, as shown in Figure 2-17. The AAR feature includes a CFNB option that allows the alternate number to be set for each IP Phone.
In the example, because the remote site does not have PSTN access, the call is not rerouted
to the IP Phone over the PSTN (instead of over the IP WAN). It is alternately rerouted to
the cell phone of the affected user. AAR and CFNB improve availability in multisite environments by providing the ability to reroute on-net calls that failed CAC over the PSTN.

Figure 2-17   *AAR and CFNB*

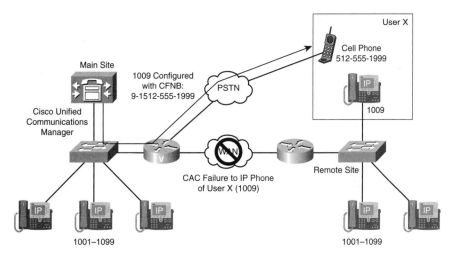

Mobility Solutions

This section provides an overview of mobility solutions that solve issues that are the result of roaming users and devices and multiple telephones (office phone, cell phone, home phone, and so on).

When users or devices roam between sites, issues arise that can be solved by mobility solutions:

- **Device Mobility:** Solves issues caused by roaming devices, including invalid device configuration settings such as regions, locations, SRST reference, AAR groups, Calling Search Spaces (CSS), and so on. The Device Mobility feature of CUCM allows device settings that depend on the physical location of the device to be automatically overwritten if the device appears in a different physical location.

- **CUCM Extension Mobility:** Solves issues that are the result of roaming users using shared guest IP phones located in other offices. Issues include wrong directory number, missing IP Phone service subscriptions, CSS, and so on. CUCM Extension Mobility allows users to log in to guest phones and replace the IP phone's configuration with the IP Phone configuration of the logged-in user.

- **Cisco Unified Mobility:** Solves issues of having multiple phones and consequently multiple phone numbers, such as an office phone, cell phone, home (office) phone, and so on. Cisco Unified Mobility allows users to be reached by a single number, regardless of the phone that is actually used.

> **NOTE**   All these mobility features are explained in Chapters 11, 12, and 13.

Dial Plan Solutions

Dial plan issues in multisite deployments can be solved in the following ways:

- **Overlapping and nonconsecutive numbers:** You can implement access codes and site codes for intersite dialing. This allows call routing that is independent of directory numbers. Appropriate digit manipulation (removing site codes in Dialed Number Identification Service [DNIS] of outgoing calls) and prefixing site codes in Automatic Number Identification (ANI) of incoming calls are required.

- **Variable-length numbering plans:** Dial string length is determined by timeout. Overlap sending and receiving is enabled, allowing dialed digits to be signaled one by one instead of being sent as one whole number.

- **Direct inward dialing (DID) ranges and E.164 addressing:** Solutions for mapping of internal directory numbers to PSTN numbers include DID, use of attendants to transfer calls, and extensions added to PSTN numbers in variable-length numbering plans.

- **Different number presentation in ISDN (Type of Number [TON]):** Digit manipulation based on TON enables the standardization of numbers signaled using different TONs.

- **Toll bypass, tail-end hop-off (TEHO), and PSTN backup:** Can be implemented by appropriate call routing and path selection based on priorities.

Dial Plan Components in Multisite Deployments

Table 2-1 lists dial plan components and their configuration elements in CUCM and in Cisco IOS gateways.

Table 2-1   *Fixed Versus Variable-Length Numbering Plans*

Dial Plan Component	Cisco IOS Gateway	CUCM
Endpoint addressing	ephone-dn, dynamic POTS, dial peers	Directory number
Call routing and path selection	Dial peers	Route patterns, route groups, route lists, translation patterns, partitions, CSSs
Digit manipulation	Voice translation profiles prefix, digit-strip, forward-digits, num-exp	Translation patterns, route patterns, route lists, significant digits
Calling privileges	COR and COR lists	Partitions, CSSs, time schedules, time periods, FACs
Call coverage	Dial peers, call applications, ephone hunt groups	Line groups, hunt lists, hunt pilots

> **NOTE**   All these elements are discussed in other books, such as *Cisco Voice over IP* and *Implementing Cisco Unified Communications Manager, Part 1 (CIPT1 v6.0)*. Information on how to use these elements to implement a dial plan in multisite deployments is provided in Chapter 4, "Implementing a Dial Plan for Multisite Deployments."

NAT and Security Solutions

When CUCM servers and IP Phones need to connect to the Internet, Cisco Unified Border Element can be used as an application proxy. When used in this way, Cisco Unified Border Element splits off-net calls inside the CUCM cluster and outside the cluster in the PSTN into two separate call legs. Cisco Unified Border Element also features signaling interworking from SIP to SIP, SIP to H.323, H.323 to SIP, and H.323 to H.323.

> **NOTE**   Cisco Unified Border Element (CUBE) used to be called Cisco Multiservice IP-to-IP Gateway.

The Cisco Unified Border Element can function in two modes:

- **Flow-around:** In this mode, only signaling is intercepted by Cisco Unified Border Element. Media exchange occurs directly between endpoints (and *flows around* Cisco Unified Border Element). Only signaling devices (CUCM) are hidden from the outside.

- **Flow-through:** In this mode, signaling and media streams are both intercepted by Cisco Unified Border Element (*flowing through* Cisco Unified Border Element). Both CUCM and IP Phones are hidden from the outside.

In flow-through mode, only Cisco Unified Border Element needs to have a public IP address, so NAT and security issues for internal devices (CUCM servers and IP Phones) are solved. Because Cisco Unified Border Element is exposed to the outside, it should be hardened against attacks.

Cisco Unified Border Element in Flow-Through Mode

In Figure 2-18, CUCM has a private IP address of 10.1.1.1, and the Cisco IP Phone has a private IP address of 10.2.1.5 with a subnet mask of 255.0.0.0. A Cisco Unified Border Element connects the CUCM cluster to the outside world—in this case, to an Internet telephony service provider (ITSP). The Cisco Unified Border Element is configured in flow-through mode and uses an internal private IP address of 10.3.1 and an external public IP address of A.

Figure 2-18   *Cisco Unified Border Element in Flow-Through Mode*

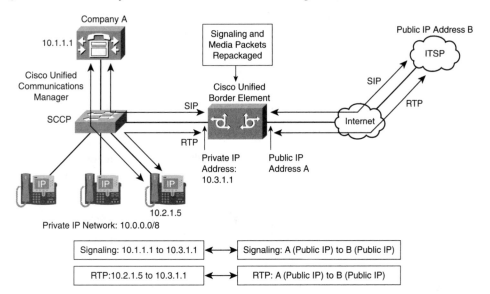

When CUCM wants to signal calls to the ITSP, it does not send the packets to the IP address of the ITSP (IP address B). Instead, it sends them to the internal IP address of the Cisco Unified Border Element (10.3.1.1) via a SIP trunk configuration. Cisco Unified Border Element then establishes a second call leg to the ITSP using its public IP address A as the source and IP address B (ITSP) as the destination. As soon as the call is set up, the Cisco Unified Border Element terminates RTP toward the ITSP using its public IP address and sends the received RTP packets to the internal IP Phone using its internal IP address.

This solution allows CUCM and IP Phones to communicate only with the internal, private IP address of the Cisco Unified Border Element. The only IP address visible to the ITSP or anyone sniffing traffic on the outside is the public IP address of Cisco Unified Border Element.

Summary

The following key points were discussed in this chapter:

- Multisite deployment solutions include QoS, efficient use of IP WAN bandwidth, backup scenarios in case of WAN failure, access and site codes, and the use of the Cisco Unified Border Element.

- QoS allows certain communication flows to be processed with higher priority than others.

- Bandwidth can be conserved by using low-bandwidth codecs, deploying mixed conference bridges or transcoders, using RTP-header compression, and deploying local media resources.

- CUCM availability features include fallback for Cisco IP Phones, CRUR, AAR and CFNB, and mobility features such as Device Mobility, Extension Mobility, and Cisco Unified Mobility.

- Multisite dial plan solutions are built using Cisco IOS gateway and CUCM dial plan tools.

- A Cisco Unified Border Element in flow-control mode hides internal devices such as CUCM and IP Phones from the outside public Internet.

References

For additional information, refer to these resources:

- Cisco Systems, Inc., Cisco Unified Communications Solution Reference Network Design (SRND), based on CUCM release 6.x, June 2007

- Cisco Systems, Inc., CUCM Administration Guide Release 6.0(1)

- Cisco Systems, Inc., Cisco Multiservice IP-to-IP Gateway Application Guide

Review Questions

Use these questions to review what you've learned in this chapter. The answers appear in Appendix A, "Answers to Chapter Review Questions."

1. Which of the following best describes QoS as a solution for multisite environments?

    a. Ensuring reliable PSTN calls

    b. Ensuring that all forms of IP traffic receive excellent performance

    c. Ensuring excellent data performance

    d. Ensuring that selected traffic such as RTP audio traffic receives excellent performance at the expense of lower-priority traffic

2. Which two of the following statements about bandwidth solutions in a multisite deployment are true?

    a. RTP header compression compresses the RTP header to 1 byte.

    b. WAN bandwidth can be conserved by using low-bandwidth codecs within a remote site.

    c. WAN bandwidth can be conserved by deploying local media resources.

    d. Voice payload compression is part of RTP header compression.

    e. Multicast MOH from branch router flash eliminates the need to send MOH over the WAN.

3. Which two of the following statements about availability are true?

    a. CFNB is required to enable main-site phones to call remote site phones during SRST fallback.

    b. SRST provides fallback for Cisco IP Phones.

    c. MGCP fallback allows the gateway to use local dial peers when the call agent cannot be reached.

    d. AAR is required to enable phones to reroute calls to another CUCM cluster over the PSTN when the IP WAN is down.

    e. MGCP fallback and SRST cannot be implemented at the same device.

4. Which two of the following are not relevant dial plan solutions for multisite CUCM deployments?

    a. Access and site codes

    b. TEHO

    c. PSTN backup

    d. Shared lines

    e. Overlap signaling

5. Which Cisco IOS feature provides a signaling and media proxy function that addresses the need for NAT?

    a. Cisco Unified Border Element

    b. Cisco PIX Firewall

    c. CUCM

    d. Cisco ASA

6. Which of the following most accurately describes the difference between flow-around and flow-through modes for CUBE?

    a. Signaling is intercepted in both modes, but media is intercepted only in flow through.

    b. Both modes intercept media and signaling.

    c. Both modes intercept only media.

    d. Both modes intercept only signaling.

7. Which of the following two protocol conversions are supported by CUBE?

    a. SCCP to SIP

    b. H.323 to SIP

    c. SIP to H.323

    d. SIP to MGCP

    e. MGCP to SCCP

8. What is the best description of MGCP fallback?

    a. If CUCM fails, MGCP fails over to SCCP dial peers for PSTN dialing.

    b. IF CUCM fails, MGCP fails over to MGCP dial peers for PSTN dialing.

    c. IF CUCM fails, MGCP fails over to H.323 dial peers for PSTN dialing.

    d. IF CUCM fails, all PSTN dialing fails.

9. What is the best benefit of multicast for MOH in a branch router?

    a. Multiple MOH files can be used in router flash.

    b. Router flash is not needed for MOH files, because the branch phones send multicast MOH to each other.

    c. MOH has only one stream of RTP to all listeners.

    d. MOH has several streams of RTP to all listeners to ensure optimal voice quality.

CHAPTER 3

Implementing Multisite Connections

CUCM multisite deployments can use a variety of connection options between sites. This chapter describes connection options and explains how to configure them.

Chapter Objectives

Upon completing this chapter, you will be able to configure gateways and trunks in multisite environments. You will be able to meet the following objectives:

- Identify the characteristics of the trunk and gateway types supported by CUCM

- Describe and implement MGCP gateways

- Describe and implement H.323 gateways

- Describe and configure Cisco IOS H.323 gateways

- Describe how to configure H.323 gateways in CUCM

- Understand different types of trunks supported by CUCM

- Describe and implement SIP trunks in CUCM

- Describe and implement intercluster, H.225, and gatekeeper-controlled intercluster trunks in CUCM

Examining Multisite Connection Options

Multisite environments have several connection options; Figure 3-1 shows a CUCM cluster at the main site, with three connections to other sites.

Figure 3-1   *Connection Options for Multisite Deployments*

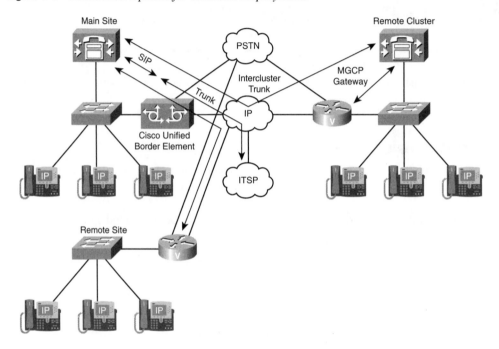

The connections are as follows:

■ Intercluster trunk (H.323) to another CUCM cluster located at a different site

■ An H.323 gateway located at a remote site

■ A session initiation protocol (SIP) trunk connected to an Internet telephony service provider (ITSP) via a Cisco Unified Border Element (CUBE), which also has a SIP trunk to CUCM

■ At the remote location an MGCP Gateway is configured to be controlled by the remote cluster CUCM.

MGCP Gateway Characteristics

A Media Gateway Control Protocol (MGCP) gateway uses the centralized call-processing model, so the gateway does not have a local dial plan and does not perform call processing on its own. Although an MGCP gateway does have dial peers, there are no phone numbers of the dial plan in the gateway. Instead, the gateway relies on a call agent such as CUCM that controls the gateway and its interfaces. Unique features on Cisco IOS MGCP gateways that are not supported by H.323 or SIP gateways include the following:

- Centralized provisioning

- Q Signaling (QSIG) supplementary services (QSIG is supported in an H.323 trunk)

- Centralized Call Detail Record (CDR) digital service level 0 granularity in CUCM CDR

- Multilevel Precedence and Preemption (MLPP)

- Hookflash transfer with CUCM

If any of these features are required, MGCP signaling must be used with the gateway.

> **NOTE**   Hookflash transfer with H.323 gateways is possible via a Tool Command Language (TCL) script, which you can download from Cisco.com.

H.323 Gateway Characteristics

H.323 gateway uses the distributed call-processing model, so the gateway has its own local dial plan with dial peers and performs call processing on its own. It does not rely on any other device but can be configured to work with CUCM or other H.323 devices. Unique features on Cisco IOS H.323 gateways not supported by MGCP or SIP gateways include the following:

- Non-Facility Associated Signaling (NFAS), which allows more than one ISDN PRI to be controlled by a single ISDN D channel

- TCL/Voice Extensible Markup Language (VoiceXML)

- Integrated voice and data access

- Fractional ISDN PRI

- Time-division multiplexing (TDM): analog direct inward dialing (A-DID), ear and mouth (E&M), PRI NFAS, Centralized Automated Message Accounting (CAMA), T1 Feature Group D (FGD)

- TDM T3 trunks

- Set the numbering plan type of outgoing calls

- The ability to reject an incoming call from the PSTN based on ANI

- If any of these features are required, H.323 signaling must be used with the gateway.

> **NOTE**   Fractional PRI support with MGCP is possible when you limit the timeslots manually at the MGCP gateway and busy out B channels in CUCM (using an advanced service parameter). However, this configuration is not officially supported.

SIP Trunk Characteristics

Session Initiation Protocol (SIP) uses the distributed call-processing model, so a SIP gateway or SIP proxy device has its own local dial plan and performs call processing on its own. A CUCM SIP trunk can connect to Cisco IOS gateways, a Cisco Unified Border Element, other CUCM clusters, or a SIP implementation with network servers (such as a SIP proxy).

SIP is a simple, customizable protocol with a rapidly evolving feature set. SIP is an Internet standard, and its support is rapidly growing in the VoIP marketplace.

> **NOTE**   When you use SIP trunks, Media Termination Points (MTP) might be required if the endpoints cannot agree on a common method of dual-tone multifrequency (DTMF) exchange.

H.323 Trunk Overview

As illustrated in Figure 3-2, CUCM supports several different types of H.323 trunks. CUCM cluster A uses a nongatekeeper-controlled intercluster trunk (ICT) to CUCM cluster B. In addition, CUCM cluster A is configured with a gatekeeper-controlled intercluster trunk. The gatekeeper-controlled intercluster trunk points to a gatekeeper, which is used for address resolution. A gatekeeper is an optional H.323 component implemented on a Cisco IOS router that allows centralized call processing and optionally call admission control (CAC). In this example, the gatekeeper can route calls between all phones controlled by CUCM clusters A, C, and D.

Figure 3-2 *H.323 Trunk Overview*

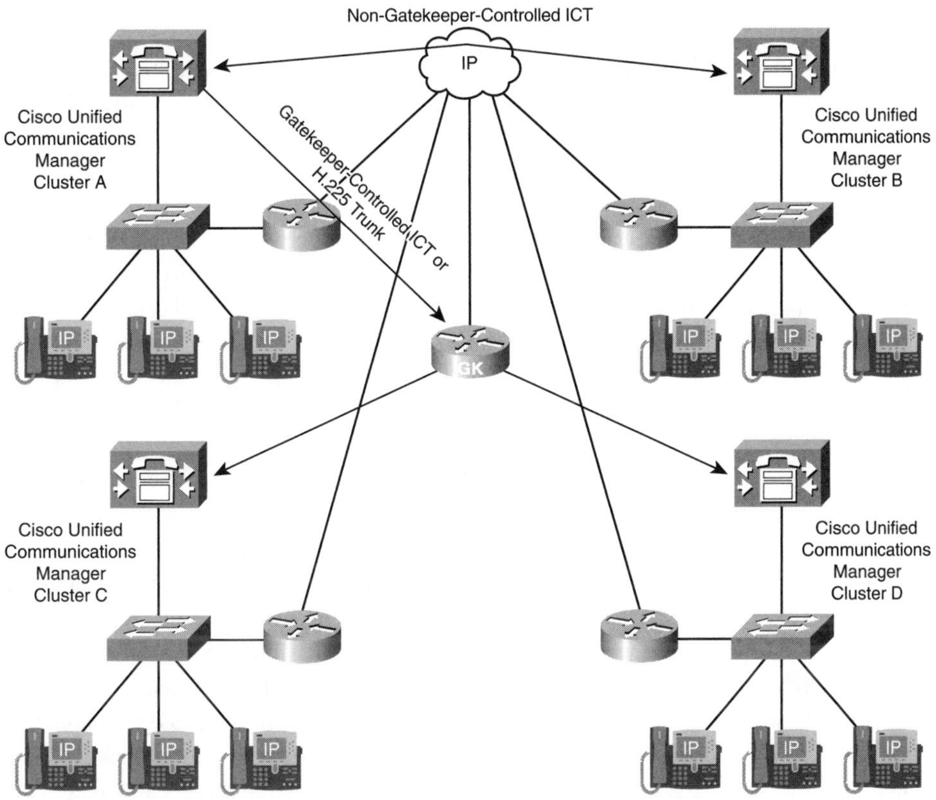

H.323 Trunk Comparison

Table 3-1 compares characteristics of the three available H.323 trunk types in CUCM.

Table 3-1 *H.323 Trunk Comparison*

	Nongatekeeper-Controlled ICT	Gatekeeper-Controlled ICT	H.225 Trunk
IP Address Resolution	IP address specified in trunk configuration	IP address resolved by H.323 RAS (gatekeeper)	
Gatekeeper Call Admission	No	Yes, by H.323 RAS (gatekeeper)	
Scalability	Limited	Scalable	
Peer	CUCM	Before Cisco CallManager 3.2	Cisco CallManager 3.2 or higher and all other H.323 devices

The nongatekeeper-controlled intercluster trunk is the simplest, because it does not use a gatekeeper. It requires the IP address of the remote CUCM server or servers to be specified, because the dialed number is not resolved to an IP address by a gatekeeper. CAC can be implemented by locations but not by gatekeeper CAC. Scalability is limited because no address resolution is used and all IP addresses have to be configured manually. The non-gatekeeper-controlled intercluster trunk points to the CUCM server or servers of the other cluster.

You may define up to three remote CUCM servers in the same destination cluster. The trunk automatically load-balances across all defined remote CUCM servers. In the remote cluster, it is important to configure a corresponding intercluster trunk (nongatekeeper-controlled) that has a CUCM group containing the same servers that were defined as remote CUCM servers in the first cluster. A similar configuration is required in each CUCM cluster that is connected by the intercluster trunks.

The gatekeeper-controlled intercluster trunk should be used instead of the nongatekeeper-controlled trunk for a larger number of clusters. The advantages of using the gatekeeper-controlled trunk are mainly the overall administration of the cluster and failover times. Nongatekeeper-controlled trunks generally require that a full mesh of trunks be configured, which can become an administrative burden as the number of clusters increases. In addition, if a subscriber server in a cluster becomes unreachable, a 5-second (the default) timeout occurs while the call is attempted. If an entire cluster is unreachable, the number of attempts before either call failure or rerouting over the public switched telephone network (PSTN) depends on the number of remote servers defined for the trunk and on the number of trunks in the route list or route group. If many remote servers and many nongatekeeper-controlled trunks exist, the call delay can become excessive.

With a gatekeeper-controlled intercluster trunk, you configure only one trunk that can then communicate via the gatekeeper with all other clusters that are registered to the gatekeeper. If a cluster or subscriber becomes unreachable, the gatekeeper automatically directs the call to another subscriber in the cluster or rejects the call if no other possibilities exist. This allows the call to be rerouted over the PSTN (if required) with little incurred delay. With a single Cisco gatekeeper, it is possible to have 100 clusters that each register a single trunk to the gatekeeper, with all clusters being able to call each other through the gatekeeper. Of course, in an enormous enterprise environment with 100 clusters, multiple gatekeepers configured as a gatekeeper cluster would eliminate the single point of failure. With nongatekeeper-controlled intercluster trunks, this same topology would require 99 trunks to be configured in each cluster. The formula for full-mesh connections is $N(N–1)/2$. There-fore, without the gatekeeper, 100 clusters would require 4950 total trunks for complete inter-cluster connectivity. The gatekeeper-controlled intercluster trunk should be used to communicate only with other CUCMs, because the use of this trunk with other H.323

devices might cause problems with supplementary services. In addition, a gatekeeper-controlled intercluster trunk must be used for backward compatibility with CUCM versions earlier than Release 3.2 (referred to as Cisco CallManager).

The H.225 trunk is essentially the same as the gatekeeper-controlled intercluster trunk, except that it can work with CUCM clusters (Release 3.2 and later). It also can work with other H.323 devices, such as Cisco IOS gateways (including CUCM Express), conferencing systems, and clients. This capability is achieved through a discovery mechanism on a call-by-call basis. This type of trunk is the recommended H.323 trunk if all CUCM clusters are at least Release 3.2.

MGCP Gateway Implementation

To implement an MGCP gateway in CUCM, as shown in Figure 3-3, you have to add the gateway to CUCM by choosing **Device > Gateway**. Then you add MGCP endpoints to the gateway, and finally you configure the endpoints. You must manually enter all the settings for the MGCP gateway in CUCM. CUCM doesn't have an automated technique such as an SNMP query of the gateway hardware to fill in the MGCP gateway fields.

Figure 3-3   *MGCP Gateway Implementation*

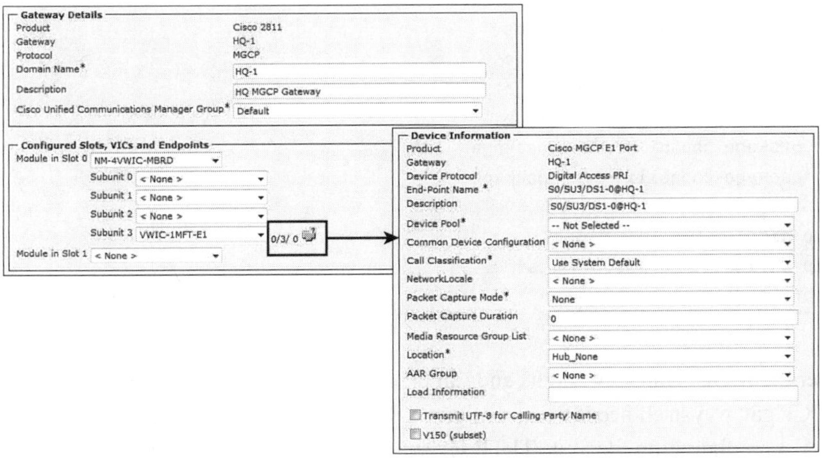

> **NOTE**   You can find more information about the MGCP protocol and MGCP gateway characteristics in *Cisco Voice over IP (CVOICE)*, Third Edition. It covers MGCP gateway implementation with CUCM in detail. This book offers only a high-level review of MGCP gateway implementation.

Example 3-1 illustrates the commands that need to be entered into the MGCP gateway for the topology shown in Figure 3-4. In this example a single E1 line is installed in the gateway and connected to the PSTN.

Only the highlighted commands were manually configured. The rest of the commands were added via TFTP.

Example 3-1 *MGCP Gateway Configuration*

```
controller E1 0/3/0
   framing hdb3
   linecode crc4
   pri-group timeslots 1-31 service mgcp
interface Serial0/3/0:15
   isdn switch-type primary-net5
   isdn incoming-voice voice
   isdn bind-l3 ccm-manager
ccm-manager mgcp
ccm-manager music-on-hold
ccm-manager config server 10.1.1.1
ccm-manager config
mgcp
mgcp call-agent 10.1.1.1 2427 service-type mgcp version 0.1
mgcp rtp unreachable timeout 1000 action notify
mgcp modem passthrough voip mode nse
mgcp package-capability rtp-package
mgcp package-capability sst-package
mgcp package-capability pre-package
no mgcp package-capability res-package
no mgcp package-capability fxr-package
no mgcp timer receive-rtcp
mgcp sdp simple
mgcp rtp payload-type g726r16 static
mgcp profile default
```

After the MGCP gateway and its endpoints have been added and configured in CUCM, the MGCP gateway itself needs to be configured. CUCM stores an Extensible Markup Language (XML) configuration file at its TFTP server, which can be downloaded by the MGCP gateway. If this configuration server feature is used, the gateway needs to be configured with only two commands (**ccm-manager config server** *IP address of Cisco TFTP* and **ccm-manager config**), as shown in Example 3-1. The rest of the configuration is automatically downloaded and applied to the Cisco IOS MGCP gateway. Additional MGCP dial peers might also be automatically added to the MGCP configuration, depending on the MGCP endpoints previously configured in CUCM.

Figure 3-4 *MGCP Gateway Implementation, Continued*

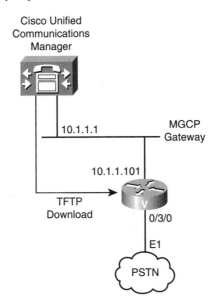

NOTE Be careful when using these automated MGCP commands, because they automatically reserve all DSP resources for all digital channels present in the gateway. Potentially, this may not leave available DSP resources for hardware conference bridges or transcoding. Many engineers choose not to enter these two commands, and instead enter all commands manually.

H.323 Gateway Implementation

Figure 3-5 illustrates the relationship between CUCM and an H.323 gateway.

H.323 gateway implementation requires configuration of CUCM and the Cisco IOS gateway. In CUCM, the important configuration steps are as follows:

Step 1 Create the gateway, and specify its IP address.

Step 2 Create a route group, and put the gateway into it.

Step 3 Create a route list, and put the route group into it.

Step 4 Create one or more route patterns pointing to the route list.

Figure 3-5 *H.323 Gateway Implementation Overview*

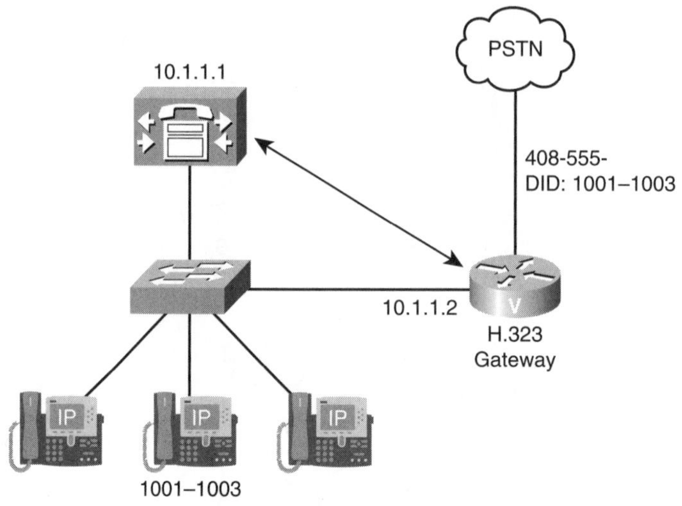

> **NOTE** The number of settings available in CUCM for an H.323 gateway is substantially less than those for an MGCP gateway. This is intentional by design, because MGCP is a client/server protocol and CUCM must contain all gateway settings. In contrast, H.323 is a peer-to-peer protocol, and CUCM simply needs to know how to talk to the gateway.

The Cisco IOS gateway configuration consists of these steps:

Step 1 Configure the H.323 gateway, specifying its H.323 ID and the IP address to use. This is done on any interface, but best practice for reliability is to use a loopback interface. Ensure that you use the same IP address you configured in CUCM for the H.323 gateway.

> **NOTE** If the IP address configured in CUCM does not match the IP address used by the gateway, CUCM considers the H.323 signaling messages to be sent from an invalid (unknown) source and ignores them, unless promiscuous operation has been permitted. (This service parameter can be configured in CUCM.)

Step 2 Configure one or more VoIP dial peers pointing to CUCM.

Step 3 Configure one or more dial peers pointing to the PSTN.

Cisco IOS H.323 Gateway Configuration

Example 3-2 shows an IOS configuration for the H.323 gateway in the network topology, illustrated in Figure 3-6.

Example 3-2 *Cisco IOS H.323 Gateway Configuration*

```
interface Loopback0
 ip address 10.1.1.101 255.255.255.255
 h323-gateway voip interface
 h323-gateway voip bind srcaddr 10.1.1.101
!
dial-peer voice 11 voip
 destination-pattern 511555....
 session target ipv4:10.1.1.1
 incoming called-number 9T
 codec g711ulaw
!
dial-peer voice 21 pots
 destination-pattern 9T
 direct-inward-dial
 port 0/0/0:23
```

Figure 3-6 *Cisco IOS H.323 Gateway Configuration*

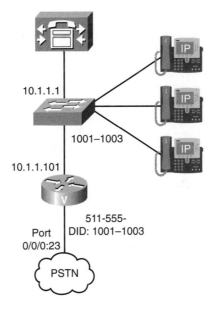

When configuring an H.323 gateway, be sure to first enable H.323 at one IP interface. If multiple IP interfaces are present, it is recommended that you use a loopback interface. Otherwise, if the interface that has been selected for H.323 is down, the H.323 application will not work, even if other interfaces could be used to route the IP packets. In this example, H.323 has been enabled on the loopback interface using the **h323-gateway voip interface** and **h323 gateway voip bind srcaddr** *IP address* commands.

In contrast to MGCP gateways, in which the call agent takes care of call routing, H.323 gateways require local dial plan configuration. In the example, the H.323 gateway is configured with a VoIP dial peer that routes calls placed to the gateway's PSTN number 511555.... toward CUCM. These are the calls that the gateway receives from the PSTN, because 511555 1001–1003 is the direct inward dialing (DID) range of the PSTN interface (port 0/0/0:23). In addition, the PSTN gateway is configured with a plain old telephone service (POTS) dial peer that routes all calls starting with 9 to the PSTN using the ISDN PRI (port 0/0/0:23).

Note that the configured digits of a destination pattern in a POTS dial peer are automatically stripped, because POTS dial peers send only wildcard (variable) digits by default. Therefore, the 9 is not sent to the PSTN. In the other direction, the gateway does not perform any digit manipulation, because VoIP dial peers do not strip any digits by default. CUCM receives H.323 call setup messages for calls that were received from the PSTN in full length (usually ten digits). Because the internal directory numbers are four digits, either CUCM or the H.323 gateway needs to be configured to strip the leading digits so that the remaining four digits can be used to route the call to internal directory numbers.

> **NOTE**   The use of 9T in dial peer 21 shown in Example 3-2 is just an example. More granular destination pattern configurations typically are used in production to allow greater call control. Additional information on how to implement digit manipulation is provided in the next chapter.

CUCM H.323 Gateway Configuration

Figure 3-7 shows an example of a CUCM H.323 gateway configuration.

To add an H.323 gateway to CUCM, choose **Device > Gateway** and click **Add New**. Then, from the Gateway Type drop-down list, choose **H.323** and click **Next**.

Figure 3-7   *CUCM H.323 Gateway Configuration*

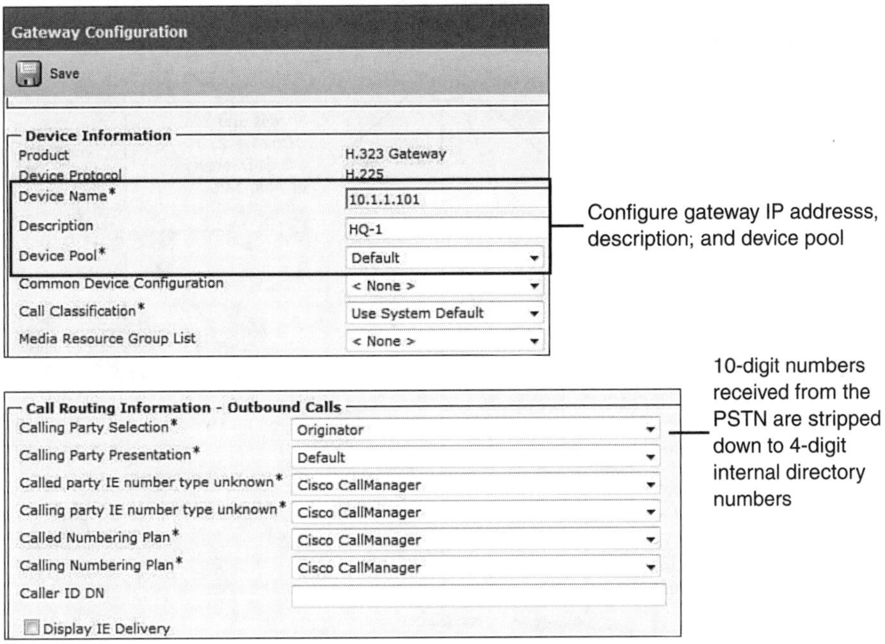

In the Gateway Configuration window, enter the IP address of the H.323 gateway in the Device Name field, select the device pool that should be used, and optionally enter a description. If CUCM should consider only some of the called digits, the significant digits parameter can be set to the number of least-significant digits that should be used to route inbound calls. In this example, in which the gateway sends full ten-digit PSTN numbers to CUCM, setting the significant digits to 4 would allow the incoming calls to be routed to internal directory numbers without any additional CUCM digit manipulation configurations, such as translation patterns.

Trunk Implementation Overview

Figure 3-8 illustrates the most important configuration elements for implementing a SIP or nongatekeeper-controlled intercluster trunk (ICT) in CUCM—the configuration of the trunk itself and the IP address of the peer. CUCM also needs to have the route group configured with the gateway, the route list, and route pattern configuration.

Figure 3-8   *Nongatekeeper-Controlled ICT and SIP Trunk Configuration Overview*

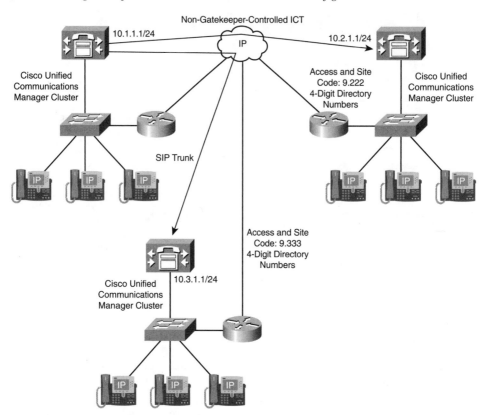

Gatekeeper-Controlled ICT and H.225 Trunk Configuration

Figure 3-9 illustrates the most important configuration elements for implementing a gatekeeper-controlled intercluster trunk or H.225 trunk in CUCM.

The required items are the configuration of the gatekeeper with its IP address and the gatekeeper-controlled ICT that points to the gatekeeper. CUCM also needs the route group connected to the gateway, route list, and route pattern configuration, similar to the previous example.

Figure 3-9   *Gatekeeper-Controlled ICT and H.225 Trunk Configuration Overview*

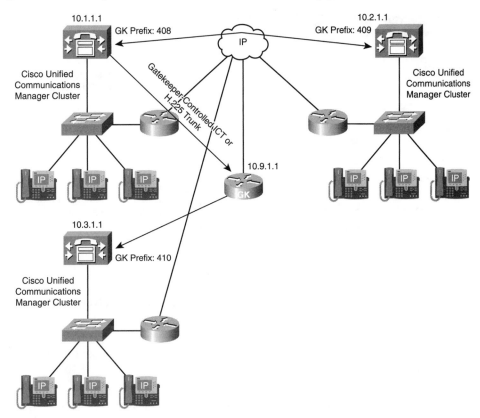

Implementing SIP Trunks

Figures 3-10 and 3-11 illustrate a CUCM SIP trunk configuration.

Figure 3-10   *CUCM SIP Trunk Configuration*

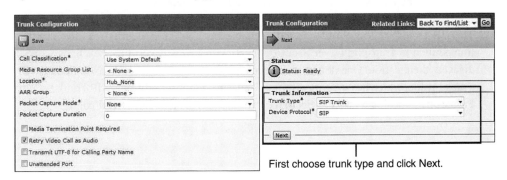

Enter trunk name and description and choose device pool.

Figure 3-11   *CUCM SIP Trunk Configuration, Continued*

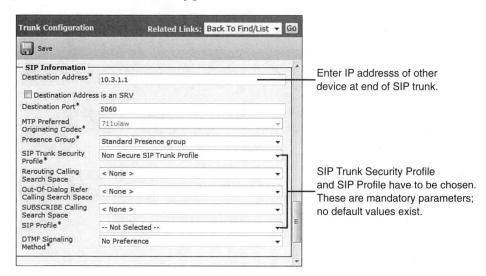

To add a SIP trunk in CUCM, choose **Device > Trunk** and click **Add New**. Then, in the Trunk Type drop-down list, choose **SIP Trunk** and click **Next**.

In the Trunk Configuration window, enter a name for the SIP trunk, choose the device pool that should be used, and optionally add a description.

In the SIP Information area of the Trunk Configuration window shown in Figure 3-11, enter the destination address of the device that is located on the other end of the SIP trunk. This device can be a Cisco Unified Border Element, CUCM Express, or any other SIP-capable device, such as a third-party SIP proxy server.

In addition, you must choose a SIP Trunk Security Profile and a SIP Profile. Both parameters are mandatory and do not have a default value.

The SIP Trunk Security Profile is used to enable and configure security features on SIP trunks, such as Transport Layer Security (TLS) with two-way certificate exchange, or SIP digest authentication. One default SIP Trunk Security Profile exists: the Non Secure SIP Trunk Profile, which has security disabled. You can configure additional SIP Trunk Security Profiles by choosing **System > Security Profile > SIP Trunk Security Profile**.

The SIP Profile is used to set timers, Real-Time Transport Protocol (RTP) port numbers, and some feature settings (such as call pickup Uniform Resource Identifiers [URIs], call hold ringback, or caller ID blocking). One default SIP profile exists called the Standard SIP Profile. You can configure additional SIP profiles by choosing **Device > Device Settings > SIP Profile**.

Implementing Intercluster and H.225 Trunks

Figures 3-12 and 3-13 demonstrate how to implement nongatekeeper-controlled intercluster trunks in CUCM. The steps are as follows:

Step 1 Choose **Device > Trunk**, and then click **Add New**.

Step 2 Choose the appropriate trunk type. After you click **Next**, the Trunk Configuration window appears, where you can configure the nongatekeeper-controlled intercluster trunk.

Step 3 Enter a device name, choose the device pool that should be used, and optionally add a description.

Step 4 Enter the IP address or addresses of the CUCM servers of the other cluster.

Figure 3-12 *Implementing Nongatekeeper-Controlled Intercluster Trunks*

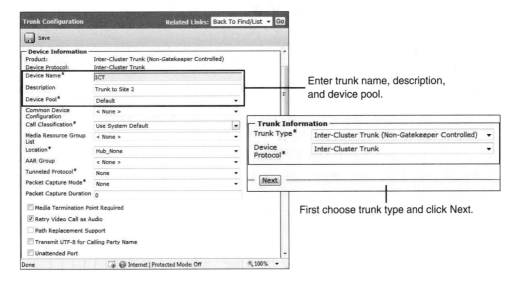

Figure 3-13 *Implementing Nongatekeeper-Controlled Intercluster Trunks, Continued*

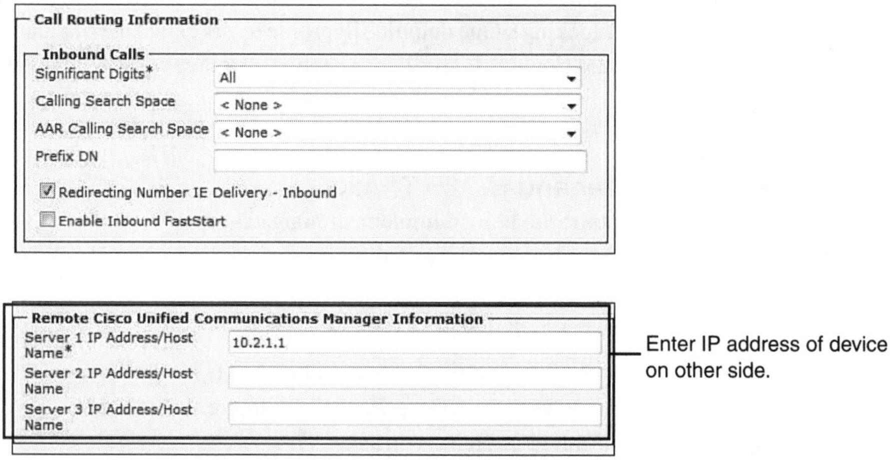

NOTE   Because the nongatekeeper-controlled intercluster trunk does not use a gatekeeper for address resolution, you must manually enter the IP address(es) of the devices on the other side.

CUCM Gatekeeper-Controlled ICT and H.225 Trunk Configuration

Figures 3-14 through 3-16 show how to implement gatekeeper-controlled intercluster trunks (an H.225 trunk or a gatekeeper-controlled intercluster trunk) in CUCM. The steps are as follows:

Step 1   Choose **Device > Gatekeeper** and click **Add New**. In the Gatekeeper Configuration window, shown in Figure 3-14, enter the IP address of the H.323 gatekeeper and optionally a description. Then make sure that the Enable Device check box is checked.

Step 2   After you have configured the gatekeeper, you can add the gatekeeper-controlled trunk, as shown in Figure 3-15. Choose **Device > Trunk** and click **Add New**. Then choose the trunk type. As discussed earlier in this chapter, there are two types of gatekeeper-controlled H.323 trunks. Gatekeeper-controlled intercluster trunks must be used when connecting to CUCM earlier than version 3.2. H.225 trunks are used to connect to CUCM version 3.2 or higher, as well as other H.323 devices such as gateways or conferencing systems.

Figure 3-14 *Implementing CUCM Gatekeeper-Controlled Intercluster Trunk Configuration: Step 1*

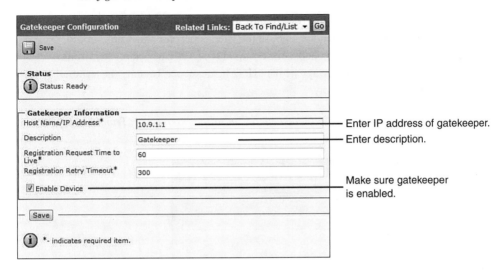

Figure 3-15 *Implementing CUCM Gatekeeper-Controlled Intercluster Trunk Configuration: Steps 2 and 3*

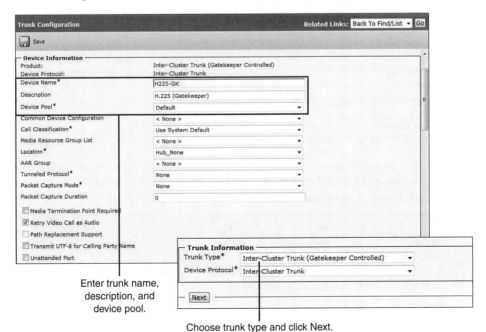

Step 3   After selecting the trunk type, enter a name for the trunk, choose the device pool that should be used, and optionally enter a description.

Step 4   As shown in Figure 3-16, you must provide the gatekeeper information. From the drop-down list, choose the gatekeeper that this trunk should register to, and then choose the terminal type. CUCM can register trunks as terminals or gateways with an H.323 gatekeeper. Usually the terminal type is set to Gateway.

Figure 3-16   *Implementing CUCM Gatekeeper-Controlled Intercluster Trunk Configuration: Steps 4 Through 6*

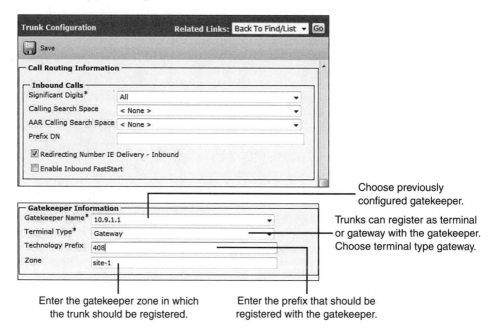

Choose previously configured gatekeeper.

Trunks can register as terminal or gateway with the gatekeeper. Choose terminal type gateway.

Enter the gatekeeper zone in which the trunk should be registered.

Enter the prefix that should be registered with the gatekeeper.

Step 5   In the Technology Prefix field, enter the prefix, which should be registered with the gatekeeper.

NOTE   The Prefix DN you enter is the prefix that the trunk will register with the gatekeeper. It can, but does not have to, include a Technology Prefix. In Figure 3-16, a Technology Prefix of 408 is used. More information about prefixes and technology prefixes is provided in *Cisco Voice over IP (CVOICE)*, Third Edition.

Step 6   Enter the gatekeeper zone in which the trunk should be registered.

> **TIP**   The H.323 zone name is case-sensitive. Make sure that it matches the zone name that was configured at the gatekeeper. In addition, if the zone name is not added and no zone security is set up, CUCM registers into the first configured zone on its assigned gatekeeper, which could cause problems.

Summary

The following key points were discussed in this chapter:

- Connection options for multisite deployments include gateways and trunks.

- When you implement MGCP gateways, most configurations are done in CUCM.

- When you implement H.323 gateways, CUCM and the gateway both have to be configured with a dial plan.

- Cisco IOS H.323 gateway configuration includes H.323 gateway and dial peer configuration tasks.

- H.323 gateway configuration in CUCM includes gateway and dial plan configuration tasks.

- Trunk support in CUCM includes SIP and three types of H.323 trunks.

- SIP trunk implementation includes trunk and dial plan configuration in CUCM.

- When configuring nongatekeeper-controlled ICTs, you must specify the IP address of the peer. Gatekeeper-controlled ICTs and H.225 trunks require you to configure an H.323 gatekeeper instead.

References

For additional information, refer to these resources:

- Cisco Systems, Inc., Cisco Unified Communications Solution Reference Network Design (SRND), based on CUCM Release 6.x, June 2007

- Cisco Systems, Inc., CUCM Administration Guide Release 6.0(1)

- Cisco Systems, Inc., Cisco IOS Voice Configuration Library: http://www.cisco.com/en/US/partner/products/ps6441/prod_configuration_guide09186a0080565f8a.html

Review Questions

Use these questions to review what you've learned in this chapter. The answers appear in Appendix A, "Answers to Chapter Review Questions."

1. Which of the following is not a connection option for a multisite CUCM deployment?

   a. SIP trunk

   b. SIP gateway

   c. H.323 gateway

   d. H.225 trunk

2. Which two commands are required to enable MGCP at the gateway when using the CUCM configuration server feature?

   a. **mgcp**

   b. **sccp**

   c. **ccm-manager config server** *IP address*

   d. **ccm-manager config**

   e. **ccm-manager sccp**

3. What is not configured in CUCM when you configure an H.323 PSTN gateway?

   a. The gateway in the route group

   b. The IP address of the gateway in the route list

   c. The route group in the route list

   d. The route pattern pointing to the route list

4. What is not configured when you configure an H.323 PSTN gateway?

   a. The IP address used for the H.323 interface

   b. The dial peer pointing to CUCM

   c. The IP address of the call agent

   d. The dial peer(s) pointing to the PSTN

5. Which parameter is set at the gateway configuration page to strip the called-party number to a certain number of digits?

   a. Called Party Transformation Mask

   b. Significant Digits

   c. Calling Party Transformation Mask

   d. Number-Length

   e. Discard Digit Instruction

6. Which two types of trunks are configured directly with the IP address of the next signaling device in the path?

   a. SIP gateway

   b. Nongatekeeper-controlled intercluster trunk

   c. SIP trunk

   d. Gatekeeper-controlled intercluster trunk

   e. MGCP trunk

7. Where do you configure SIP timers and features for a SIP trunk?

   a. SIP profile

   b. SIP security profile

   c. SIP trunk security profile

   d. Common trunk profile

8. What do you need to specify at the gatekeeper configuration page when adding a gatekeeper to CUCM?

   a. Hostname of the gatekeeper

   b. H.323 ID of the gatekeeper

   c. IP address of the gatekeeper

   d. Zone name

   e. Technology prefix

9. What is the best reason to implement a gatekeeper in a multisite implementation?

   a. To allow IP Phones to register to the gatekeeper to implement centralized call routing

   b. To prevent IP Phones from registering to the incorrect CUCM server

   c. To implement centralized call routing with CAC

   d. To implement centralized call routing, ensuring that CAC is not used incorrectly

CHAPTER 4

Implementing a Dial Plan for Multisite Deployments

Multisite dial plans have to address special issues, such as overlapping and nonconsecutive directory numbers, public switched telephone network (PSTN) access, PSTN backup, and tail-end hop-off (TEHO). This chapter describes how to build multisite dial plans using CUCM and Cisco IOS gateways.

Chapter Objectives

Upon completing this chapter, you will be able to implement a dial plan to support inbound and outbound PSTN dialing, site-code dialing, and tail-end hop-off. You will be able to meet these objectives:

- Identify dial plan issues and possible solutions

- Describe how site codes and transformation masks solve issues caused by overlapping directory numbers

- Implement PSTN access in a multisite deployment

- Implement selective PSTN breakout

- Describe how to use the PSTN as a backup for calls to other VoIP domains

- Implement TEHO

Multisite Dial Plan Overview

Several dial plan solutions exist for multisite deployments with both centralized call processing and distributed call processing.

- **Access and site codes:** By adding an access code and a site code to directory numbers of remote locations, you can do call routing based on the site code instead of directory numbers. As a result, directory numbers do not have to be globally unique, although they do need to be unique within a site. Configuration requires route patterns, translation patterns, partitions, and Calling Search Spaces (CSS). Adding access and site codes simplifies internal dialing for users in a multisite environment.

- **Implementing PSTN access:** PSTN access within a CUCM cluster is implemented using route patterns, route lists, route groups, and partitions and CSSs. When implementing TEHO, the same dial plan configuration elements are used; however, more entities have to be configured, which makes the configuration more complex. TEHO reduces the operating cost of long-distance dialing.

- **Implementing PSTN backup:** The IP WAN used in a multisite deployment with centralized call processing is backed up by Media Gateway Control Protocol (MGCP) fallback, Cisco Unified Survivable Remote Site Telephony (SRST), or CUCM Express in SRST mode, and Call Forward Unregistered (CFUR). PSTN backup ensures that calls will go through the PSTN in the event of a WAN link failure.

Implementing Access and Site Codes

Configuring access and site codes includes implementing site codes for on-net calls and setting digit manipulation by configuring route patterns, translation patterns, partitions, and calling search spaces.

Implementing Site Codes for On-Net Calls

In Figure 4-1, two sites have overlapping and nonconsecutive directory numbers. To accommodate unique addressing of all endpoints, site-code dialing is used. Users dial an access code (8 in this example), followed by a three-digit site code. A designer can choose another site code access code as well. When calling the phone with directory number 1001 at the remote site, a user located at the main site has to dial 82221001. For calls in the other direction, remote users dial 81111001. When distributed call processing is used, each CUCM cluster is only aware of its own directory numbers in detail. For all directory numbers located at the other site, the call is routed to a CUCM server at the other site based on the dialed site code.

Digit-Manipulation Requirements When Using Access and Site Codes

When you use site codes in multisite environments with distributed call processing, as shown in Figure 4-2, the access and site code have to be stripped from the Dialed Number Identification Service (DNIS) on outgoing calls. If access and site codes are configured before the . in the route pattern, they can be easily stripped using the discard digit instruction on the route pattern or route list. For incoming calls, you have to add the access code and appropriate site code that are used to get to the caller's site. You can do this easily by using translation patterns. Note that the ANI can also be properly manipulated on the outgoing CUCM servers at the main site.

Figure 4-1 *Access and Site Codes Solve Issues with Directory Numbers Used at Different Sites*

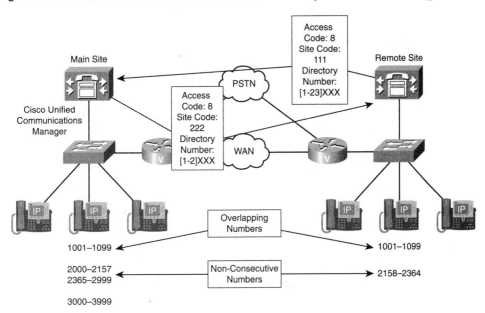

Figure 4-2 *Digit-Manipulation Requirements When Using Access and Site Codes*

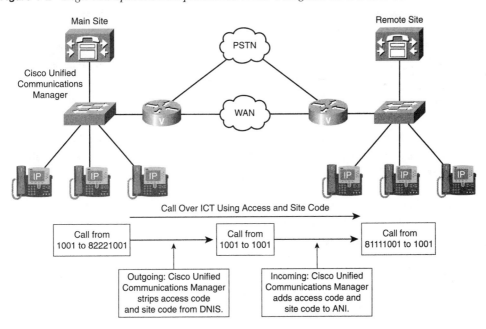

> **NOTE** If the WAN link is not functional, additional digit manipulation would be required to route the call through the PSTN, because the PSTN does not understand the Site Code.

Access and Site Code Requirements for Centralized Call-Processing Deployments

If overlapping directory numbers exist in a centralized call-processing deployment, access and site codes are implemented in a different way, as shown in Figure 4-3.

Figure 4-3 *Centralized Call Processing Deployments: Access and Site Codes*

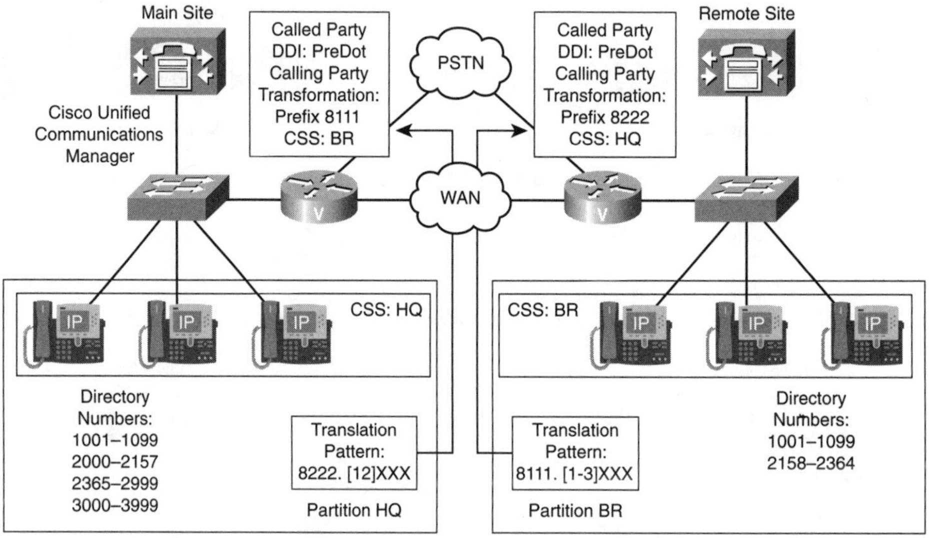

This figure shows two sites with centralized call processing. Directory numbers in the main site and the remote site partially overlap. Again, access and site codes are used to solve the problem of overlapping directory numbers.

However, in this case, partitions and CSSs need to be deployed in a way that phones at the remote site do not see directory numbers of main-site phones, and vice versa. In this case, a translation pattern is added for each site.

The translation pattern of each site includes the access and site code of the respective site. Phones at each site have a CSS assigned, which provides access to the directory numbers of the local site and the translation pattern for the other site or sites. The translation patterns are configured with a transformation mask that strips the access code and site code. Further, each translation pattern must have a CSS, which provides access to only those directory numbers that are located at the target site of the respective translation pattern. This way, all phones can dial local directory numbers and site-code translation patterns for accessing other sites. After an intersite number is dialed that consists of the access code, site code, and directory number, the directory number is extracted by the translation pattern. Then the number is looked up again in the call-routing table using a CSS that has access only to the directory numbers of the site, which was identified by the site code.

Implementing PSTN Access

When you implement PSTN access in a multisite environment, you must perform digit manipulation as described in the following list before the call is sent to the PSTN. Digit manipulation has to be done in CUCM when you use an MGCP gateway. It can be performed either in CUCM or at the H.323 gateway when using an H.323 gateway.

- Outgoing calls to the PSTN:

    —**Automatic Number Identification (ANI) transformation:** If no direct inward dialing (DID) range is used at the PSTN, transform all directory numbers to a single PSTN number in the ANI. If DID is used, extend the directory numbers to a full PSTN number.

    —**DNIS transformation:** Strip the access code.

- Incoming calls from the PSTN:

    —**ANI transformation:** Transform ANI into the full number (considering Type of Number [TON]), and add the access code so that users can easily redial the number.

    —**DNIS transformation:** If DID is used, strip the office code, area code, and country code (if present) to get to the directory number. If DID is not used, route the call to an attendant such as a receptionist or an interactive voice response (IVR) application.

Figure 4-4 shows an example of digit manipulation performed for both incoming and outgoing PSTN calls.

As shown in the figure, internal numbers have to be represented as valid PSTN numbers, and PSTN numbers should be shown with access code 9 internally. Recall from Chapter 1, "Identifying Issues in a Multisite Deployment," that the ANI is the number calling from, and the DNIS is the number calling to. Note how four-digit dialing is used internal to CUCM in this example because incoming DNISs are manipulated to four digits.

Figure 4-4   *PSTN Access Example*

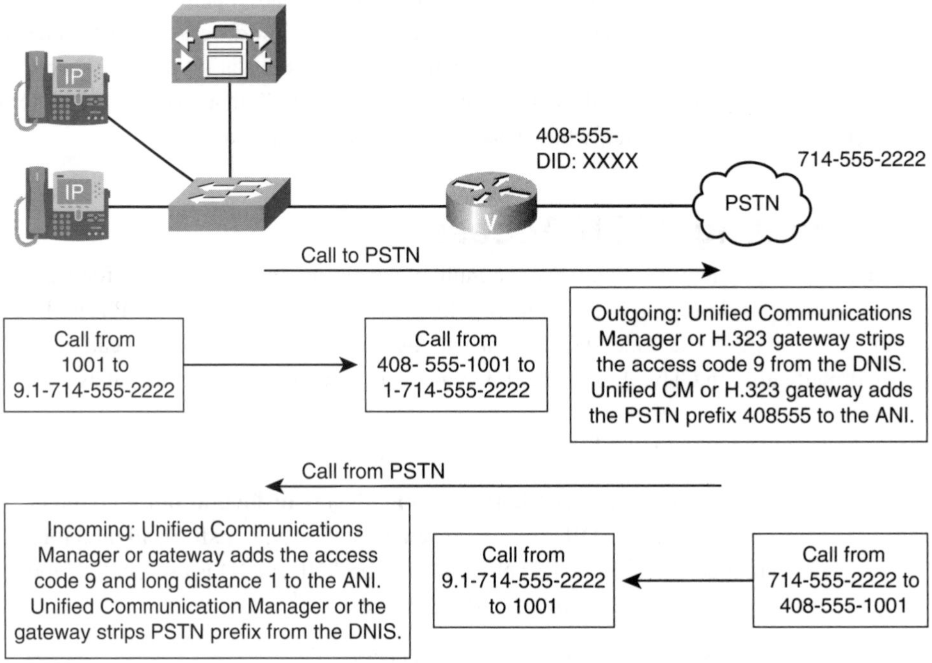

NOTE   Adding the access code (and changing ten-digit PSTN numbers to 11-digit PSTN numbers, including the long-distance 1 digit) to the ANI of incoming calls is not required. Adding it, however, allows users to call back the number from call lists (such as received calls or missed calls) without having to edit the number by adding the required access code.

Transformation of Incoming Calls Using ISDN TON

The TON is used to specify in which format a number such as ANI or DNIS is represented. To have a unique, standardized way to represent PSTN numbers in CUCM, the numbers have to be transformed based on the TON.

U.S. TON in ISDN provides information about number format:

■   Subscriber

   Seven-digit subscriber number: three-digit exchange code, four-digit station code

■   National

Ten-digit number: three-digit area code, seven-digit subscriber number

- International

Variable length (11 digits for U.S. numbers):

—Country code (one digit for U.S. country code; one, two, or three digits for all other countries)

—Area code (three digits for U.S. area code)

—Subscriber number (seven digits for U.S. subscriber number)

NOTE   This description is based on the North American Numbering Plan (NANP) , which applies to the United States, Canada, and several Caribbean nations, as described at http://www.nanpa.com.

Figure 4-5 shows an example of performing TON-based digit manipulation based on the incoming call's ANI.

Figure 4-5   *ISDN TON: ANI Transformation of an Incoming Call*

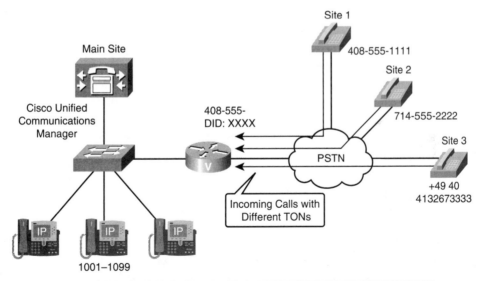

Site	TON	ANI	Required ANI Transformation
1	Subscriber	5551111	9.5551111
2	National	7145552222	9.1714555 2222
3	International	49404132673333	9.01149404132673333

In this figure, three different calls are received at the main site gateway. The first call is received from the local area with a subscriber TON and a seven-digit number. This number only needs to be prefixed with access code 9. The second call, received with national TON and ten digits, is modified by adding access code 9 and the long-distance 1, both of which are required for placing calls back to the source of the call. The third call is received from another country (Germany in this case) with an international TON. For this call, the access codes 9 and 011 have to be added to the received number, which begins with the country code of 49. Note that 011 is the NANP international access code, which is different for calls originating outside the NANP.

The end result benefits an internal user who receives but misses any calls from these sites and wants to easily call back any of these numbers without editing the number from his or her missed call list.

NOTE   This example demonstrates the commonly used access code 9 to dial out to the PSTN. It is perfectly acceptable for an organization to choose another access code such as 8, or no access code at all. The Required ANI Transformation digits in this example would be changed accordingly.

Implementing Selective PSTN Breakout

A multisite deployment, shown in Figure 4-6, typically has multiple PSTN gateways, usually one per site. Selective PSTN breakout ensures that local gateways are used to access the PSTN. From a dial plan perspective, this can be achieved by creating one 9.@ route pattern if you're using the North American Numbering Plan; otherwise, use 9.! per site. These route patterns are put into different partitions and point to different PSTN gateways. IP Phones need to be configured with a CSS that includes only the route patterns that refer to the local gateway. This way, IP Phones will always use their local PSTN gateway for PSTN breakout.

Figure 4-6   *Configure IP Phones to Use a Local PSTN Gateway*

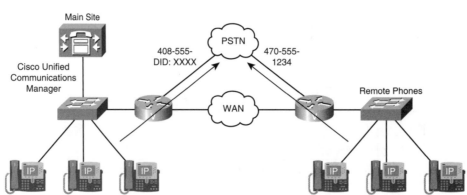

PSTN breakout occurs at the gateway located closest to the PSTN destination:

■ Route patterns for each area that can be reached at different costs—one per site, in different partitions

■ Route patterns point to route lists (with different priorities of gateways: cheapest gateway first, local gateway next, and then another gateway for additional backup if desired).

■ Phone CSS for correct route-pattern selection

NOTE If greater control over restricting outbound dialing is required, more-specific route patterns should be created instead of those using the generic @ wildcard.

Configure IP Phones to Use Remote Gateways for Backup PSTN Access

Figure 4-7 shows how a multisite dial plan can feature multiple choices for PSTN access to provide a backup in case of primary (local) gateway failure.

Figure 4-7 *Configure IP Phones to Use Remote Gateways for Backup PSTN Access*

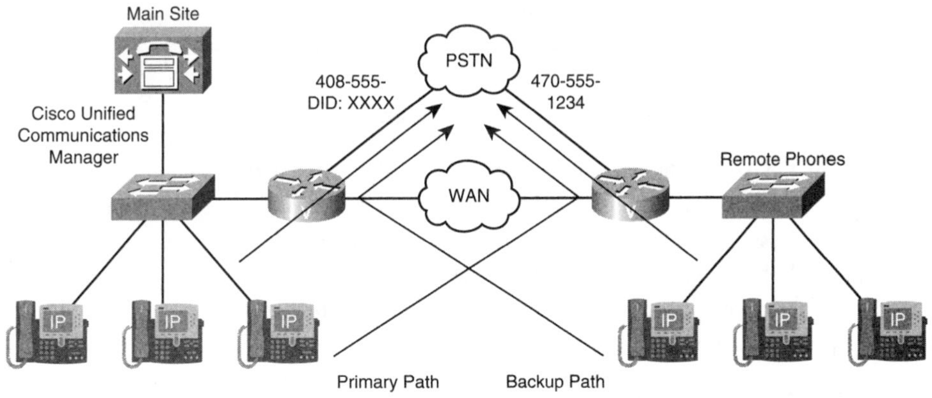

In this figure, both sites have IP Phones and a PSTN gateway. As discussed earlier in this book, IP Phones should always use their local gateway to access the PSTN, which is critical for emergency 911 calls. A user dialing 911 in Atlanta certainly wouldn't want to reach the emergency call center in Chicago. This example of geographic routing can be achieved by using multiple route patterns in partitions and CSSs at the IP Phones. If the local PSTN gateway has a failure while the WAN link is functional, you can provide backup PSTN access by using route lists and route groups with multiple gateways. Because a route list and route group is a prioritized list of devices, it is simple to specify the primary and backup path.

Careful consideration should be given to 911 calls so as to not route 911 calls remotely. The emergency number 911 is also unique within the NANP; different emergency numbers are used outside the NANP.

Considerations When Using Backup PSTN Gateways

When using backup PSTN gateways, you have to consider issues that can occur with the ANI on outgoing calls. Basically, you have two options for configuring the ANI for the outgoing call:

■ **Use the primary gateway's PSTN number on the secondary gateway.**

When using the ANI of the primary (currently unavailable) gateway to route the call out of the secondary gateway, the call is signaled the same way as it is when using the primary gateway. Callbacks to the ANI are not possible as long as the primary gateway is not operating. Users receiving the calls do not become confused, because they don't see a different number. If they use the signaled number to call later when the primary gateway is up and running again, everything works as it should.

CAUTION   Sending calls out of a gateway with the ANI of another gateway might not be permitted in your country or by your provider. There can also be issues with emergency calls. Therefore, ensure that your planned deployment complies with legal requirements.

■ **Use the secondary gateway's PSTN number.**

When the ANI of the backup gateway is used, the called party may get confused about the number that should be used when calling back. For instance, the person may update his address books with the different number and inadvertently end up sending calls through the backup gateway every time he calls. Further DID ranges would have to include remote phones or IVR scripts (automated attendants) to be able to route calls to phones located in any site, regardless of where the PSTN call was received.

CAUTION   Using a remote gateway for PSTN access might not be permitted in your country or by your provider. There can also be issues with emergency calls. Therefore, ensure that your planned deployment complies with legal requirements.

Implementing PSTN Backup for On-Net Intersite Calls

Figure 4-8 shows a multisite deployment with two sites. Each site has its own CUCM cluster. Intersite calls use the intercluster trunk (ICT) or a SIP trunk over the IP WAN to the other cluster. The route patterns with the site codes point to route lists, which point to route groups that have the ICT as the first option and the PSTN gateway as the second option. If the IP WAN link fails for any reason, because both sites have access to the PSTN, the PSTN is used as a backup for intersite calls. Note that proper digit manipulation must take place if the calls are routed through the PSTN.

Figure 4-8   *Implementing PSTN Backup for On-Net Intersite Calls*

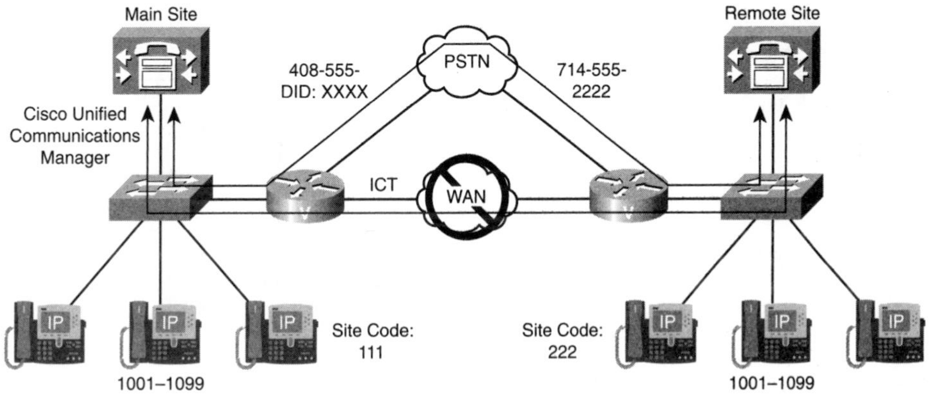

Digit-Manipulation Requirements for PSTN Backup of On-Net Intersite Calls

PSTN backup for on-net calls can be easily provided by route lists and route groups giving priority to the intercluster trunk over the PSTN gateway, as shown in Figure 4-9.

When using a PSTN backup for on-net calls, you must address internal versus external dialing. Although on-net calls usually use site codes and directory numbers, calls that are sent through the PSTN have to use E.164 numbers. Digit-manipulation requirements vary, depending on the path that is taken for the call:

- Digit-manipulation requirements when using the ICT, which is the first choice in the route list and route group:

    —**At the calling site:** The access and site code are removed from DNIS.

    —**At the receiving site:** The access and site code are added to the ANI. (This can also be done on the calling site.)

Figure 4-9 *Digit-Manipulation Requirements for PSTN Backup of On-Net Intersite Calls*

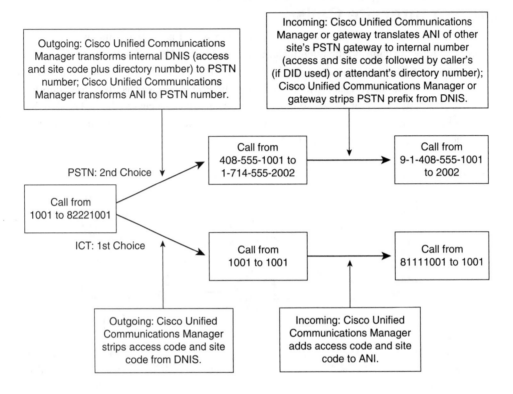

■ Digit-manipulation requirements when using the PSTN (secondary choice in the route list and route group)

—**At the calling site:** The internal DNIS comprising an access code, site code, and directory number is transformed into the PSTN number of the called phone. The ANI is transformed into the PSTN number of the calling phone.

NOTE If DID is not supported, the site's PSTN number is used in DNIS and ANI instead of the IP Phone's PSTN number.

—**At the receiving site:** The PSTN ANI is recognized as a PSTN number of an on-net connected site and is transformed into the internal number: access and site code, followed by the directory number of the calling phone (if DID is used at the calling site) or of the attendant of the calling site (if DID is not used at the calling site). The DNIS is transformed into an internal directory number and is routed to the IP Phone (if DID is used at the receiving site) or to an attendant (if DID is not used at the receiving site).

Implementing Tail-End Hop-Off

When you implement TEHO, PSTN breakout occurs at the gateway that is closest to the dialed PSTN destination. You do this by creating a route pattern for each destination area that can be reached at different costs. These route patterns are required once per site and have to be put into different partitions by identifying the site that should use a particular route pattern.

As illustrated in Figure 4-10, each route pattern points to a route list and route group or groups and has an ordered list of PSTN gateways that includes the cheapest gateway first, the local gateway next, and optionally a third gateway for additional backup. IP Phones have a CSS that selects the route patterns built for their site. This way, per originating site and per destination number, a different first-choice gateway can be selected, and the local gateway is the second option.

Figure 4-10 *Implementing Tail-End Hop-Off (TEHO)*

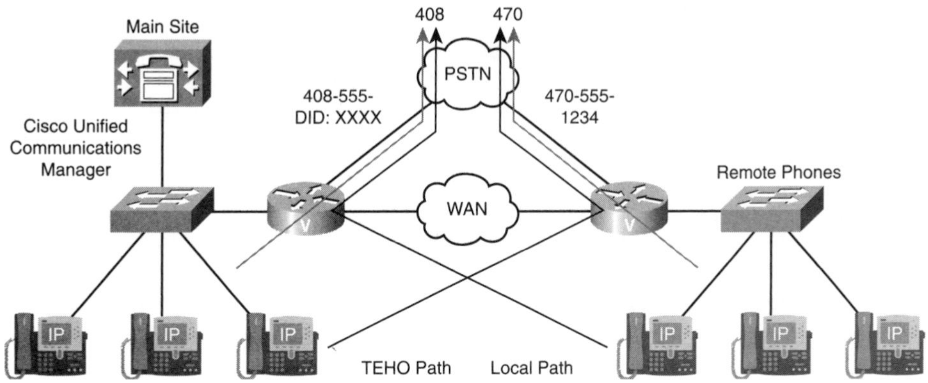

Considerations When Using TEHO

When using backup TEHO, consider the following potential issues:

- Consider what number you want to use for the ANI of the outgoing call. The factors you must consider are the same that have been discussed for PSTN backup.

- With TEHO, calls are routed based on the source (physical location) and based on the dialed number. This can require a huge number of route patterns, resulting in complex dial plans. Such dial plans are difficult to maintain and troubleshoot.

- CUCM has no automated technique to enter all the remote route patterns for TEHO. They all must be entered manually based on a specific study of area codes in different geographic regions and their associated toll charges.

- The primary purpose of TEHO is to reduce operating costs by increasing WAN utilization and decreasing PSTN toll charges. For example, PSTN long-distance toll charges within the contiguous 48 United States have dropped considerably in the last few decades, hence reducing the TEHO cost savings. However, TEHO cost savings for international calls can be considerable.

CAUTION   The use of TEHO might not be permitted in your country or by your provider. There also can be issues with emergency calls. Therefore, ensure that your planned deployment complies with legal requirements.

NOTE   You also must consider call admission control (CAC) when implementing TEHO. When the primary (TEHO) path is not admitted as a result of reaching the CAC call limit, calls should be routed through the local gateway. More information about CAC is provided in Chapter 9, "Implementing Call Admission Control."

Summary

The following key points were discussed in this chapter:

- Multisite dial plans should support selective PSTN breakout with backup gateways, PSTN backup for on-net calls, TEHO, and intersite calls using access codes and site codes.

- If you add an access code and site code to directory numbers at each site, directory numbers do not have to be globally unique anymore.

- When you route calls to the PSTN, calling directory numbers have to be transformed into PSTN numbers. Also, access codes used on dialed patterns have to be removed to ensure that ANI and DNIS are in accordance with PSTN numbering schemes.

- Selective PSTN breakout means that different gateways are used for PSTN access, depending on the caller's physical location.

- When using the PSTN as a backup for intersite calls, internal directory numbers and internally dialed patterns have to be transformed to ensure that ANI and DNIS are in accordance with PSTN numbering schemes.

- When TEHO is implemented, calls to the PSTN are routed differently based on the caller's physical location and the PSTN number that was dialed. This ensures that the call uses the IP WAN as much as possible and breaks out to the PSTN at the gateway that is closest to the dialed PSTN destination.

Review Questions

Use these questions to review what you've learned in this chapter. The answers are found in Appendix A, "Answers to Chapter Review Questions."

1. Which of the following statements about implementing PSTN backup for the IP WAN is true?

    a. In distributed deployments, PSTN backup for intersite calls requires CFUR.

    b. Route groups including the on-net and off-net path are required for PSTN backup in a centralized deployment.

    c. PSTN backup requires a PSTN gateway at each site.

    d. CFUR allows remote-site phones to use the PSTN for calls to the main site.

2. What is required for implementing access and site codes in a centralized deployment?

    a. A separate translation pattern for each destination site, configured with a CSS providing access to the destination site

    b. A separate translation pattern for each source site, configured with a CSS providing access to the source site

    c. A separate translation pattern for each source site, configured with the partition of the destination site

    d. A separate translation pattern for each destination site, configured with the partition of the destination site

3. Which two are not valid type of number (TON) codes for incoming ISDN PSTN calls?

   a. International

   b. National

   c. Subscriber

   d. Directory number

   e. Operator number

4. Which two statements about PSTN gateway selection are true?

   a. Using TEHO minimizes PSTN costs.

   b. Using local PSTN gateways minimizes PSTN costs.

   c. When you use TEHO, you must pay special attention to the configuration of the calling number.

   d. Using remote PSTN gateways for backup is never recommended.

   e. It is recommended that you use remote PSTN gateways as a backup when the IP WAN is overloaded.

5. You should perform digit manipulation at the _____ when digit-manipulation requirements vary based on the gateway used for the call.

   a. Gateway

   b. Route list as it relates to the route group

   c. Route pattern

   d. Trunk

   e. Translation pattern

6. When you implement TEHO for international calls and use the local PSTN gateway as a backup, how many route patterns are required for a cluster with three sites located in different countries?

   a. 3

   b. 6

   c. 9

   d. 12

7. What is the best benefit of using site codes for multisite deployments?

    a. Ease of administering the dial plan

    b. Ease of dialing for users with an overlapping dial plan

    c. Improved security for multisite dialing

    d. You can eliminate implementing CUBE in a multisite environment

8. What is the most desirable configuration for digit manipulation when there are outgoing calls to the PSTN?

    a. Maintain the five-digit user DN ANI.

    b. Always use digit manipulation to change the area code the user dials to reduce operating costs.

    c. Transform the ANI to a full E.164 number of the user's phone or an attendant.

    d. Always avoid digit manipulation of the ANI to preserve internal DNs.

CHAPTER 5

Examining Remote-Site Redundancy Options

This chapter provides an overview of the different options with remote-site redundancy in CUCM multisite installations. These different mechanisms are illustrated to help you understand how the technologies interact to deliver reliable communication services. This includes Media Gateway Control Protocol (MGCP) and Cisco Unified Survivable Remote Site Telephony (SRST).

Chapter Objectives

Upon completing this chapter, you will be able to describe the mechanisms for providing call survivability and device failover at remote sites, including the functions, operation, and limitations of each mechanism. You will be able to meet these objectives:

■   Describe remote-site redundancy options, and compare their characteristics

■   Describe how Cisco Unified SRST works

■   Describe how MGCP fallback works

■   Describe SRST versions, their protocol support and features, and the required Cisco IOS Software release

■   Describe dial plan requirements for MGCP fallback and SRST with the option of using CUCM Express

Remote-Site Redundancy Overview

Two different technologies are used to provide remote-site redundancy for small and medium remote sites in a CUCM environment. SRST and MGCP gateway fallback are the key components of delivering fail-safe communication services, as shown in Figure 5-1.

Figure 5-1 *SRST and MGCP Fallback*

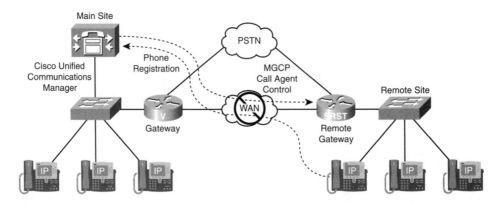

CUCM supports Cisco Unified IP Phones at remote sites that are attached to Cisco multi-service routers across the WAN. Before Cisco Unified SRST, when the WAN connection between a router and the CUCM failed, or when connectivity with the CUCM was lost for any reason, Cisco Unified IP Phones on the network became unusable for the duration of the failure. The reason is that Cisco IP Phones demand Skinny Client Control Protocol (SCCP) or session initiation protocol (SIP) connectivity to a call-processing agent such as CUCM, and in the absence of signaling connectivity, the phones become fully unusable.

Cisco Unified SRST overcomes this problem and ensures that Cisco Unified IP Phones offer continuous, although reduced, service by providing call-handling support for Cisco Unified IP Phones directly from the Cisco Unified SRST router. The system automatically detects a failure and uses Simple Network-Enabled Auto-Provision (SNAP) technology to autoconfigure the branch office router to provide call processing for Cisco Unified IP Phones that are registered with the router. When the WAN link or connection to the primary CUCM subscriber is restored, call handling reverts to the primary CUCM.

MGCP gateway fallback is a mechanism that allows a Cisco IOS router to continue providing voice gateway functions even when the MGCP call agent is not in control of the media gateway. These voice gateway functions are implemented through a fallback mechanism that activates the so-called default technology application. The gateway then works in the same way as a standalone H.323 or SIP gateway by using its configured dial peers.

Remote-Site Redundancy Technologies

Table 5-1 lists the capabilities of different remote-site redundancy technologies.

Table 5-1 *Remote-Site Redundancy Technologies*

		SRST		
	MGCP Fallback	**Cisco Unified SRST**	**Cisco Unified SIP SRST**	**Cisco Unified Communications Manager Express in SRST Mode**
Provides Redundancy For	MGCP-controlled gateways	SCCP phones	SIP phones	SCCP phones
Delivered Service	Fall back to Cisco IOS default technology	Basic telephony service	Basic SIP proxy service	Cisco Unified Communications Manager Express
Maximum Number of Phones	—	720 (C3845)	480 (C3845)	240 (C3845)
ISDN Call Preservation	No	Yes (no MGCP)	Yes (no MGCP)	Yes (no MGCP)
Analog/CAS Call Preservation	Yes	Yes	Yes	Yes

To use SRST as your fallback mode on an MGCP gateway, SRST and MGCP fallback have to be configured on the same gateway.

> **NOTE** MGCP and SRST have had the capability to be configured on the same gateway since Cisco IOS Software Release 12.2(11)T.

Cisco Unified SIP SRST provides a basic set of features to SIP-based IP Phones. It has to be enabled and configured separately on Cisco IOS routers. In Cisco Unified SRST versions before 3.4, it provides a SIP Redirect Server function; in subsequent versions, it acts as a back-to-back user agent (B2BUA).

SIP is an Internet standard discussed in many Request for Comments (RFC). If you want to supplement your knowledge of SIP, here is a good RFC to start with:

http://www.ietf.org/rfc/rfc3261.txt

Cisco Unified Communications Manager Express (CUCME) in SRST mode provides more features to a smaller maximum number of SCCP IP Phones by falling back to CUCME mode. Main feature enhancements include hunt groups and basic automatic call distribution (B-ACD) functions or support of local Cisco Unity voice-mail integrations.

> **NOTE**   Before CUCM version 6, CUCME and SRST contained similar functionality but existed as separate technologies. SRST always requires Cisco CallManager (CCM) or CUCM, whereas CUCME can exist as a separate entity. However, with CUCM version 6, CUCME in SRST mode can add functionality to SRST when configured to provide survivability with CUCM. However, only SRST or CUCME can be configured at any one time on an IOS router.

VoIP call preservation, as shown in Tables 5-2 and 5-3, sustains connectivity for topologies in which signaling is handled by an entity (such as CUCM) that is different from the other endpoint and brokers signaling between the two connected parties.

Call preservation is useful when a gateway and the other endpoint, which typically is a Cisco Unified IP Phone, are co-located at the same site, and the call agent is remote and therefore more likely to experience connectivity failures.

Table 5-2   *Call Preservation Capabilities of Different Interfaces*

Interface Type	Cisco Analog Interface Cards				
Card Type	WS-svccmm-24fxs	Ws-x6624-fxs	VG224	VG248	ATA 186 and 188
H.323 Gateway	No	No	No	Yes	No
SIP Gateway	No	No	No	Yes	No
MGCP Gateway	No	No	No	Yes	No

Table 5-3   *Call Preservation Capabilities of Different Interfaces, Continued*

Interface Type	Cisco Time-Division Multiplexing Interface Cards				
Card Type	T1 CAS	E1 CAS	T1 PRI	E1 PRI	BRI
H.323 Gateway	Yes	Yes	Yes	Yes	Yes
SIP Gateway	Yes	Yes	Yes	Yes	Yes
MGCP Gateway	Yes	Yes	No	No	No

Basic Cisco Unified SRST Usage

Cisco Unified SRST provides CUCM with fallback support for Cisco Unified IP Phones that are attached to a Cisco router on a local network.

Cisco Unified SRST enables routers to provide basic call-handling support for Cisco Unified IP Phones when they lose connection to remote primary, secondary, and tertiary CUCM servers or when the WAN connection is down.

Basic SRST supports up to 720 SCCP IP Phones on the highest supported router (3845). In addition, the VG248 Analog Phone Gateway offers basic SRST support and secure voice fallback. However, it does not support hunt groups or message waiting indication (MWI) for voice mail in fallback mode.

Cisco Unified SIP SRST Usage

Cisco Unified SIP SRST provides backup to an external SIP proxy server by providing basic registrar and redirect server services earlier than Cisco Unified SIP SRST version 3.4 or B2BUA for Cisco Unified SIP SRST version 3.4 and higher services.

A SIP phone uses these services when it is unable to communicate with its primary SIP proxy of CUCM in the event of a WAN connection outage.

Cisco Unified SIP SRST can support SIP phones with standard RFC 3261 feature support locally and across SIP WAN networks. With Cisco Unified SIP SRST, SIP phones can place calls across SIP networks in the same way that SCCP phones do.

Cisco Unified SIP SRST supports the following call combinations: SIP phone to SIP phone, SIP phone to public switched telephone network (PSTN) or router voice port, SIP phone to SCCP phone, and SIP phone to WAN VoIP using SIP.

SIP proxy, registrar, and B2BUA servers are key components of a SIP VoIP network. These servers usually are located in the core of a VoIP network. If SIP phones located at remote sites at the edge of the VoIP network lose connectivity to the network core (because of a WAN outage), they may be unable to make or receive calls. Cisco Unified SIP SRST functionality on a SIP PSTN gateway provides service reliability for SIP-based IP Phones in the event of a WAN outage. Cisco Unified SIP SRST enables the SIP IP Phones to continue making and receiving calls to and from the PSTN. They also can continue making and receiving calls to and from other SIP IP Phones by using the dial peers configured on the router.

When the IP WAN is up, the SIP phone registers with the SIP proxy server and establishes a connection to the B2BUA SIP registrar (B2BUA router). But any calls from the SIP phone go to the SIP proxy server through the WAN and out to the PSTN.

When the IP WAN fails or the SIP proxy server goes down, the call from the SIP phone cannot get to the SIP proxy server. Instead, it goes through the B2BUA router out to the PSTN.

> **NOTE** The B2BUA acts as a user agent to both ends of a SIP call. The B2BUA is responsible for handling all SIP signaling between both ends of the call, from call establishment to termination. Each call is tracked from beginning to end, allowing the operators of the B2BUA to offer value-added features to the call. To SIP clients, the B2BUA acts as a user agent server on one side and as a user agent client on the other (back-to-back) side. The basic implementation of a B2BUA is defined in RFC 3261, as mentioned earlier in this chapter.

CUCME in SRST Mode Usage

CUCME in SRST mode enables routers to provide basic call-handling support for Cisco Unified IP Phones if they lose connection to remote primary, secondary, and tertiary CUCM installations or if the WAN connection is down.

When Cisco Unified SRST functionality is provided by CUCME, provisioning of phones is automatic. Most CUCME features are available to the phones during periods of fallback, including hunt groups, Call Park, and access to Cisco Unity voice messaging services using SCCP. The benefit is that CUCM users gain access to more features during fallback without any additional licensing costs.

CUCME in SRST mode offers a limited telephony feature set during fallback mode. If the following features are required, basic SRST should be used, because these features are not supported with CUCM in SRST mode:

- More than 240 phones exist during fallback service.

- Cisco VG248 Analog Phone Gateway support is required.

- Secure voice fallback during SRST fallback service.

- Simple, one-time configuration for SRST fallback service.

Cisco Unified SRST Operation

Figure 5-2 illustrates the function of Cisco Unified SRST.

Figure 5-2   *SRST Function in a Normal Situation*

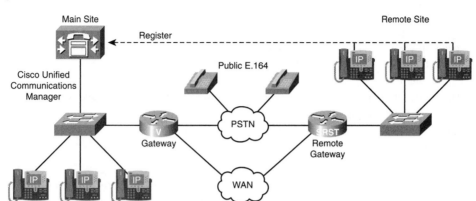

CUCM supports Cisco Unified IP Phones at remote sites attached to Cisco multiservice routers across the WAN. The remote-site IP Phones register with CUCM. Keepalive messages are exchanged between IP Phones and the central CUCM server across the WAN. CUCM at the main site handles the call processing for the branch IP Phones. Note that Cisco IP Phones cannot register SCCP or SIP through the PSTN to CUCM even if the PSTN is functional, because SCCP and SIP must run over an IP network.

SRST Function of Switchover Signaling

When Cisco Unified IP Phones lose contact with CUCM (as shown in Figure 5-3) because of any kind of IP WAN failure, they register with the local Cisco Unified SRST router to sustain the call-processing capability that is necessary to place and receive calls.

Figure 5-3   *SRST Function of Switchover Signaling*

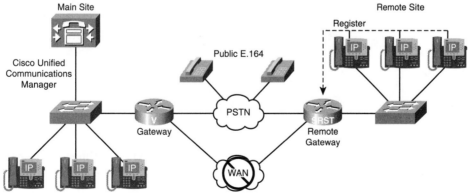

Cisco Unified SRST configuration provides the IP Phones with the alternative call control destination of the Cisco Unified SRST gateway.

When the WAN link fails, the IP Phones lose contact with the central CUCM but then register with the local Cisco Unified SRST gateway.

The Cisco Unified SRST gateway detects newly registered IP Phones, queries these IP Phones for their configuration, and then autoconfigures itself. The Cisco Unified SRST gateway uses SNAP technology to autoconfigure the branch office router to provide call processing for Cisco Unified IP Phones that are registered with the router.

> **CAUTION**   In the event of a WAN failure, when the branch IP Phones register to the SRST gateway, do not erase the settings on the phone. The phone settings, such as phone numbers, were added to the phone from CUCM when the WAN was functional, and the phone then takes its settings and uses them to register to the SRST router. If the phone has no settings, it cannot register to SRST, and the phone will not be functional.

SRST Function of the Call Flow After Switchover

Cisco Unified SRST ensures that Cisco Unified IP Phones offer continuous service by providing call-handling support directly from the Cisco Unified SRST router using a basic set of call-handling features, as shown in Figure 5-4.

Figure 5-4   *SRST Function of the Call Flow After Switchover*

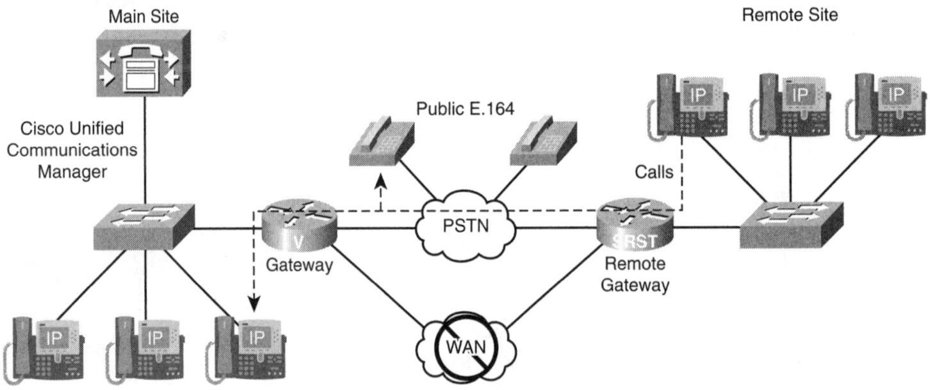

The Cisco Unified SRST gateway uses the local PSTN breakout with configured dial peers. Cisco Unified SRST features such as call preservation, autoprovisioning, and failover are supported.

During a WAN connection failure, when Cisco Unified SRST is enabled, Cisco Unified IP Phones display a message informing users that the phone is operating in CUCM fallback mode. This message can be adjusted.

While in CUCM fallback mode, Cisco Unified IP Phones continue sending keepalive messages in an attempt to reestablish a connection with the CUCM server at the main site.

SRST Function of Switchback

Figure 5-5 shows Cisco Unified IP Phones attempting to reestablish a connection over the WAN link with CUCM at the main site periodically when they are registered with a Cisco Unified SRST gateway.

Figure 5-5 *SRST Function of Switchback*

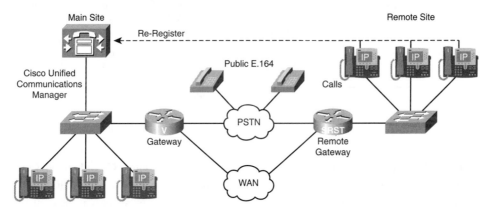

Cisco IP Phones, by default, wait up to 120 seconds before attempting to reestablish a connection to a remote CUCM.

When the WAN link or connection to the primary CUCM is restored, the Cisco Unified IP Phones reregister with their primary CUCM. Three switchback methods are available on the Cisco IOS router: immediate switchback, graceful switchback (after all outgoing calls on the gateway are completed), or switchback after a configured delay. When switchback is completed, call handling reverts to the primary CUCM, and SRST returns to standby mode. The phones then return to their full functionality provided by CUCM.

SRST Timing

Typically, a phone takes three times the keepalive period to discover that its connection to CUCM has failed. The default keepalive period, as shown in Figure 5-6, is 30 seconds.

Figure 5-6 *SRST Timing*

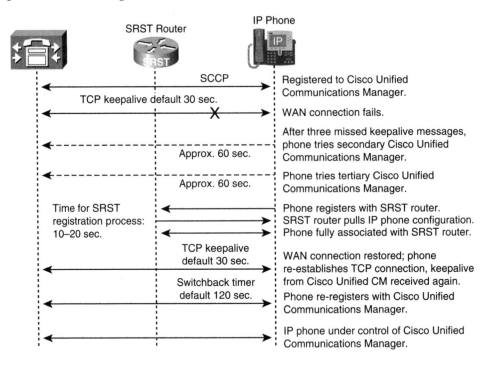

If the IP Phone has an active standby connection established with a Cisco Unified SRST router, the fallback process takes 10 to 20 seconds after the connection with CUCM is lost. An active standby connection to a Cisco Unified SRST router exists only if the phone has a single CUCM in its Cisco Unified CM Group. Otherwise, the phone activates a standby connection to its secondary CUCM.

> **NOTE** The time it takes for an IP Phone to fall back to the SRST router can vary, depending on the phone type. Phones such as the Cisco Unified IP Phone models 7902, 7905, and 7912 can take approximately 2.5 minutes to fall back to SRST mode.

If a Cisco Unified IP Phone has multiple CUCM systems in its Cisco Unified CM group, the phone progresses through its list before attempting to connect with its local Cisco Unified SRST router. Therefore, the time that passes before the Cisco Unified IP Phone eventually establishes a connection with the Cisco Unified SRST router increases with each attempt to connect to a CUCM. Assuming that each attempt to connect to a CUCM takes about one minute, the Cisco Unified IP Phone in question could remain offline for three minutes or more following a WAN link failure. You can decrease this time by setting the keepalive timer to a smaller value. You can configure the keepalive timer using the CUCM service parameter Station Keepalive Interval.

While in SRST mode, Cisco Unified IP Phones periodically attempt to reestablish a connection with CUCM at the main site.

> **NOTE**   If you want a Cisco IP Phone to come out of SRST fallback mode faster, you can manually reboot the phone by pressing "settings" and then **#**, or by going into the router mode call-manager-fallback and entering **reset all**.

MGCP Fallback Usage

A PSTN gateway can use MGCP gateway fallback configured as an individual feature if H.323 or SIP is configured as a backup service. SRST and MGCP fallback must be configured on the same gateway with Cisco IOS Software Release 12.2(11)T or later if this single gateway will provide SRST fallback service to phones and MGCP gateway fallback.

Although MGCP gateway fallback is most often used together with SRST to provide gateway functions to IP Phones in SRST mode, it can also be used as a standalone feature. For example, with a fax application server using a PRI ISDN interface controlled by MGCP, connectivity to the PSTN can be preserved by MGCP gateway fallback. An MGCP-fallback standalone configuration may also be used to allow analog interfaces that are controlled by SCCP to stay in service even when the WAN connection to the CUCM is down.

MGCP gateway fallback preserves active calls from remote-site IP Phones to the PSTN when analog or channel-associated signaling (CAS) protocols are used. For ISDN protocols, call preservation is impossible, because Layer 3 of the ISDN stack is disconnected from the MGCP call agent and is restarted on the local Cisco IOS gateway. This means that for active ISDN calls, all call-state information is lost in cases of switchover to fallback operation.

MGCP Fallback Operation

MGCP gateway fallback, shown in Figure 5-7, is a feature that improves the reliability of MGCP branch networks. A WAN link connects the MGCP gateway at a remote site to the Cisco Communications Manager at a central site, which is the MGCP call agent. If the WAN link fails, the fallback feature keeps the gateway working as an H.323 or SIP gateway and rehomes to the MGCP call agent when the WAN link is active again. MGCP gateway fallback works in conjunction with the SRST feature.

Figure 5-7   *MGCP Gateway Fallback in a Normal Situation*

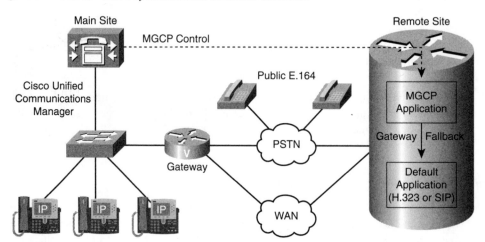

Cisco IOS gateways can maintain links to up to two backup CUCM servers in addition to a primary CUCM. This redundancy enables a voice gateway to switch over to a backup server if the gateway loses communication with the primary server. The secondary backup server takes control of the devices that are registered with the primary CUCM. The tertiary backup takes control of the registered devices if both the primary and secondary backup CUCM systems fail. The gateway preserves existing connections during a switchover to a backup CUCM server.

When the primary CUCM server becomes available again, control reverts to that server. Reverting to the primary server can occur in several ways: immediately, after a configurable amount of time, or only when all connected sessions are released.

MGCP Gateway Fallback During Switchover

The MGCP gateway performs a switchover to its default technology of H.323 or SIP (as shown in Figure 5-8) when the keepalives between CUCM and the Cisco MGCP gateway are missing.

Figure 5-8 *MGCP Gateway Fallback During Switchover*

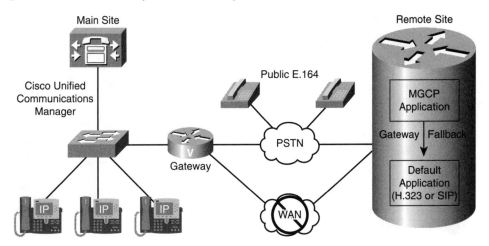

The MGCP gateway fallback feature provides the following functionality:

■ **MGCP gateway fallback support:** All active MGCP analog, E1 CAS, and T1 CAS calls are maintained during the fallback transition. Callers are unaware of the fallback transition, and the active MGCP calls are cleared only when the callers hang up. Active MGCP PRI backhaul calls are released during fallback. Any transient MGCP calls that are not in the connected state are cleared at the onset of the fallback transition and must be attempted again later.

■ **Basic connection services in fallback mode:** Basic connection services are provided for IP telephony traffic that passes through the gateway. When the local MGCP gateway transitions into fallback mode, the default H.323 or SIP session application assumes responsibility for handling new calls. Only basic two-party voice calls are supported during the fallback period. When a user completes (hangs up) an active MGCP call, the MGCP application handles the on-hook event and clears all call resources.

MGCP Gateway Fallback During Switchback

The MGCP-gateway-fallback feature provides the rehome functionality to switch back to MGCP mode. As shown in Figure 5-9, the switchback or rehome mechanism is triggered by the reestablishment of the TCP connection between CUCM and the Cisco MGCP gateway.

Figure 5-9   *MGCP Gateway Fallback During Switchback*

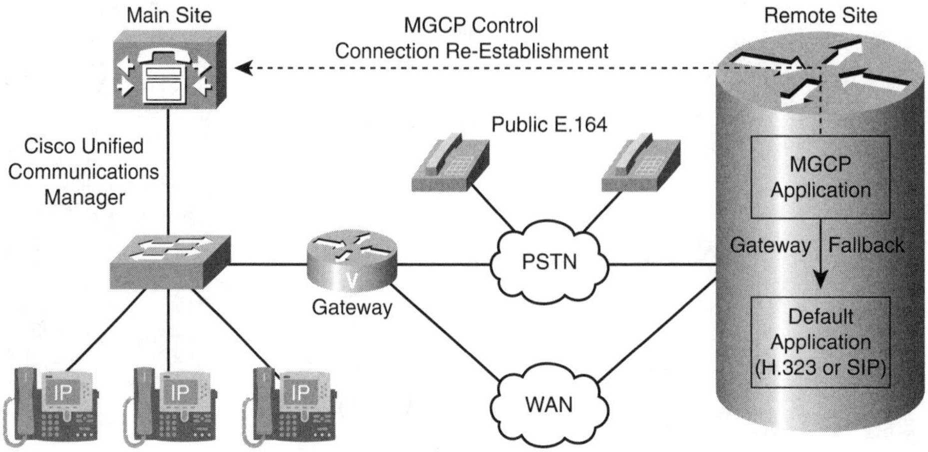

Rehome function in gateway-fallback mode detects the restoration of a WAN TCP connection to any CUCM server. When the fallback mode is in effect, the affected MGCP gateway repeatedly tries to open a TCP connection to a CUCM server that is included in the prioritized list of call agents. This process continues until a CUCM server in the prioritized list responds. The TCP open request from the MGCP gateway is honored, and the gateway reverts to MGCP mode. The gateway sends a RestartInProgress (RSIP) message to begin registration with the responding CUCM.

All currently active calls that are initiated and set up during the fallback period are maintained by the default H.323 session application, except ISDN T1 and E1 PRI calls. Transient calls are released. After rehome occurs, the new CUCM assumes responsibility for controlling new IP telephony activity.

MGCP Gateway Fallback Process

The MGCP gateway maintains a remote connection to a centralized CUCM cluster, as shown in Figure 5-10, by sending MGCP keepalive messages to the CUCM server at 15-second intervals.

Figure 5-10   *MGCP Gateway Fallback Process*

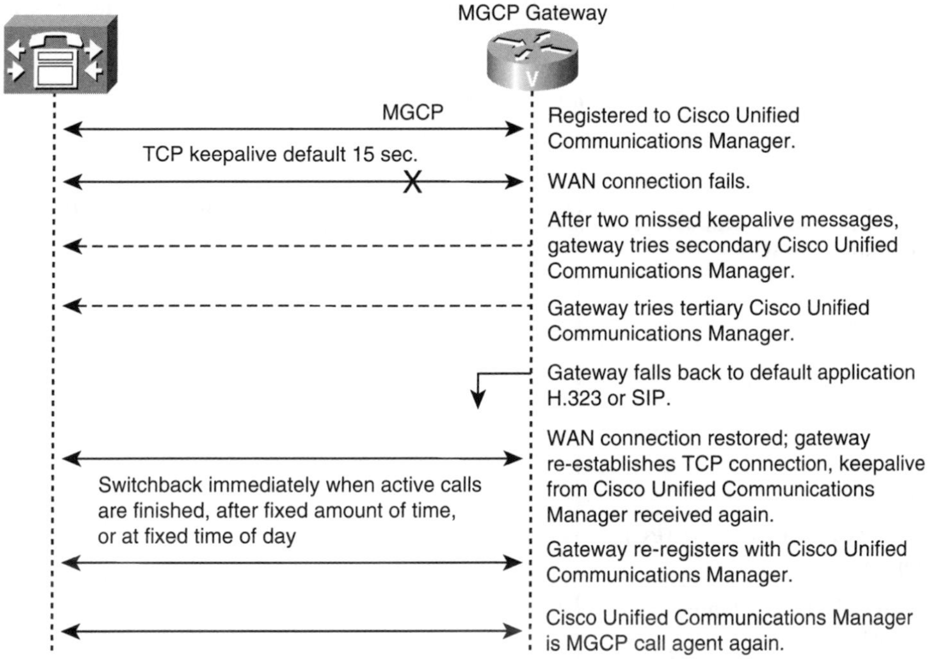

If the active CUCM server fails to acknowledge receipt of the keepalive message within 30 seconds, the gateway attempts to switch over to the next available CUCM server.

If none of the CUCM servers responds, the gateway switches into fallback mode and reverts to the default H.323 or SIP session application for basic call control.

NOTE   H.323 is a standardized communication protocol that enables dissimilar devices to communicate with each other through the use of a common set of codecs, call setup and negotiating procedures, and basic data-transport methods.

The gateway processes calls on its own using H.323 until one of the CUCM connections is restored. The same occurs if SIP is used instead of H.323 on the gateway.

Cisco Unified SRST Versions and Feature Support

Table 5-4 describes Cisco Unified SRST versions, their protocol support and features, and the required Cisco IOS Software release.

Table 5-4 *Cisco Unified SRST Versions*

Feature	CUCM Express in SRST Mode	SRST 4.0	SRST 3.2	SRST 2.1
Minimum Cisco IOS Software Release	12.4(11)XJ	12.4(4)XC	12.3(11)T	12.2(15)T1
Hunt Group	✓			
B-ACD	✓			
SIP SRST		✓		
Video	✓	✓		
Voice Security	✓	✓		
Cisco IP Communicator (CIPC) Support	✓	✓		
Analog Telephone Adaptor (ATA) Support	✓	✓	✓	
Local Music On Hold (MOH)	✓	✓	✓	
Three-Party Conference	✓	✓	✓	

The version of the Cisco Unified SRST application depends on which release of the Cisco IOS Software is running on the router. Each Cisco IOS Software release implements a particular SRST version. You upgrade to a newer version of SRST through a Cisco IOS update into router flash. Recent Cisco IOS Software releases often have higher memory requirements than older ones, so make sure that you look into this before upgrading.

For detailed information on the history of Cisco Unified SRST, refer to the *Cisco Unified SRST Administration Guide* or other documents listed in the documentation road map for Cisco Unified SRST at http://www.cisco.com.

SRST 4.0 Platform Density

The maximum number of IP Phones and directory numbers supported by the Cisco Unified SRST 4.0 feature depends on which Cisco IOS router platform is used, as shown in Table 5-5.

Table 5-5 *SRST 4.0 Platform Density*

Platform	Maximum Number of IP Phones	Maximum Directory Numbers
1751, 1760, 2801	24	256
2811, 261xXM, 262xXM	36	144
2821, 265xXM	48	192
2691	72	288
2851	96	288
3725	144	960
3745	480	960
3825	336	960
3845	720	960

This table shows the maximum number of phones and directory numbers on phones that a Cisco Unified SRST router can accommodate. For example, a Cisco 3845 Integrated Services Router can support a maximum of 720 phones and 960 directory numbers on the phones.

NOTE   These maximum numbers of IP Phones are for common SRST configurations only. Routers with large numbers of IP Phones and complex configurations may not work on all platforms and can require additional memory or a higher performance platform.

Dial Plan Requirements for MGCP Fallback and SRST Scenarios

Figure 5-11 illustrates requirements of standalone dial plans to work with MGCP fallback and SRST.

SRST failover leaves the remote site independent from the complex dial plan implemented in CUCM at the main site. The SRST router needs to have a dial plan implemented to allow all remote-site phones, all main-site phones, and all PSTN destinations to be reached with the same numbers as in standard mode.

During fallback, users should be able to dial main-site directory numbers as usual. Because these calls have to be routed over the PSTN during fallback, main-site extensions have to be translated to E.164 PSTN numbers at the PSTN gateway.

Figure 5-11   *SRST Dial Plan Requirements for Calls from the Remote Site*

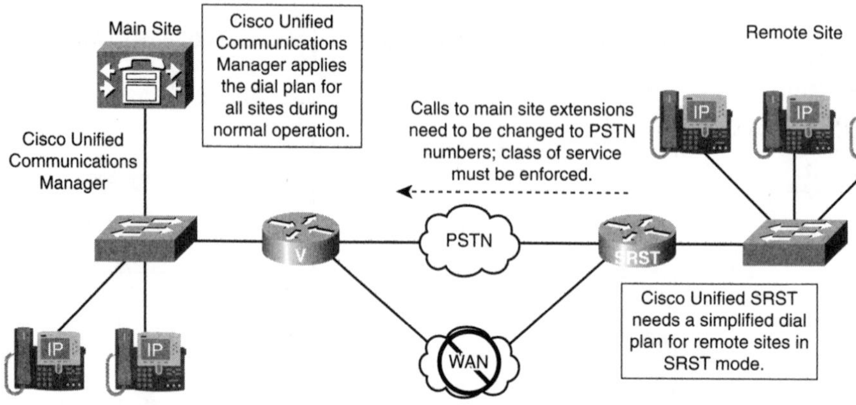

Most enterprises limit the range of destinations that can be reached from specific extensions by applying class of service to the extensions. This limitation should still be valid during times in SRST mode by applying IOS class of restriction (COR), as described in the next chapter.

Ensuring Connectivity for Remote Sites

When SRST is active, you must take several measures to ensure connectivity from remote sites to PSTN destinations, between different sites, and inside the site itself.

To guarantee PSTN connectivity, dial peers with destination patterns corresponding to the PSTN access code have to be implemented. In H.323 or SIP gateways, these dial peers must be present for normal operation. When MGCP gateways are used, dial peers are activated by the MGCP-gateway-fallback mechanism. Interdigit timeout adopts open numbering plans that do not have a fixed number of digits.

Voice translation profiles that are applied to dial peers, the voice interface, or the voice port modify the calling party ID to enable callback from call lists.

For intrasite and intersite connectivity, voice translation profiles are configured to expand called numbers to PSTN format during fallback.

The Cisco IOS command **dialplan-pattern** in call-manager-fallback configuration mode modifies incoming called numbers to match the remote-site extensions. It ensures that internal extensions can be dialed even though the lines are configured with the site code and extension. The Line Text Label settings defined in CUCM are not applied to the SRST phones, so the complete directory number applied to the line is visible to the user.

Ensuring Connectivity from the Main Site Using Call Forward Unregistered

During fallback, main-site users should still be able to call remote-site users using their extension numbers, as shown in Figure 5-12.

Figure 5-12 *Ensure Connectivity from the Main Site Using CFUR*

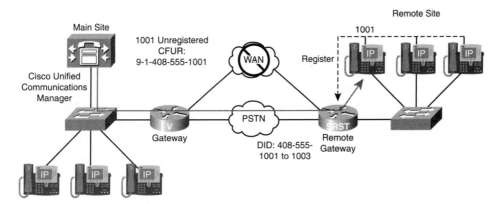

CUCM considers the remote-site phones unregistered and cannot route calls to the affected IP Phone directory numbers. Therefore, if main-site users dial internal extensions during the IP WAN outage, the calls will fail or go to voice mail.

To allow remote IP Phones to be reached from main-site IP Phones, Call Forward Unregistered (CFUR) can be configured for the remote-site phones. CFUR should be configured with the PSTN number of the remote-site gateway so that internal calls for remote IP Phones get forwarded to the appropriate PSTN number.

> **NOTE** In older versions of CCM that did not support CFUR, it was not possible to allow a main-site phone registered to CCM to call a remote-site phone in SRST mode over the PSTN during a WAN failure. This was because CCM did not have a mechanism to route calls to unregistered DNs through the PSTN.

CFUR Considerations

CFUR was first implemented in CCM Release 4.2.

As mentioned earlier, the CFUR feature allows calls placed to a temporarily unregistered IP Phone to be rerouted to a configurable number. The configuration of CFUR has two main elements:

- **Destination selection:** When the directory number is unregistered, calls can be rerouted to voice mail or to the directory number that was used to reach the IP Phone through the PSTN.

- **Calling Search Space (CSS):** CUCM attempts to route the call to the configured destination number using the CFUR CSS of the directory number that was called. The CFUR CSS is configured on the target IP Phone and is used by all devices that are calling the unregistered IP Phone. This means that all calling devices use the same combination of route pattern, route list, route group, and gateway to place the call. In addition, all CFUR calls to a given unregistered device are routed through the same unique gateway, regardless of the location of the calling IP Phone. It is recommended that you select a centralized gateway as the egress point to the PSTN for CFUR calls and configure the CFUR CSS to route calls to the CFUR destination through this centralized gateway.

  If an IP Phone is unregistered while the gateway that is associated with the direct inward dialing (DID) number of that phone is still under the control of CUCM, CFUR functionality can result in telephony routing loops. For example, if an IP Phone is simply disconnected from the network, the initial call to the phone would prompt the system to attempt a CFUR call to the DID of the phone through the PSTN. The resulting incoming PSTN call would in turn trigger another CFUR attempt to reach the directory number of the same phone, triggering yet another CFUR call from the central PSTN gateway through the PSTN. This cycle potentially could repeat itself until system resources are exhausted.

The CUCM service parameter Max Forward UnRegistered Hops To DN in the Clusterwide Parameters (Feature—Forward) section in CUCM Administration controls the maximum number of CFUR calls that are allowed for a directory number at one time. The default value of 0 means that the counter is disabled. If any directory numbers are configured to reroute CFUR calls through the PSTN, loop prevention is required. Configuring this service parameter to a value of 1 would stop CFUR attempts as soon as a single call were placed through the CFUR mechanism. This setting would also allow only one call to be forwarded to voice mail, if CFUR is so configured. Configuring this service parameter to a value of 2 would allow up to two simultaneous callers to reach the voice mail of a directory number whose CFUR setting is configured for voice mail. It would also limit potential loops to two for directory numbers whose CFUR configuration sends calls through the PSTN.

NOTE   CUCM Extension Mobility directory numbers should not be configured to send CFUR calls to the PSTN DID that is associated with the directory number. The directory numbers of CUCM Extension Mobility profiles in the logged-out state are deemed to be unregistered. Therefore, any calls to the PSTN DID number of a logged-out directory number would trigger a routing loop. To ensure that calls made to CUCM Extension Mobility directory numbers in the logged-out state are sent to voice mail, their corresponding CFUR parameters must be configured to send calls to voice mail.

Keeping Calling Privileges Active in SRST Mode

Under normal conditions in multisite deployments with centralized call processing, calling privileges are implemented using partitions and CSSs within CUCM.

However, when IP WAN connectivity is lost between a branch site and the central site, Cisco Unified SRST takes control of the branch IP Phones, and the entire configuration that is related to partitions and CSSs is unavailable until IP WAN connectivity is restored. Therefore, it is desirable to implement classes of service within the branch router when running in SRST mode.

For this application, you must define classes of service in Cisco IOS routers using the class of restriction (COR) functionality. You can adapt the COR functionality to replicate the CUCM concepts of partitions and CSSs by following these main guidelines:

■   Named tags have to be defined for each type of call that you want to distinguish.

■   Basic outgoing COR lists containing a single tag each have to be assigned to the outgoing dial peers that should not be available to all users. These outgoing COR lists are equivalent to partitions in CUCM.

■   Complex incoming COR lists containing one or more tags have to be assigned to the directory numbers that belong to the various classes of service.

SRST Dial Plan Example

Call-routing components on Cisco IOS routers and CUCM are necessary before a dial plan will work in SRST mode, as shown in Figure 5-13.

Figure 5-13 *SRST Dial Plan Example*

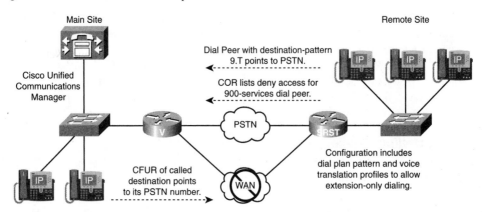

CFUR must be defined on the CUCM side. Configuring the Cisco IOS router is a little more complex when you use dial peers, COR, dial plan pattern, and voice translation profiles to define the simplified SRST dial plan. Note how this example lets you dial 9 to get out to all numbers on the PSTN from the remote site but limits 900 calls with COR to align with the same restrictions set in CUCM.

Summary

The following key points were discussed in this chapter:

- MGCP fallback works in conjunction with SRST to provide telephony service to remote IP Phones during WAN failure.

- Making the Cisco IP Phone CUCM list shorter results in faster SRST switchover.

- The Cisco Unified SRST version is linked with the Cisco IOS software release.

- The MGCP gateway fallback default application is H.323 or SIP.

- When SRST is active, several measures must be taken to ensure connectivity from remote sites to PSTN destinations, between different sites, and inside the site itself.

References

For additional information, refer to these resources:

■ Cisco Systems, Inc., Cisco Unified Communications Solution Reference Network Design (SRND), based on CUCM Release 6.x, June 2007

■ Cisco Systems, Inc., CUCM Administration Guide Release 6.0(1)

Review Questions

Use these questions to review what you've learned in this chapter. The answers appear in Appendix A, "Answers to Chapter Review Questions."

1. Which of the following CUCM and IOS gateway features provides failover for MGCP controlled gateways?

   a. MGCP SRST

   b. SRST fallback

   c. MGCP fallback

   d. MGCP in SRST mode

   e. MGCP failover

2. Which two of the following calls are not preserved during switchover of an SRST gateway?

   a. Calls between IP Phones located at the remote site

   b. Conference calls of remote-site phones using a conference bridge located at the main site

   c. Calls between IP Phones located at the remote site and the main site

   d. PSTN calls of remote phones placed through an H.323 gateway located at the remote site

   e. Calls from main-site phones that were placed to a remote-site phone and then transferred from the remote-site phone to another main-site phone

3. Which two are correct numbers of supported phones in SRST for the given platform?

    a. 2851: 24

    b. 3725: 256

    c. 3745: 480

    d. 3825: 336

    e. 3845: 1024

4. What can you use to configure the dial plan at the remote-site gateway so that branch users can still reach the headquarters when dialing internal directory numbers during fallback?

    a. This is not possible. Users have to dial headquarters users by their E.164 PSTN number while in fallback mode.

    b. Translation profiles modifying the calling number

    c. The **dialplan-pattern** command

    d. Translation profiles modifying the called number

    e. Although this is possible, it should be avoided, because it may confuse users.

5. Which two protocols are potentially used on a remote gateway with MGCP fallback in fallback mode?

    a. MGCP

    b. SCCP

    c. SIP

    d. H.323

    e. Megaco

    f. RTP

6. What IOS commands are used on a remote gateway configured with MGCP fallback to give PSTN access for IP Phones during fallback mode?

    a. This feature is unavailable. Remote phones can only dial each other.

    b. H.323 or SIP dial peers

    c. Static routes

    d. Dynamic dial peers

    e. MGCP dial peers

7. What protocol is used between the remote-office Cisco IP Phones and CUCM during fallback to maintain keepalives for SRST?

    a. MGCP

    b. SCCP

    c. H.323

    d. OSPF hello packets

    e. EIGRP keepalives

8. What method is used to maintain SIP connectivity from remote-office Cisco IP Phones to CUCM during a complete WAN failure?

    a. This is not possible. Remote-office Cisco IP Phones will fail over to the SRST remote-office router.

    b. SIP can be routed through the PSTN with POTS dial peers.

    c. SIP can be routed through the PSTN if the Local Exchange Carrier enables SIP through the PSTN connection.

    d. SIP can be routed through the PSTN with POTS dial peers combined with the Local Exchange Carrier, enabling SIP through the PSTN connection.

CHAPTER 6

Implementing Cisco Unified SRST and MGCP Fallback

This chapter describes how to configure Cisco Unified Survivable Remote Site Telephony (SRST) on Cisco IOS routers to provide redundancy to Cisco Skinny Client Control Protocol (SCCP) phones. It also describes how to configure the Media Gateway Control Protocol (MGCP) gateway fallback feature. In addition, this chapter illustrates how to configure features such as Music On Hold (MOH) and voice-mail integration for Cisco Unified SRST.

Chapter Objectives

Upon completing this chapter, you will be able to configure SRST to provide call survivability and MOH for SCCP phones, and MGCP fallback for gateway survivability. You will be able to meet these objectives:

- Describe the configuration requirements of CUCM and the SRST gateway

- Configure CUCM to enable SRST for remote phones

- Configure a Cisco IOS router for SRST

- Configure a Cisco IOS router to support MGCP fallback

- Configure CUCM to route calls to unregistered devices via the PSTN

- Configure a Cisco IOS router with a dial plan for SRST operation

- Configure SRST to support special features such as voice mail, conferences, MOH, and call transfer

MGCP Fallback and SRST Configuration

Figure 6-1 shows the topology relating to configuring Cisco Unified SRST and MGCP gateway fallback on Cisco IOS routers.

Figure 6-1 *MGCP Fallback and SRST Configuration*

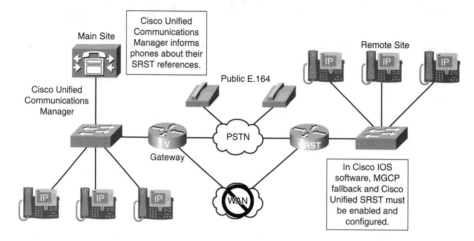

The MGCP-gateway-fallback feature is activated and configured on the Cisco IOS router. Note that Cisco Unified SRST must be configured within CUCM and within the Cisco IOS router.

Configuration Requirements for MGCP Fallback and Cisco Unified SRST

When configuring MGCP fallback and Cisco Unified SRST, you must follow these steps at different locations:

- Define the SRST references for phones in CUCM Administration.

- Configure the Call Forward Unregistered (CFUR) feature, and set the CFUR destination of lines on remote-site phones to the correct public switched telephone network (PSTN) number in CUCM Administration to enable reachable remote sites in SRST mode.

- Enable and configure the MGCP fallback and Cisco Unified SRST features on the IOS gateways.

- Implement a simplified SRST dial plan on the remote-site gateways to ensure connectivity for remote-site phones in SRST mode.

Cisco Unified SRST Configuration in CUCM

The SRST feature in CUCM provides IP Phones with the information needed to find the relative gateway to register with when they lose contact with CUCM servers.

An SRST reference must first be defined. This reference contains information about IP addresses and ports of SRST gateways for SCCP and session initiation protocol (SIP) phones. Because the SRST functions are different for SIP and SCCP, the addresses and ports are also different.

Secondly, provide a group of phones with this information by assigning the SRST reference to a proper device pool, which is then assigned to the phones.

SRST Reference Definition

An SRST reference, as shown in Figure 6-2, comprises the gateway, which can provide limited CUCM functionality when all other CUCM servers for IP Phones are unreachable. Choose **Cisco Unified Communications Manager Administration > System > SRST**.

Figure 6-2   *SRST Reference Definition in CUCM*

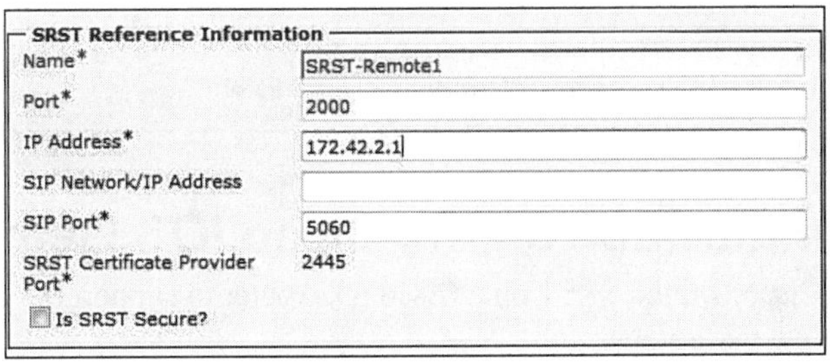

SRST references determine which gateways IP Phones will search when they attempt to complete a call if the CUCM is unavailable.

Administrators must configure CUCM with a unique SRST reference name that specifies the IP address of the Cisco Unified SRST gateway. The default TCP port number 2000 normally is used.

The SIP network and IP address apply to SIP SRST. If SIP SRST is used, the IP address and port that are used by the SIP protocol of the Cisco Unified SRST gateway have to be specified; the default port number is 5060. The configured address and port will be used by SIP phones to register with the SIP SRST gateway.

CUCM Device Pool

The SRST reference, as shown in Figure 6-3, is assigned to IP Phones using device pools. Choose **Cisco Unified Communications Manager Administration > System > Device Pool**.

Figure 6-3 *Device Pool in CUCM*

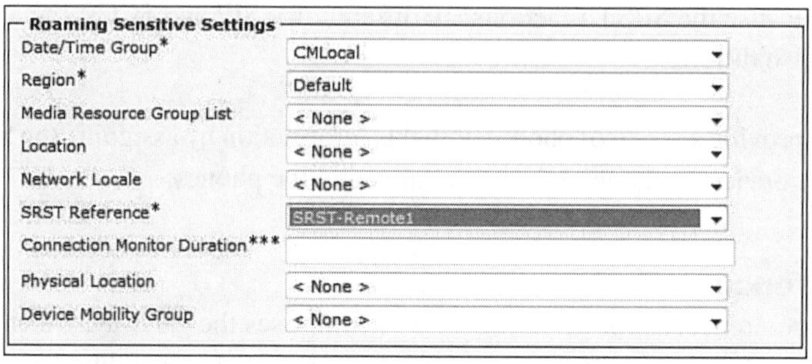

Administrators select the configured SRST reference from the drop-down menu in the device pool configuration.

> **NOTE**   If devices are associated with this SRST reference, a message appears, saying that devices need to be reset for the update to take effect.

SRST Configuration on the Cisco IOS Gateway

To configure Cisco Unified SRST on a Cisco IOS router to support the Cisco IP Phone functions, follow these steps:

Step 1   Enter call-manager-fallback configuration mode to activate SRST.

Step 2   Define the IP address and port to which the SRST service binds.

Step 3   Define the maximum number of directory numbers to support.

Step 4   Define the maximum number of IP Phones to support.

Step 5   Define the maximum number of numbers allowed per phone type.

Step 6   Define the phone keepalive interval.

> **TIP**   When Cisco Unified SRST is enabled, Cisco IP Phones in call-manager-fallback configuration mode do not have to be reconfigured, because phones retain the same configuration that was used with CUCM.

SRST Activation Commands

Example 6-1 shows the commands for the first two SRST configuration steps.

Example 6-1 *SRST Activation Commands*

```
RemoteSite#configure terminal
  RemoteSite(config)#call-manager-fallback
    RemoteSite(config-cm-fallback)#ip source-address ip-address [port port]
      [any-match | strict-match]
```

The Cisco IOS command **call-manager-fallback** enters call-manager-fallback configuration mode.

The Cisco IOS command **ip source-address** enables the router to receive messages from the Cisco IP Phones through the specified IP addresses and provides for strict IP address verification. The default port number is 2000. This IP address will be supplied later as an SRST reference IP address in CUCM Administration.

The **ip source-address** command is mandatory. The fallback subsystem does not start if the IP address of the Ethernet port to which the IP Phones are connected (typically the Ethernet interface of the local SRST gateway) is not provided. If the port number is not provided, the default value (2000) is used.

The **any-match** keyword instructs the router to permit Cisco IP Phone registration even when the IP server address used by the phone does not match the IP source address. This option lets you register Cisco IP Phones on different subnets or those with different default DHCP routers or different TFTP server addresses.

The **strict-match** keyword instructs the router to reject Cisco IP Phone registration attempts if the IP server address used by the phone does not exactly match the source address. By dividing the Cisco IP Phones into groups on different subnets and giving each group different DHCP default router or TFTP server addresses, this option restricts the number of Cisco IP Phones allowed to register.

SRST Phone Definition Commands

The commands shown in Example 6-2, **max-dn** and **max-ephones**, are mandatory because the default values for both are defined as 0.

Example 6-2 *SRST Phone Definition Commands*

```
RemoteSite#configure terminal
 RemoteSite(config)#call-manager-fallback
  RemoteSite(config-cm-fallback)#max-dn max-directory-numbers [dual-line]
    [preference preference-order]
  RemoteSite(config-cm-fallback)#max-ephones max-phones
```

The Cisco IOS command **max-dn** sets the maximum number of directory numbers or virtual voice ports that can be supported by the router and activates dual-line mode. The maximum number is platform-dependent. The default is 0.

The **dual-line** keyword is optional. It allows IP Phones in SRST mode to have a virtual voice port with two channels.

> **NOTE**   The **dual-line** keyword facilitates call waiting, call transfer, and conference functions by allowing two calls to occur on one line simultaneously. In dual-line mode, all IP Phones on the Cisco Unified SRST router support two channels per virtual voice port.

The optional parameter **preference** sets the global preference for creating the VoIP dial peers for all directory numbers that are associated with the primary number. The range is from 0 to 10. The default is 0, which is the highest preference.

> **NOTE**   The router must be rebooted to reduce the limit on the directory numbers or virtual voice ports after the maximum allowable number is configured.

To configure the maximum number of Cisco IP Phones that an SRST router can support, use the **max-ephones** command in call-manager-fallback configuration mode. The default is 0, and the maximum configurable number is platform-dependent. The only way to increase the maximum number of Cisco IP Phones supported is to upgrade to a higher hardware platform.

> **NOTE**   The router must be rebooted to reduce the limit on Cisco IP Phones after the maximum allowable number is configured.

SRST Performance Commands

To optimize performance of the system, best practice dictates that you use the **limit-dn** and **keepalive** commands, as shown in Example 6-3.

Example 6-3   *SRST Performance Commands*

```
RemoteSite#configure terminal
  RemoteSite(config)#call-manager-fallback
    RemoteSite(config-cm-fallback)#limit-dn {7910 | 7935 | 7940 | 7960} max-lines
    RemoteSite(config-cm-fallback)#keepalive seconds
```

The optional Cisco IOS command **limit-dn** limits the directory number lines on Cisco IP Phones during SRST mode, depending on the Cisco IP Phone model.

> **NOTE**   This command must be configured during the initial Cisco Unified SRST router configuration, before any IP Phone actually registers with the Cisco Unified SRST router. However, you can change the number of lines later.

The setting for the maximum number of directory lines is from 1 to 6. The default is 6. If any active phone has the last line number greater than this limit, warning information is displayed for phone reset.

The optional Cisco IOS command **keepalive** sets the time interval, in seconds, between keepalive messages that are sent to the router by Cisco IP Phones. The range is 10 to 65535. The default is 30.

The keepalive interval is the period of time between keepalive messages that are sent by a network device. A keepalive message is a message that is sent by one network device to inform another network device that the virtual circuit between the two is still active.

> **NOTE**   If the default time interval between messages of 30 seconds will be used, this command does not have to be used.

Cisco Unified SRST Configuration Example

Figure 6-4 shows a multisite topology that supports SCCP-controlled IP Phones at the remote SRST site. The configuration is shown in Example 6-4.

Figure 6-4   *Multisite Topology Supporting SCCP-Controlled IP Phones at the Remote SRST Site*

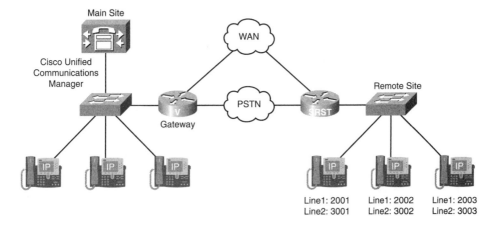

Example 6-4 *Cisco Unified SRST Configuration Example*

```
RemoteSite#configure terminal
  RemoteSite(config)#call-manager-fallback
    RemoteSite(config-cm-fallback)#ip source-address 172.47.2.1 port 2000
    RemoteSite(config-cm-fallback)#max-ephones 3 dual-line
    RemoteSite(config-cm-fallback)#max-dn 6
    RemoteSite(config-cm-fallback)#limit-dn 7960 2
    RemoteSite(config-cm-fallback)#keepalive 20
    RemoteSite(config-cm-fallback)#end
RemoteSite#
```

NOTE More commands might be necessary, depending on the complexity of the deployment.

MGCP-Gateway-Fallback Configuration on the Cisco IOS Gateway

To configure the MGCP gateway fallback on a Cisco IOS router to support the MGCP fallback function, follow these steps:

Step 1 Activate MGCP gateway fallback.

Step 2 Define the service to fall back to.

To enable outbound calls while in SRST mode on an MGCP gateway, you must configure two fallback commands on the MGCP gateway. These two commands allow SRST to assume control over the voice port and over call processing on the MGCP gateway. With Cisco IOS Software releases before 12.3(14)T, configuring MGCP gateway fallback involves the **ccm-manager fallback-mgcp** and **call application alternate** commands. With Cisco IOS Software releases after 12.3(14)T, configuring MGCP gateway fallback uses the **ccm-manager fallback-mgcp** and **service** commands.

NOTE Both commands have to be configured. Configurations will not work reliably if only the **ccm-manager fallback-mgcp** command is configured.

To use SRST on an MGCP gateway, you must configure SRST and MGCP gateway fallback on the same gateway.

MGCP Fallback Activation Commands

The Cisco IOS command **ccm-manager fallback-mgcp**, shown in Example 6-5, enables the gateway fallback feature and allows an MGCP voice gateway to provide call-processing services through SRST or other configured applications when CUCM is unavailable.

Example 6-5 *MGCP Fallback Activation Commands*

```
RemoteSite#configure terminal
 RemoteSite(config)#ccm-manager fallback-mgcp
 RemoteSite(config)#call application alternate Default
  RemoteSite(config-app-global)#service alternate Default
```

The **call application alternate Default** command specifies that the default voice application takes over if the MGCP call agent is unavailable. This allows a fallback to H.323 or SIP, which means that local dial peers are considered for call routing.

The **service alternate Default** command is entered in the global-configuration submode of the application-configuration submode. To navigate to this location, follow these steps:

Step 1 To enter application configuration mode to configure applications, use the **application** command in global configuration mode.

Step 2 To enter application-configuration global mode, use the **global** command in application configuration mode.

Enter either of the two commands, depending on the Cisco IOS Software release. The newer configuration method is the **service** command.

As discussed in the preceding chapter, analog calls are preserved in the event of MGCP fallback. To provide call preservation during switchback, call preservation for H.323 has to be enabled using the commands shown in Example 6-6.

Example 6-6 *H.323 Call Preservation Activation Commands*

```
RemoteSite#configure terminal
 RemoteSite(config)#voice service voip
  RemoteSite(conf-voi-serv)#h323
   RemoteSite(conf-serv-h323)#no h225 timeout keepalive
```

MGCP Fallback Configuration Example

Figure 6-5 shows an MGCP-controlled remote-site gateway with an MGCP-gateway-fallback configuration for an SRST-enabled Cisco IOS router, as shown in Example 6-7.

Figure 6-5 *MGCP Fallback Example*

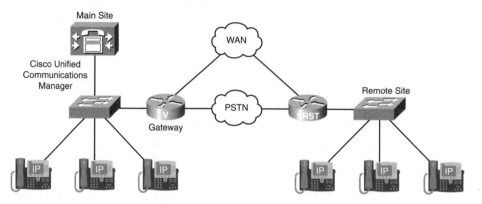

Example 6-7 *MGCP Fallback Configuration Example*

```
RemoteSite#configure terminal
  RemoteSite(config)#ccm-manager fallback-mgcp
  RemoteSite(config)#application
    RemoteSite(config-app)#global
      RemoteSite(config-app-global)#service alternate Default
      RemoteSite(config-app-global)#end
RemoteSite#
```

> **NOTE**   More commands might be necessary, depending on the complexity of the deployment.

Dial Plan Configuration for SRST Support in CUCM

This section describes the configuration to adjust the CUCM dial plan to work with Cisco Unified SRST.

The CUCM dial plan has to be adjusted to ensure the reachability of remote-site phones by their extensions even if the remote site runs in SRST mode. The parameter that enables this adjustment is the CFUR destination setting, which has to be defined on every line of an SRST enabled remote-site phone. This parameter was introduced in Cisco Unified Communication Manager Release 4.2.

The CFUR feature forwards calls to unregistered (disconnected or logged out) directory numbers for the defined destination. The destination might be the PSTN number of a phone at a remote site or the voice mail for a user in a CUCM Extension Mobility setting.

To ensure that the feature works even if a major WAN breakdown disconnects all the remote sites, only voice gateways located at the main site should be used. This can be ensured by selecting the correct Calling Search Space (CSS) for the CFUR destination.

CFUR causes routing loops whenever there is a single disconnected SRST phone in which the remote location is not in SRST mode. Internal calls to that directory number are forwarded to the CFUR (PSTN) destination and are received by the remote-site gateway in normal mode. This gateway handles the call as usual, sending the signaling to its CUCM subscriber. CUCM then again forwards the call to the PSTN, causing an inevitable routing loop.

To limit the impact of these routing loops, Cisco introduced a CUCM service parameter called Max Forward UnRegistered Hops to DN. When activated, this counter limits the calls that are forwarded to one CFUR destination.

SRST Dial Plan of CFUR and CSS

The CFUR feature is a way to reroute calls placed to a temporarily unregistered destination phone. The configuration of CFUR consists of the two main elements of destination selection and CSS, as shown in Figure 6-6. Choose **Cisco Unified Communications Manager Administration > Call Routing > Directory Number**.

Figure 6-6   *SRST Dial Plan Configuration of CFUR and CSS*

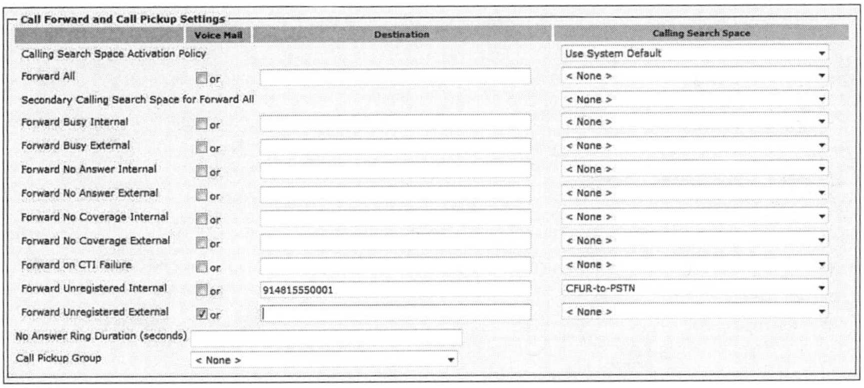

When the directory number is unregistered, calls can be rerouted to the voice mail that is associated with the extension or to a directory number that is used to reach the phone through the PSTN. The latter approach is preferable when a phone is located within a site whose WAN link is down. If the site is equipped with SRST, the phone (and its co-located PSTN gateway) reregisters with the co-located SRST router. The phone then can receive calls placed to its PSTN direct inward dialing (DID) number.

In this case, the appropriate CFUR destination is the corresponding PSTN DID number of the original destination directory number. Configure this PSTN DID in the destination field, along with applicable access codes and prefixes. For this example, the number would be 9-1-481-555-0001.

CUCM attempts to route the call to the configured destination number using the CFUR CSS of the called directory number. The CFUR CSS is configured on the target phone and is used by all devices that are calling the unregistered phone. This means that all calling devices use the same combination of route pattern, route list, route group, and gateway to place the call, and that all CFUR calls to a given unregistered device are routed through the same unique gateway, regardless of where the calling phone is located. It is recommended that you select a centralized gateway as the egress point to the PSTN for CFUR calls. You also should configure the CFUR CSS to route calls that are intended for the CFUR destination to this centralized gateway.

SRST Dial Plan: Max Forward UnRegistered Hops to DN

The CUCM service parameter **Max Forward UnRegistered Hops to DN** reduces the impact caused by CFUR routing loops, as shown in Figure 6-7. Choose **CUCM Administration > System > Service Parameter > Cisco CallManager**.

Figure 6-7   *SRST Dial Plan Configuration of Max Forward UnRegistered Hops to DN*

Clusterwide Parameters (Feature - Forward)		
Forward Maximum Hop Count *	12	12
Forward No Answer Timer *	12	12
Max Forward Hops to DN *	12	12
Retain Forward Information *	False	False
Forward By Reroute Enabled *	False	False
Transform Forward by Reroute Destination	True	True
Always Forward Switch Voice Mail Calls *	True	True
Forward By Reroute T1 Timer *	10	10
Include Original Called Info for Q.SIG Call Diversions *	Only after the first diversion	Only after the first diversion
Max Forward UnRegistered Hops to DN *	0	0
CFA CSS Activation Policy *	With Configured CSS	With Configured CSS
There are hidden parameters in this group. Click on Advanced button to see hidden parameters.		

This parameter specifies the maximum number of forward unregistered hops that are allowed for a directory number at one time. It limits the number of times the call can be forwarded because of the unregistered directory number when a forwarding loop occurs. Use this count to stop forward loops for external calls that have been forwarded by CFUR, such as intercluster IP Phone calls and IP Phone-to-PSTN phone calls that are forwarded to each other. CUCM terminates the call when the value that is specified in this parameter is exceeded. The default 0 disables the counter but not the CFUR feature. The allowed range is from 0 to 60.

MGCP Fallback and SRST Dial Plan Configuration in the Cisco IOS Gateway

A dial plan in SRST mode, at a minimum, enables the remote-site users to place and receive calls from the PSTN.

At least one dial peer needs to be configured to enable calls to and from the PSTN. The destination pattern of that dial peer has to correspond to the PSTN access code (for example, 9T). The more elegant way is to configure several dedicated dial peers with destination patterns that match the number patterns in a closed numbering plan, such as 91.......... (91 followed by ten dots).

In countries that have variable dial plans, the only destination pattern that is needed is 9T. Because of the variable length of dialed numbers, the router waits for the interdigit timeout (T302) or for a hash (#) sign to indicate the end of the dial string. Cisco Unified SRST version 4.1 and Cisco Unified Communications Manager Express Release 4.1 do not support the overlap sending feature to the PSTN. The receiving of ISDN overlap dialing from PSTN is supported but has to be enabled on the interfaces. To shorten the wait time for users after they complete the dial string, it is possible to reduce the interdigit timeout from the SRST default of 10 seconds.

SRST Dial Plan Components for Normal Mode Analogy

A good SRST dial plan is as close as possible between the dialing functionality in normal mode and in SRST mode. The telephony service should have the same look and feel for the user, regardless of the mode the system is in. For example, it would be an unacceptable failover design if the remote user required an awareness of WAN link connectivity when he dials his headquarters.

The numbers in the call lists (such as missed calls) must have the correct format (PSTN access code plus PSTN phone number) to enable users to use the list entries for dialing. The calling party ID of incoming calls from the PSTN needs to be modified by voice translation profiles and voice translation rules.

Abbreviated dialing between sites of the site code plus the extension number is possible in SRST mode. Voice translation profiles have to be used to expand the called numbers to PSTN format for intersite dialing.

If the calling privileges (which normally are controlled by the CUCM) have to be preserved in SRST mode, class of restriction (COR) configuration must be used.

SRST Dial Plan Dial Peer Commands

The **dial-peer** command is the main component for configuring dial plans on Cisco IOS routers, as shown in Example 6-8.

Example 6-8 *Dial Peer Commands for an SRST Dial Plan*

```
RemoteSite#configure terminal
  RemoteSite(config)#dial-peer voice tag pots
    RemoteSite(config-dial-peer)#destination-pattern [+]string[T]
    RemoteSite(config-dial-peer)#port slot-number/port
```

You define a particular dial peer, specify the voice encapsulation method, and enter dial peer configuration mode using the **dial-peer voice** command in global configuration mode. The following list defines the keywords and parameters used in the configuration shown in Example 6-8:

- The parameter *tag* specifies digits that define a particular dial peer. The range is from 1 to 2147483647.

- The keyword **pots** indicates that this is a plain old telephone service (POTS) peer. The option **voip** also exists, indicating that this is a VoIP peer, but is not mentioned in Example 6-8 because POTS dial peers are predominately used for SRST. POTS dial peers contain a port, whereas VoIP dial peers contain a configured IP address.

- You specify either the prefix or the full E.164 telephone number to be used for a dial peer using the **destination-pattern** command in dial peer configuration mode.

- The optional character + indicates that an E.164 standard number follows.

- The parameter *string* defines a series of digits that specify a pattern for the E.164 or private dialing plan telephone number. Valid entries are the digits 0 through 9, the letters A through D, and the following special characters:

  *

  #

  ,

  .

  +

  ^

  $

  \

  ?

  []

  ()

- The optional control character **T** indicates that the **destination-pattern** value is a variable-length dial string. Using this control character enables the router to wait until all digits are received before routing the call.

- To associate a dial peer with a specific voice port, use the **port** command in dial peer configuration mode.

- The parameter *slot-number* defines the number of the slot in the router in which the voice interface card (VIC) is installed. Valid entries depend on the number of slots that the router platform has.

- The parameter *port* defines the voice port number. Valid entries are 0 and 1.

Table 6-1 lists common classes of PSTN calls in the North American Numbering Plan (NANP) and lists the pattern that is used for each class. An access code of 9 should be used to indicate a PSTN call. The exception is 911, which should be configured with and without the access code 9. The patterns outlined in Table 6-1 must be reachable in SRST mode.

Table 6-1   *SRST Dial Plan Dial Peer Commands*

Call Type	Pattern
Emergency	911
Services	[2–8]11
Local	[2–9]xx-xxxx
Long-distance or national	1[2–9]xx [2–9]xx-xxxx
International	011+country code+number
Toll-free	1[800,866,877,888]xxx-xxxx
Premium	1 900 xxx-xxxx 1 976 xxx-xxxx

An access code of 9 typically is used to indicate a PSTN call; however, other access codes such as 8 are also permissible.

The patterns in the table are the minimum number of patterns that need to be reachable in SRST mode.

Example 6-9 provides a sample configuration of dial peers only, demonstrating outbound dialing to the PSTN in an SRST router. This example is in the NANP, which also shows local ten-digit dialing in area code 919. The configuration as written can be directly pasted into a router.

Example 6-9   *Dial Peer Example for an SRST Dial Plan*

```
!
dial-peer voice 1 pots
  description PSTN-emergency dial 9 first
  destination-pattern 9911
  port 0/1/0:23
  forward-digits 3
!
dial-peer voice 2 pots
  description PSTN-emergency
  destination-pattern 911
  port 0/1/0:23
  forward-digits all
!
dial-peer voice 3 pots
  description PSTN-Local Services
```

Example 6-9   *Dial Peer Example for an SRST Dial Plan (Continued)*

```
  destination-pattern 9[2-8]11
  port 0/1/0:23
  forward-digits 3
!
dial-peer voice 4 pots
  description PSTN-Local 7 digit dialing
  destination-pattern 9[2-9]......
  port 0/1/0:23
  forward-digits 7
!
dial-peer voice 5 pots
  description PSTN-10 Digit Local Dialing for Area Code 919
  destination-pattern 9919[2-9]......
  port 0/1/0:23
  forward-digits 10
!
dial-peer voice 6 pots
  description PSTN-Long Distance Dialing
  destination-pattern 91[2-9]..[2-9]......
  port 0/1/0:23
  forward-digits 11
!
dial-peer voice 7 pots
  description PSTN-International Dialing
  destination-pattern 9011T
  port 0/1/0:23
  prefix 011
```

NOTE   This example does not contain any class of restriction (COR), which currently allows all SRST registered phones to dial all numbers, including long-distance, 900, and international, without any constraint. COR is discussed later in this chapter. In addition, dial peers 3 and 4 do not require the **forward-digits** command, and are added only for clarity.

SRST Dial Plan Commands: Open Numbering Plans

Example 6-10 defines the configuration commands for open numbering plans in an SRST dial plan.

Example 6-10 *SRST Dial Plan Commands for an SRST Dial Plan*

```
RemoteSite#configure terminal
  RemoteSite(config)#interface serial0/1/0:23
    RemoteSite(config-if)#isdn overlap-receiving [T302 ms]
    RemoteSite(config-if)#exit
  RemoteSite(config)#call-manager-fallback
    RemoteSite(config-cm-fallback)#timeouts interdigit sec
    RemoteSite(config-cm-fallback)#dialplan-pattern tag pattern
      extension-length length [extension-pattern extension-pattern] [no-reg]
```

The following list defines the commands, keywords, and parameters used in the configuration shown in Example 6-10:

- To activate overlap receiving on ISDN interfaces, you use the **isdn overlap-receiving** command in interface configuration mode. This command is applicable on BRI interfaces or on the ISDN interface of E1/T1 controllers in PRI mode.

- The optional parameter **T302** defines how many milliseconds the T302 timer should wait before expiring. Valid values for the *ms* argument range from 500 to 20000. The default value is 10000 (10 seconds).

> **CAUTION**   Modifying the **T302** parameter, when connected to public networks, might disable the function. The **T302** describes the interdigit timeout for all phones in the CUCM cluster.

- Configure the timeout value to wait between dialed digits for all Cisco IP Phones that are attached to a router using the **timeouts interdigit** command in call-manager-fallback configuration mode.

- The parameter *sec* defines the interdigit timeout duration, in seconds, for all Cisco IP Phones. Valid entries are integers from 2 to 120.

- Create a global prefix that can be used to expand the extension numbers of inbound and outbound calls into fully qualified E.164 numbers using the **dialplan-pattern** command in call-manager-fallback configuration mode.

- The parameter *tag* is the unique identifier that is used before the telephone number. The tag number is from 1 to 5.

- The parameter *pattern* is the dial plan pattern, such as the area code, the prefix, and the first one or two digits of the extension number, plus wildcard markers or dots (.) for the remainder of the extension-number digits.

- The keyword **extension-length** sets the number of extension digits that will appear as a caller ID followed by the parameter *length*, which is the number of extension digits. The extension length must match the setting for IP Phones in CUCM mode. The range is from 1 to 32.

- The optional keyword **extension-pattern** sets the leading digit pattern of an extension number when the pattern is different from the leading digits defined in the pattern variable of the E.164 telephone number. An example is when site codes are used. The parameter *extension-pattern* that follows defines the leading digit pattern of the extension number. It is composed of one or more digits and wildcard markers or dots (.). For example, **5..** would include extensions 500 to 599, and **5...** would include extensions 5000 to 5999. The extension pattern configuration should match the mapping of internal to external numbers in CUCM.

- The optional keyword **no-reg** prevents the E.164 numbers in the dial peer from registering with the gatekeeper.

Example 6-11 demonstrates the use of the **dialplan-pattern** command, which shows how to create a dial plan pattern for directory numbers 500 to 599 that is mapped to a DID range of 408-555-5000 to 5099. If the router receives an inbound call to 408-555-5044, the dial plan pattern command is matched, and the extension of the called E.164 number, 408-555-5000, is changed to directory number 544. If an outbound calling party extension number (544) matches the dial plan pattern, the calling-party extension is converted to the E.164 number 408-555-5044. The E.164 calling-party number appears as the caller ID.

Example 6-11 *SRST Dial Plan Example for Mapping Directory Numbers*

```
RemoteSite#configure terminal
 RemoteSite(config)#call-manager-fallback
  RemoteSite(config-cm-fallback)#dialplan-pattern 1 40855550..
    extension-length 3 extension-pattern 5..
```

SRST Dial Plan Voice Translation-Profile Commands for Digit Manipulation

The combination of **voice translation-profiles** and **voice translation-rules** creates a very powerful tool for modifying numbers so that they match dial plan needs. Example 6-12 shows the configuration commands for voice translation profiles.

Example 6-12   *Voice Translation-Profile Commands*

```
RemoteSite#configure terminal
  RemoteSite(config)#voice translation-profile name
    RemoteSite(cfg-translation-profile)#translate {called | calling |
      redirect-called | redirect-target} translation-rule-number
```

You define a translation profile for voice calls using the **voice translation-profile** command in global configuration mode. The *name* parameter of this command defines the name of the translation profile. The maximum length of the **voice translation-profile** name is 31 alphanumeric characters.

You associate a translation rule with a voice translation profile using the **translate** command in **voice translation-profile** configuration mode. The following list defines the keywords and parameter for the **translate** command:

■   **called** associates the translation rule with called numbers.

■   **calling** associates the translation rule with calling numbers.

■   **redirect-called** associates the translation rule with redirected called numbers.

■   **redirect-target** associates the translation rule with transfer-to numbers and call-forwarding final destination numbers.

■   *translation-rule-number* is the number of the translation rule to use for the call translation. The valid range is from 1 to 2147483647. There is no default value.

> **NOTE**   The prior IOS digit manipulation tool **translation rule** has been replaced by **voice translation-rule**. The commands are similar but are incompatible with each other.

SRST Dial Plan Voice Translation-Rule Commands for Number Modification

Example 6-13 shows the configuration commands for voice translation-rules.

Example 6-13   *Voice Translation-Rule Commands*

```
RemoteSite#configure terminal
  RemoteSite(config)#voice translation-rule number
    router(cfg-translation-rule)#rule precedence /match-pattern/
      /replace-pattern/[type {match-type replace-type} [plan
      {match-type replace-type}]]
```

You define a translation rule for voice calls using the **voice translation-rule** command in global configuration mode. The *number* parameter identifies the translation rule. The range of the number is from 1 to 2147483647. The choice of the number does not affect usage priority.

You define a translation rule using the **rule** command in voice translation-rule configuration mode. The following list defines the keywords and parameters for the **rule** command, as shown in Example 6-13:

■ The parameter *precedence* defines the priority of the translation rule. The range is from 1 to 15.

■ The parameter **/match-pattern/** is a stream editor (SED) expression used to match incoming call information. The slash (/) is a delimiter in the pattern.

■ The parameter **/replace-pattern/** is a SED expression used to replace the match pattern in the call information. The slash is a delimiter in the pattern.

■ The optional construct **type** *match-type replace-type* lets you modify the call's number type. Valid values for the *match-type* argument are **abbreviated**, **any**, **international**, **national**, **network**, **reserved**, **subscriber**, and **unknown**. Valid values for the *replace-type* argument are **abbreviated**, **international**, **national**, **network**, **reserved**, **subscriber**, and **unknown**.

■ The optional construct **plan** *match-type replace-type* lets you modify the call's numbering plan. Valid values for the *match-type* argument are **any**, **data**, **ermes**, **isdn**, **national**, **private**, **reserved**, **telex**, and **unknown**. Valid values for the *replace-type* argument are **data**, **ermes**, **isdn**, **national**, **private**, **reserved**, **telex**, and **unknown**.

SRST Dial Plan Profile Activation Commands for Number Modification

Voice translation profiles can be bound to dial peers, source groups, trunk groups, voice ports, and the voice service POTS.

Example 6-14 shows the configuration commands for voice translation profile activation.

Example 6-14   *Voice Translation Rule Activation Commands*

```
RemoteSite#configure terminal
 RemoteSite(config)#voice-port 0/1/0:23
  RemoteSite(config-voiceport)#translation-profile {incoming | outgoing} name
  RemoteSite(config-voiceport)#exit
 RemoteSite(config)#call-manager-fallback
  router(config-cm-fallback)#translation-profile {incoming | outgoing} name
```

In this example, the **voice translationprofile** is bound to a voice port. The **voice translationprofile** can also be bound to all the dial peers, but the voice port needs to be done only once.

You assign a translation profile to a voice port using the **translation-profile** command in **voice-port** configuration mode. The following list defines the keywords and parameter for the **translation-profile** command:

- The keyword **incoming** specifies that this translation profile handles incoming calls.

- The keyword **outgoing** specifies that this translation profile handles outgoing calls.

- The parameter *name* is the name of the translation profile.

In addition to the configuration shown in Example 6-14, the voice translation profiles can be bound to the **call-manager-fallback** Cisco IOS service. The structure of the command is identical.

> **NOTE**   The incoming direction of the **voice translation-profile** bound to the **call-manager-fallback** Cisco IOS service handles the calls coming from IP Phones that are registered with the router.

For more information about voice translation profiles, refer to the following documents at Cisco.com, which you should be able to locate by searching by title:

- *TechNotes Number Translation Using Voice Translation Profiles*

- *TechNotes Voice Translation Rules*

SRST Dial Plan Class of Restriction Commands

Calling privileges can be assigned to IP Phones when they are in SRST mode using COR commands. In the absence of COR in SRST dial peers, all phones can dial all numbers.

Example 6-15 shows the dial plan configuration commands for COR as they apply to SRST.

Example 6-15   *Class of Restriction Commands*

```
RemoteSite#configure terminal
  RemoteSite(config)#call-manager-fallback
    RemoteSite(config-cm-fallback)#cor {incoming | outgoing} cor-list-name
      [cor-list-number starting-number - ending-number | default]
```

The command **cor** configures a COR on dial peers that are associated with directory numbers. The following list defines the keywords and parameters for the **cor** command:

- The keyword **incoming** defines that a COR list is to be used by incoming dial peers.

- The keyword **outgoing** defines that a COR list is to be used by outgoing dial peers.

- The parameter *cor-list-name* is the COR list name.

- The parameter *cor-list-number* is a COR list identifier. The maximum number of COR lists that can be created is 20, composed of incoming or outgoing dial peers. The first six COR lists are applied to a range of directory numbers. The directory numbers that do not have a COR configuration are assigned to the default COR list, as long as a default COR list has been defined.

- The parameters *starting-number - ending-number* define the directory number range, such as 2000 to 2025.

- The keyword **default** instructs the router to use an existing default COR list.

Table 6-2 summarizes the functions of COR dialed calls.

Table 6-2　*COR Dialing Possibilities*

COR List on Incoming Dial Peer	COR List on Outgoing Dial Peer	Result
No COR	No COR	The call succeeds.
No COR	A COR list is applied for outgoing calls.	The call succeeds. By default, the incoming dial peer has the highest COR priority when no COR is applied. If you apply no COR for an incoming call leg to a dial peer, the dial peer can make a call out of any other dial peer, regardless of the COR configuration on the outgoing dial peer.
A COR list is applied for incoming calls.	No COR	The call succeeds. By default, the outgoing dial peer has the lowest priority. Because some COR configurations exist for incoming calls on the incoming or originating dial peer, it is a superset of the outgoing-call COR configuration for the outgoing or terminating dial peer.
A COR list is applied for incoming calls (a superset of the COR list applied for outgoing calls on the outgoing dial peer).	A COR list is applied for outgoing calls (subsets of the COR list applied for incoming calls on the incoming dial peer).	The call succeeds. The COR list for incoming calls on the incoming dial peer is a superset of the COR list for outgoing calls on the outgoing dial peer.
A COR list is applied for incoming calls (a subset of the COR list applied for outgoing calls on the outgoing dial peer).	A COR list is applied for outgoing calls (supersets of the COR list applied for incoming calls on the incoming dial peer).	The call does not succeed. The COR list for incoming calls on the incoming dial peer is not a superset of the COR list for outgoing calls on the outgoing dial peer.

NOTE　The complete configuration of COR is handled in the Cisco Voice over IP course. Table 6-2 presents an overview only.

SRST Dial Plan Example

Figure 6-8 shows a multisite topology with a Cisco Unified SRST-enabled Cisco IOS router in the remote site.

Figure 6-8 *SRST Dial Plan Topology*

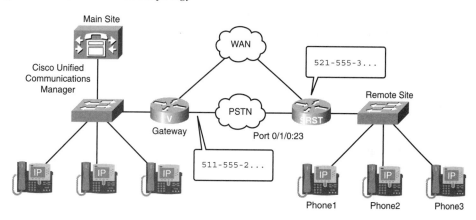

This figure shows a main site with a PSTN number of 511-555-2xxx and a remote site with a PSTN number of 521-555-3xxx. Four digits are used for all internal calls, including calls between the main site and remote site. The remote-site gateway has a single ISDN PRI connection to the PSTN configured on port 0/1/0:23.

For the SRST remote-site configuration shown in Example 6-16, assume that the remote site has only three phones, with one DN each. During SRST fallback, Phone 1 is configured with directory number 3001 and has unlimited PSTN dialing access. Phone 2 is configured with directory number 3002 and is not be allowed to place international calls. Phone 3 is configured with directory number 3003 and is allowed to place only internal calls. Four-digit dialing to headquarters is configured, and calls should be sent to the main site over the PSTN when in SRST mode.

The remote-site router also requires MGCP configurations, as discussed previously, but they are not included in Example 6-16 for simplicity.

Example 6-16 *Remote-Site SRST Dial Plan Configuration Example*

```
application
  global
    service alternate default
!
call-manager-fallback
  ip source-address 10.1.250.101 port 2000
  max-ephones 3
  max-dn 3
  cor incoming phone1 1 3001
  cor incoming phone2 2 3002
```

continues

Example 6-16 *Remote-Site SRST Dial Plan Configuration Example (Continued)*

```
    cor incoming phone3 3 3003
    dialplan-pattern 1 5215553...
    extension-length 4
!
dial-peer cor custom
  name internal
  name pstn
  name pstn-intl
!
dial-peer cor list internal
  member internal
!
dial-peer cor list pstn
  member pstn
!
dial-peer cor list pstn-intl
  member pstn-intl
!
dial-peer cor list phone1
  member internal
  member pstn
  member pstn-intl
!
dial-peer cor list phone2
  member internal
  member pstn
!
dial-peer cor list phone3
  member internal
!
dial-peer voice 1 pots
  description Internal dialing from the PSTN
  incoming called-number .
  direct-inward-dial
  port 0/1/0:23
!
dial-peer voice 9 pots
  description PSTN dial 9 first
  corlist outgoing pstn
  destination-pattern 9T
  port 0/1/0:23
!
dial-peer voice 9011 pots
  description International dial 9 first
  corlist outgoing pstn-intl
```

Example 6-16   *Remote-Site SRST Dial Plan Configuration Example (Continued)*

```
  destination-pattern 9011T
  port 0/1/0:23
  prefix 011
!
dial-peer voice 2000 pots
  description Internal 4 digit dialing to HQ
  corlist outgoing internal
  translation-profile outgoing to-HQ
  destination-pattern 2...
  port 0/1/0:23
!
voice translation-rule 1
  rule 1 /^2/ /15115552/
!
voice translation-profile to-HQ
  translate called 1
!
```

The first part of the SRST configuration includes the **dialplan-pattern** command configured under **call-manager-fallback** configuration mode, which maps the internal four-digit directory numbers to the E.164 PSTN number.

COR lists are configured for internal destinations called internal, for international PSTN destinations named pstn-intl, and for all other PSTN destinations labeled pstn. These COR lists are applied to dial peers as outgoing COR lists. Their function is equivalent to partitions in CUCM.

Additional COR lists are configured, one per phone. These are applied as incoming COR lists to phone directory numbers using the **cor incoming** command in **call-manager-fallback** configuration mode. The configuration shown in Example 6-16 applies the incoming COR list phone1, which is equivalent to CSSs in CUCM, to phone 1, which registers with the SRST gateway with a directory number of 3001, incoming COR list phone2 to the phone with directory number 3002, and incoming COR list phone3 to the phone with directory number 3003.

Outgoing COR lists are applied to the dial peers that are used as outgoing dial peers: dial peer 9011 for international PSTN calls, dial peer 9 for PSTN calls, and dial peer 2000 for calls to headquarters.

> **NOTE** For simplicity, Example 6-16 does not show all the outbound dial peers, as shown previously in Example 6-9. Using the destination pattern 9T as shown in dial peer 9 typically is avoided when possible for local or national calls to avoid the interdigit timeout associated with the T wildcard.

Dial peer 1 is configured for inbound dialing from the PSTN with the **incoming called-number** command to identify all destination phone numbers. Direct inward dialing is enabled, which turns off the second dial tone at ISDN port 0/1/0:23 for external calls dialing in.

The called E.164 numbers (521-555-3xxx) are mapped to four-digit extensions because of the **dialplan-pattern** command that is configured in call-manager-fallback configuration mode. As a result, incoming PSTN calls are sent to the four-digit extensions.

Outgoing calls to phones located at the main site at extensions 2xxx match a destination pattern in dial peer 2000. Dial peer 2000 sends calls to port 0/1/0:23 after performing digit manipulation using the to-HQ voice translation profile. This profile translates the four-digit called number to an 11-digit E.164 PSTN number. The result is that during SRST fallback, users can still dial four-digit extensions to reach phones in headquarters.

Telephony Features Supported by Cisco Unified SRST

The Cisco Unified SRST system provides the following features to phones in SRST mode:

- Alias-based call rerouting lets you define alternative extensions for up to 50 specific PSTN or directory numbers, which also supports hunting of alternative extensions.

- Call Pickup works in conjunction with the Alias function to allow a pickup function that is similar to Call Pickup in CUCM.

- Call Forward Busy / No Answer enables call forwarding to one specific extension.

- Call Transfer has to be enabled and configured in the call-manager-fallback Cisco IOS service where possible call-transfer destinations have to be specified.

- Three-party G.711 ad hoc conferencing has to be enabled and configured under call-manager-fallback.

- MOH can be provided for G.711 VoIP and PSTN calls. MOH can use internal .wav files stored in the router's flash memory. Multicast MOH is supported.

- SRST supports voice-mail integration to a local voice-mail system or to a remote voice-mail system that is accessed over the PSTN during SRST fallback.

Special Requirements for Voice-Mail Integration Using Analog Interfaces

When providing voice-mail access during SRST and using Foreign Exchange Office (FXO) or Foreign Exchange Station (FXS) interfaces, a special configuration is required, as shown in Figure 6-9.

Figure 6-9 *Special Requirements for Voice-Mail Integration Using Analog Interfaces*

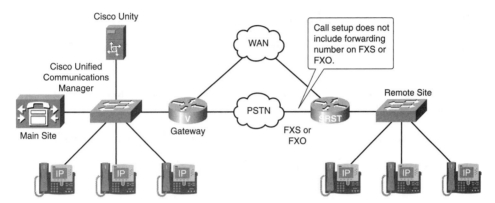

If voice mail is connected to the SRST system using ISDN BRI or PRI, the outgoing setup message contains all the information that the voice mail needs to find the mailbox of the called party. Voice-mail systems accessed over FXO and FXS interfaces cannot send this required information (such as the redirecting number) when setting up the call. Therefore, the SRST gateway can be configured to send the required information using dual-tone multifrequency (DTMF) tones.

Voice-mail integration is configured using the **voicemail** command in call-manager-fallback configuration mode. DTMF tones that are used to send information about the call-forwarding number over analog lines are configured using the **pattern** command under **vm-integration**.

> **NOTE**   Refer to the section "Integrating Voice Mail with Cisco Unified SRST" in *Cisco Unified Survivable Remote Site Telephony Version 4.1 System Administrator Guide* for more information about voice-mail integration with Cisco SRST.

Summary

The following key points were discussed in this chapter:

- A simplified SRST dial plan has to be implemented on the remote-site gateways to ensure connectivity for remote sites in SRST mode.

- SRST reference is assigned via device pool membership.

- Basic Cisco IOS gateway SRST configuration requires only six configuration steps.

- Cisco IOS gateway MGCP fallback configuration requires only two configuration steps.

- CFUR forwards calls made to unregistered directory numbers to the defined destination.

- ISDN overlap dialing has to be enabled in countries with open numbering plans.

- SRST supports numerous telephony features. Voice-mail integration over FXS/FXO lines requires special configuration.

References

For additional information, refer to this resource:

- *Cisco Unified SRST 4.1 System Administrator Guide* (search by title at Cisco.com)

Review Questions

Use these questions to review what you've learned in this chapter. The answers appear in Appendix A, "Answers to Chapter Review Questions."

1. When implementing MGCP Fallback and SRST, what configuration is not performed at CUCM?

    a. Adding SRST references

    b. Enabling MGCP fallback at the MGCP gateway configuration page

    c. Configuring CFUR to reach remote-site phones during SRST mode

    d. Applying SRST references to phones

2. The SRST reference can be applied only per phone at the phone configuration page.

    a. True

    b. False

3. Which command is used for SRST configuration at the Cisco IOS router?

   a. **telephony-server**

   b. **ccm-manager fallback**

   c. **service alternate default**

   d. **call-manager-fallback**

4. Which command is not used for MGCP fallback configuration?

   a. **ccm-manager fallback-mgcp**

   b. **application**

   c. **global**

   d. **telephony-server**

   e. **service alternate default**

5. Where do you configure the CFUR-Max-Hop-Counter?

   a. Service parameter

   b. Enterprise parameter

   c. SRST gateway configuration

   d. Phone configuration

6. How can calling privileges be implemented for individual SRST phones?

   a. You can do this only when using CUCM Express in SRST mode.

   b. By preconfiguring the phones that need calling privileges assigned

   c. By configuring an ephone-dn template

   d. By configuring COR lists for directory numbers

7. Why would you configure voice-mail integration with ISDN using DTMF tones at the SRST gateway?

   a. In SRST mode, the gateway does not know the forwarding number.

   b. On FXS or FXO interfaces, the called number cannot be sent in signaling messages.

   c. The forwarding number cannot be sent in signaling messages.

   d. The used voice-mail system supports only in-band DTMF.

8. What digits will be sent to the PSTN through port 0/1/0:23 in the following SRST dial peer if 9011443335343 is dialed?

```
dial-peer voice 9011 pots
  description International dial 9 first
  corlist outgoing pstn-intl
  destination-pattern 9011T
  port 0/1/0:23
  prefix 011
```

a. 9011443335343

b. 011443335343

c. 443335343

d. 3335343

e. No digits will be sent to the PSTN.

9. How can remote-site IP Phones be configured to dial four digits to get to headquarters phones in the event of a WAN link failure?

a. Configure failover dialing in CUCM.

b. Configure a translation rule in CUCM for four-digit dialing.

c. Configure a voice translation rule on the remote-site router to translate four-digit dialing into the full E.164 number to route over IP.

d. Configure a voice translation rule on the remote-site router to translate four-digit dialing into the full E.164 number to route through the PSTN.

10. What is the effect of omitting the **max-ephone** command in call-manager-fallback configuration mode?

a. An unlimited number of remote IP Phones will register to the SRST router in fallback mode.

b. A limited number of remote IP Phones based on router hardware model will register to the SRST router in fallback mode.

c. A limited number of remote IP Phones based on the IOS license will register to the SRST router in fallback mode.

d. No remote IP Phones will register to the SRST router in fallback mode.

CHAPTER 7

Implementing Cisco Unified Communications Manager Express in SRST Mode

Cisco Unified Communications Manager Express (CUCME) has many features, benefits, and limitations compared to CUCM. This chapter explains those features, as well as the process of registering IP Phones with CUCME for Survivable Remote Site Telephony (SRST). This chapter also discusses the basic telephony-service commands for configuring **ephones** and **ephone-dns**. This includes some basic hunting, a desirable feature of CUCME in SRST mode over (basic) Cisco Unified SRST.

Chapter Objectives

Upon completing this chapter, you will be able to configure CUCME to provide telephony service, basic hunting, and Music On Hold (MOH) to Skinny Client Control Protocol (SCCP) and session initiation protocol (SIP) phones if the connection to the centralized call agent is lost. You will be able to meet these objectives:

- Describe CUCME and the modes in which it can be used

- Describe CUCME versions, their protocol support and features, and the required Cisco IOS Software release

- Describe general CUCME configuration parameters and their functions

- Configure CUCME to support SRST fallback

- Phone Provisioning Options

- Advantages of CUCME SRST

- Phone Registration Process

- Configuring CUCME for SRST

CUCME Overview

Cisco Unified Communications Manager Express (CUCME) is an IOS-based IP telephony solution that is an alternative to CUCM for branch offices or small businesses. CUCME is the call-control device using SCCP or SIP to control 240 or fewer IP Phones. CUCME can work independently of CUCM or integrated with SRST, as described in this chapter. CUCME is based on the IOS feature set and does not require any unique router hardware, but it can leverage the modular hardware of the Cisco gateway.

Figure 7-1 shows a deployment of a CUCME router with several phones and devices connected to it. The CUCME router is connected to the public switched telephone network (PSTN) and WAN.

Figure 7-1 *Standalone CUCME*

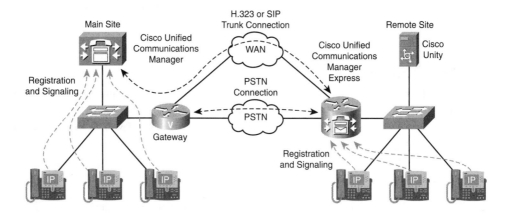

CUCME in SRST Mode

Figure 7-2 shows a topology that can use SRST fallback support using CUCME. SRST is an IOS feature that enables routers to provide call-handling support for Cisco IP Phones if they lose their connection to a remote primary, secondary, or tertiary CUCM installation, which can occur if the WAN connection to the main site is down.

When CUCME provides Cisco Unified SRST functionality, provisioning of phones is automatic. Most CUCME features are available to the phones during periods of fallback, including hunt groups, Call Park, and access to Cisco Unity voice messaging services using SCCP. The benefit is that CUCM users gain access to more features during fallback without any additional licensing costs.

Figure 7-2 *CUCME in SRST Mode*

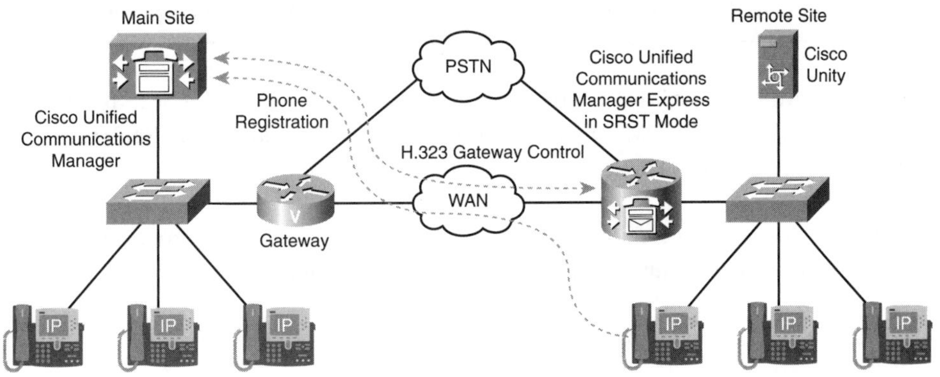

Standalone CUCME Versus CUCM and CUCME in SRST Mode

Consider the differences in features listed in Table 7-1 when choosing between standalone CUCME and CUCM or CUCME in SRST mode.

Table 7-1 *Standalone CUCME* Versus CUCM and CUCME in SRST Mode*

Feature	CUCM and CUCME for SRST	Standalone CUCME
Enterprise size	Small to large	Small
CUCM clustering	Yes. CUCME for SRST leverages the CUCM cluster, but CUCME routers are not cluster members.	No. Standalone CUCME is fully independent of the CUCM cluster.
API	AXL, JTAPI, TAPI	AXL, TAPI (light), TCL
Voice security	TLS, SRTP, IPsec	TLS, IPsec, SRTP
Video	Cisco Unified Video Advantage, 7985	Cisco Unified Video Advantage only
Centralized call processing	Yes	For small sites only

You need to take into account other considerations when choosing the correct system. The server-based CUCM telephony solution also provides scalability for large enterprises. CUCM servers can be grouped in a cluster to provide fault-tolerant telephony for up to 30,000 IP Phones per cluster. Multiple clusters can be configured in an enterprise as previously discussed for larger enterprises. Customers can make use of extensive server-based application programming interfaces (API) with CUCM.

NOTE   Although Cisco IOS gateways can work with CUCM in many configuration options, the IOS gateway never actually replicates the database from the CUCM servers.

Both CUCME and CUCM offer voice security through Transport Layer Security (TLS) and IP Security (IPsec). CUCM offers additional voice security with Secure Real-Time Transport Protocol (SRTP).

CUCM is a centralized architecture but also allows for distributed call processing. CUCME is a distributed architecture but also allows centralized call processing for small sites.

CUCM offers a greater choice of voice codecs and video product selection.

CUCME does not support all CUCM features. For example, it only supports video calls with Cisco Unified Video Advantage.

The CUCM call-processing solution offers feature-rich telephony services to medium or large enterprises. CUCME can serve small deployments on its own or is used as a backup for a centralized call-processing CUCM deployment (CUCME in SRST mode).

The CUCME solution is based on the Cisco access router and Cisco IOS Software. It is simple to deploy and manage, especially for customers who already use Cisco IOS Software products. This allows customers to take advantage of the benefits of IP communication without the higher costs and complexity of deploying a server-based solution. However, it supports only up to 240 users, dependent on the Integrated Service Router (ISR) IOS gateway model.

NOTE   For more information on Cisco ISR models and phone limitations, go to Cisco.com/go/isr.

Although multiple CUCME systems can be interconnected using trunks, the features that are supported across trunks are limited.

CUCME cannot be used if features such as CUCM Extension Mobility, Device Mobility, location-based call admission control (CAC) (including RSVP-enabled locations), call hunting, call pickup, presence, and many others are required to operate across multiple sites. In this case, or simply because of the size of the deployment, CUCM is the better choice. When using CUCM, it is common to use centralized call processing for some sites when IP Phones register to a CUCM across the IP WAN. In this case, CUCME in SRST mode is a better choice than standard SRST functionality, because CUCME in SRST mode offers more features than standard SRST.

In summary, use CUCM when CUCME does not scale to the number of endpoints or does not provide all the features required. If CUCM is used, CUCME in SRST mode should be used if standard SRST features do not meet the requirements for backup scenarios.

CUCME Features

CUCME delivers capabilities that were previously available only to larger enterprises to the small or medium-sized business.

CUCME integrates with voice-mail systems such as Cisco Unity, Cisco Unity Connection, Cisco Unity Express, and third-party voice-mail systems, as shown in Figure 7-3. CUCME can also use the voice gateway features of the ISR router for connectivity to analog phones and faxes, connection to an IP WAN or the Internet, and digital and analog connectivity to the PSTN.

Figure 7-3 *CUCME Features*

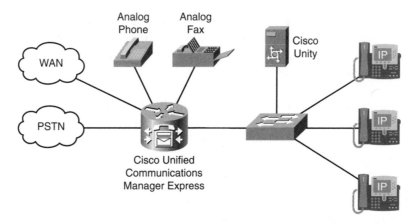

Administration of CUCME can be done using a GUI or command-line interface (CLI).

CUCME Features and Versions

The version of the CUCME depends on the release of the Cisco IOS Software that is running on the router, as shown in Table 7-2.

Table 7-2   *CUCME Features and Versions*

Feature	CUCME 4.2	CUCME 4.1	CUCME 4.0(1)	CUCME 3.3
Recommended Cisco IOS Software release	12.4(11)XW	12.4(15)T	12.4(9)T	12.4(3)
Extension mobility	✓			
Media security	✓			
Presence with Busy Lamp Field (BLF) status	✓	✓		
Video	✓	✓	✓	
Phone security	✓	✓	✓	
Local MOH	✓	✓	✓	✓
SIP phone support	✓	✓	✓	
SCCP phone support	✓	✓	✓	✓

Each Cisco IOS Software release implements a particular CUCME version. You upgrade to a newer version of CUCME through a Cisco IOS update. Often the recent Cisco IOS Software releases have greater memory requirements than older ones, so verify your memory capacity before upgrading.

For detailed information on the feature history of CUCME, refer to the most recent *Cisco Unified Communications Manager Express Administration Guide* and the other documents described in the documentation road map for CUCME on Cisco.com. CUCME version 4.3 requires a minimum IOS version of 12.4(15)XZ.

Other CUCME Features

CUCME also includes the following features that are similar to legacy low-end PBX and key system features:

- Call Transfer, Call Transfer Blocking, paging, intercom, call coverage

- Call Park, Park Call Recall, dedicated park slot per extension, MOH, multicast MOH

- Hunt groups, basic automatic call distribution (B-ACD) and reporting

- Ad-hoc conferencing, retain conference when initiator drops

- Night bell, night service call forwarding

- Headset autoanswer, distinctive ring patterns for internal and external

- Support for Cisco Unified Video Advantage

- Support for Cisco IP Communicator

General Configuration of CUCME

At a minimum, the following commands must be configured to deploy a CUCME system:

- **telephony-service:** The **telephony-service** command enters telephony-service configuration mode, where global settings of CUCME are configured.

- **max-ephones:** CUCME must be configured with the maximum number of **ephones** using the **max-ephones** command in telephony-service configuration mode.

- **max-dn:** CUCME must be configured with the maximum number of extension numbers (**ephone-dns**) using the **max-dn** command in telephony-service configuration mode.

> **NOTE**   The default value of **max-ephones** and **max-dn** is 0. This default must be modified to allow the configuration of **ephones** and **ephone-dns**. The maximum number of supported **ephones** and **ephone-dns** is version-specific and platform-specific. The number displayed in Cisco IOS Software Help files does not always reflect the actual limit.

- **ip source-address:** This command is entered in telephony-service configuration mode. It is used to define the IP address to which CUCME is bound.

- **create cnf-files:** This command is entered in telephony-service configuration mode. It is used to generate Extensible Markup Language (XML) configuration files for phones.

- **ephone-dn:** This global configuration command is used to create a directory number. After this command is entered, the router is in **ephone-dn** subconfiguration mode.

- **number:** The **number** command defines a directory number for an **ephone-dn** (extension), which then can be assigned to an IP Phone.

- **ephone:** The **ephone** command is entered in global configuration mode. It is used to create a phone in CUCME.

- **mac-address:** This command is entered in **ephone** configuration mode. It specifies the device ID of an **ephone**. When a phone registers with CUCME, it has to provide a device ID (which is based on the phone's MAC address) that is configured in CUCME.

- **type:** This command is entered in **ephone** configuration mode. It specifies the phone type of this **ephone**.

- **button:** This command is entered in **ephone** configuration mode. It is used to assign one or more **ephone-dns** to an **ephone**.

- **dialplan-pattern:** This command is entered in telephony-service configuration mode. It is used to map E.164 PSTN numbers to internal extension numbers.

CUCME Basic Configuration

Example 7-1 shows a basic CUCME configuration.

Example 7-1   *Cisco Unified CME Basic Configuration*

```
telephony-service
  max-ephones 5
  max-dn 10
  ip source-address 10.1.250.102 port 2000
  create cnf-files
!
ephone-dn  6
  number 3001
ephone-dn  7
  number 3002
!
ephone  3
  mac-address 0012.0154.5D98
  type 7960
  button  1:6
ephone  4
  mac-address 0007.0E57.6F43
  type 7961
  button  1:7
!
dialplan-pattern 3 5215553... extension-length 4
!
```

This example shows a CUCME configuration of two **ephones**—one with directory number 3001 and one with directory number 3002. In this very simple example, only two Cisco IP Phones are configured to register to CME as an **ephone**. An **ephone** is an Ethernet phone, which is a Cisco IP Phone identified by its burned-in MAC address from manufacturing. The four-digit extensions are expanded to a ten-digit E.164 PSTN address (521-555-3*xxx*).

CUCME Configuration Providing Phone Loads

CUCME can be configured to provide specific phone loads to IP Phones for each type of phone.

CUCME needs to be configured so that IP Phone firmware files are available through the TFTP server. The command **tftp-server flash:***filename* allows the specified file that resides in flash memory to be downloaded via TFTP.

Example 7-2 shows a configuration with firmware files made available by the CME router.

Example 7-2   *Cisco Unified CME Phone Load Configuration*

```
tftp-server flash:P0030702T023.bin
tftp-server flash:cmterm_7920.4.0-02-00.bin
!
telephony-service
  load 7960-7940 P0030702T023
  load 7920 cmterm_7920.4.0-02-00
!
```

This example shows the following Cisco IP Phone firmware files that are made available:

■ cmterm_7920.4.0-02-00.bin (Cisco Unified Wireless IP Phone 7920)

■ P0030702T023.bin (Cisco Unified IP Phones 7940G and 7960G)

To associate a type of Cisco IP Phone with an IP Phone firmware file, use the **load** *model firmware-file* command in telephony-service configuration mode.

> **TIP**   You can see a list of IP Phone models supported by the CUCME router by entering the **load ?** command in telephony-service configuration mode.

> **NOTE**   Firmware filenames are case-sensitive.

CUCME Configuration for Music On Hold

Music On Hold (MOH) is an audio stream played to PSTN and VoIP G.711 or G.729 callers who are placed on hold by phones in a CUCME system. This audio stream is intended to reassure callers that they are still connected to their calls. Example 7-3 shows the configuration of MOH on Cisco Unified CME.

Example 7-3 *Cisco Unified CME Music On Hold Configuration*

```
telephony-service
  moh moh-file.au
  multicast moh 239.1.1.1 port 16384
!
```

Keep in mind the following points when configuring MOH:

- MOH is enabled by the **moh** command under telephony service.

- For multicast MOH, add the **multicast moh** command.

- CUCME supports only G.711 for MOH.

- Transcoders are required to allow G.729 to be used for MOH.

When the phone receiving MOH is part of a system that uses a G.729 codec, transcoding is required between G.711 and G.729. The G.711 MOH must be translated into G.729. Note that because of compression, MOH using G.729 is of significantly lower fidelity than MOH using G.711. The G.729 codec was designed to accommodate human voice, not more complex sounds from musical instruments.

If the MOH audio stream is also identified as a multicast source, the CUCME router additionally transmits the stream on the physical IP interfaces of the CUCME router that you specify during configuration. This gives external devices access to the MOH audio stream.

Certain IP Phones do not support IP multicast and therefore do not support multicast MOH. You can disable multicast MOH to individual phones that do not support multicast. Callers hear a repeating tone when they are placed on hold as an alternative to MOH.

In CUCME Release 4.1 and later releases, the MOH feature is supported when a call is put on hold from a SIP phone and when the user of a SIP phone is put on hold by a SIP, SCCP, or plain old telephone service (POTS) endpoint. The holder (the party who pressed the hold key) or the holdee (the party who is put on hold) can be on the same CUCME group or on a different CUCME group that is connected through a SIP trunk. MOH is also supported for call transfers and conferencing, with or without a transcoding device.

Configuring MOH for SIP phones is the same as configuring MOH for SCCP phones.

Configuring CUCME in SRST Mode

An SRST reference in CUCM can be a standard SRST gateway or a CUCME router. Unlike standalone CUCME, when you are configuring CUCME in SRST mode, no phones have to be configured, because they can be learned by Simple Network-Enabled Auto-Provision (SNAP).

However, CUCME in SRST mode allows any combination of the following configurations:

■ **Manually configured ephones with associated ephone-dns:** In this case, the phone is fully configured; both the **ephone** and an **ephone-dn**, which is associated with the **ephone**, exist. This is used for phones that require additional configuration settings that cannot be learned from the phone via SNAP. These settings should be applied only to this phone (or few phones). Therefore, an **ephone** template or **ephone-dn** template cannot be used (because these apply to all learned phones and/or directory numbers).

■ **Manually configured ephones with no associated ephone-dn:** This configuration is useful if specific phone configuration parameters are required (which cannot be assigned from a template) but no specific directory number is required. If an **ephone** is preconfigured in CUCME and is not associated with a directory number, the directory number is not learned via SNAP. Therefore, the phone won't have a directory number unless through auto-assignment. This is equivalent to auto-registration in CUCM, where essentially a random directory number is assigned to the phones.

NOTE This combination is not very common, because it combines the need for specific phone configuration parameters with the dynamic assignment of directory numbers.

■ **Manually configured ephone-dns:** These **ephone-dns** are not associated with an **ephone**. The reason to configure the **ephone-dn** but not the **ephone** is that only individual **ephone-dn** configuration is required, but default settings or a single template can be used for the **ephone**. (This is added after the phone registers.)

■ **No manual configuration:** In this case, the **ephone-dn** and the **ephone** are learned by SNAP. You can apply configuration settings that are not supported by SNAP to such newly added phones and directory numbers by configuring the appropriate templates.

Phone-Provisioning Options

Table 7-3 summarizes the phone-provisioning options and shows the relevant configuration parts.

Table 7-3 *Phone-Provisioning Options*

	ephone and ephone-dn	ephone and Auto-Assignment	ephone-dn and SRST Provisioning	Full SRST Provisioning
Cisco IOS Configuration	ephone 1 mac-address...type 7960 button 1:6 ephone-dn 6 number 3001	ephone 1 mac-address...type 7960 (no button...) telephony-service auto assign...	ephone-dn 6 number 3001 telephony-service srst mode auto-provision...	telephony-service srst mode auto-provision...
Resulting Directory Number Configuration	Existing CUCME configuration	CUCME ephone-dn configuration referenced by auto-assignment	CUCME ephone-dn configuration of matching phone directory number	Phone directory number configuration (plus CUCME SRST ephone-dn template)
Resulting Phone Configuration	Existing CUCME configuration	Existing CUCME configuration	CUCME ephone template	CUCME ephone template

As shown in this table, if an **ephone** and **ephone-dn** are configured in CUCME, a phone that registers with the configured MAC address gets the complete configuration of the phone and its DN applied as configured in CUCME. CUCME does not use SNAP to configure the phone.

If an **ephone** is configured but not associated with an **ephone-dn**, auto-assignment has to be enabled. Otherwise, the phone does not have a line and cannot place or receive calls. The **ephone-dn** configuration is determined based on the arguments of the **auto-assign** command. SNAP is not used to learn phone settings or directory number configuration parameters.

If only **ephone-dns** are configured, the **ephone** configuration is learned by SNAP. The **ephone-dn** configuration that is configured in CUCME is used instead of the phone directory-number configuration provided by SNAP. **ephone** templates (if configured) are applied to the learned **ephone** configuration.

If neither an **ephone** with its MAC address nor a directory number exists for the registering phone, Cisco Unified CME learns everything, including the **ephone** and **ephone-dn** configuration, by SNAP. **ephone** and **ephone-dn** templates are applied if they are configured.

Advantages of CUCME SRST

Using CUCME in SRST mode has several advantages compared to using standard SRST:

■ CUCME provides more telephony features than SRST.

■ CUCME in SRST mode allows a mix of preconfigured phones and/or directory numbers for phones and directory numbers (DN) that require individual settings and phones that are not configured but are learned by SNAP.

■ The additional features of CUCME can be leveraged by preconfiguring the required individual settings in CUCME to benefit SRST.

■ **ephone** configuration is based on MAC addresses. **ephone-dn** configuration is based on the directory number.

■ All phones and/or directory numbers that collectively require identical configuration not provided by SNAP do not have to be preconfigured, but the additional configuration can be applied using templates.

■ These features allow flexible configuration of any CUCME feature in a scalable way, because only those devices have to be preconfigured, which requires individual settings.

Phone Registration Process

When a phone loses connectivity to its Cisco Unified Communications Manager, it registers to its configured SRST reference.

If that SRST reference is CUCME in SRST mode, the CUCME router first searches for an existing preconfigured **ephone** with the MAC address of the registering phone. If an **ephone** is found, the stored **ephone** configuration is used. No phone configuration settings provided by SNAP are applied, and no **ephone** template is applied. If the **ephone** is configured with one or more **ephone-dns**, the stored configuration is used for the phone's **ephone-dn** or **ephone-dns**. Neither information provided by SNAP nor the **ephone** template configured under telephony-service is applied. If the configured **ephone** is not configured with an **ephone-dn**, auto-assignment has to be enabled for the phone to be able to be associated with an **ephone-dn**. SNAP is not an option in this case.

If no **ephone** is found for the MAC address of the registering phone, CUCME adds the **ephone** (and applies the **ephone** template if it is configured) using SNAP. If the directory number exists, it is bound to the added phone; otherwise, the directory number is learned using SNAP. If it is configured, the **ephone-dn** template is applied.

Configuring CUCME for SRST

The configuration of CUCME in SRST mode is performed in telephony-service configuration mode, as shown in Example 7-4. As soon as the command **telephony-service** is active, the command **call-manager-fallback** is not accepted by the CLI, and vice versa.

Example 7-4 *Configuring CUCME for SRST*

```
CMERouter#configure terminal
 CMERouter(config)#telephony-service
 CMERouter(config-telephony)#srst mode auto-provision {all | dn | none}
 CMERouter(config-telephony)#srst dn line-mode {dual | dual-octo | octo | single}
```

To enable SRST mode for CUCME, use the **srst mode auto-provision** command in **telephony-service** configuration mode:

■ The keyword **all** includes information for learned **ephones** and **ephone-dns** in the running configuration.

■ The keyword **dn** includes information for learned **ephone-dns** in the running configuration.

■ The keyword **none** does not include information for learned **ephones** or **ephone-dns** in the running configuration. Use this keyword when CUCME is providing SRST fallback services for Cisco Unified Communications Manager.

> **NOTE** If the administrator saves the running configuration after learning **ephones** and **ephone-dns**, the fallback IP Phones are treated as locally configured IP Phones on the CUCME SRST router. This could adversely impact the fallback behavior of those IP Phones.

To specify the line mode for the **ephone-dns** that are automatically created in SRST mode on a CUCME router, use the **srst dn line-mode** command in telephony-service configuration mode:

■ The keyword **dual** specifies dual-line **ephone-dns**.

■ The keyword **single** specifies single-line **ephone-dns** (this is the default).

- The keyword **dual-octo** specifies that fallback **ephone-dns** are dual-line or octo-line. This is a new keyword in CUCME v4.3 and later versions.

- The keyword **octo** specifies that fallback **ephone-dns** are single-line. This is a new keyword in CUCME v4.3 and later versions.

> **NOTE**   If single-line **ephone-dns** is used with multiple-line features such as call waiting, call transfer, and conferencing, a phone must have more than one single-line directory number.

To specify an **ephone-dn** template to be used in SRST mode on a CUCME router, use the **srst dn template** command in telephony-service configuration mode, as shown in Example 7-5.

Example 7-5 *Configuring CUCME for SRST, Continued*

```
CMERouter#configure terminal
  CMERouter(config)#telephony-service
  CMERouter(config-telephony)#srst dn template template-tag
  CMERouter(config-telephony)#srst ephone template template-tag
  CMERouter(config-telephony)#srst ephone description string
```

To specify an **ephone-dn** template to be used in SRST mode on a CUCME router, use the **srst dn template** command in **telephony-service** configuration mode according to the following points:

- The parameter *template-tag* is the identifying number of an existing **ephone-dn** template. The range is from 1 to 15.

- To specify an **ephone-template** to be used in SRST mode on a CUCME router, use the **srst ephone template** command in **telephony-service** configuration mode.

  The parameter *template-tag* is the identifying number of an existing **ephone-template**. The range is from 1 to 20.

- To specify a description to be associated with an **ephone** in SRST mode on a CUCME router, use the **srst ephone description** command in telephony-service configuration mode.

  The maximum length of the parameter *string* is 100 characters.

CUCME for SRST Mode Configuration

Figure 7-4 shows a topology example of Cisco Unified CME in SRST mode. Example 7-6 shows the SRST Mode configuration. Ten IP Phones are configured, with a maximum of 30 directory numbers among all ten.

Figure 7-4   *CUCME Topology*

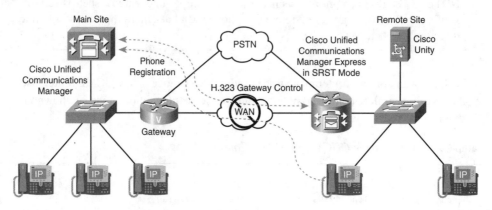

Example 7-6   *CUCME for SRST Mode Configuration*

```
CMERouter#configure terminal
 CMERouter(config)#telephony-service
  CMERouter(config-telephony)#srst mode auto-provision all
  CMERouter(config-telephony)#srst dn line-mode dual
  CMERouter(config-telephony)#srst ephone template 1
  CMERouter(config-telephony)#srst dn template 3
  CMERouter(config-telephony)#srst ephone description
  CMERouter(config-telephony)#max-ephone 10
  CMERouter(config-telephony)#max-dn 30
  CMERouter(config-telephony)#exit
 CMERouter(config)#ephone-template 1
      CMERouter(config-ephone-template)#keep-conference local-only
 CMERouter(config)#ephone-dn-template 3
   CMERouter(config-ephone-template)#hold-alert 25 idle
```

In this example, CUCME uses **ephone-template 1** for newly added phones. This template configures conferences to drop if no internal members are left in the conference.

ephone-dns, which are learned using SNAP, are configured to alert the user if a call is on hold for 25 seconds and the phone is idle.

The description of learned phones should be CUCME SRST, and the **ephone-dns** should be **dual-mode** lines.

Summary

The following key points were discussed in this chapter:

- CUCME cannot be a member of a CUCM cluster.

- CUCME supports Extension Mobility, phone and media security, Busy Lamp Field (BLF), and video.

- Basic configuration of CUCME includes **telephony-service** configuration, **ephone** configuration, and **ephone-dn** configuration.

- The **srst mode** command in telephony-service confirmation mode is required to allow CUCME to learn **ephones** and **ephone-dns** via SNAP.

References

For additional information, refer to this resource:

- Cisco Systems, Inc., *Cisco Unified Communications Manager Express System Administrator Guide* on Cisco.com

Review Questions

Use these questions to review what you've learned in this chapter. The answers appear in Appendix A, "Answers to Chapter Review Questions."

1. Which two statements about CUCME are true?

   a. Cisco IP Phones register with CUCME in standalone mode when CUCME is part of the Cisco Unified CM Group specified in the phone's device pool.

   b. During SRST fallback, IP Phones register with CUCME in SRST mode when CUCME is configured as the SRST reference for the IP Phone.

   c. CUCME in SRST mode provides more features than standard SRST.

   d. The same platform can serve more phones when running CUCME in SRST mode versus running standard SRST.

   e. Standalone CUCME routers can be clustered for redundancy.

2. Which two features were added in CUCME version 4.2 that were not available in CME with all previous versions?

   a. Extension Mobility

   b. Media Security

   c. Presence with BLF status

   d. Video

   e. Local MOH

3. Which of the following three commands are not configured in telephony-service configuration mode?

   a. **create cnf-files**

   b. **ephone**

   c. **ephone-dn**

   d. **max-ephones**

   e. **max-dn**

   f. **ip source-address**

   g. **dialplan-pattern**

4. Which statement about CUCME in SRST mode is not true?

   a. If only the **ephone-dn** is preconfigured, only the **ephone** is learned by SNAP.

   b. If **ephone** and **ephone-dn** are preconfigured, SNAP is not used.

   c. If neither the **ephone** nor **ephone-dn** is preconfigured, **ephone** and **ephone-dn** are learned by SNAP.

   d. If only the **ephone** is preconfigured, only the **ephone-dn** is learned by SNAP.

5. Which of the following statements is the most accurate about the relationship between IOS routers in a remote site and CUCM?

   a. The CUCM database can be configured to replicate its content onto an IOS router in SRST mode.

   b. The CUCM database can be configured to replicate its content onto an IOS router in SRST mode on version 4.0 and later.

   c. The CUCM database can be configured to replicate its content onto an IOS router in SRST mode only with CME.

   d. The CUCM database cannot be configured to replicate its content onto an IOS router in any mode.

6. Which of the following statements about IOS Routers in a remote site is the most accurate?

    a. **call-manager-fallback** and **telephony-service** should both be configured on the remote router for optimal performance.

    b. **call-manager-fallback** and **telephony-service** should both be configured on the remote router with standalone CME.

    c. **call-manager-fallback** and **telephony-service** should both be configured on the remote router to enable the maximum features to remote Cisco IP Phones in fall-back mode.

    d. **call-manager-fallback** and **telephony-service** can never be configured on a remote router at the same time.

7. Which protocol do you need to configure to copy the phone firmware files from the CME router to the Cisco IP Phones?

    a. FTP

    b. SFTP

    c. TFTP

    d. Secure TFTP

    e. HTTP

8. What is the benefit of multicast MOH in a remote router?

    a. Maximum MOH functionality

    b. Reduced bandwidth utilization when two or more phones are receiving MOH

    c. Compliance with Internet standards

    d. Improved audio quality by using G.729

CHAPTER 8

Implementing Bandwidth Management

When an IP WAN connects different sites in a Cisco Unified Communications network, bandwidth consumption at the IP WAN should be minimized. Techniques that can help conserve bandwidth on the IP WAN in a multisite deployment include reducing the required bandwidth of voice streams, keeping some voice streams such as local media resources away from the IP WAN, and employing special features such as multicast Music On Hold (MOH) from branch router flash or using transcoders.

This chapter describes all these techniques and features and their implementation.

Chapter Objectives

Upon completing this chapter, you will be able to implement techniques to reduce bandwidth requirements on IP WAN links in CUCM multisite deployments. You will be able to meet these objectives:

■ Describe methods of minimizing bandwidth requirements for Cisco Unified Communications

■ Configure CUCM to control the codec used for a call

■ Implement local conference bridges to avoid accessing conference bridges over the IP WAN even if all participants are local

■ Implement transcoders to allow low-bandwidth codecs to be used when low-bandwidth codecs are not supported by both endpoints

■ Implement multicast MOH from branch router flash to avoid MOH streams over the IP WAN

Bandwidth Management Overview

Valuable IP WAN bandwidth can be conserved by various techniques, including reducing the required bandwidth of voice streams by using Real-Time Transport Protocol (RTP) header compression, a quality of service (QoS) link efficiency mechanism, or low-bandwidth audio codecs.

> **NOTE**   QoS is discussed in *End-to-End QoS Network Design: Quality of Service in LANs, WANs, and VPNs* (Cisco Press, 2004) and *Cisco QOS Exam Certification Guide (IP Telephony Self-Study)*, Second Edition (Cisco Press, 2004).

Other options for IP WAN bandwidth management are techniques that influence where voice streams are sent. If three phones, all located at a remote site, establish an ad hoc conference, there is a great difference in bandwidth usage if the conference bridge is located at the remote site local to the phones that are members of the conference. If the conference is located at the main site and has to be accessed over the IP WAN, WAN bandwidth is used inefficiently. In the case of the conference resources at the main site, all three remote IP Phones send their voice stream to the conference bridge over the IP WAN. The conference bridge across the WAN mixes the received audio and then streams it back to all conference members in three separate unicast streams. Although the call appears to be local to the remote site because all conference members are located at that site because of the remotely located conference bridge, the IP WAN is occupied by three calls.

> **NOTE**   The term Multipoint Control Unit (MCU) is often used in the VoIP industry to refer to a physical device dedicated to mixing multiple RTP audio streams in a conference call. In this chapter, a hardware conference bridge in an IOS router or software conference bridge running in a CUCM server plays the role of an MCU.

Other bandwidth-management solutions include the use of transcoders or the implementation of special features such as multicast MOH from branch router flash.

Transcoders are devices that can *transcode* voice streams; that is, they change how the audio payload is encoded. For example, transcoding can take a G.711 audio stream and change it into a G.729 audio stream. Transcoders allow the use of low-bandwidth codecs over the IP WAN even if one of the endpoints requires a high-bandwidth codec such as G.711.

Multicast MOH from branch router flash allows a multicast MOH stream to be generated by a Cisco IOS router located at the remote site, instead of being sent over the IP WAN from a centralized MOH server.

CUCM Codec Configuration

To conserve IP WAN bandwidth, low-bandwidth codecs such as G.729 should be used in the IP WAN. For calls within a LAN environment, high-bandwidth codecs such as G.711 should be used for optimal audio quality. When choosing the right codec for your configuration, it is important to remember that low-bandwidth codecs such as G.729 are designed for human speech; they do not work well for other audio streams. The audio quality of G.729 can sound quite poor when used to play music.

As stated previously, other methods exist for limiting the bandwidth required for MOH streams. If multicast MOH from branch router flash cannot be used, but MOH streams are not desired on the IP WAN, MOH can be disabled for remote-site phones.

Review of CUCM Codecs

The codec to be used for a call depends on CUCM region configuration. Each device is assigned with a region via the device pool configuration.

For each region, the administrator can configure the codec with the highest permitted bandwidth requirement within a region, to other specifically listed regions, and to all other unlisted regions as well.

When a call is placed between two devices, the codec is determined based on the regions of the two devices and on the devices' capabilities. The devices use the codec that is best supported by both devices and that does not exceed the bandwidth requirements of the codec permitted for the region or regions that are involved in the call. If the two devices cannot agree on a codec when a region configuration allows a G.729 codec but a device on the other end supports only G.711, a transcoder is invoked if available.

Figure 8-1 shows a sample scenario for codec configuration in CUCM.

Figure 8-1 *Codec Configuration Topology*

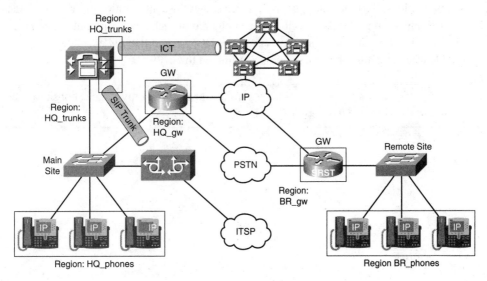

In this figure, phones located at headquarters are configured with region HQ_phones. An intercluster trunk that connects to another CUCM cluster and a SIP trunk connecting to an Internet telephony service provider (ITSP) are in region HQ_trunks. The PSTN gateway that is located at headquarters is configured with region HQ_gw. At the remote site, phones are in region BR_phones, and the PSTN gateway is in region BR_gw.

CUCM regions are configured in the following way:

- Within HQ_phones: G.711

- Within HQ_gw: G.711

- HQ_phones to HQ_gw: G.711

- Within BR_phones: G.711

- Within BR_gw: G.711

- BR_phones to BR_gw: G.711

- All others: G.729

As a result of this configuration, all calls that use the IP WAN between the remote site and headquarters use G.729. Calls that are sent through the intercluster or SIP trunk use G.729 as well. Calls between phones within headquarters, calls between phones within the remote site, calls from headquarters phones to the headquarters PSTN gateway, and calls from remote-site phones to the remote-site PSTN gateway use G.711.

This scenario is illustrated in Figure 8-2, which shows the configuration of the HQ_phones and BR_phones regions. Both regions are configured in such a way that calls within the region and calls to the local gateway for regions HQ_gw and BR_gw are allowed to use G.711, whereas calls to all other regions are limited to G.729.

NOTE   The example in Figure 8-2 is a partial configuration only. It does not show the configuration of the other regions.

Figure 8-2 *CUCM Codec Configuration*

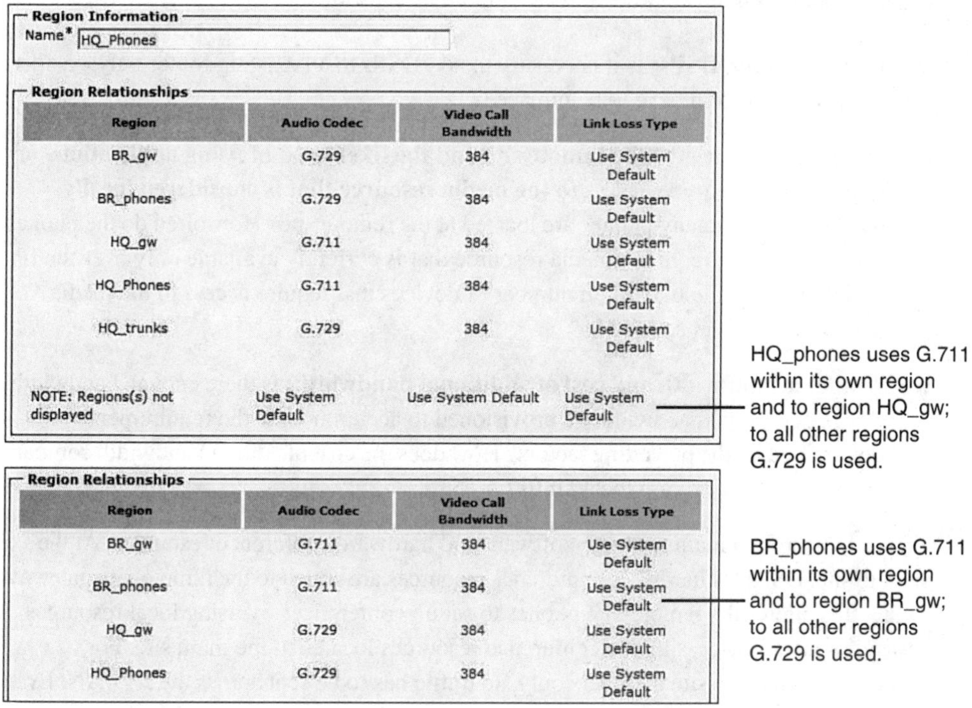

Region Information
Name* HQ_Phones

Region Relationships

Region	Audio Codec	Video Call Bandwidth	Link Loss Type
BR_gw	G.729	384	Use System Default
BR_phones	G.729	384	Use System Default
HQ_gw	G.711	384	Use System Default
HQ_Phones	G.711	384	Use System Default
HQ_trunks	G.729	384	Use System Default
NOTE: Regions(s) not displayed	Use System Default	Use System Default	Use System Default

HQ_phones uses G.711 within its own region and to region HQ_gw; to all other regions G.729 is used.

Region Relationships

Region	Audio Codec	Video Call Bandwidth	Link Loss Type
BR_gw	G.711	384	Use System Default
BR_phones	G.711	384	Use System Default
HQ_gw	G.729	384	Use System Default
HQ_Phones	G.729	384	Use System Default

BR_phones uses G.711 within its own region and to region BR_gw; to all other regions G.729 is used.

Local Conference Bridge Implementation

When local conference bridges or media termination points (MTP) are deployed at each site, traffic does not have to cross the IP WAN if all endpoints are located at the same site. Local media resources such as conference bridges and MTPs can be implemented by providing appropriate hardware digital signal processors (DSP) in the routers located at the remote sites. All voice gateways require DSPs, but additional DSP resources are required for hardware conference calls and transcoding.

NOTE   Search for the "DSP Calculator" tool on Cisco.com after logging in with your CCO account for exact calculations of DSP requirements.

Whether the extra cost of providing the DSP resources for hardware conference calls will pay off depends on the answers to these important questions:

- **Cost of adding DSPs:** Is it necessary to add DSPs to an existing router only, or does the whole platform have to be replaced?

- **Number of devices at the remote site and the likelihood of using applications or features that require access to the media resource that is considered locally deployed:** How many phones are located at the remote site? How often do the phones use features that require a media resource that is currently available only over the IP WAN? What is the maximum number of devices that require access to the media resource at the same time?

- **Available bandwidth and cost of additional bandwidth:** Is there enough bandwidth, or can additional bandwidth be provisioned to accommodate the requirements determined by the preceding factors? How does the cost of adding bandwidth compare to the cost of deploying local DSPs?

Figure 8-3 shows a main site with software and hardware conference resources. At the remote site, DSPs for hardware conference resources are added to the remote-site gateway. Doing this allows the remote-site phones to set up conferences by using local resources instead of always accessing the conference resources located at the main site. For conferencing remote-site members only, no traffic has to be sent across the IP WAN. Even if a few callers from the main site are in the same conference call as the others in the remote site, the WAN utilization is still minimized.

Figure 8-3 *Implementing Local Conference Bridges at Two Sites*

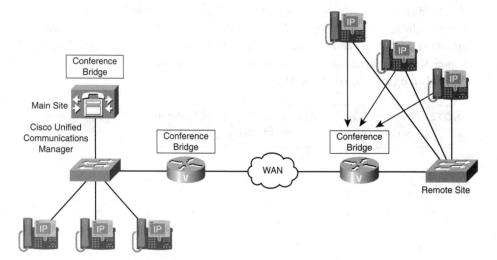

> **NOTE** When an ad hoc conference includes members of different sites, a separate voice stream for each remote member has to be sent across the IP WAN. However, if a Meet-Me conference is set up, the users located at the remote site could first establish an ad hoc conference by using a media resource that is local to the remote users by using the DSP resources in their local gateway. Then they could add a call to the remote Meet-Me conference to their local ad hoc conference. In this case, only a single voice stream is sent across the IP WAN connecting the two conferences.

Figure 8-4 illustrates how media resource groups (MRG) and media resource group lists (MRGL) are used logically in CUCM to ensure that headquarters phones use the conference resources at headquarters and that remote-site phones use the remote-site conference resource when establishing a conference.

Figure 8-4 *Implementing Local Conference Bridges at Two Sites, Continued*

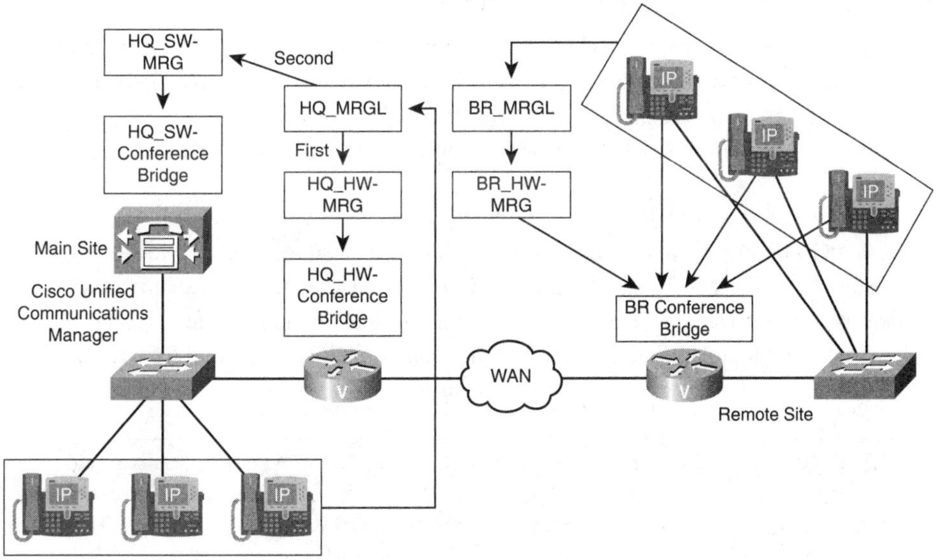

The following three media resource groups are created:

- **HQ_HW-MRG:** Includes the hardware conference bridge provided by the voice gateway located at headquarters.

- **HQ_SW-MRG:** Includes the software conference bridge provided by a CUCM server located at headquarters.

- **BR_HW-MRG:** Includes the hardware conference bridge provided by the voice gateway located at the remote site.

HQ_HW-MRG is the first entry of the media resource group list called HQ_MRGL, and HQ_SW-MRG is the next entry. Headquarters phones are configured with HQ_MRGL. Because media resource groups are used in a prioritized way, headquarters phones that invoke a conference first use the available hardware conference resources. When all of them are in use, the software conference resources are accessed. Software conference resources run on a CUCM server and use the server CPU to mix the calls. Note that the remote site does not have a software conference bridge because the remote site does not have CUCM servers.

At the remote site, all phones refer to the BR_MRGL, which includes only the BR_HW-MRG. This configuration allows remote phones to use their local conference bridge when they invoke conferences instead of accessing conference resources located across the IP WAN.

Transcoder Implementation

Transcoders are devices that can *transcode* voice streams; that is, they change how the audio payload is encoded. For instance, G.711 audio streams are changed into G.729 audio streams. Transcoders are deployed to allow the use of low-bandwidth codecs over the IP WAN even if one of the endpoints supports only high-bandwidth codecs such as G.711.

The transcoder has to be deployed close to the device that supports only G.711. That device sends a G.711 stream to the transcoder, which transcodes the audio to a low-bandwidth codec such as G.729, all in real time. The G.729 voice stream is then sent from the transcoder to the other device, such as a phone located at a remote site, over the IP WAN. It is important to avoid transcoding more than one time in a single call flow whenever possible, because the audio quality may be significantly reduced.

> **NOTE**   It is important for the media resource group list to be configured so that the device that is limited to the higher-bandwidth codec is the one that requests the transcoder media resource. For example, if only G.729 is permitted between two IP Phones, but one IP Phone supports only G.711, the phone using G.729 that cannot comply with the permitted codec is the one that requests a transcoder. Therefore, the media resource group list of this phone requires access to a transcoder, which should be physically located close to the requesting device. Regions have to be set up in such a way that the requesting phone is allowed to use G.711 to the transcoder. Note that this call leg is also subject to region configuration.

As with local conference bridges, these factors must be taken into account before transcoders are deployed:

- **Cost of adding DSPs:** Is it necessary to add DSPs to an existing router only, or does the whole platform have to be replaced?

- **Number of phones at the remote site and the number of calls that are placed to G.711-only phones over the IP WAN:** How many phones are located at the remote site? How often do the phones need to communicate with phones located at headquarters that support G.711 only and hence require a transcoder when G.729 must be used over the IP WAN? How many of these calls occur at the same time?

- **Available bandwidth and the cost of additional bandwidth:** Is there enough bandwidth (or can additional bandwidth be provisioned) to allow G.711 for calls to devices that do not support G.729? How does the cost of adding bandwidth compare to the cost of deploying local DSPs?

Implementing a Transcoder at the Main Site

Figure 8-5 illustrates implementing a transcoder at the main site for remote-site phones calling in to G.711-only devices in the main site.

Figure 8-5 *Implementing a Transcoder at the Main Site*

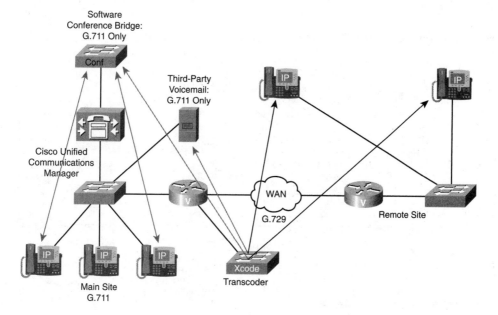

At the main site, two devices support G.711 only. One is a CUCM software conference bridge, the other one is a third-party voice-mail application.

Regions are configured in such a way that all voice traffic between the remote site and the main site has to use the G.729 codec.

Because software conference bridges support only G.711, remote users configured with G.729 are not permitted to join the conference unless transcoding is configured.

If you add a transcoder resource at the main-site gateway, the remote-site user can now send a G.729 voice stream, saving WAN bandwidth. The voice stream is transcoded to G.711 and is passed on to the conference bridge by the transcoder located at the main site.

The same approach can be used for calls to the G.711-only voice-mail system from the remote site. For example, Cisco Unity Express voice mail supports only G.711.

NOTE   Cisco Unity supports both G.711 and G.729. If G.729 were implemented on Cisco Unity, DSP transcoding in this example would not be required. However, it is not recommended that you have Unity perform transcoding.

Figure 8-6 illustrates how the transcoding solution shown in Figure 8-5 is logically implemented in CUCM.

Figure 8-6   *Implementing a Transcoder at the Main Site, Continued*

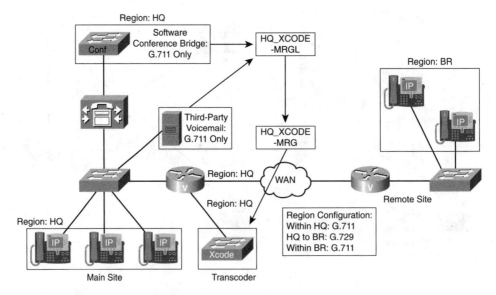

All headquarters devices—such as phones, voice-mail system, software conference bridge, and transcoder—are in region HQ. Remote-site phones are in region BR.

CUCM region configuration allows G.711 to be used within region HQ and region BR. Calls between regions HQ and BR are limited to G.729.

When a call is placed from a remote-site phone to the voice-mail system, CUCM identifies the need for a transcoder based on the capabilities of the devices. In this example, only G.711 is used at the voice-mail system, and the maximum permitted codec over the WAN is G.729. If the device that supports only a codec with higher bandwidth requirements than permitted by the region configuration can access a transcoder, the call is set up and invokes the transcoder resource. The call would otherwise fail.

Configuration Procedure for Implementing Transcoders

To implement transcoders, perform these steps:

Step 1 Add a transcoder resource in CUCM.

Step 2 Configure the transcoder resource in Cisco IOS Software.

Step 3 Configure media resource groups.

Step 4 Configure media resource group lists.

Step 5 Assign the media resource group lists to devices, and logically link these in CUCM.

> **NOTE**   Steps 1 and 2 are described in this chapter. Steps 3, 4, and 5—configuring media resource group lists and assigning them to devices—are discussed in *Implementing Cisco Unified Communications Manager, Part 1 (CIPT1)*.

Step 1: Add a Transcoder Resource in CUCM

To add a transcoder resource in CUCM, choose **Media Resources > Conference Bridge** and click **Add New**. The Transcoder Configuration window opens, as shown in Figure 8-7. Here you choose the type of Cisco transcoder media resource. The options are as follows:

■   Cisco IOS Enhanced Media Termination Point for the Cisco NM-HDV2, NM-HD-1V/2V/2VE, 2800 series, and 3800 series routers

■   Cisco IOS Media Termination Point in the Cisco NM-HDV and 1700 series routers

■   Cisco Media Termination Point Hardware for Cisco Catalyst WS-X6608-T1 and WS-X6608-E1

■   Cisco Media Termination Point WS-SVC-CMM

Figure 8-7   *Adding a Transcoder Resource in Cisco Unified Communications Manager*

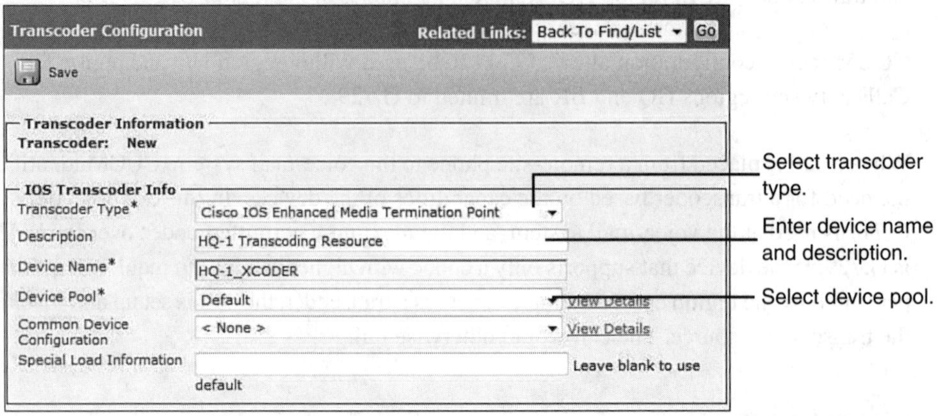

Choose the type of Cisco transcoder media resource, enter a device name and description for it, and then choose a device pool.

The device name has to match the name listed at the Cisco IOS router that provides the media resource. The name is case-sensitive. If the transcoding resource is provided by Cisco IOS Enhanced Media Termination Point hardware, the name can be freely chosen. In all other cases, the name is MTP followed by the MAC address of the interface that is configured to be used for registering the media resource with CUCM.

Step 2: Configure the Transcoder Resource in Cisco IOS Software

Example 8-1 shows a portion of the output display of **show running-config** of the Cisco IOS gateway as it relates to providing transcoding resources to CUCM.

Example 8-1   *Configuring the Transcoder Resource in Cisco IOS Software*

```
interface Loopback0
  ip address 10.6.9.1 255.255.255.255
!
voice-card 0
  dspfarm
  dsp services dspfarm
!
sccp local Loopback0
sccp ccm 10.1.1.1 identifier 1 version 6.0
sccp
!
sccp ccm group 1
  associate ccm 1 priority 1
  associate profile 1 register HQ-1_XCODER
```

Example 8-1 *Configuring the Transcoder Resource in Cisco IOS Software (Continued)*

```
!
dspfarm profile 1 transcode
  codec g711ulaw
  codec g711alaw
  codec g729ar8
  codec g729abr8
  maximum sessions 2
  associate application SCCP
  no shutdown
```

In Example 8-1, a Cisco IOS Enhanced Media Termination Point type transcoder can be configured with the following options:

- **dspfarm (DSP farm):** To enable DSP farm service, use the **dspfarm** command in global configuration mode. The DSP farm service is disabled by default.

- **dsp services dspfarm:** To enable DSP farm services for a particular voice network module, use the **dsp services dspfarm** command in interface configuration mode.

- **sccp local:** Skinny Client Control Protocol (SCCP) is required to select the local interface that is used to register the media resources with Cisco Unified Communications Manager. Enter the **sccp local** command in global configuration mode.

- **sccp ccm:** Use this command in global configuration mode to use SCCP to add a CUCM server to the list of available servers. You also can set various parameters, including IP address or Domain Name System (DNS) name, port number, and version number.

- **sccp:** To enable the SCCP protocol and its related applications (for example, transcoding and conferencing), use the **sccp** command in global configuration mode. If this command is removed, registration will fail with CUCM.

- **sccp ccm group:** To create a CUCM group and enter SCCP CUCM configuration mode, use the **sccp ccm group** command in global configuration mode.

- **associate ccm:** To associate a CUCM with a CUCM group and establish its priority within the group, use the **associate ccm** command in SCCP CUCM configuration mode.

- **associate profile:** To associate a DSP farm profile with a CUCM group, use the **associate profile** command in SCCP CUCM configuration mode.

> **NOTE**   The name specified in the Cisco IOS device must match the name in the CUCM exactly, because the names are case-sensitive. In addition, it is critical for the DSP resources to register to CUCM with SCCP. If the registration fails, the hardware resources will be unavailable.

> **NOTE**   When a Cisco IOS Enhanced Media Termination Point is being configured, any name can be configured with the **associate profile** command. When a Cisco IOS conference bridge is being configured, the name cannot be configured. It is MTP(*MAC*), where (*MAC*) is the MAC address of the interface that was specified in the **sccp local** command.

- **dspfarm profile:** To enter DSP farm profile configuration mode and define a profile for DSP farm services, use the **dspfarm profile** command in global configuration mode.

- **codec** (dsp): To specify call density and codec complexity based on a particular codec standard, use the **codec** command in DSP interface DSP farm configuration mode.

- **associate application sccp:** To associate SCCP to the DSP farm profile, use the **associate application sccp** command in DSP farm profile configuration mode.

- **maximum sessions** (DSP farm profile): To specify the maximum number of sessions that the profile supports, use the **maximum sessions** command in DSP farm profile configuration mode.

- **no shutdown:** If you fail to issue the **no shutdown** command for the DSP farm profile, registration to CUCM will not occur.

To verify the Cisco IOS media resource configuration, use the following **show** commands:

- **show sccp:** Shows you whether the Cisco IOS router successfully established a TCP connection with the configured CUCM or Managers to exchange SCCP signaling messages.

- **show sccp ccm group** *1*: Shows you which media resources are registered with the CUCM(s) that are configured in the specified group.

- **show dspfarm profile** *1*: Shows you the status of the media resource of the specified profile at the Cisco IOS router.

- **show sccp connections**: Shows you the active RTP streams connected to the DSP resources for hardware conferencing, transcoding, or both.

Multicast MOH from Branch Router Flash Implementation

Multicast MOH from branch router flash is a feature that allows multicast MOH streams to be generated by gateways located at remote sites instead of streaming MOH from the main site to the remote site over the IP WAN.

The feature is based on multicast MOH, so CUCM must be configured to use multicast MOH instead of unicast MOH. This configuration is recommended to reduce the load at the MOH server and to reduce bandwidth utilization. This feature multicasts only one stream that can be received by all devices, instead of streaming MOH individually for each endpoint in separate unicast RTP sessions.

Multicast MOH from branch router flash is a feature of the Survivable Remote Site Telephony (SRST) configuration. Therefore, the remote-site router that will generate the multicast MOH stream for the devices located at the remote site has to be configured for SRST. SRST does not have to be active (there is no need for a fallback scenario), because an SRST gateway that is configured for multicast MOH streams MOH continuously, regardless of its state of standby mode or SRST mode.

Because the MOH server located at the main site has to be configured for multicast MOH, multicast routing has to be enabled to allow the multicast stream to be routed from the CUCM server network to the phone network(s). If the MOH server is on the same network that the IP Phones are on, multicast routing is not required. However, such a scenario is not recommended for security reasons, because servers should be separated from endpoints with VLANs.

Each SRST router can stream only one file and use one multicast address and port. If you provide different MOH files, however, different MOH can be played for each site.

If you want different MOH streams for the main site, separate MOH servers should be used, each with a different multicast address. It is not sufficient to use different multicast port addresses, because IP Phones join multicast groups by multicast group address only, not by address-and-port combination.

When multicast MOH is used, IP Phones and CUCM are unaware that the IP Phones listen to locally generated MOH streams. From a signaling perspective, the IP Phone is instructed to listen to a certain multicast stream. The local SRST gateway must generate a multicast MOH stream by using identical settings, such as destination address (multicast group), destination port, and codec.

Multicast MOH in SRST gateways supports only the G.711 codec. Therefore, G.711 must also be configured between the CUCM MOH server and the branch IP Phones. If CUCM signaled a codec other than G.711 to the IP Phone, the IP Phone could not play the locally generated MOH stream because of a codec mismatch. The signaling would be G.729, but the received RTP stream would be G.711.

To ensure that CUCM sends signaling messages to the phone that instruct the phone to listen to a G.711 stream, configure regions in the following manner:

- Put the CUCM MOH server or servers into a dedicated region such as MOH.

- Put all branch devices into a site-specific region such as Branch-1.

- Allow G.711 between regions MOH and Branch-1.

- Make sure that region Branch-1 is limited to G.729 for calls to and from all other regions.

Implementing Multicast MOH from Branch Router Flash

In the topology shown in Figure 8-8, a MOH server is located at the main site and is configured for multicast MOH. Assume that multicast routing has been enabled in the whole network, including the IP WAN link to the remote site.

Figure 8-8 *Implementing Multicast MOH from Branch Router Flash*

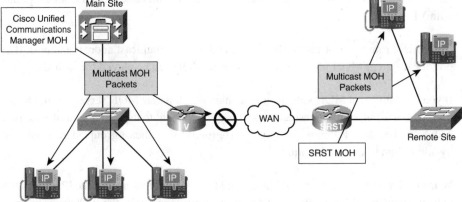

The main-site router, however, should no longer route multicast MOH to the remote site. The remote-site SRST gateway should instead generate multicast MOH streams to the phones located at the remote site.

Because CUCM is unaware that the multicast packets generated by the MOH server at the main site are filtered on the IP WAN interface and then locally generated by the remote-site SRST gateway, CUCM instructs the IP Phones located at the remote site to join the multicast group IP address that is configured at the CUCM MOH server. To allow the phones to receive MOH for the multicast group IP address they join, the SRST gateway has to be configured to use exactly the same multicast address and port that are used by the CUCM MOH server located at the main site. Example 8-2 shows a portion of the output of **show running-config** at the main site. Example 8-3 shows a portion of the output of **show running-config** at the remote site.

Example 8-2 *Main-Site Configuration*

```
ip access-list extended drop-moh
  deny udp any host 239.1.1.1 eq 16384
  permit ip any any
!
interface serial 0/0
  ip access-group drop-moh out
  no ip pim sparse-mode
```

Example 8-3 *Remote-Site Configuration*

```
call-manager-fallback
  max-ephones 1
  max-dn 1
  ip source-address 10.1.5.102
  moh moh-file.au
  multicast moh 239.1.1.1 port 16384
```

It is assumed that the baseline configuration provides multicast routing in the whole network and that the CUCM MOH server is already configured for multicast MOH.

NOTE Multicast routing uses Class D addresses for the destination of the MOH RTP streams. The source address streaming MOH is a Class A, B, or C address, never a multicast address.

The multicast MOH stream that is sent toward the remote site needs to be blocked to avoid unneeded WAN utilization. Also, multicast MOH from branch router flash needs to be implemented at the remote site. Of course, if other WAN data traffic is currently being blocked at the main site in an existing production router, the command line **deny udp any host 239.1.1.1 eq 16384** must be properly integrated with the existing access list.

Therefore, the SRST configuration of the remote-site router is extended to include multicast MOH. The SRST configuration uses the same multicast IP address and port that are configured at the CUCM MOH server located at the main site.

To stop multicast MOH generated by the main-site CUCM MOH server from being sent over the IP WAN, one of three options can be chosen:

■ **Set TTL to a low-enough value at the Cisco Unified Communications Manager MOH server:** If the TTL value in the IP header of the generated multicast MOH packets is set to a low-enough value, the packets are not routed out to the IP WAN. However, if the IP WAN link is one hop away from the CUCM MOH server, and if the main-site phones are also one hop away from the server, this method cannot be used, because the main-site IP Phones would also be affected by the dropped packets. In the current example, Time to Live (TTL) is set to 1, and it is assumed that the IP Phones are in the same VLAN, like the CUCM MOH server.

■ **Filter the packets by an IP access control list (ACL):** At the main-site router, an ACL can be configured that drops the multicast MOH packets at the IP WAN interface.

> **NOTE**   When multicast MOH in CUCM is configured, it is necessary to specify how to increment multicast streams based on IP addresses or port numbers. Depending on the setting, the IP ACL needs to be configured appropriately to include all possible IP addresses and port numbers. It is recommended that you increment the IP addresses by contiguous numbering. Note that each enabled codec has a separate MOH stream.

■ **Disable multicast routing at the IP WAN interface:** If you disable multicast routing at the IP WAN interface, multicast packets are not routed out that interface.

At the branch router, the multicast MOH stream is sent out the interface specified in the **ip source-address** command in call-manager-fallback configuration mode or in telephony-server configuration mode, when CUCM Express in SRST mode is used. Therefore, the multicast MOH stream generated at the branch router does not have to be blocked at the branch router WAN interface.

Configuration Procedure for Implementing Multicast MOH from Branch Router Flash

Implementing multicast MOH from branch router flash involves the following steps:

Step 1   Enable multicast routing in the network.

Step 2 Configure multicast MOH in CUCM:

    a. Configure MOH audio sources for multicast MOH.

    b. Configure MOH audio server for multicast MOH.

    c. Configure the maximum hop value to prevent multicast MOH streams from being sent over the IP WAN.

Step 3 Enable multicast MOH from branch router flash at the branch router.

Step 4 Optional: Use alternative methods to prevent multicast MOH streams from being sent over the IP WAN:

    a. Use IP ACL at the IP WAN router interface.

    b. Disable multicast routing on the IP WAN router interface.

Perform only the first two steps when only multicast MOH will be implemented without unicast MOH, and when the multicast MOH from the branch router flash feature won't be used because the router at the remote location doesn't support it. In this case, the maximum hop value configured in Step 2c has to be set to a high-enough value to allow the multicast MOH packets to be sent all the way to the remote phones.

If multicast MOH from branch router flash is used, the maximum hop value configured in Step 2c must be low enough to ensure that the multicast MOH packets generated by the MOH server do not reach the IP WAN. Step 4 provides two alternative methods of preventing the multicast MOH packets that are generated by the MOH server from reaching the IP WAN. Either of these methods can be used instead of setting the maximum hop parameter to a low value. Preventing the packets from reaching the IP WAN is important when phones located at the main site require a maximum hop value that is too high to block the traffic from WAN interfaces.

> **NOTE** All IP Phones must be able to access the main-site CUCM MOH server from their media resource group list. This access is required as soon as multicast MOH is configured, whether or not multicast MOH from branch router flash is used. If the IP Phones at the remote site do not have access to the CUCM MOH server from their media resource group list, CUCM cannot instruct the IP Phones to join the multicast group, and it makes the phone use Tone On Hold instead of MOH.
>
> Furthermore, the **Use Multicast for MOH Audio** check box has to be checked at the media resource group that includes the multicast-enabled MOH server.
>
> Finally, make sure that the G.711 codec is used between the MOH server and the branch phones, because SRST multicast MOH supports only G.711.

Step 1: Enable Multicast Routing on Cisco IOS Routers

Example 8-4 shows a portion of **show running-config** in the IOS gateway that enables multicast routing at the main site and remote site.

Example 8-4 *Step 1: Enabling Multicast Routing in Cisco IOS Routers*

```
ip multicast-routing
!
interface FastEthernet0/0
  description HQ-Voice-Servers
  ip address 10.1.1.101 255.255.255.0
  ip pim sparse-dense-mode
!
interface FastEthernet0/1
  description HQ-Phones
  ip address 10.1.2.101 255.255.255.0
  ip pim sparse-dense-mode
!
interface Serial0/1
  description IP WAN
  ip address 10.1.5.101 255.255.255.0
  ip pim sparse-dense-mode
```

NOTE   The same configuration is required at the branch router.

Two commands are required to enable multicast routing in the network so that multicast MOH streams can be sent:

- **ip multicast-routing:** This command is configured in global configuration mode. It enables multicast routing on the Cisco IOS router in general.

- **ip pim sparse-dense-mode:** This command needs to be configured on each interface where multicast routing should be enabled.

Step 2a: Configure MOH Audio Sources for Multicast MOH

To enable multicast MOH, first multicast MOH must be allowed on MOH audio sources, as shown in Figure 8-9. In CUCM, choose **Media Resources > Music On Hold Audio Source** and **Media Resources > Fixed MOH Audio Source**.

NOTE   The configuration shown in Example 8-4 enables multicast routing in the whole network. When multicast MOH from branch router flash is used, multicast streams are not sent to the IP WAN. They can be blocked based on the maximum hops parameter (the TTL field in the IP header by IP ACLs) or by disabling multicast routing on the interface. The last option, however, can be used only if no other multicast routing applications are required in the network. In the example shown here, the maximum hops parameter cannot be used, because the HQ-Phones network and the IP WAN network have the same distance to the HQ-Voice-Servers network. To allow multicast MOH to be sent to the HQ phones, a maximum hop value of 2 is required. This value, however, allows the multicast MOH packets to be sent out the WAN interface. Therefore, IP ACLs have to be used, or multicast routing has to be disabled at the WAN interface, provided that multicast routing is not required by other applications.

Figure 8-9   *Step 2a: Configuring MOH Audio Sources for Multicast MOH*

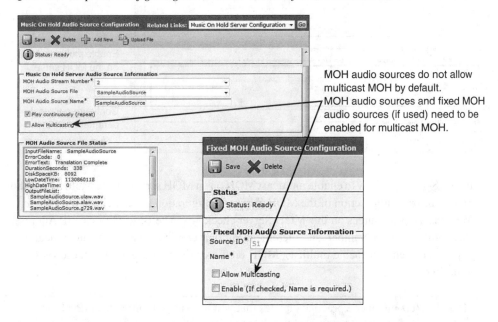

Check the **Allow Multicasting** check box for each MOH audio that is allowed to be sent as a multicast stream. This applies to MOH audio sources and to fixed MOH audio sources.

NOTE   You can find more information about configuring the MOH server and MOH audio sources in *Implementing Cisco Unified Communications Manager, Part 1 (CIPT1)*.

Step 2b: Configure Multicast MOH in CUCM

After multicast MOH on audio sources has been allowed, the MOH server has to be enabled for multicast MOH, as shown in Figure 8-10. In CUCM, choose **Media Resources > Music On Hold Server**.

Figure 8-10 *Step 2b: Configuring Multicast MOH in CUCM*

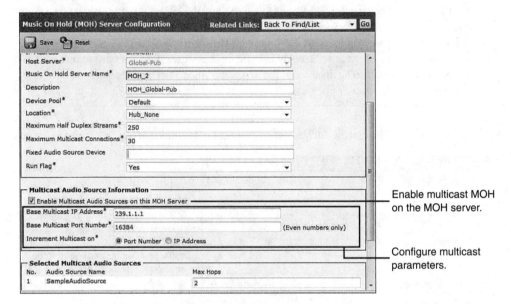

Figure 8-10 shows how to enable multicast MOH on an MOH server. In the Multicast Audio Source Information section of the MOH Server Configuration screen, check the Enable Multicast Audio Sources on this MOH Server check box. The Base Multicast IP Address, Base Multicast Port Number, and Increment Multicast on parameters are automatically populated when you enable multicast MOH on the server. You can modify these values as desired.

> **NOTE** Recommended practice dictates that you increment multicast on IP address instead of port number to avoid network saturation in firewall situations. Doing this means that each multicast audio source has a unique IP address and helps avoid network saturation. If multiple codecs are enabled for the MOH server, additional IP addresses are in use, with one per codec and per audio source.

Step 2c: Configure the Maximum Hops to Be Used for MOH RTP Packets

Continue the multicast MOH server configuration by setting the maximum hop value, as shown in Figure 8-11.

Figure 8-11 *Step 2c: Configuring the Maximum Hops to Be Used for MOH RTP Packets*

Set maximum hops (time to live) value per audio source for multicast packets.

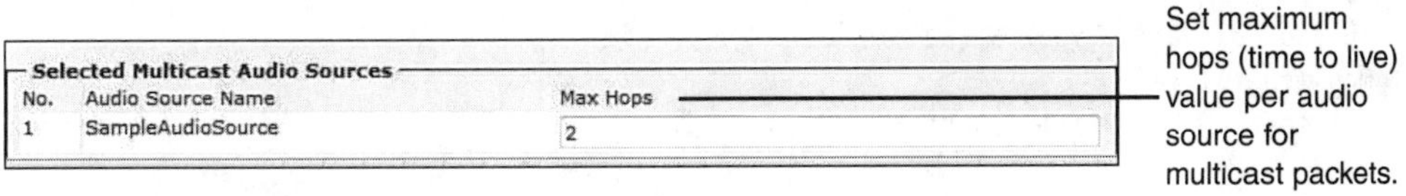

All MOH audio sources that were configured for multicasting in the previous step are listed in the Selected Multicast Audio Sources section of the MOH server configuration screen. You can set the Max Hops value for each audio source. The Max Hops default value is 2. This parameter sets the TTL value in the IP header of the multicast MOH RTP packets to the specified value. TTL in an IP packet indicates the maximum number of routers that an audio source is allowed to cross. If Max Hops is set to 0, the multicast MOH RTP packets remain in the subnet of the multicast MOH server.

When you implement multicast MOH without using the multicast MOH from branch router flash feature, make sure that the maximum hop value is high enough to allow the packets to be sent all the way to the remote phones.

When multicast MOH from branch router flash is used, one way of preventing the multicast MOH packets generated by the MOH server from being sent over the WAN link is to set Max Hops to a value that is lower than the hop count toward the WAN interface of the main-site router. This value, however, might conflict with the needs within the main site (when IP Phone networks have the same or a higher distance to the MOH server than the WAN network). In such a case, use alternative options, as shown in Step 4.

Step 3: Enable Multicast MOH from Branch Router Flash at the Branch Router

Example 8-5 shows a portion of **show running-config** that demonstrates how to configure a Cisco IOS router for multicast MOH from branch router flash.

Multicast MOH from branch router flash is part of the SRST feature. Therefore, SRST must be configured before you can enable multicast MOH from branch router flash.

> **NOTE**   Additional SRST configuration options were discussed in Chapter 6, "Implementing Cisco Unified SRST and MGCP Fallback."

Example 8-5   *Enabling Multicast MOH from Branch Router Flash at the Branch Router*

```
ip multicast-routing
!
call-manager-fallback
  max-ephones 1
  max-dn 1
  ip source-address 10.1.5.102
  moh moh-file.au
  multicast moh 239.1.1.1 port 16384
!
interface FastEthernet0/0
  description BR-Phones
  ip address 10.1.5.102 255.255.255.0
 !
interface Serial0/1
  description IP WAN
   ip address 10.1.4.102 255.255.255.0
```

Based on an existing SRST configuration, only two commands are required to enable multicast MOH from branch router flash:

■ **moh** *file-name*: This command specifies the MOH audio source file. The specified file has to be stored in flash memory of the SRST gateway.

■ **multicast moh** *multicast-group-address* **port** *port*: This command specifies the multicast address and port that are used for the multicast MOH packets. The specified address and port must exactly match the values that were configured at the MOH server in Step 2b.

> **NOTE**   The SRST gateway permanently streams MOH, regardless of an IP WAN failure or IP Phones being registered with the SRST gateway.

Step 4a: Use an IP ACL at the IP WAN Router Interface

Example 8-6 shows a portion of **show running-config** that demonstrates how to configure a Cisco IOS router to drop multicast MOH packets by using an IP ACL.

Example 8-6   *Step 4a: Using IP ACL at the IP WAN Router Interface*

```
ip multicast-routing
!
ip access-list extended drop-moh
  deny ip any host 239.1.1.1 eq 16384
  permit ip any any
```

Example 8-6 *Step 4a: Using IP ACL at the IP WAN Router Interface (Continued)*

```
!
interface FastEthernet0/0
  description HQ-Voice-Servers
  ip address 10.1.1.101 255.255.255.0
  ip pim sparse-dense-mode
!
interface FastEthernet0/1
  description HQ-Phones
  ip address 10.1.2.101 255.255.255.0
  ip pim sparse-dense-mode
!
interface Serial0/1
  description IP WAN
  ip address 10.1.4.101 255.255.255.0
  ip access-group drop-moh out
  ip pim sparse-dense-mode
```

The ACL matches the MOH group address and port number that are used by the MOH server for the MOH RTP packets. The ACL is applied to the IP WAN interface in the outgoing direction and therefore does not allow multicast MOH packets to be sent out the IP WAN.

NOTE   If the MOH server is configured to use more than one codec, the access list has to include additional IP addresses or port numbers. By default, only G.711 is enabled in the Supported MOH Codecs service parameter of the Cisco IP Voice Media Streaming App service. The MOH server can be configured to increment on either IP addresses or port numbers.

Step 4b: Disable Multicast Routing on the IP WAN Router Interface

Example 8-7 shows a portion of **show running-config** that illustrates how to configure a Cisco IOS router to disable multicast routing at the IP WAN interface.

If no other multicast applications are used over the IP WAN, the simplest way of preventing the multicast MOH packets from being sent to the WAN is to disable multicast routing at the WAN interface.

Example 8-7   *Step 4b: Disabling Multicast Routing on the IP WAN Router Interface*

```
ip multicast-routing
!
interface FastEthernet0/0
  description HQ-Voice-Servers
  ip address 10.1.1.101 255.255.255.0
  ip pim sparse-dense-mode
!
interface FastEthernet0/0
  description HQ-Phones
  ip address 10.1.2.101 255.255.255.0
  ip pim sparse-dense-mode
!
interface Serial0/1
  description IP WAN
  ip address 10.1.4.101 255.255.255.0
  no ip pim sparse-dense-mode
```

Summary

The following key points were discussed in this chapter:

- Bandwidth-management methods include techniques that reduce required bandwidth of voice streams, techniques that keep voice streams off the IP WAN, and other techniques such as deploying transcoders.

- The highest bandwidth-consuming codec for a call between two devices is determined by the CUCM region configuration of the two devices.

- When you are deploying local conference bridges at multiple sites, use media resource groups and media resource group lists to control which conference bridge is used by which device.

- Transcoders allow low-bandwidth codecs to be used over the IP WAN when low-bandwidth codecs are not supported by both endpoints.

- Multicast MOH from branch router flash is a feature that allows MOH streams to be generated locally at the remote site instead of being sent across the IP WAN from the main site.

References

For additional information, refer to these resources:

- Cisco Systems, Inc., Cisco Unified Communications Solution Reference Network Design (SRND), based on CUCM Release 6.x, June 2007

- Cisco Systems, Inc., *CUCM Administration Guide Release 6.0(1)*

- Cisco Systems, Inc., *Cisco Unified SRST 4.1 System Administrator Guide*

Review Questions

Use these questions to review what you've learned in this chapter. The answers appear in Appendix A, "Answers to Chapter Review Questions."

1. Which of the following features does not conserve bandwidth in the IP WAN?

   a. RTP header compression

   b. Low-bandwidth codecs

   c. Local media resources

   d. Quality of service

2. How can the bandwidth per call be limited in CUCM?

   a. By specifying the maximum permitted codec between pairs of regions

   b. By specifying the maximum permitted codec between pairs of locations

   c. By specifying the maximum bandwidth per stream with the **bandwidth zone local** command

   d. By specifying the maximum permitted codec for calls going out of or coming into a region

3. When deploying local conference bridges at each site, what is the minimum number of media resource group lists that is required?

   a. The number of sites multiplied by (the number of sites minus 1) divided by 2

   b. One per site

   c. One per site and one per conference bridge

   d. One

4. Which device requires access to the transcoder from its media resource group list when transcoding is required for a call?

   a. Both endpoints of the original call

   b. The calling device

   c. The device that supports only codecs not permitted for the original call

   d. The called device

5. Which statement about multicast MOH from branch router flash is true?

   a. Multicast MOH from branch router flash requires an SRST router to be in fall-back mode to work.

   b. Multicast MOH from branch router flash can also be used for unicast MOH.

   c. The branch router can stream only a single MOH file and supports G.711 and G.729 only.

   d. Regions in CUCM have to be configured such that G.711 is allowed between the CUCM MOH server and the branch phones.

6. Which of the following is the best use of transcoding resources?

   a. Configure transcoding with DSP resources to use G.711 over the WAN and with G.729 in the LAN

   b. Configure transcoding with DSP resources to use G.729 over the WAN and with G.711 in the LAN

   c. Configure transcoding with DSP resources on both routers to use G.711 over the WAN and with G.729 in the LAN

   d. Configure transcoding with DSP resources on both routers to use G.711 over the WAN and with G.711 in the LAN

7. Which VoIP signaling protocol or protocol options must be used to configure transcoding resources on a router to communicate with CUCM?

   a. SIP

   b. SCCP

   c. MGCP

   d. H.323

   e. SIP and H.323 with CUBE

   f. Any VoIP signaling protocol may be used.

8. Which of the following best describes how multicast MOH streams RTP?

   a. A source Class D address streams to a destination Class D address.

   b. A source Class A, B, or C address streams to a destination Class D address.

   c. A source Class D address streams to a destination Class A, B, or C address.

   d. A source Class A, B, or C address streams to a destination Class A, B, or C address.

9. What is the procedure to ensure that remote-site phones correctly use the DSP resources for hardware conference calls, which minimizes WAN utilization?

   a. Put the phones in an MRG that links to an MRGL that links to the remote-site conference bridge.

   b. Put the phones in an MRGL that links to an MRG that links to the remote-site conference bridge.

   c. Put the phones in an MRG that links to an MRGL that links to the main-site conference bridge.

   d. Put the phones in an MRGL that links to an MRG that links to the main-site conference bridge.

10. Which two of the following are acceptable ways to avoid main-site multicast MOH traffic from traversing the IP WAN?

   a. Prevent dynamic routing protocols from routing over the WAN.

   b. At the main-site router, an ACL can be configured that drops the multicast MOH packets at the IP WAN interface.

   c. Disable multicast routing at the IP WAN interface at the main site.

   d. Disable multicast routing at the IP WAN interface at the remote site.

   e. Use only static routes for IP routing over the IP WAN.

CHAPTER 9

Implementing Call Admission Control

Implementing multiple-site IP telephony deployments over an IP WAN requires additional planning to ensure the quality and availability of voice calls.

When an IP WAN connects multiple sites in a Cisco Unified Communications deployment, quality of service (QoS) has to be implemented to prioritize voice packets over data packets. However, to avoid an oversubscription that is caused by too many voice calls, a mechanism is needed to limit the number of calls that are allowed at the same time between certain locations. Call admission control (CAC) is the mechanism that ensures that voice calls do not oversubscribe the IP WAN bandwidth and thus impact voice quality. If CAC is not configured, CUCM assumes that all links everywhere have infinite bandwidth, which can result in oversubscription of WAN links at the expense of audio quality.

This chapter describes how to implement three CAC mechanisms that are provided by CUCM and explains how automated alternate routing (AAR) can be used in some scenarios to reroute calls that were denied by CAC over the public switched telephone network (PSTN) ultimately to the remote site.

Chapter Objectives

Upon completing this chapter, you will be able to describe and configure CAC mechanisms and AAR in CUCM. You will be able to meet these objectives:

- Describe the CAC options provided by CUCM

- Implement locations-based CAC in CUCM

- Implement RSVP-enabled locations-based CAC in CUCM

- Implement AAR to reroute calls over the PSTN if not enough bandwidth is available for an on-net call

- Implement H.323 gatekeeper-based CAC in CUCM

Call Admission Control Overview

CAC limits the number of calls between certain parts of the network to avoid bandwidth oversubscription, with too many voice calls over WAN links. This result cannot be achieved by QoS mechanisms alone, because QoS provides only the means to prioritize voice over data traffic. For example, the QoS best-practice mechanism for prioritizing voice of Low-Latency Queuing (LLQ) does not resolve the situation in which too many voice and/or video streams are sent over the network.

If oversubscription occurs, any packets of any voice stream can be affected, not just packets of the particular call or calls that exceed the bandwidth limit. The result is packet delays and packet drops of all voice calls; hence, oversubscription degrades the quality of all voice calls.

Therefore, to ensure good voice quality, CAC has to be used to limit the number of voice calls.

Call Admission Control in CUCM

CUCM supports different CAC methods, as shown in Figure 9-1.

Figure 9-1 *Call Admission Control in CUCM*

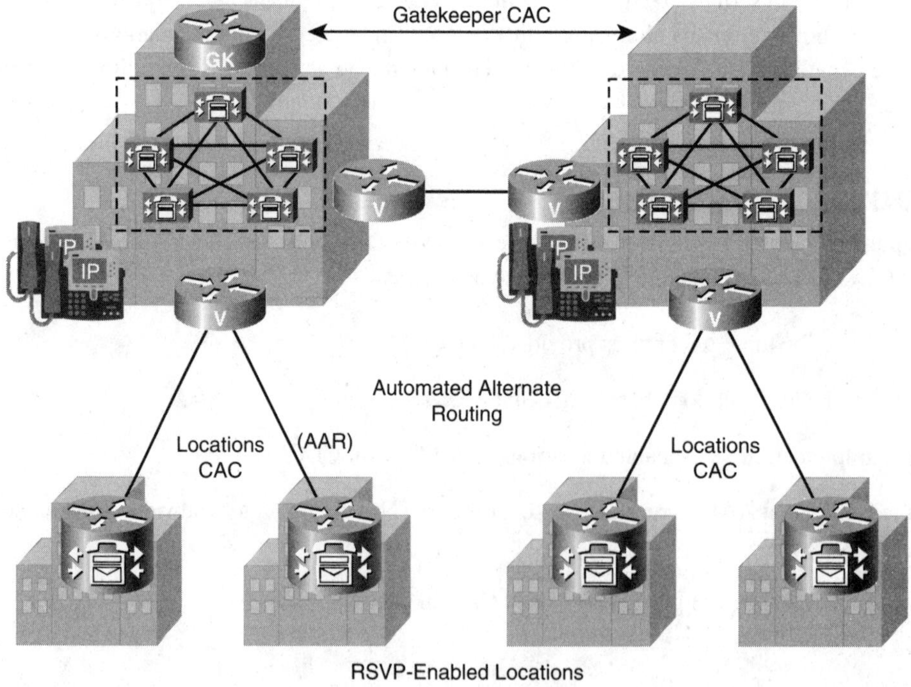

In centralized call-processing deployments with CUCM, standard locations and Resource Reservation Protocol (RSVP)-enabled locations can be used to provide CAC. If a call is not admitted by one of these two CAC methods because of bandwidth limitations, AAR can be used to reroute the call over the PSTN as an off-net call instead of just denying the call. AAR provides a service similar to PSTN backup, except that the event is not a call failure on the on-net path but a lack of available bandwidth from a CAC point of view. AAR is designed to work within each CUCM cluster.

In distributed call-processing environments with two or more CUCM clusters, an H.323 gatekeeper configured with CAC can be used in conjunction with H.323 trunks. Cisco offers two types of H.323-based trunks for gatekeepers: an inter-cluster trunk (gatekeeper-controlled) and an H.225 trunk (gatekeeper-controlled). If the call is not admitted by the H.323 gatekeeper, standard backup functionality of route lists and route groups is applied. For example, to route calls that have not been admitted by the gatekeeper to be sent over the trunk, one or more PSTN gateways can be configured in another lower-priority route group of the same route list. In this way, the gatekeeper-controlled trunk is preferred over the PSTN as long as calls are admitted, but if admission is rejected, calls are sent over the PSTN. AAR is not used with gatekeeper CAC.

Locations

Each device in a CUCM cluster has one location assigned. The assignment can be direct and/or via a device pool. Assigning locations to each device based on the device pool significantly simplifies the CUCM configuration when there are many devices. If both types of assignment are used, the device configuration has higher priority, because it is more specific than the more-general device pool.

Calls are limited by permitting a certain bandwidth for all calls coming into and going out of a location. CUCM calculates the actual audio codec bandwidth plus IP overhead (assuming a packetization period of 20 ms). This means that each G.711 call is assumed by the location to be 80 kbps, and a G.729 call is assumed to be 24 kbps.

NOTE Calls within a location do not decrease the bandwidth limit, because they are unlimited. Only calls that go out of a location or that are received from outside the location are considered by the locations-based CAC algorithm.

The configured bandwidth limit is independent of the call's destination location. Unlike region configuration, in which the maximum permitted codec is configured *for each pair of regions*, the bandwidth limit of a location applies to *all interlocation calls, regardless of the other location.*

Locations provide CAC for calls within clusters. However, because locations can also be configured for gateways and trunks, they do allow some control over calls leaving the cluster.

Locations-based CAC in CUCM is totally unaware of the network's topology. It is a purely logical assignment and does not reflect the actual topology or the actual bandwidth available.

Locations: Hub-and-Spoke Topology

Figure 9-2 shows a hub-and-spoke CUCM topology with locations-based CAC.

Figure 9-2   *Locations with a Hub-and-Spoke Topology*

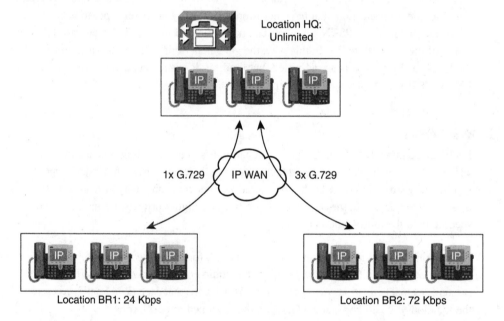

As shown in this figure, the three sites are headquarters (HQ) and two branches (BR1 and BR2). Assuming that there is a hub-and-spoke WAN provider with no direct connection between the branches, all traffic between branches goes via headquarters.

This scenario is ideal for locations-based CAC, which works relatively well in hub-and-spoke topologies. If the intention is to allow only one G.729 call on the link between BR1 and HQ and three G.729 calls on the link between BR2 and HQ, the following location configuration would work:

- Location HQ: Unlimited

- Location BR1: 24 kbps

- Location BR2: 72 kbps

This configuration ensures that no more than one G.729 call will be sent over the IP WAN toward location BR1 and that no more than three G.729 calls will be sent over the IP WAN toward location BR2.

> **NOTE**   The configuration also allows one G.729 call between BR1 and BR2. CUCM CAC is based on a hub-and-spoke topology, in which all calls over the WAN are monitored for CAC as if they go through HQ. Because the configured bandwidth limit does not consider the destination location, the 24-kbps limit of BR1 allows any call to go out or in, regardless of where it goes to or comes from. The headquarters limit is unaffected by such a call. Only locations BR1 and BR2 subtract 24 kbps from their limits. Because locations-based CAC does not provide topology awareness, CUCM does not even know that the call physically flows through headquarters.

Locations: Full-Mesh Topology

Figure 9-3 shows a full-mesh topology with locations-based CAC.

Figure 9-3   *Locations with a Full-Mesh Topology*

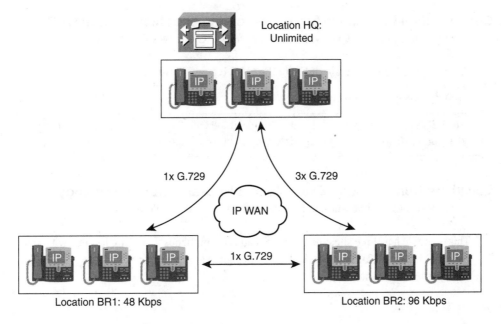

In this figure, a direct IP WAN link has been added between BR1 and BR2. One G.729 call is allowed on the WAN link from BR1 toward headquarters, one G.729 call is allowed on the WAN link between BR1 and BR2, and three G.729 calls are allowed on the WAN link from BR2 toward headquarters.

Such a scenario reveals issues that arise when locations-based CAC is used in topologies other than hub-and-spoke. To allow the additional G.729 call that is permitted on the WAN link between BR1 and BR2, the bandwidth limit of these two locations has been increased by 24 kbps, which allows one more G.729 call. Doing this, however, can lead to the following undesirable situations:

- **Two G.729 calls from BR1 to HQ:** Because the BR1 location now has a limit of 48 kbps, it allows two G.729 calls. Location bandwidth limits are not configured per destination, so any call coming into or going out of a location is considered, regardless of the other location involved in the call. Therefore, there is no way to divide the available 48 kbps between one call toward the HQ and one call to BR2.

- **Four G.729 calls from BR2 to HQ:** The same problem occurs with the BR2 location. The additional bandwidth that was added to accommodate the desired call toward BR1 can be used toward the HQ, occupying that link with one more call than intended.

NOTE   The problems that are encountered here are caused by the fact that the bandwidth limit is configured per location, regardless of the other location where the call goes to or comes from.

Configuration Procedure for Implementing Locations-Based CAC

The implementation of CUCM locations-based CAC involves the following steps:

Step 1   Add locations and configure the CAC bandwidth limit.

Step 2   Assign locations to devices.

NOTE   To know how much bandwidth has to be calculated per call, regions should be designed and configured to negotiate codecs before locations are implemented.

Locations Configuration Example of a Hub-and-Spoke Topology

Figure 9-4 shows a hub-and-spoke locations-based CAC implementation.

This example has three sites: headquarters and two branches. Each site has its own location (HQ, BR1, and BR2). The physical WAN design is a hub-and-spoke topology where headquarters is the hub.

Figure 9-4   *Locations Configuration of a Hub-and-Spoke Topology*

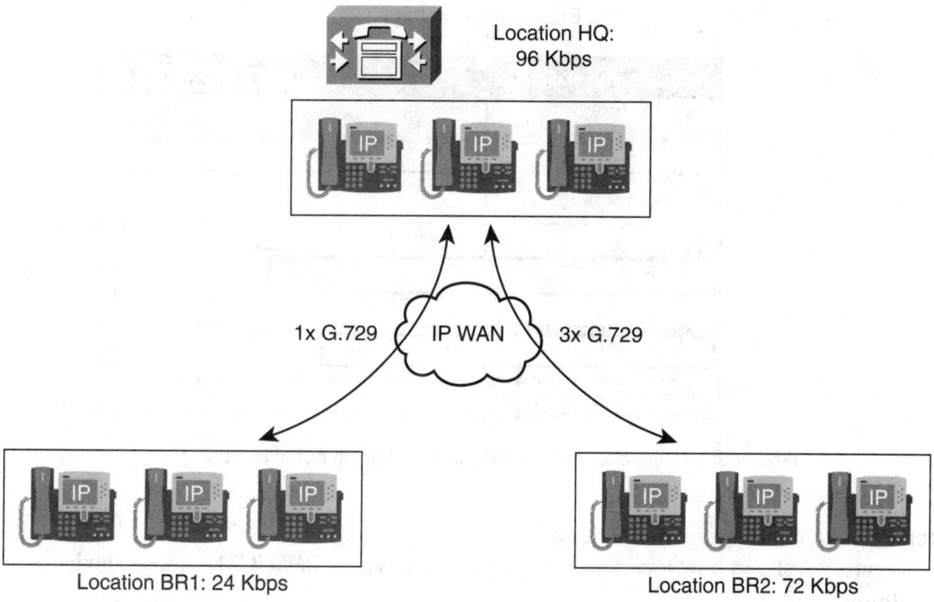

Location HQ:
96 Kbps

1x G.729   IP WAN   3x G.729

Location BR1: 24 Kbps

Location BR2: 72 Kbps

The link between branch 1 and headquarters should not carry more than one G.729 call, and the link between branch 2 and headquarters should not carry more than three G.729 calls. There is no WAN link directly between the WAN sites.

The following figures show how to implement locations-based CAC for this scenario.

Step 1: Configure Locations

Figure 9-5 shows how you configure the locations in CUCM by choosing **System > Location**.

One location exists by default—the Hub_None location. This location is the default location for all devices. To add a new location, click **Add New**.

In the **Location Configuration** window, enter a name for the location in the **Name** field, and set the bandwidth for audio calls. The default Location bandwidth is unlimited.

Calculations of calls for CUCM CAC include Layer 3 to 7 overhead minus the Layer 2 overhead. This results in a G.729 call calculated with 24 kbps and a G.711 at 80 kbps. The actual bandwidth of a voice call contains the Layer 2 overhead. CUCM's "view" of the call does not include the Layer 2 overhead. Be aware that unless RSVP-enabled locations (which are discussed in a moment) are used, standard locations-based CAC considers calls coming into the location and going out of the location, regardless of the location of the other device.

Figure 9-5 *Step 1: Configure Locations in CUCM*

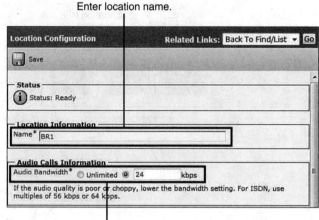

Enter location name.

Set bandwidth permitted for calls coming into and going out of location.

Step 2: Assign Locations to Devices

Figure 9-6 shows how locations are assigned to devices. In CUCM, choose **Device > Phone**.

Figure 9-6 *Step 2: Assign Locations to Devices*

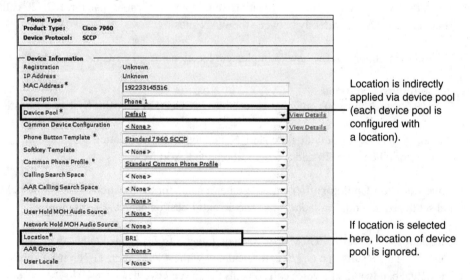

Location is indirectly applied via device pool (each device pool is configured with a location).

If location is selected here, location of device pool is ignored.

Locations are a mandatory setting in a device pool, and each device needs a device pool assigned. Therefore, a device always has a location assigned indirectly through its device pool. If a device uses a different location than the one specified in its device pool, that location can be chosen at the device itself. A location that is assigned at the device level has higher priority than the location of the device pool. A good way to remember this in Cisco voice technologies is a simple rule: "More-specific overrides more-general."

RSVP-Enabled Locations

RSVP-enabled locations are based on CUCM standard locations. RSVP-enabled locations differ from standard locations in two ways. First, RSVP can be enabled selectively between pairs of locations. Because endpoints such as Cisco IP Phones do not support RSVP, the solution requires separate RSVP agents.

An RSVP agent is a device called a Media Termination Point (MTP) through which the call has to flow. RSVP is used only between the two RSVP agents. The Real-Time Transport Protocol (RTP) stream from the IP Phone to the RSVP agent does not use RSVP.

The second and most important difference between RSVP-enabled locations and standard locations is that the use of RSVP makes this CAC mechanism WAN topology-aware, because RSVP will communicate over the WAN. Standard locations do not contain in their configurations details of the WAN topology. RSVP-enabled locations work well with all topologies (full-mesh, partial-mesh, and hub-and-spoke) and adapt to network changes by considering the actual topology. Advantages include consideration of the following:

- **Link failures:** If one link in the IP network goes down and packets are routed on different paths, RSVP is aware of the change and calculates the bandwidth that is now available at the actual routed path.

- **Backup links:** If backup links are added after link failures, or if bandwidth on demand is used to add dial-on-demand circuits, RSVP again is fully aware of the routing path that is currently used and the bandwidth available on each link along that path.

- **Load-share paths:** If load sharing is used, RSVP is aware of the overall bandwidth provided by multiple load-sharing links.

Using RSVP for CAC lets you admit or deny calls based on actual oversubscriptions. The result is always based on the *currently* available bandwidth and interfaces, not on a logical configuration that ignores the physical topology.

Three Call Legs with RSVP-Enabled Locations

When RSVP-enabled locations are used, the end-to-end call is split into three separate call legs, as shown in Figure 9-7.

Figure 9-7   *Three Call Legs with RSVP-Enabled Locations*

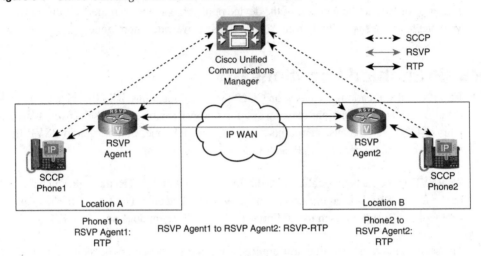

In this figure, Phone1, which is in Location A, places a call to Phone2, which is in Location B. CUCM location configuration specifies that RSVP has to be used for calls between these two locations.

CUCM instructs the two involved RSVP agents in Location A and the other in Location B to use RSVP to try to set up the call between each other. If the call is admitted because enough bandwidth is available in the network path between these two devices, the RSVP agents inform CUCM that the RSVP call leg was successfully set up.

CUCM now tells the phones to set up their call legs, each to its respective RSVP agent. If the RSVP call setup between the two RSVP agents is denied, CUCM considers the call to have failed CAC.

It is important to realize that there are three separate RTP streams: Phone1 talks to RSVP Agent1, RSVP Agent1 talks to RSVP Agent2, and RSVP Agent2 talks to Phone2.

RSVP CAC is used only between the RSVP agents. In this case the RSVP agents are the routers in the two locations, not the Cisco IP Phones.

Characteristics of Phone-to-RSVP Agent Call Legs

Standard location algorithms apply to the call leg between an IP Phone and its RSVP agent, which are usually in the same location. If they are in different locations, standard locations-based CAC is first performed for this call leg between the phone and the RSVP agent. The two RSVP agents try to set up their call leg by using RSVP only if enough bandwidth is available for the IP Phones to reach their RSVP agents.

An RSVP agent registers with CUCM as a special MTP device. CUCM uses the media resource group list of the IP Phone to determine which RSVP agent is to be used by which IP Phone. The association of a phone to its RSVP agent is *not* performed by searching for an RSVP agent in the same location as the phone. As mentioned earlier, the IP Phone and its RSVP agent can be in different locations. Only media resource group lists are used to identify the RSVP agent to be used by an IP Phone.

From a design perspective, the RSVP agent that is used by a certain IP Phone or group of phones should be as close as possible to the IP Phone or phones. Such a design ensures that no suboptimal paths such as phones are accessing RSVP agents over the IP WAN. In addition, this ensures that RSVP-based CAC performed for the phone to RSVP agent is a short network path, ideally over the LAN only.

The RSVP agent supports pass-through codec configuration, which allows any codec to be used. The benefit is that the codec does not have to be known or supported by the RSVP agent, including secure RTP (SRTP), where the RTP payload is encrypted.

Characteristics of RSVP Agent-to-RSVP Agent Call Legs

The call leg between two RSVP agents uses standard RSVP, as implemented in Cisco IOS routers. The IP network between the RSVP agents is RSVP-enabled, which requires each interface to be configured with a maximum amount of bandwidth that can be used for RSVP calls. When not enough bandwidth is available end to end (between the two RSVP agents in this case), RSVP CAC denies the call.

If RSVP is not enabled on any hop in the path, the CAC algorithm ignores the appropriate link (that is, it is always admitted on this link).

CUCM RSVP agent CAC uses the Integrated Services (IntServ) QoS model for the RSVP call leg. This means that RSVP is used only for CAC (the "control" plane), not with RSVP reservable queues for providing QoS to the streams. Instead, standard low-latency queuing (LLQ) configuration is required to provision QoS for the RTP voice stream (the "data" plane).

The end-to-end call—that is, the incorporation of all three call legs—is established only after the RSVP call leg has been admitted. If the RSVP call leg is not admitted, the call fails because of CAC denial caused by insufficient bandwidth.

RSVP Basic Operation

As shown in Figure 9-8, the RSVP-enabled sender (in this case, an RSVP agent) sends a PATH message toward the RSVP-enabled receiver (again, an RSVP agent in this case) along the path that requests bandwidth for the call to be set up. The receiver responds with a Resv message that is routed back along the path. Each RSVP-enabled device checks to see if the requested bandwidth is available and sends the appropriate information in the downstream path toward the sender.

Figure 9-8   *RSVP Functionality over Multiple Hops*

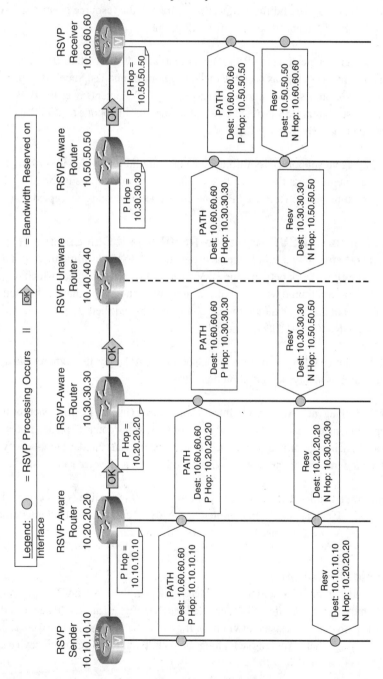

If no RSVP-enabled device on the path denies the reservation because of insufficient bandwidth, the reservation succeeds, and the call is admitted by RSVP CAC.

A more detailed description of the key RSVP messages follows:

- **Path messages (PATH):** An RSVP path message is sent by each sender along the unicast or multicast routes that are provided by the routing protocol. A PATH message is used to store the path state in each node. The path state is used to route reservation request (Resv) messages in the reverse direction.

- **Reservation-request messages (Resv):** A reservation request message is sent by each receiver host toward the senders. This message follows in reverse the routes that the data packets use, all the way to the sender hosts. A reservation request message must be delivered to the sender hosts so that they can set up appropriate traffic control parameters for the first hop. RSVP does not send any positive acknowledgment messages.

Other RSVP messages are as follows:

- **Error and confirmation messages:** Reservation request acknowledgment messages are sent when a reservation confirmation object appears in a reservation request message. This acknowledgment message contains a copy of the reservation confirmation. An acknowledgment message is sent to the unicast address of a receiver host, and the address is obtained from the reservation confirmation object. A reservation request acknowledgment message is forwarded to the receiver hop by hop to accommodate the hop-by-hop integrity-check mechanism.

    —Path error messages result from path messages, and they travel toward senders. Path error messages are routed hop by hop using the path state. At each hop, the IP destination address is the unicast address of the previous hop.

    —Reservation request error messages result from reservation request messages and travel toward the receiver. Reservation request error messages are routed hop by hop using the reservation state. At each hop, the IP destination address is the unicast address of the next-hop node. Information carried in error messages can include the following:

    Admission failure

    Bandwidth unavailable

    Service not supported

    Bad flow specification

    Ambiguous path

■ **Teardown messages:** RSVP teardown messages remove the path and reservation state without waiting for the cleanup timeout period. Teardown messages can be initiated by an application in an end system (sender or receiver) or a router as the result of state timeout. RSVP supports the following two types of teardown messages:

—**Path teardown:** Path teardown messages delete the path state (which deletes the reservation state), travel toward all receivers downstream from the point of initiation, and are routed like path messages.

—**Reservation-request teardown:** Reservation-request teardown messages delete the reservation state, travel toward all matching senders upstream from the point of teardown initiation, and are routed like corresponding reservation request messages.

> **NOTE**   The mechanism that RSVP creates the call path by checking for an available resource each step from source to destination is somewhat analogous to traditional circuit switching through the PSTN, because hops through central offices are established during a long-distance phone call.

RSVP-Enabled Location Configuration

Figure 9-9 shows a conceptual example of a CAC implementation configured in CUCM, based on RSVP-enabled locations that will be implemented in the steps listed in the following section.

Figure 9-9   *RSVP-Enabled Location CUCM Configuration*

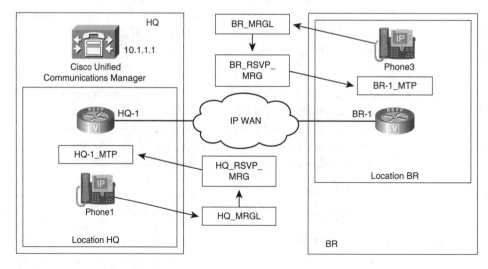

This example has two sites: headquarters (HQ) and branch (BR). Phones located at headquarters are in location HQ, and phones located at the branch are in location BR. RSVP agents exist at each site where HQ-1_MTP is provided by router HQ-1, and BR-1_MTP is provided by router BR-1. The RSVP agents are assigned to their respective locations.

Headquarters phones have media resource group list HQ_MRGL applied. This media resource group list includes a media resource group named HQ_RSVP_MRG, which includes the HQ-1_MTP RSVP agent media resource. Branch phones have media resource group list BR_MRGL applied. This media resource group list includes a media resource group BR_RSVP_MRG, which includes the BR-1_MTP RSVP agent media resource.

Regions, although not shown in this figure, are configured so that G.729 has to be used for calls between headquarters phones and branch phones.

Configuration Procedure for Implementing RSVP-Enabled Locations-Based CAC

The implementation of CUCM RSVP-enabled locations involves the following steps:

Step 1   Configure RSVP service parameters.

Step 2   Configure RSVP agents in Cisco IOS.

Step 3   Add RSVP agents to CUCM.

Step 4   Enable RSVP between location pairs.

Step 5   Configure media resource groups.

Step 6   Configure media resource group lists.

Step 7   Assign media resource group lists to devices.

Because implementation of media resource groups and media resource group lists (Steps 5 to 7) are discussed in detail in *Implementing Cisco Unified Communications Manager, Part 1 (CIPT1)* and have been used in earlier chapters of this book, only Steps 1 to 4 are described here.

Step 1: Configure RSVP Service Parameters

The following important RSVP service parameters can be configured:

■ **Default inter-location RSVP Policy:** This parameter sets the clusterwide default RSVP policy. You can set this service parameter to one of the following values:

—**No Reservation:** No RSVP reservations get made between any two locations.

—**Optional (Video Desired):** A call can proceed as a best-effort, audio-only call if failure to obtain reservations for both audio and video streams occurs. The RSVP agent continues to attempt an RSVP reservation for audio and informs CUCM if the reservation succeeds.

—**Mandatory:** CUCM does not ring the terminating device until RSVP reservation succeeds for the audio stream and, if the call is a video call, for the video stream as well.

—**Mandatory (Video Desired):** A video call can proceed as an audio-only call if a reservation for the audio stream succeeds but the reservation for the video stream does not succeed.

■ **RSVP Retry Timer:** This parameter defines the interval in seconds after which the RSVP agent retries the reservation if a failure occurs. If you set this parameter to 0, you disable RSVP retry on the system. If the RSVP policy is optional, the call can still proceed even if an RSVP failure occurs during call setup. An RSVP failure indicates insufficient bandwidth at the time of setup, so the call is likely to begin with poor voice quality. However, this condition may be transient, and the automatic reservation retry capability may succeed during the course of the call, at which point adequate bandwidth will be assured for the remainder of the call. The CUCM administrator can configure the icon or message displayed to the user. It should convey something like "Your call is proceeding despite network congestion. If you experience impaired audio quality, you may want to try your call again later." If reservation retry succeeds, the icon or message should be removed or replaced by one that conveys a return to normal network conditions and assured audio quality.

■ **Mandatory RSVP Mid-call Retry Counter:** This parameter specifies the mid-call RSVP retry counter when the RSVP policy specifies Mandatory and when the mid-call error-handling option "call fails following retry counter exceeds" is set. The default value specifies one time. If you set the service parameter to –1, retry continues indefinitely until either the reservation succeeds or the call gets torn down.

■ **Mandatory RSVP mid call error handle option:** This parameter specifies how a call should be handled if the RSVP reservation fails during a call. You can set this service parameter to the following values:

—**Call becomes best effort:** If RSVP fails during a call, the call becomes a best-effort call. If retry is enabled, RSVP retry attempts begin simultaneously.

—**Call fails following retry counter exceeded:** If RSVP fails during a call, the call fails after n retries of RSVP if the Mandatory RSVP Mid-call Retry Counter service parameter specifies n.

Table 9-1 shows the interaction of these policy settings.

Table 9-1 *RSVP Policy Settings*

RSVP Policy	When Reservation Failure (Non-Multilevel Precedence and Preemption [MLPP]) Occurs	Mandatory RSVP Mid-Call Error Handling	Mandatory RSVP Retry Counter	Behavior/Call Result
Mandatory	Audio or video RSVP failure in initial call setup	—	—	Call rejected
Mandatory	Audio or video RSVP failure in mid-call	Call fails following retry counter exceeded	n	Call released if reservation does not succeed after n retries
Mandatory	Audio or video RSVP failure in mid-call	Call becomes best-effort	n	Call proceeds as best-effort, and reservation is retried infinitely
Mandatory (video desired)	Audio RSVP failure in initial call setup	—	—	Call rejected
Mandatory (video desired)	Video RSVP failure in initial call setup	—	—	Call proceeds as audio-only
Mandatory (video desired)	Audio RSVP failure in mid-call	Call fails following retry counter exceeded	n	Call released if reservation does not succeed after n retries
Mandatory (video desired)	Video RSVP failure in initial call setup	—	—	Call proceeds as audio-only
Mandatory (video desired)	Audio RSVP failure in mid-call	Call becomes best-effort	n	Call proceeds; audio stream in call becomes best-effort if reservation does not succeed after n retries
Mandatory (video desired)	Video RSVP failure in mid-call	Call fails following retry counter exceeded	n	Call proceeds as audio-only

continues

Table 9-1   *RSVP Policy Settings (Continued)*

RSVP Policy	When Reservation Failure (Non-Multilevel Precedence and Preemption [MLPP]) Occurs	Mandatory RSVP Mid-Call Error Handling	Mandatory RSVP Retry Counter	Behavior/Call Result
Mandatory (video desired)	Video RSVP failure in mid-call	Call becomes best-effort	n	Call proceeds; video stream in call becomes best-effort if reservation does not succeed after n retries
Optional (video desired)	Audio or video RSVP failure in initial call setup	—	—	Call proceeds as audio-only with best-effort; RSVP is tried until reservation succeeds or call is torn down
Optional (video desired)	Audio or video RSVP failure in mid-call	—	—	Call proceeds as audio-only; if audio stream had reservation failure, it becomes best-effort
Mandatory	Audio or video RSVP failure in initial call setup	—	—	Call rejected

Figure 9-10 shows the configuration of the previously described service parameters. It also shows the service parameters that are used to set the Differentiated Services Code Point (DSCP) values that should be used for the RTP packets of calls for which RSVP failed. These parameters can be audio channel (for which RSVP failed at the call setup if the policy was set to Optional) or video or audio channel (if the RSVP failure occurs mid-call and the Mandatory RSVP mid-call error-handling option is set to Call Becomes Best Effort).

You can configure all these service parameters from CUCM Administration by choosing **System > Service Parameters** under the **Cisco CallManager** service. All these parameters are clusterwide, which means that they apply to all servers in the cluster running the **Cisco CallManager** service.

Figure 9-10   *Step 1: Configure RSVP Service Parameters*

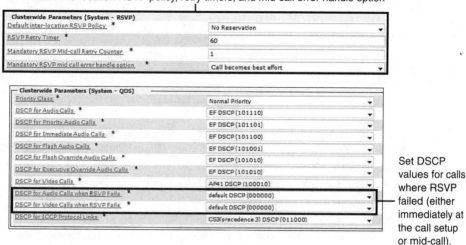

Set default interlocation RSVP policy, retry timers, and mid-call error handle option

Set DSCP values for calls where RSVP failed (either immediately at the call setup or mid-call).

Step 2: Configure RSVP Agents in Cisco IOS Software

Example 9-1 shows a portion of the configuration from **show running-config**. It demonstrates how to configure a Cisco IOS router to enable RSVP agent functionality.

Example 9-1   *Step 2: Configure RSVP Agents in Cisco IOS Software*

```
!
interface Loopback0
  ip address 10.5.9.1 255.255.255.255
!
sccp local Loopback0
sccp ccm 10.1.1b1 identifier 1 version 6.0
sccp
!
sccp ccm group 1
  associate ccm 1 priority 1
  associate profile 1 register HQ-1_MTP
!
dspfarm profile 1 mtp
  codec pass-through
  rsvp
  maximum sessions software 20
  associate application SCCP
```

continues

Example 9-1 *Step 2: Configure RSVP Agents in Cisco IOS Software (Continued)*

```
!
interface Serial0/1
  description IP-WAN
  ip address 10.1.4.101 255.255.255.0
  duplex auto
  speed auto
  ip rsvp bandwidth 40
!
```

As with other Cisco IOS-provided media resources, such as conference bridges and transcoders, the configuration starts with global Skinny Client Control Protocol (SCCP) settings, followed by the CUCM group configuration. Any functional IP address on the router may be chosen for SCCP. However, a loopback interface is best practice (as shown in Example 9-1), because it is reliable by not being directly associated with any one physical interface. The configuration of the media resource is performed in **dspfarm profile** configuration mode. Three commands are specific to the implementation of a software MTP RSVP agent:

- **codec pass-through:** This command specifies that the actual content of the RTP stream is not modified. Media resources usually have to interpret and modify the audio stream; examples are transcoders that change the codec of the audio stream, and hardware media termination points that are used to convert out-of-band signaling into in-band dual-tone multifrequency (DTMF). The RSVP agent repackages RTP only at Layers 3 and 4. It terminates the incoming call leg by decapsulating RTP and then reencapsulating the identical RTP into a new call leg. Because this simple repackaging does not require interpreting and modifying the audio payload, which is required with transcoders or hardware media termination points that are used for DTMF, the router can perform this function in software.

- **rsvp:** This command specifies that this media termination point is used as an RSVP agent that will set up a call leg to another RSVP agent where RSVP with IntServ over DiffServ has to be used.

- **maximum sessions software** *sessions*: This command specifies the maximum number of sessions for the media resource. Note that the keyword **software** is used. It indicates that this RSVP agent should not use DSPs but that it should perform its function in software: Using software MTP is possible only when codec pass-through has been configured.

After the MTP RSVP agent has been set up, you must enable RSVP on the WAN interface or interfaces by using the **ip rsvp bandwidth** *bandwidth* command. The specified bandwidth determines how much bandwidth is allowed to be reserved by RSVP.

> **NOTE**   The bandwidth reserved for a call depends on the codec that is used. As with standard non-RSVP-enabled CUCM locations, it is 80 kbps for G.711 and 24 kbps for G.729. During call setup, however, the RSVP agent always requests an additional 16 kbps, which is released immediately after the RSVP reservation is successful. Therefore, the interface bandwidth has to be configured in such a way that it can accommodate the desired number of calls, considering the codec that will be used plus the extra 16 kbps. For example, if two G.729 calls are permitted on the interface, 64 kbps must be configured. For two G.711 calls, 176 kbps is required.
>
> In Example 9-1, only one G.729 call is permitted.

Step 3: Add RSVP Agents to CUCM

Figure 9-11 shows how to add an RSVP agent in CUCM.

Figure 9-11 *Step 3: Add RSVP Agents to CUCM*

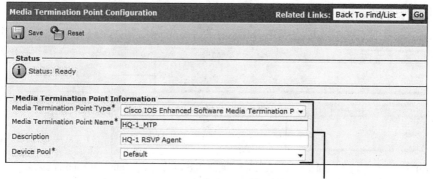

Select media termination point type and device pool.
Enter media termination point name and description.

After the RSVP agent function at the Cisco IOS gateway has been configured, the corresponding media resource has to be added to CUCM. In CUCM, choose **Media Resources > Media Termination Point** and click **Add New**.

In the Media Termination Point Configuration window, choose the type of the media termination point. Currently the only option is Cisco IOS Enhanced Software Media Termination Point. Enter a name and description, and then choose the device pool that should be used.

> **NOTE**   The name of the media termination point has to match the name that was configured at the Cisco IOS router with the **associate profile** *id* **register** command entered in **sccp ccm group** *id* configuration mode. The name is case-sensitive.

> **NOTE**   Because RSVP-enabled locations allow RSVP to be used between two RSVP agents that are between the two endpoints of a call, at least two RSVP agents have to be configured in a cluster to make it work. In our example, these would be HQ-1 and BR-1. Example 9-1 is an example for the HQ-1 router.

Step 4: Enable RSVP Between Location Pairs

After the RSVP agents in Cisco IOS routers have been configured and added to CUCM, RSVP has to be enabled between one or more pairs of locations, as shown in Figure 9-12.

Figure 9-12   *Step 4: Enable RSVP Between Location Pairs*

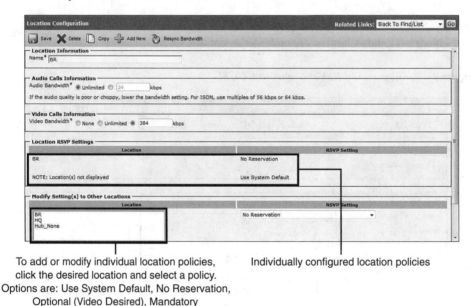

To add or modify individual location policies, click the desired location and select a policy. Options are: Use System Default, No Reservation, Optional (Video Desired), Mandatory

Individually configured location policies

This task is performed in the Location Configuration window, which can be accessed from CUCM Administration by choosing **System > Location**. Choose the location for which RSVP should be enabled for calls to one or more other locations. In the Location Configuration window, under Modify Setting(s) to Other Locations, the currently configured location and all other locations are listed.

Choose the **Location** to which RSVP should be used, and then choose the **RSVP Setting**. The options are the same as those for the Default Inter-location RSVP Policy service parameter:

- **No Reservation:** No RSVP reservations get made between any two locations.

- **Optional (Video Desired):** A call can proceed as a best-effort, audio-only call if failure to obtain reservations for both audio and video streams occurs. The RSVP agent continues to attempt an RSVP reservation for audio and informs CUCM if the reservation succeeds.

- **Mandatory:** CUCM does not ring the terminating device until RSVP reservation succeeds for the audio stream and, if the call is a video call, for the video stream as well.

- **Mandatory (Video Desired):** A video call can proceed as an audio-only call if a reservation for the audio stream succeeds but a reservation for the video stream does not succeed.

In addition, the option Use System Default applies the value of the Default Inter-location RSVP Policy service parameter for calls to the chosen location.

After you click **Save**, the changes are displayed in the Location RSVP Settings part of the window. Only locations that are *not* configured to use the system default are listed.

NOTE RSVP can also be enabled *within* a location. For the currently configured location, Use System Default is not an option. Only No Reservation, Optional (Video Desired), Mandatory, or Mandatory (Video Desired) can be chosen within a location. The default for calls to Own Location is No Reservation, and to all other locations the default is Use System Default.

NOTE When RSVP-enabled locations are used, it is extremely important that the phones use the appropriate RSVP agent. Note that there will be three call legs: The calling phone to *its* RSVP agent, between the RSVP agents, and the remote RSVP agent to the called phone.

CUCM determines which RSVP agent should be used by a given phone based solely on the media resource group lists assigned to the phones that attempt to establish a call. Errors in the media resource group list configuration can result in suboptimal traffic flows. Therefore, proper assignment of phones to RSVP agents, by using Media Resource Group Lists (MRGL) and Media Resource Groups (MRG), is extremely important when RSVP-enabled locations are implemented. The sample scenario at the beginning of this configuration section provides all the information needed for how to assign the RSVP agents to the phones. Further configuration of MRGLs and MRGs is covered in detail in *Implementing Cisco Unified Communications Manager, Part 1 (CIPT1)*.

Automated Alternate Routing

As illustrated in Figure 9-13, AAR allows calls to be rerouted through the PSTN using an alternate number when CUCM blocks a call because of insufficient location bandwidth from CAC. With AAR, the caller does not need to hang up and redial the called party. Without AAR, the user would get a reorder tone, and the IP Phone would display "Not enough bandwidth." The administrator can change this Cisco IP Phone display message in CUCM to a different text response.

Figure 9-13   *AAR Overview*

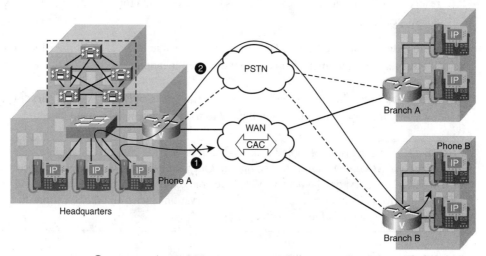

❶ – Cisco Unified Communications Manager CAC blocks a call over the IP WAN.
❷ – The call is automatically rerouted over the PSTN.

AAR applies to centralized call-processing deployments for internal calls within the same CUCM cluster. For instance, if a Cisco IP Phone at company headquarters calls a Cisco IP Phone in branch B, and the available bandwidth for the WAN link between the branches is insufficient as computed by the locations mechanism, AAR can reroute the call through the PSTN. The audio path of the call would be IP-based from the calling phone to its local headquarters PSTN gateway, time-division multiplexing (TDM)-based from that gateway through the PSTN to the branch B gateway, and IP-based from the branch B gateway to the destination IP Phone.

AAR is transparent to users. It can be configured so that users dial only the four-digit directory number of the called phone without any other user input to reach the destination through an alternative network, such as the PSTN. Digit manipulation through the PSTN must be appropriately configured because four digits will not be routable in the PSTN.

In Figure 9-13, a call is placed from Phone A to Phone B, but the locations-based CAC denies the call because of insufficient bandwidth. With AAR, CUCM now *automatically* composes the required route pattern to reach Phone B via the PSTN and sends the call off-net.

Automated Alternate Routing Characteristics

AAR provides a fallback mechanism for calls denied by locations-based CAC or RSVP-enabled locations-based CAC by rerouting calls over the PSTN in the event of CAC failure.

AAR works only for calls placed to internal directory numbers. It does not apply to calls placed to route patterns or feature patterns such as Meet-Me or Call Park. However, it does work for hunt pilots and computer telephony interface (CTI) ports. These entities can be configured with an AAR group and an AAR Calling Search Space (CSS).

The alternative number used for the PSTN call is composed of the dialed directory number, a prefix configured per AAR source and destination group, and the external phone number mask of the called device.

Alternatively, calls can be routed to voice mail, or an AAR destination mask can be configured per device that allows any number to be used for the rerouted call. The number specified at the AAR destination mask is also known as the Call Forward No Bandwidth (CFNB) destination.

> **NOTE**   AAR is a fallback mechanism for calls that are denied by locations-based CAC or RSVP-enabled locations-based CAC. It does not apply to voice calls that are denied by gateways because they exceed the available or administratively permitted number of channels. It also does not apply to calls that have been rejected on trunks, such as gatekeeper-controlled H.225 or intercluster trunks. If such calls fail for any reason, fallback mechanisms are provided by route lists and route groups.
>
> AAR is invoked only when the locations-based call admission control denies the call because of a lack of network bandwidth. AAR is not invoked when the IP WAN is unavailable or other connectivity issues cause the called device to become unregistered with CUCM. In such cases, the calls are redirected to the target specified in the Call Forward No Answer field of the called device.

AAR Example

Figure 9-14 shows two sites with centralized call processing within a single CUCM cluster. At headquarters are a CUCM cluster, IP Phones, and a Cisco IOS router (HQ-1) acting as a PSTN gateway and providing access to the IP WAN.

Figure 9-14 *AAR Example*

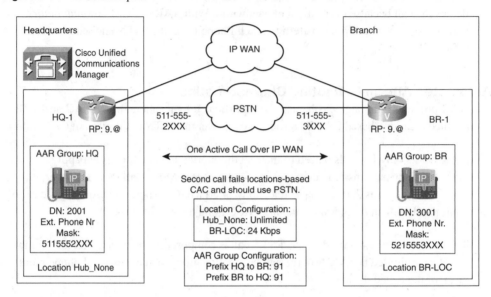

The branch site has IP Phones and a Cisco IOS router (BR-1) acting as a PSTN gateway and providing access to the IP WAN.

Headquarters phones are in location Hub_None; branch phones are in location BR-LOC. Location Hub_None is unlimited, and location BR-LOC is limited to 24 kbps to allow one G.729 call over the IP WAN. Regions, which are not shown in the figure, are configured so that G.729 is negotiated for calls between the branch and headquarters.

Directory numbers of headquarters phones in the range 2XXX are in AAR group HQ; directory numbers of branch phones with range 3XXX are in AAR group BR. The AAR groups HQ to BR and BR to HQ are both configured with a prefix of 91.

The PSTN number of the headquarters gateway is 5115552XXX, and the PSTN number of the branch gateway is 5215553XXX. The external phone number masks of the IP Phone directory numbers are configured correspondingly.

Two route patterns, one of which is 9.@, exist in different partitions (not shown in the figure). Headquarters phones use the route pattern that refers to the headquarters gateway, and branch phones use the route pattern that refers to the branch gateway based on the CSS of the phones.

When an active call occurs between a headquarters phone and a branch phone, the following happens if the phone with directory number 2001 attempts to call 3001:

CUCM determines the locations of the two phones involved in the call: Hub_None and BR-LOC. CUCM checks if the desired call exceeds the bandwidth limit of one of these two locations. This circumstance exists at the BR-LOC location, which is limited to 24 kbps and is fully occupied by the existing call.

CUCM therefore identifies a CAC failure and checks whether AAR is (globally) enabled. Because AAR is assumed to be enabled in this example, CUCM then determines the AAR groups of the two devices: HQ and BR.

CUCM then composes a PSTN number based on the directory number (3001) of the called phone, its external phone number mask (5215553XXX), and the prefix configured for at the HQ group that has to be used toward the BR group (91). The resulting number is 915215553001.

CUCM then uses the AAR CSS, not shown in Figure 9-14, configured at the calling phone to redirect the call to 915215553001. The AAR CSS of the calling phone includes the partition of the 9.@ route pattern, which points to the headquarters PSTN gateway HQ-1. The call is rerouted through the HQ-1 gateway over the PSTN.

AAR Considerations

You must consider several important points when implementing AAR. AAR supports the following call scenarios:

- The call originates from an IP Phone within one location and terminates at an IP Phone within another location.

- An incoming call through a gateway device within one location terminates at an IP Phone within another location.

AAR does *not* work with Survivable Remote Site Telephony (SRST). AAR is activated only after a call is denied by CAC, not by WAN failures.

If the AAR-composed number results in a number with the same area code as the gateway, the area code must not be dialed. To deal with this situation, a translation pattern can be created that strips the area code before the AAR composed number is dialed. Depending on the dial plan implementation and the type of call (international, multiple countries, and so on), additional modifications might be required.

AAR does not support CTI route points as the origin or destination of calls, and AAR is incompatible with extension mobility for users who roam to different sites.

> **NOTE**   When tail-end hop-off (TEHO) is used, it is important to configure the AAR
> CSS in such a way that the local gateway is always used for calls being rerouted by using
> AAR. Calls will fail otherwise, because the call leg to the remote PSTN gateway again
> runs into the same issue as the initial call: It needs to go over the IP WAN. This typically
> means it goes out of the location of the originating phone, but doing that is impossible,
> because no bandwidth is left for the location. This is why the initial call ends up in a CAC
> failure.

AAR Configuration Procedure

The implementation of AAR involves the following steps:

Step 1   Configure AAR service parameters (Cisco CallManager service).

Step 2   Configure partitions and CCSs.

Step 3   Configure AAR groups.

Step 4   Configure phones for AAR:

- Apply AAR CSS and (source) AAR group to IP Phones.

- Configure IP Phone directory number(s):

    — Apply (destination) AAR group.

    — Set individual AAR destination mask (CFNB).

    — Forward to voice mail no bandwidth.

Step 2 is discussed in detail in *Implementing Cisco Unified Communications Manager, Part
1 (CIPT1)*.

The partitions and AAR CSS have to be designed in such a way that the AAR CSS of
the calling device includes the partition required to route the redirected call to the number
composed of destination directory number, external phone number mask, and AAR prefix
according to the AAR group configuration. If an individual AAR destination mask or
forward to voice mail is configured, the AAR CSS has to provide access to these numbers,
which is the number composed of the called directory number and AAR destination mask
or voice-mail pilot number.

Step 1: Configure AAR Service Parameters

Figure 9-15 shows how to enable AAR and set AAR-related parameters. In CUCM, choose
System > Service Parameters > Cisco CallManager.

Figure 9-15 *Step 1: Configure AAR Service Parameters*

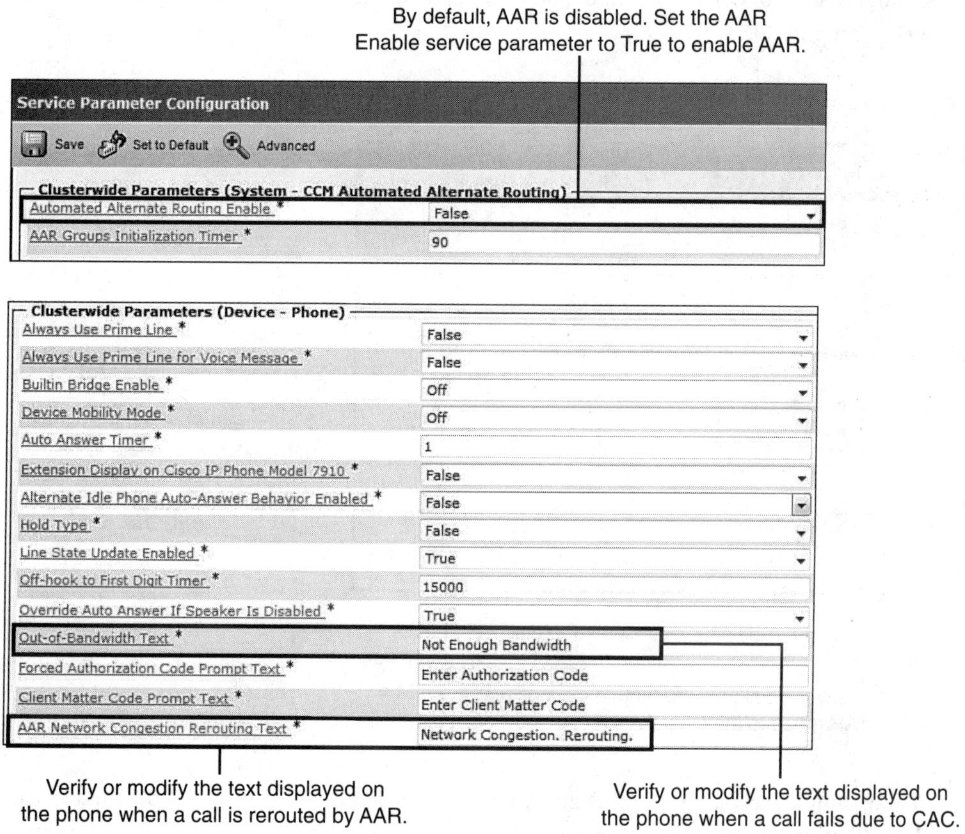

By default, AAR is disabled. Set the AAR
Enable service parameter to True to enable AAR.

Service Parameter Configuration

💾 Save   🔄 Set to Default   🔍 Advanced

Clusterwide Parameters (System – CCM Automated Alternate Routing)

Automated Alternate Routing Enable *	False
AAR Groups Initialization Timer *	90

Clusterwide Parameters (Device - Phone)

Always Use Prime Line *	False
Always Use Prime Line for Voice Message *	False
Builtin Bridge Enable *	Off
Device Mobility Mode *	Off
Auto Answer Timer *	1
Extension Display on Cisco IP Phone Model 7910 *	False
Alternate Idle Phone Auto-Answer Behavior Enabled *	False
Hold Type *	False
Line State Update Enabled *	True
Off-hook to First Digit Timer *	15000
Override Auto Answer If Speaker Is Disabled *	True
Out-of-Bandwidth Text *	Not Enough Bandwidth
Forced Authorization Code Prompt Text *	Enter Authorization Code
Client Matter Code Prompt Text *	Enter Client Matter Code
AAR Network Congestion Rerouting Text *	Network Congestion. Rerouting.

Verify or modify the text displayed on
the phone when a call is rerouted by AAR.

Verify or modify the text displayed on
the phone when a call fails due to CAC.

You enable AAR by setting the CUCM service parameter Automated Alternate Routing
Enable to True. False is the default.

Another AAR-related service parameter is Out-of-Bandwidth Text, where you can specify
the text that is displayed on an IP Phone when a call fails due to a lack of available bandwidth. With the AAR Network Congestion Rerouting Text parameter, you specify the text
that is displayed on an IP Phone when AAR reroutes a call.

Step 2: Configure Partitions and CSSs

The configuration of partitions and CSS is covered in *Implementing Cisco Unified
Communications Manager, Part 1 (CIPT1)*.

Step 3: Configure AAR Groups

As shown in Figure 9-16, you configure AAR groups from CUCM Administration by
choosing **Call Routing > AAR Groups**. Each added AAR group can be configured with

a dial prefix for its own group and two dial prefixes for each of the other AAR groups. Configure one for calls going to the other group and one for calls being received from the other group.

Figure 9-16 *Step 3: Configure AAR Groups*

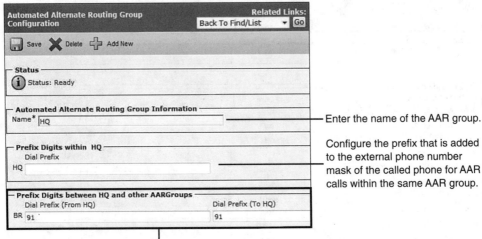

Enter the name of the AAR group.

Configure the prefix that is added to the external phone number mask of the called phone for AAR calls within the same AAR group.

For each other AAR group, configure the dial prefix that is added to the external phone number mask of the called phone.

Specify the dial prefix for both directions (call from this AAR group to the other AAR group and vice versa).

This example has only two AAR groups. The same dial prefix is used in both directions. Instead of assigning one AAR group to some phones and assigning the other AAR group to the remaining phones, a single AAR group could be configured and applied to all phones. Configuring a dial prefix for this single group within the group would have the same effect. However, it is recommended that you group phones into separate AAR groups based not only on the current situation but also on the possibilities for growth. From this perspective, it might be useful to have different sites in different AAR groups.

> **TIP** In complex scenarios, especially when centralized call processing across different countries is used, international numbering plans might make it difficult to implement AAR based on only a directory number, external phone number mask, and dial prefix. In such situations, it can be helpful to use the dial prefix not so that it is the final PSTN number, but so that it includes special digits such as * that can be used in translation patterns. Pointing to translation patterns provides more flexibility than simply prefixing an external phone number.

Step 4: Configure Phones for AAR

Configure phones for AAR by choosing **Call Routing > Phone** in CUCM, as shown in Figure 9-17.

Figure 9-17 *Step 4: Configure Phones for AAR*

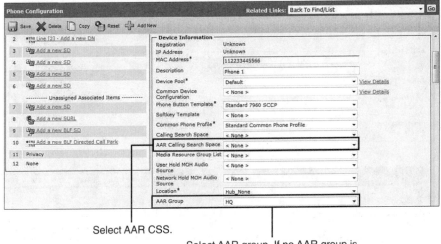

Select AAR CSS.

Select AAR group. If no AAR group is selected here, AAR group of DN is used.

When enabling AAR on a phone, the Phone Configuration window has two possible settings:

- **AAR Calling Search Space:** This is the CSS that is used if a call that originated at this phone is rerouted using AAR.

- **AAR Group:** The AAR group at the phone does not need to be set when AAR is used. If no AAR group is set at the phone, the AAR group of the directory number is used.

The IP Phone directory numbers must be configured for AAR, as shown in Figure 9-18.

Figure 9-18 *Step 4: Configure Phones for AAR, Continued*

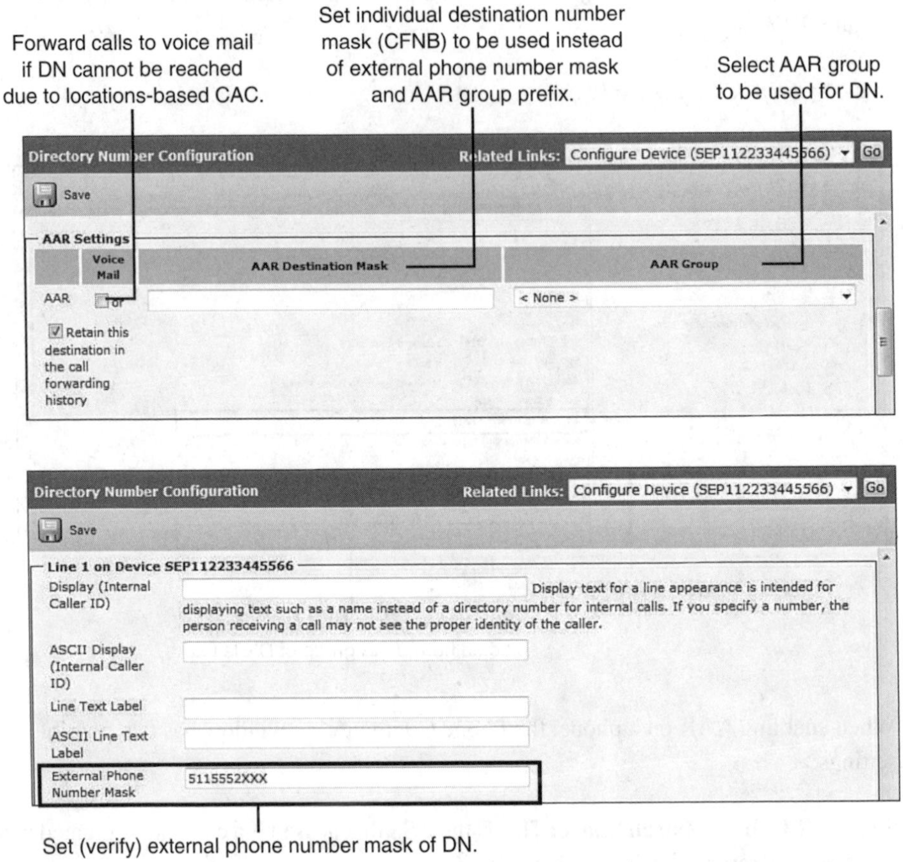

The relevant settings in the Directory Number Configuration window are as follows:

- **AAR Settings: Voice Mail checkbox:** If this option is activated, calls to this phone are forwarded to voice mail if this directory number cannot be reached because of locations-based CAC.

- **AAR Destination Mask:** If this is set, it is the number where calls are rerouted if this directory number cannot be reached because locations-based CAC is composed of this mask and this directory number instead of this directory number, the external phone number mask, and an AAR group prefix. Because this setting is configured per directory number, it allows *any* destination to be specified. If the mask does not contain *n* wildcard digits, calls are rerouted to the specified number without considering any digits of the directory number. Therefore, this setting is often called CFNB.

- **AAR Group:** Select the AAR group to be used for the directory number (DN).

- **External Phone Number Mask:** This is the external phone number mask of the directory number. It should always be set, because it is used by other features, such as digit manipulation at route patterns or route lists.

H.323 Gatekeeper CAC

CUCM can connect to other CUCM clusters or to any other H.323 devices via H.323 trunks. H.323 trunks can be configured on their own without using a gatekeeper for address resolution and CAC, or as gatekeeper-controlled trunks. Two types of gatekeeper-controlled trunks can be configured in CUCM:

- **Gatekeeper-controlled intercluster trunk:** This trunk is intended to work with CUCM releases before 3.2, although it can be used on later versions.

- **H.225 trunk:** This trunk can be used to work with CUCM 3.2 or later and all other Cisco or third-party H.323 devices. The H.225 trunk features a peer-discovery mechanism. Hence, it can identify the device located at the other end of the trunk and use the appropriate feature set.

A CUCM gatekeeper-controlled trunk registers as an H.323 gateway with the gatekeeper. Alternatively, it can be configured to register as H.323 terminals. When a trunk is registered, CUCM provides the following information to the gatekeeper, as you can see with the command **show gatekeeper endpoints**:

- **H.323 device type:** The device type can be either gateway or terminal. CUCM is usually configured to register as a gateway.

- **H.323 ID:** The H.323 ID is based on the name of the trunk that is configured in CUCM, with the string _x at the end. The x is a number that uniquely identifies each call-processing CUCM server of the cluster where the Cisco CallManager service is activated.

NOTE The H.323 ID has to be unique. CUCM keeps the H.323 ID that is used by the members of a cluster unique by adding the individual ending _x. Furthermore, because CUCM does not allow multiple trunks to use the same name, no duplicate H.323 IDs can be presented to the gatekeeper from a cluster. However, if the same trunk name is configured in multiple clusters, the call-processing servers of two or more clusters will try to register with the same H.323 ID. The gatekeeper does not allow these duplicate H.323 IDs to register, so the trunk is not operational. Therefore, it is important to use unique trunk names across all CUCM clusters that register with a gatekeeper.

■ **H.323 zone:** H.323 zones are used to group devices. Call routing and CAC are performed based on these zones. For instance, a default technology prefix can be configured per zone that identifies the gateway (or gateways) to which calls should be routed when the gatekeeper does not know which gateway to use. Also, CAC can be configured differently for calls within a zone versus interzone calls.

NOTE The H.323 zone name configured at the gatekeeper-controlled trunk is case-sensitive and has to exist at the gatekeeper.

■ **Technology prefix:** H.323 gateways including CUCM can register prefixes. These are number ranges they can route calls to at the gatekeeper. The prefix can consist only of numbers (such as 511), or it can include a technology prefix (such as 1# or 2#). One way of using an H.323 technology prefix is for a gateway to indicate the services it provides by specifying an appropriate technology prefix (for instance, 1# for voice services, 2# for fax services, and so on). Calls that include the technology prefix in their numbers (for example, a call placed to 1#5115551000) can be routed to the gateway in the zone that registered the appropriate technology prefix. Technology prefixes can also be used for TEHO over a gatekeeper-controlled WAN.

As just mentioned, a gatekeeper can be configured to route calls to the gateway or gateways that register with a prefix that is configured to be the default technology. For example, if only one CUCM cluster registers per zone, the trunk in each cluster can be configured with a technology prefix of 1#, and the gatekeeper can be configured to send all calls to the gateway that registered with the configured default technology prefix of 1# in this case. The gatekeeper needs only a configuration of number prefixes, which is a number to find the correct zone. When the outgoing zone is determined, the gatekeeper just sends the call to one of the gateways or CUCM clusters that registered in the zone with the default technology prefix.

NOTE More information about how a gatekeeper routes call is provided in the *Cisco Voice Over IP* course.

H.323 Gatekeeper Used for Call Routing for Address Resolution Only

Figure 9-19 shows an example of gatekeeper-controlled trunks in a distributed CUCM deployment. In the example, two CUCM clusters are shown. Each cluster has an H.225 trunk configured.

Figure 9-19 *H.323 Gatekeeper Used for Call Routing for Address Resolution Only*

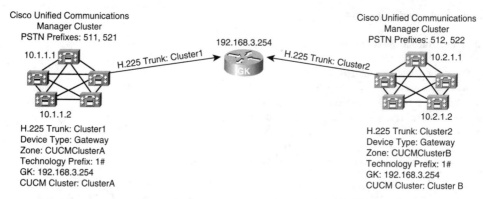

Cisco Unified Communications
Manager Cluster
PSTN Prefixes: 511, 521

10.1.1.1

H.225 Trunk: Cluster1

192.168.3.254

H.225 Trunk: Cluster2

Cisco Unified Communications
Manager Cluster
PSTN Prefixes: 512, 522

10.2.1.1

10.1.1.2

H.225 Trunk: Cluster1
Device Type: Gateway
Zone: CUCMClusterA
Technology Prefix: 1#
GK: 192.168.3.254
CUCM Cluster: ClusterA

10.2.1.2

H.225 Trunk: Cluster2
Device Type: Gateway
Zone: CUCMClusterB
Technology Prefix: 1#
GK: 192.168.3.254
CUCM Cluster: Cluster B

NOTE A * is a gatekeeper wildcard that denotes all possible phone numbers, analogous to the gateway of last resort static route in data routing. If a technology prefix is properly entered without the * wildcard, the * often shows up automatically in the IOS configuration after the technology prefix, as illustrated in Example 9-2.

Example 9-2 is a sample of the gatekeeper configuration from **show running-config**. CAC is not configured; therefore, the gatekeeper assumes that infinite bandwidth is available to calls on all WAN links. This example has no gatekeeper fault tolerance.

Example 9-2 *Sample Gatekeeper Configuration for Call Routing Without CAC*

```
gatekeeper
 zone local CUCMClusterA lab.com 192.168.3.254
 zone local CUCMClusterB lab.com 192.168.3.254
 zone prefix CUCMClusterA 511*
 zone prefix CUCMClusterA 521*
 zone prefix CUCMClusterB 512*
 zone prefix CUCMClusterB 522*
 gw-type-prefix 1#* default-technology
 no shutdown
```

The call-processing servers of ClusterA are registered in zone CUCMClusterA, and the call-processing servers of ClusterB are registered in zone CUCMClusterB. This can be verified by using the command **show gatekeeper endpoints**. All endpoints are registered with prefix 1#*, which is configured to be the default technology prefix. You can verify this by using the command **show gatekeeper gw-type-prefix**. The result of these two commands entered in privileged EXEC mode is shown aggregated as an example into one combined output in Example 9-3.

Example 9-3 *Aggregated Output of* **show gatekeeper** *Commands*

```
show gatekeeper endpoints

show gatekeeper gw-type-prefix

GATEKEEPER ENDPOINT REGISTRATION
================================
H323-ID    IPAddr    ZoneName     Type     Prefix
Cluster1_1 10.1.1.1  CUCMClusterA VOIP-GW  1#*
Cluster1_2 10.1.1.2  CUCMClusterA VOIP-GW  1#*
Cluster2_1 10.2.1.1  CUCMClusterB VOIP-GW  1#*
Cluster2_2 10.2.1.2  CUCMClusterB VOIP-GW  1#*
```

The H.225 trunks use different names for each cluster to keep the H.323 IDs unique. ClusterA uses Cluster1, and ClusterB uses Cluster2. Each cluster has two call-processing nodes—10.1.1.1 and 10.1.1.2 in ClusterA, and 10.2.1.1 and 10.2.1.2 in ClusterB.

The trunk in ClusterA, with the name Cluster1, is configured with zone ClusterA and technology prefix 1#*. The trunk in ClusterB, with the name Cluster2, is configured with zone ClusterB and the same technology prefix (1#*). Both trunks refer to the IP address of the same gatekeeper of 192.168.3.254.

The gatekeeper has two local zones named CUCMClusterA and CUCMClusterB. It is configured to route calls to prefixes 511 and 521 to zone CUCMClusterA, and to route calls to prefixes 512 and 522 to zone CUCMClusterB. In addition, the gatekeeper is configured to use technology prefix 1#* as the default technology. Therefore, calls to prefixes for which the gatekeeper does not know what gateway to use are routed to the gateway or gateways that registered a technology prefix of 1#*.

This gateway configuration means that the gatekeeper has four gateways registered. Cluster1_1 is the first call-processing server of the CUCM Group that is configured in the device pool of the trunk. Cluster1_2 is the second call-processing server of ClusterA and the two call-processing servers of ClusterB. Note that CUCM automatically gives an added numeric designator of _1 or _2 in the name.

They all use different H.323 IDs because different trunk names have been configured in the two clusters and because CUCM adds the _1 and _2 to the trunk name to uniquely identify the call-processing servers per cluster.

NOTE If the same trunk name were configured in the two clusters, registrations would fail because of duplicate H.323 IDs.

If the gatekeeper receives an admission request (ARQ) message from one of the H.323 gateways (in this case a Cisco Unified Communications Server), it looks up its call-routing table of the list of configured zone prefixes to find out in which zone the requested prefix can be found.

> **NOTE**   The command **debug ras** shows the ARQ message followed by an acceptance (ACF) or a rejection (ARJ) based on the CAC settings and number of simultaneous calls. Example 9-2 does not have CAC configured; this is addressed in the next section.

You can verify the list of configured prefixes and their zones using the command **show gatekeeper zone prefix**.

If an ARQ message was sent from 10.1.1.1 to the gatekeeper that requests a call to 5125551234, the gatekeeper determines that the call has to be routed to zone CUCM ClusterB. The only prefix registered by gateways in this zone is 1#*, which is the default technology prefix; it is registered by 10.2.1.1 and 10.2.1.2. Therefore, the gatekeeper chooses one of these two gateways in a round-robin fashion to be the terminating gateway. It tells the originating gateway, the CUCM server of ClusterB that sent the ARQ message, to set up an H.323 call with the determined terminating gateway of 10.2.1.1 or 10.2.1.2.

> **NOTE**   At this point, the gatekeeper is configured only to perform call-routing address resolution. It resolves a dialed number to the IP address where the call has to be routed.

Using an H.323 Gatekeeper for CAC

To use an H.323 gatekeeper for CAC, bandwidth limitations have to be configured. In Cisco IOS, H.323 gatekeeper CAC is implemented by using the **bandwidth** command:

```
router(config-gk)#bandwidth {interzone | total | session}
  {default | zone zone-name} bandwidth-size
```

> **NOTE**   The command **bandwidth** exists in other IOS modes as well, such as QoS and interface modes. When used in different IOS modes, this command takes on entirely different meanings.

Table 9-2 lists the parameters used with the **bandwidth** command in gatekeeper mode for configuring CAC options.

Table 9-2 *bandwidth* Parameters

Syntax	Description
Interzone	Specifies the total amount of bandwidth for H.323 traffic from the zone to any other zone.
Total	Specifies the total amount of bandwidth for H.323 traffic allowed in the zone.
Session	Specifies the maximum bandwidth allowed for a session in the zone.
Default	Specifies the default value for all zones.
zone *zone-name*	Specifies a particular zone by name.
bandwidth-size	Maximum bandwidth. For **interzone** and **total**, the range is from 1 to 10,000,000 kbps. For **session**, the range is from 1 to 5000 kbps.

NOTE The bandwidth that is assumed by the gatekeeper for each call is twice the bandwidth of the audio codec. A G.729 call is configured for 16 kbps, and a G.711 call is configured for 128 kbps. This is not the actual bandwidth seen on the wire, but it's the standard used when configuring gatekeeper CAC to represent a call. Multiple calls are simply calculated as an even multiple of these numbers, 16 and 128. Therefore, it is critical to know which codec is being used when configuring gatekeeper CAC.

Bandwidth limitations are configured differently on different Cisco products and for different features. Again, these different settings do not change the bandwidth seen on the wire; they only show the expected configuration on these products all representing the same call. Table 9-3 summarizes how to configure bandwidth limitations for CAC in CUCM.

Table 9-3 *Bandwidth Parameters in CUCM and the H.323 Gatekeeper*

	CUCM Region	CUCM Location	Cisco IOS H.323 Gatekeeper
Audio-Only Call Configuration	Audio codec only	Audio codec bit rate plus Layer 3 overhead	Twice the audio codec bit rate
Example: G.711 Call	G.711	80 kbps	128 kbps
Video Call Configuration	Audio codec and video call speed	Video call speed	Twice the video call speed
Example: 384-kbps Video Call	G.711 and 384 kbps	384 kbps	768 kbps
Example: G.729 Call	G.729	24 kbps	16 kbps

NOTE   Video calls have not been discussed in this chapter but are shown for completeness.

H.323 Gatekeeper Also Used for Call Admission Control

Figure 9-20 shows a sample topology of a Cisco IOS H.323 gatekeeper that has CAC enabled with the configuration in Example 9-4.

Figure 9-20   *H.323 Gatekeeper with Call Admission Control*

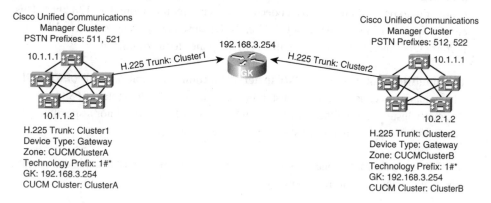

Cisco Unified Communications
Manager Cluster
PSTN Prefixes: 511, 521

10.1.1.1

H.225 Trunk: Cluster1

192.168.3.254

GK

H.225 Trunk: Cluster2

10.1.1.1

10.1.1.2

H.225 Trunk: Cluster1
Device Type: Gateway
Zone: CUCMClusterA
Technology Prefix: 1#*
GK: 192.168.3.254
CUCM Cluster: ClusterA

Cisco Unified Communications
Manager Cluster
PSTN Prefixes: 512, 522

10.2.1.2

H.225 Trunk: Cluster2
Device Type: Gateway
Zone: CUCMClusterB
Technology Prefix: 1#*
GK: 192.168.3.254
CUCM Cluster: ClusterB

Example 9-4 shows a sample of the output of **show running-config** of the gatekeeper configuration with CAC.

Example 9-4   *H.323 Gatekeeper with Call Admission Control Configuration*

```
gatekeeper
  zone local CUCMClusterA lab.com 192.168.3.254
  zone local CUCMClusterB lab.com 192.168.3.254
  zone prefix CUCMClusterA 511*
  zone prefix CUCMClusterA 521*
  zone prefix CUCMClusterB 512*
  zone prefix CUCMClusterB 522*
  bandwidth interzone default 64
  bandwidth interzone zone CUCMClusterB 48
  bandwidth session default 128
  bandwidth total zone CUCMClusterB 688
  gw-type-prefix 1#* default-technology
  no shutdown
```

Example 9-4 is based on Example 9-2, but now the H.323 gatekeeper also performs CAC.

The **bandwidth interzone default 64** command specifies that 64 kbps is permitted for calls going out of and coming into a zone. Because no specific zone is specified, but the keyword **default** is used, this setting applies to all zones that are not explicitly configured with a different setting.

The **bandwidth interzone zone CUCMClusterB 48** command specifies that the previously configured default interzone bandwidth limit should not apply to ClusterB but that ClusterB should instead be limited to only 48 kbps. Note again how "more specific" takes precedence over "more general." The **bandwidth session default 128** command limits the bandwidth to be used per call to a codec that does not require more than 128 kbps. This equates to one G.711 call or eight G.729 calls. Because no different session bandwidth is configured for any specific zone, this default applies to all zones.

The **bandwidth total zone CUCMClusterB 688** command limits all calls of ClusterB, which applies to calls within the cluster and intercluster calls, to a total of 688 kbps. Because ClusterA has neither a **bandwidth total default** command nor a specific **bandwidth total** command, ClusterA has no total limit applied.

If G.729 is used for interzone calls and G.711 is used for intrazone calls, this configuration effectively would permit the following:

■   There can be a maximum of three G.729 calls between ClusterA and ClusterB because ClusterB is limited to 48 kbps based on 3 * 16 kbps. ClusterA could have four G.729 calls to other zones. However, because the example shows only two zones and the other zone, ClusterB, is limited to three G.729 calls, ClusterA will never be able to use the permitted interzone bandwidth.

■   The maximum audio bandwidth is limited to 64 kbps. Calls requiring more bandwidth, for media such as wideband audio codecs or video calls with a video call bandwidth of more than 64 kbps, are not permitted in any zone.

■   The total of all calls of both interzone and intrazone calls in zone ClusterB must not exceed 688 kbps. As an example, this configuration allows three G.729 calls to ClusterA based on 3 * 16 kbps and five G.711 calls within ClusterB based on 5 * 128 kbps. Intrazone calls in zone ClusterA are unlimited.

> **NOTE** Some of the bandwidth commands in the example are for illustration only and are not useful in this scenario because only two zones are shown. Furthermore, intrazone limitations have been configured but would never apply in this scenario, because the H.323 gateways of CUCM systems only use the gatekeeper for calls to the other cluster. Note that all H.323 gatekeeper bandwidth limitations apply only to calls that are routed by using the gatekeeper. A call between IP Phones of the same cluster does not use the gatekeeper-controlled trunk and therefore is not subject to any of the bandwidth commands entered at the gatekeeper.

Provide PSTN Backup for Calls Rejected by CAC

Backup paths can be provided for calls that are rejected by a gatekeeper because of CAC, as shown in Figure 9-21.

Figure 9-21 *Provide PSTN Backup for Calls Rejected by CAC*

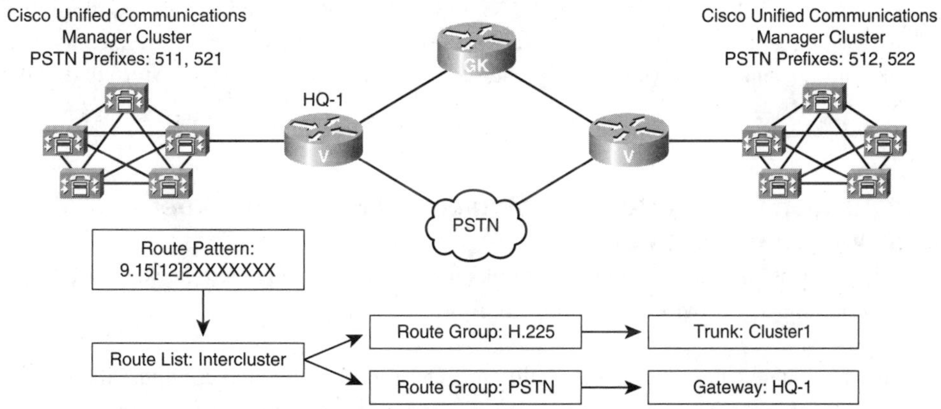

Route lists and route groups provide backup paths if the preferred path fails. In the example, if the calls cannot be established over the H.225 trunk because of CAC, the calls use the PSTN gateway (HQ-1) as backup.

When a call placed to a gateway or trunk fails, there can be multiple causes. The appropriate device can be down, resulting in a timeout when trying to place a call to an H.323 gateway. CAC can limit a call when an ARQ message is sent to an H.323 gatekeeper. Also, there can be keepalives that are not exchanged with an MGCP gateway because of lost connectivity. There can be other problems in communicating with the gateway successfully, such as sending H.323 messages to the IP address of an interface other than the one where the H.323 has been bound, or failing gatekeeper registration because of an invalid zone name or because the call is rejected because of lack of resources. The latter may occur when no channel is available on an E1 or T1 trunk, when an administratively configured limit of calls is reached at a dial peer, or because of CAC.

CUCM uses the same backup method for all these types of call failures based on route lists and route groups configured with route patterns. If the currently attempted device of a route group cannot extend the call for any reason, CUCM tries the next device according to the route group and route list configuration for each route pattern.

Therefore, providing a backup for calls that have been rejected because of H.323 gatekeeper CAC is as simple as having a route list and route groups that prefer the gatekeeper-controlled trunk over one or more PSTN gateways. If the call cannot be set up over the trunk, CUCM reroutes the call to the PSTN gateways. Note that AAR is not used in any of these examples.

> **NOTE** For a PSTN backup, digit manipulation has to be performed in such a way that the calling number and, more importantly, the called number are transformed to always suit the needs of the device that is actually used. This transformation is usually done at the route list, where digit manipulation can be configured per route group. In the example, the called number 9-1-511-555-1234 has to be changed to a ten-digit number for the H.225 trunk because the gatekeeper is configured with area code prefixes without the long-distance 1 and to an 11-digit number in case the call needs to be rerouted to the PSTN gateway.

Configuration Procedure for Implementing H.323 Gatekeeper-Controlled Trunks with CAC

To implement gatekeeper-controlled trunks for call routing only, add gatekeeper CAC functionality, and provide a backup path, follow these steps:

Step 1   Enable gatekeeper functionality at a Cisco IOS router, and configure the gatekeeper for call routing. This configuration typically includes zones, zone prefixes, and the default technology prefix.

Step 2   Add the gatekeeper to CUCM.

Step 3   Add the gatekeeper-controlled trunk, either a gatekeeper-controlled intercluster trunk or an H.225 trunk, to CUCM, and configure the trunk.

Step 4   Configure route groups, route lists, and route patterns to route calls that match a certain route pattern. An example is 9.5[12][12]....... for the examples shown earlier in this topic to the gatekeeper-controlled trunk.

> **NOTE**   Steps 2 through 4 are described in *Implementing Cisco Unified Communications Manager, Part 1 (CIPT1)*.

To implement gatekeeper-controlled CAC, configure the Cisco IOS gatekeeper with bandwidth commands to enable bandwidth limitations. Typically this is required only for interzone calls.

> **NOTE** The command syntax and a sample configuration were shown earlier in this chapter.

To provide backup paths for the gatekeeper-controlled trunk, add PSTN gateways to route groups, and add these gateways to the route lists that are using the gatekeeper-controlled trunks.

> **NOTE** PSTN backup was configured in earlier examples of this book. More information about gatekeeper configuration is provided in the *Cisco Voice over IP* course.

Summary

The following key points were discussed in this chapter:

- CAC limits the number of calls to avoid voice-quality issues caused by bandwidth oversubscription because of too many voice calls.

- CUCM locations can be used for CAC within a CUCM cluster that has a hub-and-spoke topology.

- CUCM RSVP-enabled locations provide topology-aware CAC between RSVP agents.

- AAR allows calls that were denied by locations-based CAC to be rerouted over the PSTN.

- H.323 gatekeepers can provide CAC on CUCM H.323 trunks.

References

For additional information, refer to these resources:

- Cisco Systems, Inc., Cisco Unified Communications Solution Reference Network Design (SRND), based on CUCM Release 6.x, June 2007

- Cisco Systems, Inc., *CUCM Administration Guide Release 6.0(1)*

- Cisco Systems, Inc., *Cisco IOS H.323 Configuration Guide—Configuring H.323 Gatekeepers and Proxies*

Review Questions

Use these questions to review what you've learned in this chapter. The answers appear in Appendix A, "Answers to Chapter Review Questions."

1. Which of the following CAC-related features applies to intercluster calls?

   a. Locations

   b. H.323 gatekeeper CAC

   c. AAR

   d. RSVP-enabled locations

2. Which of the following is an accurate description of a limitation of locations-based CAC?

   a. Locations-based CAC does not let you configure a different limit per pair of locations. Only a total limit for all calls coming into or going out of a location can be configured.

   b. Locations-based CAC is primarily designed for CAC between two or more CUCM clusters.

   c. Locations-based CAC can only be configured to allow a maximum of ten calls.

   d. Locations-based CAC does not have any CAC limitations.

3. Which statement about RSVP-enabled locations is false?

   a. They adapt to the actual topology considering network changes.

   b. RSVP provides QoS for each RTP stream.

   c. The RSVP agent to be used by a phone is determined by the phone's media resource group list.

   d. The RSVP agent is configured as an MTP in CUCM.

   e. Cisco IP Phones do not support RSVP.

4. AAR reroutes calls to the PSTN for which two kinds of calls?

   a. Calls rejected by an H.323 gatekeeper

   b. Calls rejected by locations-based or RSVP-enabled locations-based CAC

   c. Calls placed to unregistered phones

   d. Calls placed to a gateway that is busy

   e. Calls placed to internal directory numbers

   f. Calls placed to the PSTN

5. How can calls that are rejected by an H.323 gatekeeper be rerouted using a different path?

   a. By configuring route lists and route groups with backup devices

   b. By putting the gatekeeper-controlled intercluster trunk or H.225 trunk into a location that is set to unlimited

   c. This is not possible, because AAR supports only internal calls.

   d. By configuring a second route pattern in the same partition referring to the backup device

6. Which statement about AAR and SRST is true?

   a. AAR does not work with SRST.

   b. AAR works well with SRST in all topologies.

   c. AAR works well with SRST in only hub-and-spoke topologies.

   d. AAR works well with SRST in only full-mesh topologies.

7. When a gatekeeper is configured to implement CAC between multiple CUCM clusters, what VoIP signaling protocol is used?

   a. SIP

   b. H.323

   c. MGCP

   d. SCCP

   e. SIP and H.323 working together with CUBE

8. Which configuration would give the best user experience if a gatekeeper configured with multiple gatekeeper-controlled intercluster trunks limited additional calls with CAC?

   a. Ensure that the additional calls blocked with CAC always give the users the reorder tone to train them when best to make calls.

   b. Use AAR to send additional calls blocked with CAC through the PSTN.

   c. Use route groups configured with the route lists and route patterns to send additional calls blocked with CAC through the PSTN.

   d. Use AAR combined with route groups configured with the route lists and route patterns to send additional calls blocked with CAC through the PSTN.

9. Which statement is the most accurate comparing locations-based CAC and RSVP-enabled locations for implementing CAC within CUCM?

   a. Both methods are optimal for full-mesh topologies.

   b. RSVP-enabled locations work better with full-mesh topologies than locations-based CAC.

   c. Locations-based CAC works better with full-mesh topologies than RSVP-enabled locations.

   d. Both methods are unacceptable for full-mesh topologies.

10. What is the proper syntax to implement CAC on a gatekeeper?

    a. Use the **bandwidth** command in interface mode.

    b. Use the **bandwidth** command in gatekeeper mode.

    c. Use the **cac** command in interface mode.

    d. Use the **cac** command in gatekeeper mode.

11. Which statement is the most accurate about locations and regions in CUCM?

    a. Locations configure CAC, and regions negotiate codecs.

    b. Regions configure CAC, and locations negotiate codecs.

    c. Both regions and locations together configure CAC.

    d. Both regions and locations together negotiate codecs.

12. Which protocol or protocols must be configured on the router to enable an IOS RSVP agent to communicate with CUCM?

    a. SIP

    b. H.323

    c. SCCP

    d. MGCP

    e. None of the above

    f. SIP and SCCP working together with CUBE

13. What is the effect of having a non-RSVP-enabled IP router in the path of an RSVP stream?

    a. The RSVP agents cannot implement CAC.

    b. The RSVP agents can implement CAC end to end fully, provided that the source and destination agents are properly configured.

    c. The RSVP agents can implement CAC without a guarantee from the non-RSVP-enabled IP router.

    d. CAC is undesirable in this topology.

CHAPTER **10**

Implementing Call Applications on Cisco IOS Gateways

This chapter describes the functions of gateway call applications and explains the differences between Tool Command Language (Tcl) scripting and Voice Extensible Markup Language (VoiceXML or VXML) functions.

Also discussed is the process of obtaining voice applications by loading an auto-attendant Tcl script to a gateway. This script allows outside callers to enter the internal directory number they want to be connected to using their telephone keypad. The auto-attendant script collects the dual-tone multifrequency (DTMF) tones and then routes the call accordingly.

Chapter Objectives

Upon completing this chapter, you will be able to download and implement Tcl scripting and VoiceXML applications on Cisco Unified Survivable Remote Site Telephony (SRST) or Cisco Unified Communications Manager Express (CUCME) IOS gateways to enable interactive voice response (IVR) functions. You will be able to meet these objectives:

- Describe the different methods available in Cisco IOS Software to implement call applications

- Describe how Tcl scripts and VoiceXML applications are supported in Cisco IOS Software

- Describe the application of the auto-attendant script

- Configure call applications in Cisco IOS Software

Call Applications Overview

Voice applications can be developed in the Cisco IOS by using one or both of these scripting languages:

- **Tcl IVR 2.0:** Tcl-based scripting with a proprietary Cisco application programming interface (API). Provides extensive call-control capabilities, signaling, and Generic Transparency Descriptor (GTD) manipulation.

- **VoiceXML:** Standards-based markup language for voice browsers. Existing web server and application logic can be used for VoiceXML applications, so less time and money are needed to build infrastructure and perform development than when traditional proprietary IVR systems are used.

For information on developing and implementing a VoiceXML document or Tcl script for use with your voice application, see the following guides at Cisco.com:

- *Cisco VoiceXML Programmer's Guide*

- *Tcl IVR API Version 2.0 Programmer's Guide*

> **NOTE**   For releases earlier than Cisco IOS Software Release 12.3(14)T, see the previous version of the *Cisco IOS Tcl IVR and VoiceXML Application Guide* at Cisco.com.

Tcl Scripting Language

Tcl (usually pronounced "tickle") is an easy-to-learn open-source scripting language that allows for rapid application development.

Tcl is related to UNIX shell scripting languages. Its syntax is similar to the C programming language, but it also has similarities to Lisp.

The motto of Tcl is "radically simple," referring to its very simple but unusual syntax.

Features and characteristics include the following:

- Everything is a command, including language structures that are in prefix notation (also known as Polish notation, which is a form of notation for logic, arithmetic, and algebra developed by the Polish logician Jan Lukasiewicz in 1920).

- Everything can be dynamically redefined and overridden. TCL scripts do not need to be compiled after they are edited.

- All data types can be manipulated as strings, including code.

- Extremely simple syntactic rules.

- Event-driven interface to sockets and files. Time-based and user-defined events are also possible.

- Flexible scope, with variable visibility restricted to lexical (static) scope by default, but with uplevel- and upvar-allowing procedures to interact with the scopes of the enclosing functions.

- Simple exception handling by using exception code returned by all command executions.

- Readily extensible, via C, C++, Java, and Tcl.

- An interpreted language that uses bytecode for improved speed while maintaining dynamic modifiability.

- Full Unicode (3.1) support, first released in 1999.

- Platform-independent: Win32, UNIX, Linux, Mac, and so on.

- Close integration with windowing (GUI) interface Tk.

- Easy-to-maintain code. Tcl scripts often are more compact and readable than functionally equivalent code in other languages.

- Can be used for many purposes and in many environments: as a text-only scripted language, as a GUI-capable language for applications, as an embedded language in web pages (server-side, or client-side as Tclets) and databases (server-side, in PostgreSQL).

- Exists as a development version, such as ActiveState Tcl; as tclkit, which is a kind of runtime version, only about 1 MB in size; as starpack, which is a single-file executable of a script/program; and as BSD-licensed freely distributable source.

VoiceXML Markup Language

VoiceXML, also known as VXML, is a standard language for designing voice-driven applications, as shown in Figure 10-1.

Figure 10-1 *VoiceXML Markup Language*

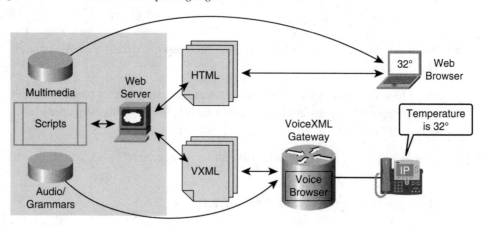

VoiceXML was created in 1999. Its first versions came from the merging of several proprietary languages developed by telecommunications system manufacturers such as AT&T, IBM, Lucent, and Motorola.

The first draft of the language was adopted by the World Wide Web Consortium (W3C) in May 2000. It has become the key industrial standard for developing voice servers and has been adopted by the major players in the market.

The current draft is the VoiceXML 2.1 Recommendation of the W3C from June 2007.

The Analogy Between HTML and VoiceXML

The similarity between HTML and VoiceXML is that HTML is a language for creating web pages, and VoiceXML is a language for writing voice-driven scenarios.

The voice browser is the equivalent of the web browser and is integrated into the voice platform (IVR). You navigate your way through a website using the keyboard and mouse. With a voice browser, you use your telephone keypad or speech recognition to navigate.

This similarity between HTML and VoiceXML makes it possible to use the same infra-structures web servers use to gain access to the information systems of the enterprise. Therefore, existing investments in security, gateways, database management systems (DBMS), and application servers are preserved, and their life is extended.

Advantages of VoiceXML

One of the many advantages of the VoiceXML language is that it is based on web technologies and has been adopted by web developers who no longer need special expertise in the voice realm to develop voice portals. Other advantages include the following:

- Standardization of scenario writing

- Application software detached from the voice interface

- Integration of Automatic Speech Recognition (ASR) and Text to Speech (TTS)

- Use of web infrastructures

- Based on web technologies adopted de facto by web developers

- Fast deployment of rapid application development (RAD) and reuse of web applications

- E-business through a multichannel portal

- No proprietary development language

Cisco IOS Call Application Support

Tcl and VoiceXML can be integrated with Cisco IOS on a Cisco IOS router configured as a gateway, as shown in Figure 10-2.

Figure 10-2 *Cisco IOS Call Application*

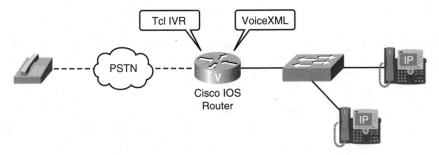

Tcl and VoiceXML applications on the Cisco gateway provide IVR features and call-control functionality such as call forwarding, conference calling, and voice mail.

IVR systems provide information through the telephone in response to user input in the form of spoken words or DTMF signaling. The Cisco voice gateway allows an IVR application to be used during call processing. A Cisco voice gateway can have several IVR applications to accommodate many different services, and you can customize the IVR applications to present different interfaces to various callers.

Tcl Versus VoiceXML Features in Cisco IOS

Tcl IVR 2.0 and VoiceXML APIs each have strengths and weaknesses, as shown in Table 10-1.

Table 10-1   *Tcl Versus VoiceXML Features in Cisco IOS Software*

	Tcl IVR 2.0	VoiceXML
Flexible Call Control	Strong	Weak
Multiple Call Legs	Strong	Weak
Collect User Input	Weak	Strong
Play Prompts	Weak	Strong

Tcl IVR 2.0 is very flexible when it comes to call control. It can describe multiple call legs based on how they should be controlled and how they should interwork. A weak point, however, is that user interface primitives are limited to digit collection and media playing commands.

VoiceXML, on the other hand, is both familiar and easy to use when designing voice user interfaces, but it is very limited in its call-control capabilities. For example, VoiceXML dialog is good at IVR activities, such as collecting user input or playing prompts.

It would be advantageous, therefore, to use Tcl IVR 2.0 to describe the call legs, and the call-flow and call-control interactions between them, while using VoiceXML to describe user interface dialogs on one or more of the legs it is controlling.

It is possible to use the handoff mechanism to have separate application instances in Tcl IVR 2.0 and to use VoiceXML to deal with the application's call-control and dialog aspects. However, it is difficult to clearly partition the call-control and dialog activities. This task requires that the call-control script and dialog execution share control of the call leg, which is difficult to do with the handoff approach.

Cisco IOS Release 12.2(11)T introduces the ability for developers to use Tcl and VoiceXML scripts to develop hybrid applications. Tcl IVR 2.0 extensions allow Tcl applications to leverage support for ASR and TTS by invoking and managing VoiceXML dialogs from within Tcl IVR scripts. Hybrid applications can be developed by using Tcl IVR for call control and VoiceXML for dialog management. This allows applications to use both Tcl IVR 2.0 and VoiceXML APIs and yet behave as a single application instance.

Cisco IOS Call Application Support Requirements

Cisco IOS routers need to meet the following prerequisites to support call applications:

- Cisco IOS version:

    —Tcl supported since 12.0(6)T, current version Tcl IVR 2.0

    —VoiceXML supported since 12.2(2)XB, current version VoiceXML 2.1

    —New Cisco voice application command-line interface structure since 12.3(14)T

- Cisco IOS enterprise router platforms supporting VXML:

    —Cisco 2800 and 3800 Series Integrated Services Routers (ISR)

    —Cisco 3700 Series

- Memory requirements for VoiceXML:

    —Minimum memory allocated is approximately 128 KB; maximum allowed is approximately 380 KB

    —The system itself allocates approximately 120 KB, whereas the maximum allowed per VoiceXML application document is approximately 65 KB.

Cisco IOS Software Release 12.0(6)T, with support for Tcl 1.0, is the first to support Tcl call applications. Tcl 2.0 is the currently supported release. Cisco IOS Software Release 12.2(2) XB is the first release to support VoiceXML. The currently supported release is VoiceXML 2.1. Since Cisco IOS Software Release 12.3(14)T, new Cisco IOS command-line interface (CLI) commands are used to configure call applications.

Cisco IOS VoiceXML browser functionality is supported and recommended on the Cisco 2800 and 3800 Integrated Services Routers, the Cisco 3700 Series Multiservice Access Routers, and on service-provider-class routers such as the Cisco AS5400HPX, AS5350XM, and AS5400XM Universal Gateways. Performance, stress, and regression tests are periodically performed and published on a representative number of these platforms.

Technically, the Cisco 1751 and 1760 Modular Access routers, the Cisco 2600XM Series, and the Cisco 2691 Multiservice Platform also support the Cisco IOS VoiceXML browser. However, these products are not in production anymore and are not recommended for Cisco IOS VoiceXML Browser sessions.

For the smallest document, the minimum memory that the Cisco IOS Software and VoiceXML interpreter uses for a call is approximately 128 KB. The maximum memory allowed is approximately 380 KB. This is allocated as follows:

- The underlying system, including the telephony signaling software and JavaScript Expressions context, requires approximately 120 KB for a call.

- Each VoiceXML document can use a maximum of 65 KB of internal memory. The amount of memory that each document requires cannot be calculated by counting tags or lines in a VoiceXML document, but generally the memory required correlates to the size of the document.

Examples of Cisco IOS Call Applications Available for Download at Cisco.com

Call applications can be self-written, obtained from third-party vendors, or downloaded from Cisco.com, where some Tcl and VoiceXML call applications are made available. The following are examples of Cisco IOS call applications that are available for download at Cisco.com:

- CUCME and Survivable Remote Site Telephony (SRST) Auto-Attendant

- CUCME Basic Automatic Call Distribution (B-ACD)

- Hookflash transfer with CUCM for H.323 gateways

- H.450 transfer for CUCME 3.2

- Voice store-and-forward support with VoiceXML handoff

- Tcl script that supports Malicious Call ID (MCID) triggering from DTMF sequence

- T.37 fax on-ramp and off-ramp scripts

Cisco call applications provide the services described in Table 10-2.

Table 10-2 *Call Application Feature Descriptions*

Call Application	Feature Description
CUCME and Cisco SRST AutoAttendant	Provides auto-attendant functionality to a Cisco IOS gateway that is in SRST mode or that runs CUCME.
CUCME Basic Automatic Call Distribution (B-ACD)	Provides automatic call distribution functionality to CUCME.
Hookflash transfer with CUCM for H.323 gateways	Enables H.323 gateways to use hookflash transfers with CUCM. By default, only Media Gateway Control Protocol (MGCP) gateways support hookflash transfer.
Voice store-and-forward support with VoiceXML handoff	This application is used at service providers to handle emails at off-ramp gateways.
H.450 transfer for CUCME 3.2	Adds H.450 transfer capabilities to CUCME 3.2.
Tcl script that supports Malicious Call ID (MCID) triggering from DTMF sequence	Allows MCID triggering based on a DTMF sequence entered by a user who wants to flag the call as malicious.

Call Application Auto-Attendant Script Example

Figure 10-3 shows the implementation of a call application using the automated attendant Tcl script. In the figure, a centralized call-processing deployment uses CUCM. At the remote site, no direct inward dialing (DID) range is used at the PSTN connection of the gateway. All incoming calls are sent to an attendant located at the main site, who transfers calls to the desired user.

Figure 10-3 *Cisco Auto-Attendant Tcl Script at the Remote-Site Cisco IOS Router*

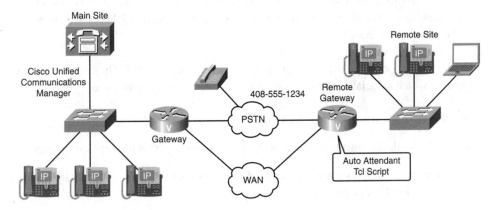

The remote gateway is MGCP, controlled by CUCM servers located at the main site. To provide survivability during WAN failures, MGCP fallback and SRST are enabled at the remote-site gateway.

Because the remote site has no dedicated attendant, a Tcl script that provides auto-attendant functionality is implemented at the remote-site gateway in the event of a WAN failure. Thus, PSTN users who are calling the remote-site gateway can choose the internal directory number of the remote-site user they want to be transferred to.

The Tcl IVR script (its_Cisco.2.0.1.0.tcl) is designed to work with CUCME and Cisco Unified SRST. The IVR script plays a welcome prompt, which prompts the user to enter a destination number when he or she dials the auto-attendant number, called the aa-pilot, which is configured in the CLI. The script collects the digits that the user has entered and places the call to the destination based on the dial plan pattern configured in the dial peer. Operator support is also included. If the user does not dial any number or enters 0, he or she is transferred to an operator, assuming that the operator number is configured in the CLI. If the user enters an invalid number, he or she is prompted to reenter the number up to three times before the system disconnects the call.

> **NOTE**   The Tcl script that has just been described is one choice for sites that do not have DID PSTN ranges and do not want all PSTN calls to go through an operator. Other approaches are possible, including the use of a B-ACD Tcl script, or when the Cisco Unity Express auto-attendant function is implemented.

To enable a call application on a Cisco IOS gateway, first the Tcl script and associated voice prompt files have to be loaded to the flash memory of the routers. Then the call application has to be provided, with its parameters in the configuration of the Cisco IOS routers. The pilot number of the call application service has to be assigned to a dial peer, which then has to be service-enabled.

Dial peers are central to the configuration of Cisco voice gateways. They act as the focal point at which associated elements come together, including the following:

- Name of the voice application to invoke

- VoiceXML documents, Tcl IVR scripts, and audio files that the application uses

- Destination telephone number and Dialed Number Identification Service (DNIS) maps that link callers to the voice application

Remote-Site Gateway Using an Auto-Attendant Script During a WAN Failure

Figure 10-4 shows the logical operation of the auto-attendant script for an inbound call from the PSTN.

Figure 10-4 *Remote-Site Gateway Using an Auto-Attendant Script During a WAN Failure*

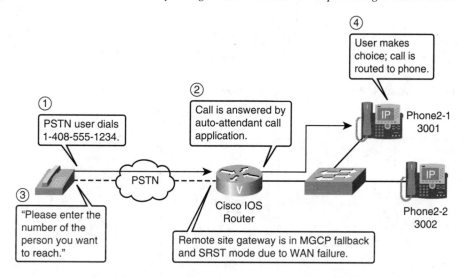

The Tcl IVR script named Cisco.2.0.1.0.tcl is designed to work with CUCME and Cisco Unified SRST. The script is loaded into router flash. As shown in Figure 10-4, the following transactions occur when a call is placed to the remote-site gateway where the script has been configured:

1. A PSTN user dials the number of the remote-site gateway, which is in SRST mode because of WAN failure.

2. Because the gateway is in MGCP fallback mode, the call is handled by the H.323 application. The incoming call is detected, an incoming dial peer is chosen, and the call application is configured at the incoming dial peer. The Tcl IVR auto-attendant script is then started.

3. The IVR script plays a welcome prompt to the caller and prompts the caller to enter a directory number.

4. The script collects the digits entered by the user and places the call to the destination based on the locally configured dial plan within the SRST configuration.

Optionally, operator support can be enabled. When the caller does not dial any number or enters 0, he or she can be transferred to the number of an operator if an operator number is configured in the CLI.

If the user enters an invalid number, he or she is prompted to reenter the number up to three times before the system disconnects the call.

Auto-Attendant Tcl Script Flowchart

Figure 10-5 shows the call flow of the auto-attendant script.

Figure 10-5 *Auto-Attendant Tcl Script Flowchart*

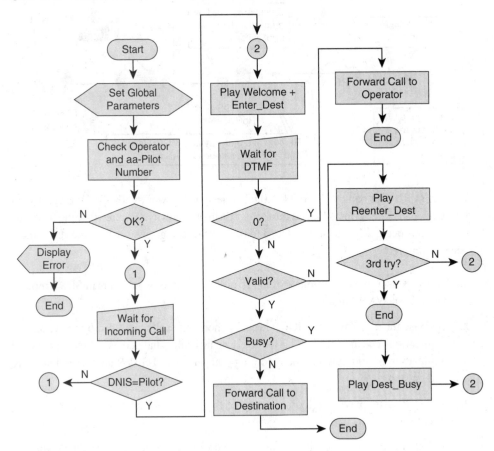

The flow of the auto-attendant script is as follows:

1. The script sets global parameters, such as the language English, according to the application configuration in Cisco IOS.

2. The script checks whether aa-pilot number (the auto-attendant pilot number) and operator numbers are configured in the CLI. The aa-pilot number configuration is mandatory for handling call transfers successfully. Therefore, an error message is displayed if no aa-pilot number is configured.

3. On an incoming call, the DNIS is checked. If the DNIS matches the configured pilot number, the script continues; otherwise, the script waits for the next incoming call.

4. For calls placed to the configured pilot number of the script, the welcome prompt en_welcome.au is played, and the en_enter_dest.au prompt asks the user to enter the destination number.

5. If the user does not dial any number or dials 0, he or she is connected to the operator, provided that an operator number was configured.

6. If the user dials an invalid destination number, the en_reenter_dest.au prompt asks the user to reenter the destination number. The user is prompted up to three times before the system disconnects the call.

7. If the user dials a valid destination number and the destination is busy, the user hears a message from the audio file dest_busy.au, stating that the destination is busy. The user is prompted to again enter a destination number from en_enter_dest.au. The script continues from Step 5.

8. If the dialed number is valid and not busy, the call is forwarded to the dialed number.

> **NOTE**   The .au audio files must also be copied into the same router flash as the TCL script.

Call Application Configuration

The steps for configuring a call application downloaded from Cisco.com vary from application to application. The following configuration steps use the auto-attendant script:

Step 1   Download the application from Cisco.com.

Step 2   Upload and uncompress the script files to flash from any TFTP server.

Step 3   To configure the call application:

   a.   Enter the service definition.

   b.   Configure service parameters.

Step 4   Associate the call application with a dial peer.

> **NOTE**   For detailed configuration steps for call applications, refer to the included documentation.

Step 1: Download the Application from Cisco.com

This first step describes how to load a VoiceXML document or Tcl script onto the Cisco gateway. Log in to Cisco.com and search for the filename cme-aa-2.0.1.0.tar.

A service is a standalone application. The application service name can then be configured under a dial peer to provide services.

> **TIP**   When you download a Tcl script from the Cisco Software Center at Cisco.com, review the ReadMe file that is included with the downloaded file. It may contain additional script-specific information, such as configuration parameters for configuring basic functionality for Tcl IVR and VoiceXML applications and user interface descriptions. You must have an account on Cisco.com to access the Software Center.

> **CAUTION**   Depending on the call application, multiple downloadable files may appear to provide the same functionality, but for different platforms. For example, auto-attendant scripts exist for CUCME and SRST. Applying the wrong script will cause unexpected results.

Step 2: Upload and Uncompress the Script to Flash

For .tar files, use the **archive tar** command to load the files from the source URL and extract all the content files to flash memory with a single command:

```
RemoteRouter# archive tar /xtract source-url flash:/file-url
```

For example, the following command designates the TFTP server with IP address 192.168.1.10, and the filename is cme-aa-2.0.1.tar:

```
RemoteRouter# archive tar /xtract tftp://192.168.1.10/cme-aa-2.0.1.tar flash:
```

Step 3a: Configure the Call Application Service Definition

The commands to define a call application are as follows:

```
RemoteRouter(config)# application
  RemoteRouter(config-app)# service service-name service-location
```

To enter the application configuration mode, you use the **application** command in global configuration mode.

The **service** command defines a new application and enters service configuration mode.

You use the parameter *service-name* to specify a meaningful service name and the parameter *service-location* to specify the location of the Tcl script.

Step 3b: Configure the Call Application Service Parameters

To provide the call application with its parameters, use the following commands:

```
RemoteRouter(config-app-param)# param parameter value
RemoteRouter(config-app-param)# paramspace language {language
  language | index index | location location | prefix prefix}
  paramspace language {location location | index number | language prefix}
```

The **paramspace language** command keywords and parameters are as follows:

- *language*: Name of the language package. Cisco IOS Software includes some built-in language packages, such as English.

- **location** *location*: URL of the audio files. Valid URLs refer to TFTP, FTP, HTTP, or RTSP servers, flash memory, or the removable disks on the Cisco 3600 series.

- **index** *number*: Category group of the audio files (from 0 to 4). For example, audio files representing days and months can be category 1, audio files representing units of currency can be category 2, and audio files representing units of time—seconds, minutes, and hours—can be category 3. The range is from 0 to 4; 0 means all categories.

- **language** *prefix*: The two-character code that identifies the language associated with the audio files. Valid entries are as follows:

    —**en**: English

    —**sp**: Spanish

    —**ch**: Mandarin

    —**aa**: All

The **param** command in service configuration mode specifies a parameter for a defined service. The parameter *parameter* defines the parameter name, and the parameter *value* assigns its value.

Some parameters are grouped by using the **paramspace** command. These parameters can also be referenced by other applications, or have their values set on the dial-peer configuration. One example is the **paramspace** *language* command, which specifies language settings for an application.

One of the biggest improvements of the revised call application syntax is the **paramspace** command. This command lets you share parameters between different call applications.

As a comparison of these commands, **param** is a locally declared variable, and **paramspace** is a globally defined variable. **param** can be referenced only in the service, whereas **paramspace** can be referenced by any service running.

> **NOTE**   The **param** and **paramspace** commands, which are used to specify parameters for the application, are nested under the service configuration. Before Cisco IOS Software Release 12.3(14)T, only parameters existed. If you use applications that were developed before 12.3(14)T, you may get warning messages about parameters not being registered. You can ignore these messages.

Step 4: Associate the Call Application with a Dial Peer

Finally, you need to bind the call application to a dial peer to enable its activation using the following command:

```
RemoteRouter(config-dial-peer)# service service-name [out-bound]
```

You must use the **service** command in dial-peer configuration mode to associate a call application with an inbound dial peer. If the application should be used for an outbound dial peer, you must set the optional keyword **out-bound**.

Call Application Configuration Example

Figure 10-6 shows a topology of a Cisco IOS router with a four-internal-digit dial plan and the auto-attendant script configured in Example 10-1.

Figure 10-6 *Call Application Sample Topology*

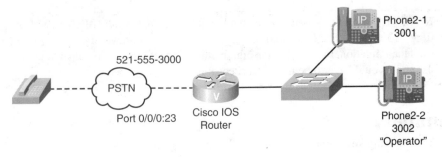

Example 10-1 *Call Application Configuration Example*

```
application
  service aa flash:its-CISCO.2.0.1.0.Tcl
    param operator 3002
    paramspace english language en
    paramspace english index 0
    paramspace english location flash:
    paramspace english prefix en
    param aa-pilot 3000
!
dial-peer voice 90
  service aa
  incoming called number 5215553000
  translation-profile incoming pstn-in
  destination-pattern 9T
  port 0/0/0:23
!
voice translation-profile pstn-in
  translate called 1
!
voice translation-rule 1
  rule 1 /^5215553/ /3/
```

The auto-attendant script is configured with the **aa-pilot 3000** parameter, which means that the script performs the auto-attendant function for calls placed to number 3000.

Example 10-1 shows the configuration of the incoming dial peer 90 on the ISDN port 0/0/0:23. The translation profile and translation rules are used to reduce the incoming called ten-digit number to four digits to match the number of digits on the internal dial plan. This way, calls placed to 521-555-3000 are seen as calls with a destination of 3000, which is the aa-pilot number configured in the call application.

The operator is configured at the Cisco IP Phone at extension 3002.

> **NOTE** Example 10-1 assumes that the Local Exchange Carrier (LEC) is sending in ten digits from the PSTN. It is common for the LEC to send in fewer digits after it performs digit manipulation. In that case, the digit manipulation by the voice translation rule in this example would have to be modified accordingly.

Summary

The following key points were discussed in this chapter:

- Voice applications can be developed using Tcl IVR or VoiceXML.

- Cisco IOS VoiceXML Browser sessions are supported and recommended on the Cisco 2800 and 3800 Integrated Services Routers.

- The Tcl IVR script its_Cisco.2.0.1.0.tcl provides auto-attendant functions for CUCME and Cisco Unified SRST.

- When uploading Tcl scripts in tar format, you can use the **archive tar** command to load the files from the source URL and extract all the content files to flash memory with a single command.

References

For additional information, refer to these resources on Cisco.com:

- *Cisco IOS Tcl IVR and VoiceXML Application Guide*

- *Tcl IVR API Version 2.0 Programming Guide*

- *Cisco VoiceXML Programmer's Guide*

Review Questions

Use these questions to review what you've learned in this chapter. The answers appear in Appendix A, "Answers to Chapter Review Questions."

1. Which two of the following characteristics apply to VoiceXML?

    a. It's a standards-based markup language for voice browsers.
    b. It's event-driven.
    c. Existing web server and application logic can be used.
    d. It's based on standard Tcl scripting language.
    e. It provides extensive call-control and signaling capabilities.

2. Which of the following is not a feature of VoiceXML?

   a. It collects user input.

   b. It plays prompts.

   c. It can be combined with Tcl scripts in the same call application.

   d. It has multiple call legs.

3. What is the function provided by the auto-attendant Tcl script that can be downloaded from Cisco.com?

   a. It allows incoming PSTN callers to enter the directory number they want to reach and transfers the call to the entered number.

   b. It integrates Unity's auto-attendant features with an IOS router.

   c. It provides Unity auto-attendant direct failover.

   d. It is a substitute for IOS SRST.

4. Which command is not entered in application service configuration mode when you configure the auto-attendant Tcl script on a Cisco IOS router?

   a. **param operator**

   b. **param aa-pilot**

   c. **telephony-service**

   d. **paramspace english language en**

5. Which two of the following are examples of TCL Script call application implementations?

   a. Centralized CUCM dial plan implementation

   b. CUCME and SRST Auto-Attendant

   c. CUCME B-ACD

   d. Cisco IP Phone services

   e. CUCM cluster replication script

6. What function does a dial peer serve when a TCL script for the auto-attendant is configured?

   a. The dial peer redirects incoming calls to CUCM in the main site.

   b. The dial peer redirects incoming calls to CUCM in the main site when in SRST fallback mode.

   c. The dial peer redirects incoming calls to the TCL script stored in the remote-site router flash.

   d. The dial peer redirects incoming calls to CUCM to the TCL script stored in the main-site router flash.

7. What is the best reason to implement a TCL auto-attendant script in remote-site router flash?

   a. To provide direct integration of Unity and an IOS auto-attendant

   b. To provide the remote site with an auto-attendant that is not dependent on IP connectivity to the main site

   c. To replace Unity with a more cost-effective auto-attendant enterprise solution

   d. To provide an alternative to SRST for outbound dialing in remote sites

8. Which of the following is the best benefit of using TCL in a Cisco telephony environment?

   a. Compiling the TCL script after it is created provides added script reliability.

   b. TCL ensures the highest level of audio security for inbound dialers.

   c. TCL scripts can be modified with a text editor and redeployed without compiling the source code.

   d. TCL scripts provide extension mobility for Cisco IP Phones.

9. Where are TCL scripts for an auto-attendant stored?

   a. On CUCM TFTP Server

   b. In remote-site router flash

   c. In remote-site router NVRAM

   d. On a dedicated Media Convergence Server

   e. On Cisco IP Phones

CHAPTER 11

Implementing Device Mobility

It is common in multisite environments for some users to roam between sites on a regular basis. When such users take their Cisco Unified Communications endpoints with them, such as Cisco Unified Wireless IP Phones or Cisco IP Communicator (softphone) phones, the standard configuration of their endpoints needs to be adapted to suit the needs of the current physical location. It is important for a professional unified communications solution to provide such a solution.

This chapter describes Device Mobility. This new feature of CUCM allows CUCM endpoints to be dynamically reconfigured based on their actual location as determined by the IP address that is used by the device.

Chapter Objectives

Upon completing this chapter, you will be able to meet the following objectives:

- List the issues with devices roaming between sites

- Describe the Device Mobility feature

- Describe the Device Mobility configuration elements and their interaction

- Describe Device Mobility operation

- Implement Device Mobility

Issues with Devices Roaming Between Sites

Figure 11-1 shows a phone device roaming between two internal sites as a user brings along his or her phone for business travel.

Figure 11-1   *Roaming Devices Between Internal Sites*

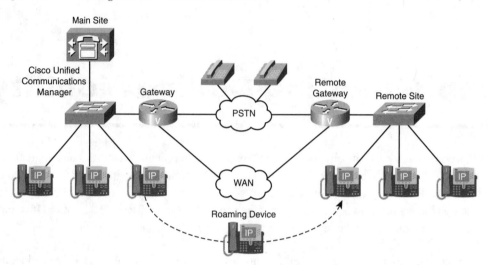

When users roam between sites, they might take their phones with them. This typically does not apply to Cisco IP Phones, but it's very common with softphones such as Cisco IP Communicator running on a laptop or Cisco Unified Wireless IP Phones.

Issues with Roaming Devices

When phones move between different CUCM sites, inaccurate phone settings may occur.

The configuration of an IP Phone includes personal settings and location-dependent settings that are all bound statically to the phone's MAC address and hence to the device itself. The physical device location has traditionally been assumed to be constant.

If a phone (or, more likely, a softphone such as IP Communicator) is moved between sites, the location-dependent settings become inaccurate. Some of these settings and their errors are as follows:

- **Region:** Might cause wrong codec settings.

- **Location:** Might cause wrong call admission control (CAC) and bandwidth settings.

- **Survivable Remote Site Telephony (SRST) reference:** Might cause a malfunction of Cisco Unified SRST.

- **Automated Alternate Routing (AAR) group:** Might cause a malfunction of the call redirection on no bandwidth.

- **Calling Search Space:** Might cause usage of remote gateways instead of local ones.

- **Media Resource Groups and Media Resource Group Lists:** Might cause allocation of wrong media resources such as conference bridges or transcoders.

For correct settings, CUCM needs to be aware of the physical location of all phones, including roaming devices.

Device Mobility Solves Issues of Roaming Devices

Device Mobility offers functionality that is designed to enhance the mobility of devices within an IP network. Table 11-1 summarizes the challenges and solutions of Device Mobility.

Table 11-1   *Device Mobility Solves Issues of Roaming Devices*

Issue Without Device Mobility	Device Mobility Feature to Solve the Issue
When the mobile user moves to a different location, Call Admission Control settings are not adjusted.	Location settings are dynamically assigned.
PSTN gateways to be used are fixed.	Dynamic phone CSS allows for site-independent local gateway access.
SRST reference is fixed.	SRST reference is dynamically assigned.
When the mobile user moves to a different region, codec settings are not adjusted.	Region settings are dynamically assigned.
AAR does not work for mobile users.	The AAR calling search space and the AAR group of the DN are dynamically assigned.
Media resources are assigned location-independently.	The media resource list is dynamically assigned.
AAR has Extension Mobility issues.	Extension Mobility also benefits from dynamic assignment.

Although devices such as IP Phones and IP Communicator still register with the same CUCM cluster with SCCP or SIP, they now will adapt some of their behavior based on the actual site where they are located. Those changes are triggered by the IP subnet in which the phone is located.

Basically, all location-dependent parameters can be dynamically reconfigured by Device Mobility. Thus, the phone keeps its user-specific configuration, such as directory number, speed dials, and call-forwarding settings. However, it adapts location-specific settings such as region, location, and SRST reference to the actual physical location. Device Mobility can also be configured so that dial plan-related settings such as the device Calling Search Space (CSS), AAR group, and AAR CSS are modified.

Device Mobility Overview

The following are key characteristics and features of Device Mobility:

- Device Mobility can be used in multisite environments with centralized call processing within a single CUCM cluster.

- Device Mobility allows users to roam between sites with their Cisco IP Phones, which typically are Cisco IP Communicator or Cisco Unified Wireless Phones.

- IP Phones are assigned with a location-specific IP address by DHCP scopes specific to each location.

- CUCM determines the physical location of the IP Phone based on the IP address used by the IP Phone.

- Based on the physical location of the IP Phone, the appropriate device configuration is applied.

Device Mobility allows users to roam between sites with their IP Phones. Typically, these are Cisco Unified Wireless IP Phones or Cisco IP Communicator Phones.

When the device is added to the network of roaming sites, it is first assigned with an IP address. Because the IP networks are different in each site, CUCM can determine the physical location of the IP Phone based on its IP address.

Based on the physical location of the IP Phone, CUCM reconfigures the IP Phone with site-specific settings.

Dynamic Device Mobility Phone Configuration Parameters

Two types of phone configuration parameters can be dynamically assigned by Device Mobility: Roaming-Sensitive Settings and Device Mobility-Related Settings.

Device Mobility can reconfigure site-specific phone configuration parameters based on the phone's physical location. Device Mobility does not modify any user-specific phone parameters or any IP Phone button settings such as directory numbers or phone services.

The phone configuration parameters that can be dynamically applied to the device configuration are grouped in two categories:

■   Roaming-Sensitive Settings

—Date/Time Group

—Region

—Location

—Connection Monitor Duration

NOTE   The Date/Time Group, Region, Location, and Connection Monitor Duration are configured at device pools only.

—Network Locale

—SRST Reference

—Media Resource Group List (MRGL)

NOTE   The Network Locale, SRST Reference, and Media Resource Group List are overlapping parameters; that is, they can be configured at phones and device pools.

—Physical Location

—Device Mobility Group

NOTE   The Physical Location and Device Mobility Group parameters are used to determine which settings should be applied to a roaming phone. The options are none, the roaming-sensitive settings only, or the roaming-sensitive settings and the settings that are related to Device Mobility. They are not phone-configuration parameters themselves, so they are not applied to the phone configuration like the other listed roaming-sensitive settings are. Instead, they are used only at the phone configuration. Consequently, they cannot be overlapping and can be configured only at device pools.

■   Device Mobility-Related Settings

—Device Mobility Calling Search Space

—AAR Calling Search Space

—AAR Group

> **NOTE**   The Device Mobility Calling Search Space, AAR Calling Search Space, and
> AAR Group are overlapping parameters. Therefore, they can be configured at phones
> and device pools. However, the Device Mobility Calling Search Space is called the
> Calling Search Space only in the Phone Configuration window. It does not overlap with
> the calling search space configured at lines. It relates specifically to a phone's device
> calling search space.

Roaming-sensitive settings are settings that do not have an impact on call routing. Device
Mobility-related settings, on the other hand, have a direct impact on call routing, because
they modify the device CSS, AAR group, and AAR CSS. Depending on the implementation
of Device Mobility, roaming-sensitive settings only, or both roaming-sensitive settings and
Device Mobility-related settings, can be applied to a roaming phone.

Device Mobility Dynamic Configuration by Location-Dependent Device Pools

Figure 11-2 illustrates the location-dependent parameters such as roaming-sensitive settings and Device Mobility-related settings that are configured at device pools. Based on the
IP subnet that is used by the phone associated with a device pool, CUCM can choose the
appropriate device pool and apply the location-dependent parameters. With the introduc-
tion of Device Mobility, CUCM is aware of the physical location of a device based on its
IP address within its subnet and applies the appropriate location-specific configuration by
selecting the corresponding device pool.

Figure 11-2   *Device Mobility with a Dynamic Configuration by Location-Dependent Device Pools*

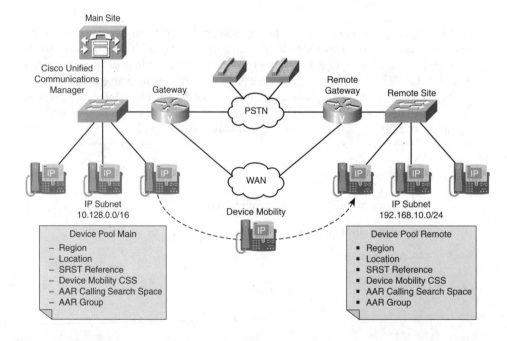

Device Mobility Configuration Elements

Table 11-2 lists the Device Mobility-related configuration elements and describes their functions. The newly introduced elements are Device Mobility Info (DMI), Physical Location (PL), and Device Mobility Group (DMG).

Table 11-2 *Device Configuration Element Functions*

Configuration Element Name	Configuration Element Function
Device Pool (DP)	Defines a set of common characteristics for devices. The device pool contains only device- and location-related information. One device pool has to be assigned to each device.
Device Mobility Info (DMI)	Specifies an IP subnet and associates it with one or more device pools. DMIs can be associated with one device pool.
Physical Location (PL)	A tag assigned to one or more device pools. It is used to identify whether a device is roaming within a physical location or between physical locations.
Device Mobility Group (DMG)	A tag assigned to one or more device pools. It is used to identify whether a device is roaming within a Device Mobility Group or between Device Mobility Groups.

The DMI is configured with a name and an IP subnet and is associated with one or more device pools. Multiple DMIs can be associated with the same device pool.

The Physical Location and the Device Mobility Group are just tags. They are configured with a name only and do not include any other configuration settings. Both are nonmandatory device pool configuration parameters. Therefore, at the device pool you can choose no physical location or one physical location and one or no Device Mobility Group. They are used to determine whether two device pools are at the same physical location and/or in the same Device Mobility Group.

The Relationship Between Device Mobility Configuration Elements

Figure 11-3 shows how the different Device Mobility configuration elements relate to each other.

Figure 11-3 *Relationship Between Device Mobility Configuration Elements*

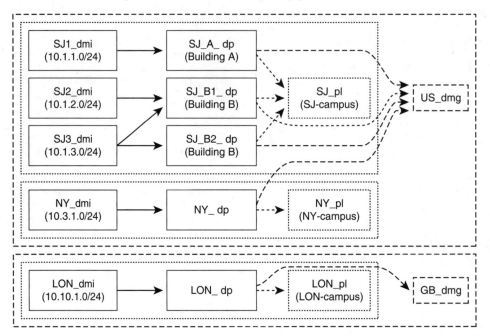

The figure shows five DMIs for three physical locations—San Jose, New York, and London. They are configured as follows:

- **SJ1_dmi:** The IP subnet of this Device Mobility Info is 10.1.1.0/24. This DMI is used at Building A of the San Jose campus and is associated with DP SJ_A_dp.

- **SJ2_dmi:** The IP subnet of this DMI is 10.1.2.0/24. This DMI is used at Building B1 of the San Jose campus and is associated with device pool SJ_B1_dp.

- **SJ3_dmi:** The IP subnet of this DMI is 10.1.3.0/24. Like SJ2_dmi, this DMI is used at Building B1, which is associated with device pool SJ_B1_dp, but it is also used at Building B2 and is associated with device pool SJ_B2_dp.

- **NY_dmi:** The IP subnet of this DMI is 10.3.1.0/24. This DMI is used at the New York campus and is associated with device pool NY_dp.

- **LON_dmi:** The IP subnet of this DMI is 10.10.1.0/24. This DMI is used at the London campus and is associated with device pool LON_dp.

Device pools SJ_A_dp, SJ_B1_dp, and SJ_B2_dp are all configured with the same physical location (SJ_pl) because they are all used for devices located at the San Jose campus.

Device pool NY_dp, serving the New York campus, is configured with physical location NY_pl. Device pool LON_dp, serving the London campus, is configured with physical location LON_pl.

All device pools that are assigned with a U.S. physical location (that is, SJ_A_dp, SJ_B1_dp, SJ_B2_dp, and NY_dp) are configured with Device Mobility Group US_dmg. This setting means that all U.S. device pools are in the same Device Mobility Group. The London campus is in a different DMG: GB_dmg.

In summary, the U.S. Device Mobility Group consists of two physical locations: San Jose and New York. At San Jose, IP subnets 10.1.1.0/24, 10.1.2.0/24, and 10.1.3.0/24 are used; New York uses IP subnet 10.3.1.0/24, and London is configured with IP subnet 10.10.1.0/24. Device Mobility Groups are used to recognize differences in dial patterns in different geographic locations.

Based on the IP address of an IP Phone, CUCM can determine one or more associated device pools and the physical location and Device Mobility Group of the device pool or pools. If an IP Phone uses an IP address of IP subnet 10.1.3.0/24, the device pool has two candidates. However, in this example, the physical location and Device Mobility Group are the same for these two device pools.

Device Mobility Operation

As discussed earlier, each phone is configured with a device pool, similar to previous versions of Cisco CallManager (CCM). This device pool is the phone's home device pool.

IP subnets are associated with device pools by configuring DMIs.

The following occurs when a Device Mobility-enabled phone registers with CUCM with an IP address that matches an IP subnet configured in a DMI:

- The current device pool is chosen as follows:

    —If the DMI is associated with the phone's home device pool, the phone is considered to be in its home location. Therefore, Device Mobility does not reconfigure the phone.

    —If the DMI is associated with one or more device pools other than the phone's home device pool, one of the associated device pools is chosen based on a round-robin load-sharing algorithm.

■ If the current device pool is different from the home device pool, the following checks are performed:

—If the physical locations are not different, the phone's configuration is not modified.

—If the physical locations are different, the roaming-sensitive parameters of the current roaming device pool are applied.

—If the Device Mobility Groups are the same, in addition to different physical locations, the Device Mobility-related settings are also applied, along with the roaming-sensitive parameters.

In summary, the roaming-sensitive parameters are applied when the physical location of the current device pool is different from the physical location of the home device pool. The Device Mobility-related settings are also applied when the physical locations are different and the Device Mobility Groups are the same. This occurs when roaming between physical locations within the same Device Mobility Group.

As a consequence, physical locations and Device Mobility Groups should be used as follows:

■ **Physical locations:** Configure physical locations in such a way that codec choice and CAC truly reflect the device's current location. Also, local SRST references and local media resources at the roaming site should be used instead of those located at the currently remote home network. Depending on the network structure, subnetting, and allocation of services, you may define physical locations based on a city, enterprise campus, or building.

■ **Device Mobility Groups:** A Device Mobility Group should define a group of sites with similar dialing patterns or dialing behavior. Device Mobility Groups represent the highest-level geographic entities in your network. Depending on the network size and scope, your Device Mobility Groups could represent countries, regions, states or provinces, cities, or other geographic entities. Device Mobility-related settings that are applied only when roaming within the same Device Mobility Group impact call routing. Therefore, different Device Mobility Groups should be set up whenever a roaming user should not be forced to adapt his dialing behavior. In this case, when roaming between different Device Mobility Groups, the phone Device Mobility-related settings that impact call routing are not modified.

Device Mobility Operation Flowchart

Figure 11-4 illustrates the flow of Device Mobility operation.

Figure 11-4   *Device Mobility Operation Flowchart*

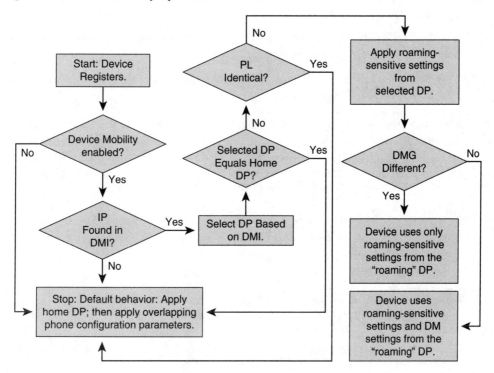

The process of a phone registration with Device Mobility is as follows:

1. A phone device attempts to register with CUCM. Phones that do not register with CUCM cannot be part of the CUCM cluster and therefore do not have any Device Mobility configuration. If the phone successfully registers to a CUCM server, continue.

2. CUCM checks whether Device Mobility is enabled for the device. If it isn't, the default behavior applies; go to Step 10. Otherwise, continue.

3. CUCM checks whether the IP address of the IP Phone is found in one of the Device Mobility Groups (DMG). If it is not found, the default behavior applies; go to Step 10. Otherwise, continue.

4. If the home device pool (DP) is associated with the DMI in which the phone's IP address was found, the home device pool is chosen. If the home device pool is not associated with the DMI in which the phone's IP address was found, the device pool is chosen based on a load-sharing algorithm. The load-sharing algorithm applies if more than one device pool is associated with the DMI.

5. If the chosen device pool is the home device pool, the default behavior applies; go to Step 10. Otherwise, continue.

6. If the physical locations (PL) of the chosen device pool and the home device pool are the same, the default behavior applies; go to Step 10. Otherwise, continue.

7. The roaming-sensitive settings of the chosen device pool of the roaming device pool are used to update the phone's configuration.

> **NOTE**   In this case, overlapping settings that exist at the phone as well as at the device pool (namely, Media Resource Group List, Location, and Network Locale of the roaming device pool) have priority over the corresponding settings at the phone. This behavior is different from the default behavior of Step 10.

8. If the Device Mobility Groups (DMG) of the chosen device pool and the home device pool are different, the device uses only the roaming-sensitive settings from the "roaming" DP. If they are not different, the device uses the roaming settings and the Device Mobility (DM) settings from the "roaming" DP.

> **NOTE**   In this case, all settings are overlapping settings that are Device Mobility-related settings that exist at the phone as well as at the device pool. Therefore, the parameters of the roaming device pool have priority over the corresponding settings at the phone. This behavior is different from the default behavior in Step 10.

9. Next, where the phone configuration has been updated with either the roaming-sensitive settings only, or with the roaming-sensitive settings and the Device Mobility-related settings, the phone is reset for the updated configuration to be applied to the phone.

> **CAUTION**   This is the end of the process. Step 10 applies only in the conditions outlined in the previous steps.

10. The default behavior is the settings of the home device pool (DP), which is the device pool configured on the phone. Some configuration parameters of the device pool can also be set individually at the phone. These overlapping phone configuration parameters are the Media Resource Group List, Location, Network Locale, Device Mobility Calling Search Space (which is just called Calling Search Space at the phone), AAR Calling Search Space, and AAR Group. If these are configured at the phone, implying they are not set to [None], the phone configuration settings have priority over the corresponding setting at the device pool.

Device Mobility Considerations

Roaming-sensitive settings ensure that the roaming device uses local media resources and SRST references. In addition, they ensure the correct use of codecs and CAC between sites. Typically, this is always desired when a device roams between different sites. It is not required when the device moves only between IP subnets within the same site. Therefore, the recommendation is to assign all device pools that are associated with IP subnets (DMI) that are used at the same site to the same physical location. This results in phone configuration changes only when the phone roams between sites (physical locations) and not in a situation where a phone is only moved between different networks of the same site.

Device Mobility-related settings impact call routing. By applying the device CSS, AAR group, and AAR, CSS calls are routed differently. The settings at the roaming device pool determine which gateway will be used for PSTN access and AAR PSTN calls based on the device CSS and AAR CSS. They also determine how the number to be used for AAR calls is composed based on the AAR group.

Such changes can result in different dialing behavior. For instance, when you roam between different countries, the PSTN access code and PSTN numbering plans might be different. For example, to dial the Austrian destination +43 699 18900009, users in Germany dial 0.0043 699 18900009, whereas users in the U.S. have to dial 9.01143 699 18900009.

German users who roam with their softphones to the U.S. might be confused when they have to use U.S. dialing rules access code 9 instead of 0 and 011 instead of 00 for international numbers. To prevent this confusion, suppress the application of Device Mobility-related settings. You do this by assigning device pools that are to be used at sites with different dialing rules to different Device Mobility Groups and different physical locations. Now, when a user roams with a device from Germany to the U.S., all the roaming-sensitive settings are applied, but the Device Mobility-related settings are not applied. The phone now uses the PSTN gateway and dial rules of its home location even though the user moved to another site. The user does not have to adapt to the dial rules of the local site to which the phone was moved.

Review of Line and Device CSSs

An IP Phone can be configured with a line CSS and a device CSS. If both exist, the partitions configured to the line CSS are considered before the partitions of the device CSS when routing a call. (This is another example of "more specific overrides more general.")

These two CSSs allow the use of the line/device approach for implementing calling privileges and the choice of a local gateway for PSTN calls. With the line/device approach, all possible PSTN route patterns exist once per location, which is configured with a site-specific partition. This partition is included in the device CSS of the phones and therefore enables the use of a local gateway for PSTN calls. To implement class of service (CoS), PSTN route patterns that should not be available to all users (for example, international calls, long-distance calls, or all toll calls) are configured as blocked route patterns and are assigned to separate partitions. The line CSS of a phone now includes the partitions of the route patterns that should be blocked for this phone. Because the line CSS has priority over the device CSS, the blocked pattern takes precedence over the routed pattern that is found in a partition listed at the device CSS.

Device Mobility and CSSs

Device Mobility never modifies the line CSS of a phone. It does, however, change the device CSS and AAR CSS of a phone when the phone is roaming between different physical locations within the same Device Mobility Group.

The line CSS implements CoS configuration by permitting internal destinations such as phone directory numbers, Call Park, and Meet-Me conferences but blocking PSTN destinations. Because the line CSS is not changed by Device Mobility, CoS settings of the device are kept when the device is roaming.

The device CSS is modified when roaming within the same Device Mobility Group. In this case, the device CSS that is used at the home location is replaced by a device CSS that is applicable to the roaming location. This device CSS refers to the local gateway of the roaming site instead of the gateway that is used at the home location.

If the traditional approach of using only one CSS combining class of service and gateway choice is used, the device CSS must be used, because Device Mobility cannot modify the line CSS, and the line CSS has priority over the device CSS. These settings can be modified by Device Mobility.

The AAR CSS can be configured only at the device level. Therefore, it is always correctly replaced when roaming between physical locations within the same Device Mobility Group.

Examples of Different Call-Routing Paths Based on Device Mobility Groups and TEHO

Table 11-3 shows how calls are routed in different Device Mobility scenarios.

Calls are routed differently depending on the configuration of Device Mobility Groups. Call-routing factors depend on whether Device Mobility-related settings are applied, the dialed destination, and the use of tail-end hop-off (TEHO). In some scenarios, calls might take suboptimal paths.

Table 11-3 *Examples of Different Call-Routing Paths Based on Device Mobility Groups and TEHO*

Scenario	Result
Same DMG, call to PSTN destination close to home location, no TEHO.	The call uses the *local PSTN gateway* at the roaming location to place a *long-distance PSTN* call.
Same DMG, call to PSTN destination close to home location, TEHO.	The call uses the IP WAN to the gateway at the home location to place a local PSTN call.
Same DMG, call to PSTN destination close to roaming location.	The call uses the local PSTN gateway at the roaming location to place a local PSTN call.
Different DMG, call to PSTN destination close to home location.	The call uses the IP WAN to the gateway at the home location to place a local PSTN call.
Different DMG, call to PSTN destination close to roaming location, no TEHO.	The call uses the *IP WAN to the gateway* at the home location to place a *long-distance PSTN* call.
Different DMG, call to PSTN destination close to roaming location, TEHO.	The call uses the local PSTN gateway at the roaming location to place a local PSTN call.

For example, assume that a user from London roams to the U.S. office with Cisco IP Communicator. For simplicity, assume that there is only one U.S. office.

For the following three scenarios, the home device pool and the roaming device pool are assigned to the same Device Mobility Group, which means that Device Mobility applies Device Mobility-related settings. As a result, PSTN calls placed from the roaming device are treated like PSTN calls of standard U.S. phones.

- If a call to a PSTN destination close to the home location such as a U.K. PSTN number is placed and TEHO is not configured, the call uses the local U.S. PSTN gateway to place an international PSTN call. From a toll perspective, this is a suboptimal solution, because the IP WAN is not used as much as it could be when implementing TEHO. This factor applies not only to the roaming user, but also to U.S. users who place calls to PSTN destinations in Great Britain.

- If the same call to a U.K. PSTN number is placed and TEHO is configured, the call uses the IP WAN to the London site and breaks out to the PSTN at the London gateway with a local call. This solution is the optimal one from a toll perspective.

- If a call to a U.S. destination number is placed, the U.S. gateway is used for a local or national call. This event is optimal from a toll perspective.

NOTE   In all the examples shown that are based on Table 11-3, the user has to dial PSTN destinations by following the NANP dial rules.

For the next three scenarios, the home device pool and the roaming device pool are assigned to different Device Mobility Groups. This means that the Device Mobility-related settings are not applied. Therefore, calls placed from the roaming device are routed the same way as they are when the device is in its home location:

■   If a call from the U.S. to a U.K. PSTN destination is placed, the call uses the IP WAN to the London site and breaks out to the PSTN at the London gateway with a local or national call. This solution is the optimal one from a toll perspective.

■   If a call from the U.S. to a PSTN destination close to the roaming location such as a U.S. PSTN number is placed and TEHO is not configured, the call uses the IP WAN from the U.S. office to the London site and breaks out to the PSTN at the London gateway to place an international call back to the U.S. From a toll perspective, this is the worst possible solution, because the call first goes from the U.S. to London over the IP WAN, wasting bandwidth, and then goes back from London to the U.S. via a costly international call.

■   If a call from the U.S. to a PSTN destination close to the roaming location such as a U.S. PSTN number is placed and TEHO is configured, the U.S. gateway is used for a local or national call. This event is optimal from a toll perspective.

NOTE   In these three examples, the user has to dial PSTN destinations by following the dial rules of the home location (the U.K.).

In summary, when allowing the Device Mobility-related settings to be applied by using the same Device Mobility Group, calls to the home location use a local PSTN gateway to place a long-distance or international call when not implementing TEHO. All other calls are optimal.

When the Device Mobility-related settings are not applied by using different Device Mobility Groups and by not using TEHO, calls to the roaming location first use the IP WAN to go from the roaming location to the home location and then use the home gateway to place a long-distance or international call back to the roaming location. All other calls are optimal.

Device Mobility Configuration

The following steps describe how to configure Device Mobility:

Step 1   Configure physical locations.

Step 2   Configure Device Mobility Groups.

Step 3   Configure device pools.

Step 4   Configure DMIs (that is, IP subnets).

Step 5   Set the Device Mobility mode using the following:

* A Cisco CallManager service parameter to set the default for all phones.

* The Phone Configuration window for an individual configuration for each phone.

Steps 1 and 2: Configure Physical Locations and Device Mobility Groups

To configure physical locations and Device Mobility Groups, as shown in Figure 11-5, in CUCM choose **System > Physical Location**. For each physical location, a name and a description are configured. Device Mobility Groups are configured under **System > Device Mobility > Device Mobility Group**. For each Device Mobility Group, a name and description are configured.

Figure 11-5   *Steps 1 and 2: Configure Physical Locations and Device Mobility Groups*

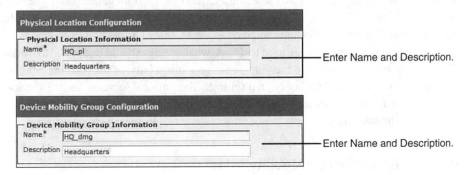

Step 3: Configure Device Pools

To configure a device pool when Device Mobility is used, as shown in Figure 11-6, in CUCM choose **System > Device Pool**.

Figure 11-6 *Step 3: Configure Device Pools*

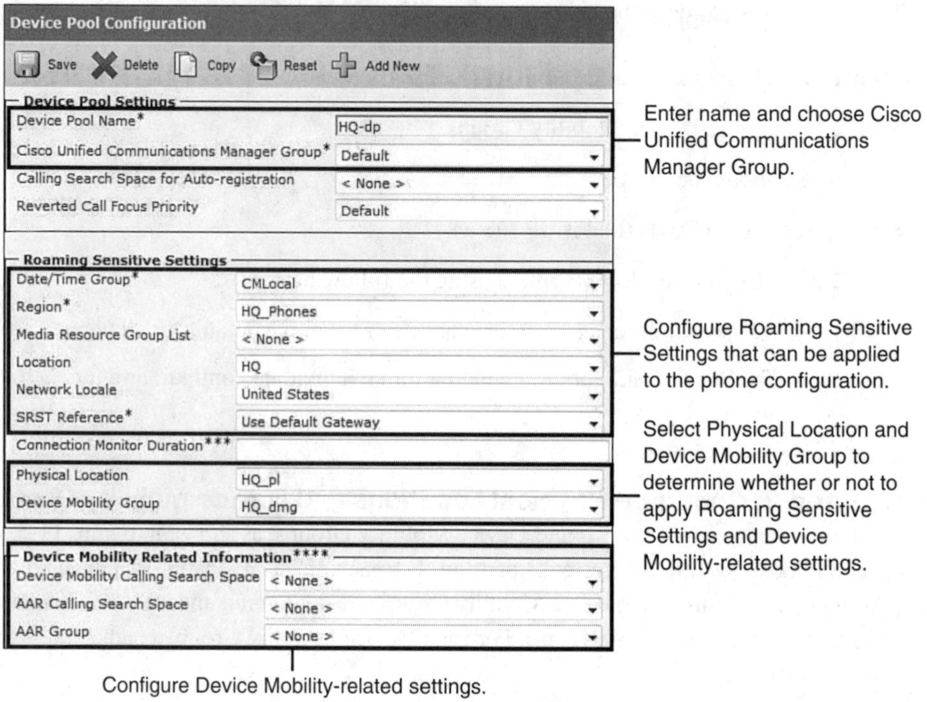

Configure Device Mobility-related settings.

A device pool is configured with a name and a CUCM group. It includes roaming-sensitive settings and Device Mobility-related settings configured under **Device Mobility Related Information**. The physical location and the Device Mobility Group, both configured under **Roaming Sensitive Settings**, are used to decide what settings should be applied to a phone. The options are no settings, the roaming-sensitive settings only, or the roaming-sensitive settings and the Device Mobility-related settings. The physical location and the Device Mobility Group themselves are not applied to the configuration of a phone but are used only to control which settings to apply.

Step 4: Configure Device Mobility Infos

To configure a device pool when Device Mobility is used, as shown in Figure 11-7, in CUCM choose **System > Device Mobility > Device Mobility Info**. The DMIs are configured with a name, a subnet, and a subnet mask. Then they are associated with one or more device pools.

Figure 11-7 *Step 4: Configure Device Mobility Infos*

Device Mobility Info
Configuration

— Device Mobility Info Information —

Name*	HQ_dmi
Subnet*	10.1.2.0
Subnet Mask*	24

Enter Name, Subnet,
and Subnet Mask.

— Device Pools for this Device Mobility Info —

Available Device Pools   Default

Selected Device Pools*   HQ-dp

Assign Device Mobility Info
to device pool(s).

Step 5a: Set the Device Mobility Mode CCM Service Parameter

Device Mobility is off by default and can be configured per phone. The default for the Device Mobility mode, if it's not set differently at the phone, is set under **System > Service Parameter**, as shown in Figure 11-8. Choose the **Cisco CallManager** service, and set the **Device Mobility Mode** to **On** or **Off**. Note that **Off** is the default. The parameter is found in the **Clusterwide Parameters (Device - Phone)** section.

> **TIP** There are quite a few entries in CUCM under **System > Service Parameter** after you choose **Cisco CallManager**. Press Ctrl-F in Internet Explorer and search for the specific title or entry.

Figure 11-8 *Step 5a: Set the Device Mobility Mode CCM Service Parameter*

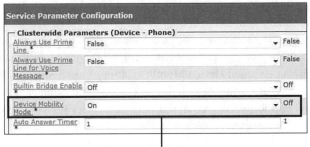

Service Parameter Configuration

— Clusterwide Parameters (Device - Phone) —

Always Use Prime Line *	False	False
Always Use Prime Line for Voice Message *	False	False
Builtin Bridge Enable *	Off	Off
Device Mobility Mode *	On	Off
Auto Answer Timer *	1	1

Set the default Device Mobility mode for all phones.

Step 5b: Set the Device Mobility Mode for Individual Phones

As shown in Figure 11-9, you set the Device Mobility mode per phone by choosing **Device > Phone**.

Figure 11-9 *Step 5b: Set the Device Mobility Mode for Individual Phones*

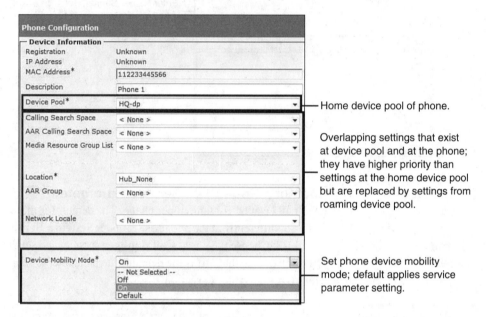

In the Phone Configuration window, you enable or disable Device Mobility for the phone by either setting the **Device Mobility Mode** to **On** or **Off** or leaving the default value **Default**. If the Device Mobility mode is set to **Default**, the Device Mobility mode is set at the **Cisco CallManager service** parameter.

Figure 11-9 also shows the configuration of the overlapping parameters, which are parameters that can be configured at both the phone and the device pool. The overlapping parameters for roaming-sensitive settings are Media Resource Group List, Location, and Network Locale. The overlapping parameters for the Device Mobility-related settings are Calling Search Space (called Device Mobility Calling Search Space at the device pool), AAR Group, and AAR Calling Search Space. Overlapping parameters configured at the phone have higher priority than settings at the home device pool and lower priority than settings at the roaming device pool.

Summary

The following key points were discussed in this chapter:

- Issues with roaming devices include inappropriate region, location, time zone, and SRST reference configuration. PSTN calls use the home gateway instead of the local gateway at the roaming site.

- Device Mobility allows roaming devices to be identified by their IP addresses. It also allows configuration settings to be applied that are suitable for the device's current physical location.

- Device Mobility configuration elements are Device Mobility Groups, physical locations, device pools, and DMIs.

- Roaming-sensitive settings are applied to devices that roam between physical locations. In addition, Device Mobility-related settings are applied to devices that roam within the same Device Mobility Group.

- After you configure Device Mobility Groups, physical locations, device pools, and DMIs, you need to enable Device Mobility either clusterwide as a service parameter or individually per phone.

References

For additional information, refer to these resources:

- Cisco Systems, Inc., Cisco Unified Communications Solution Reference Network Design (SRND), based on CUCM Release 6.x, June 2007

- Cisco Systems, Inc., *CUCM Administration Guide Release 6.0(1)*

Review Questions

Use these questions to review what you've learned in this chapter. The answers appear in Appendix A, "Answers to Chapter Review Questions."

1. Which setting is not modified on an IP Communicator when a user roams between sites when Device Mobility is enabled?

   a. Region

   b. Directory number

   c. Location

   d. SRST reference

2. Which two statements about the relationship between Device Mobility configuration elements are true?

    a. Device Mobility Infos refer to one or more device pools.

    b. Device pools refer to one or more physical locations.

    c. Device pools refer to one Device Mobility Group.

    d. Device pools refer to one Device Mobility Info.

    e. Physical locations refer to Device Mobility Groups.

3. Which statement about Device Mobility operation is false?

    a. A device pool is selected based on the device's IP address.

    b. If the selected device pool is the home device pool, no changes are made.

    c. If the selected device pool is in a different Device Mobility Group than the home device pool, the Device Mobility-related settings of the roaming device pool are applied.

    d. If the selected device pool is in a different physical location than the home device pool, the roaming-sensitive settings of the roaming device pool are applied.

4. If no physical location is configured at the device pool, the physical location configured at the phone is used.

    a. True

    b. False

5. Which two of the following are valid issues that Device Mobility fixes by changing the settings for roaming (mobile) phones in CUCM v6?

    a. SRST References for mobile phones are dynamically assigned.

    b. Phone speed dials for mobile phones are dynamically assigned.

    c. Phone services for mobile phones are dynamically assigned.

    d. Region settings for mobile phones are dynamically assigned.

    e. Call Forward settings for mobile phones are dynamically assigned.

6. Which of the following statements about Device Mobility is the most accurate?

    a. Device Mobility is essentially the same as Extension Mobility.

    b. Device Mobility has been available in CUCM and CCM since version 3.0.

    c. Device Mobility is a new feature added in CUCM.

    d. Device Mobility greatly enhances Cisco IP Phone services for mobile users.

7. What is the correct configuration relationship between Device Pools and Device Mobility in CUCM?

  a. IP Phones may optionally be configured to use Device Pools when enabling Device Mobility.

  b. IP Phones must be configured to use Device Pools when enabling Device Mobility.

  c. Device pools can optionally be configured to work with Device Mobility.

  d. Device pools are not used when enabling Device Mobility.

8. Which statement about configuring Device Mobility in a CUCM cluster is true?

  a. Device Mobility is enabled by default in the cluster and must be enabled for devices in CUCM v6.

  b. Device Mobility is disabled by default and must be enabled for the CUCM Cluster and then configured for individual devices in CUCM v6.

  c. Device Mobility is enabled by default in the cluster and must be enabled for devices in all versions of CCM and CUCM.

  d. Device Mobility is disabled by default and must be enabled for the CUCM Cluster and then configured for individual devices in all versions of CCM and CUCM.

9. Which three of the following are valid Device Mobility Configuration Elements?

  a. Device pool

  b. Region

  c. Physical location

  d. Device Mobility Group

  e. CUCM server

  f. Cisco IP Phone

CHAPTER 12

Implementing Extension Mobility

In multisite environments, it is common for some users to roam between sites on a regular basis. When such users use phones that are provided at the sites they visit, they would like to, but traditionally cannot, use their personal phone settings, such as their directory number, speed dials, calling privileges, and Message Waiting Indication (MWI). A Unified Communications solution can solve this problem.

This chapter describes Extension Mobility, a feature of CUCM that allows CUCM users to log in to an IP Phone and get their personal profile applied, regardless of the device and physical location that they are using.

Chapter Objectives

Upon completing this chapter, you will be able to describe and configure Extension Mobility to allow roaming users to log in to any device and have the device reconfigured with their personal settings. You will be able to meet these objectives:

- Identify issues with users roaming between sites

- Describe the Cisco Extension Mobility feature

- Describe the Cisco Extension Mobility configuration elements and their interaction

- Describe Cisco Extension Mobility operation

- Configure and implement Cisco Extension Mobility

Issues with Users Roaming Between Sites

Chapter 11, "Implementing Device Mobility," addressed the situation when users travel to other sites within their organization and bring their phone, such as IP communicator on their laptop, with them. This chapter addresses issues that can occur if users temporarily change their workplace and roam between different sites but do not travel with a device and instead use any available phone at the current location. When users roam between sites and do not have their phone with them (see Figure 12-1), they might want to use any available phone at the site they have traveled to. Some organizations call this "hoteling" and often provide offices or cubicles for traveling employees.

Figure 12-1 *Roaming Users*

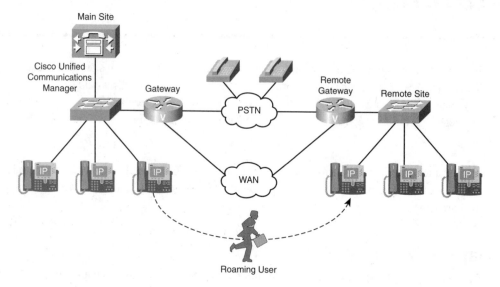

Issues with Roaming Users

Without Extension Mobility, when a user uses a different guest phone in a different site, this leads to the following issues:

- Extensions are traditionally bound to constant devices.

- The user gets the wrong extension on that phone.

- The user gets the wrong calling privileges.

- The user does not have speed dials available.

- The user has the wrong services assigned.

- Message Waiting Indicator (MWI) status does not work with a different extension.

To effectively address these issues, the user would require CUCM to reconfigure the phone that is used with user-specific configuration instead of having device-specific settings applied to the phone.

Extension Mobility Solves Issues of Roaming Users

Extension Mobility offers functionality that is designed to enhance the mobility of users within a CUCM cluster. It also resolves the issues of roaming users with Extension Mobility, which are summarized in Table 12-1.

Table 12-1 *Extension Mobility Solves Issues of Roaming Users*

Issue Without Extension Mobility	Extension Mobility Feature to Solve the Issue
Extensions are bound to physical devices.	Extensions are bound to device profiles.
Speed dials are assigned to physical devices.	Speed dials are assigned to device profiles.
Services are assigned to physical devices.	Services are assigned to device profiles.
MWI status is defined for physical devices.	MWI status is updated during Extension Mobility login.
Calling privileges are defined for physical devices and locations.	Calling privileges result from merging line settings (device-based) and physical device settings (location-related).

Although the device is not the user's home device, it is reconfigured with user-specific settings that are stored in profiles. This action lets you separate user-specific parameters configured in user profiles from device-specific parameters that are still stored at the phone configuration along with default values for user-specific settings. The phone adapts some of its behavior based on the individual user who is currently using the phone.

The configuration changes are triggered by a user login where the user is identified by a user ID and PIN. The phone configuration adapts to the individual user. When the user stops using the phone, he or she logs out, and the default configuration is reapplied.

The use of profiles on a Cisco IP Phone is analogous to a user profile on a computer on most desktop operating systems. When two or more different users share the same computer, their login profile customizes their desktop for settings such as wallpaper, desktop icons, taskbar settings, and so on. Similarly, when two or more traveling users share the same Cisco IP Phone, their login profile customizes their phone settings and functionality.

CUCM Extension Mobility Overview

CUCM Extension Mobility allows users to log in to any phone and get their individual user-specific phone configuration applied to that phone. Thus, users can be reached at their personal directory number, regardless of their location or the physical phone they are using. Extension Mobility is implemented as a phone service and works within a single CUCM cluster.

The user-specific configuration is stored in device profiles. After successful login, the phone is reconfigured with user-specific parameters, and other device-specific parameters remain the same. If a user is associated with multiple device profiles, he or she must choose the device profile to be used.

If a user logs in with a user ID that is still logged in at another device, one of the following options can be configured:

- **Allow multiple logins:** When this method is configured, the user profile is applied to the phone where the user is logging in, and the same configuration remains active at the device where the user logged in before. The line number or numbers become shared lines because they are active on multiple devices.

- **Deny login:** In this case, the user gets an error message. Login is successful only after the user logs out at the other device where he or she logged in before.

- **Auto-logout:** Like the preceding option, this option ensures that a user can be logged in on only one device at a time. However, it allows the new login by automatically logging out the user at the other device.

On a phone that is configured for Extension Mobility, either another device profile that is a logout device profile can be applied, or the parameters as configured at the phone are applied. The logout itself can be triggered by the user or enforced by the system after expiration of a maximum login time.

Extension Mobility: Dynamic Phone Configuration Parameters

Two types of configuration parameters are dynamically configured when CUCM Extension Mobility is used:

- **User-specific device-level parameters:** These are user-specific phone configuration parameters such as user Music On Hold (MOH) audio source, phone button templates, softkey templates, user locales, Do Not Disturb (DND), privacy settings, and phone service subscriptions. All these parameters are configured at the device level of an IP Phone.

- **Configuration of phone buttons, including lines:** All phone buttons—not only the button types as specified in the phone button template but also the complete configuration of the phone buttons—are updated by Extension Mobility. This update includes all configured lines, with all the line-configuration settings, speed dials, service URLs, Call Park buttons, and any other buttons that are configured in the device profile that is to be applied.

Extension Mobility with Dynamic Phone Configuration by Device Profiles

Figure 12-2 illustrates how user-specific settings roam with the user when the user logs out of one phone at the main site and then logs in to an Extension Mobility-enabled phone located at the remote site.

Figure 12-2 *Extension Mobility Dynamic Phone Configuration by Device Profiles*

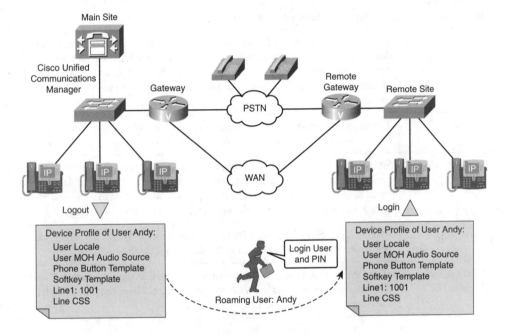

As shown in the figure, the user-specific parameters, such as device-level parameters and all phone button settings including line configurations, are configured in device profiles. Based on the user ID entered during login, CUCM can apply the user's personal device profile and reconfigure the phone with the configuration profile of the individual user who logs in.

With Extension Mobility, CUCM is aware of the end user sitting behind a device and applies the appropriate user-specific configuration based on a device profile associated with the logged-in user.

CUCM Extension Mobility Configuration Elements

Table 12-2 lists the configuration elements related to Extension Mobility and describes their functions. The configuration elements that are introduced with Extension Mobility are the device profile and the default device profile.

Table 12-2 *Extension Mobility Configuration Elements*

Configuration Element Name	Configuration Element Function
Phone	Stores the configuration of physical phones. Configuration parameters include device-specific phone parameters (such as device CSS, location, or MRGL), user-specific phone parameters (such as user MOH audio source, DND, or softkey template), and (user-specific) button configuration (such as lines or speed dials).
End user	The end user is associated with one or more device profiles. The user ID and the PIN are used to log in to a phone with Extension Mobility.
Device profile	Stores user-specific phone configuration in logical profiles. Configuration parameters include user-specific phone and button parameters (such as lines and speed dials). The parameters of the device profile are applied to a physical phone after a user logs in to the phone using Extension Mobility.
Phone service	Extension Mobility is implemented as a phone service. Hardware phones and device profiles have to be subscribed to the service.
Default device profile	Stores the default device configuration parameters that should be applied when the phone model of a user's device profile is different from the phone model of the phone where the user logs in.

The device profile is configured with all user-specific settings that are found at the device level of an IP Phone, such as user MOH audio source, phone button templates, softkey templates, user locales, DND and privacy settings, phone service subscriptions, and all phone buttons, including lines and speed dials. One or more device profiles are applied to an end user in the End User Configuration window.

The default device profile stores default device configuration parameters that are applied by Extension Mobility when there is a mismatch between the actual phone model where the user logs in and the phone model configured in the user's device profile. The default device profile exists once per phone model type and per protocol for SIP and SCCP. All the parameters that cannot be applied from the user's device profile are taken from the default device profile.

For example, a user is associated with a device profile for a Cisco Unified IP Phone 7940 running SCCP. If this user logs on to a Cisco Unified IP Phone 7961 running SIP, some features exist on the target phone that cannot be configured at the Cisco Unified IP Phone 7940 device profile. In this case, the configuration parameters that are unavailable on the user's device profile are taken from the default device profile of the Cisco Unified IP Phone 7940 SCCP.

If a device profile includes more parameters than are supported on the target phone, the additional settings are ignored when the target phone with the user-specific settings is reconfigured.

> **NOTE**   For ease of administration, configuration is much simpler if an organization chooses and standardizes a single Cisco IP Phone model at its different locations for Extension Mobility.

The Relationship Between Extension Mobility Configuration Elements

As shown in Figure 12-3, an end user is associated with one or more device profiles. For each possible IP Phone model, whether SCCP or SIP, a default device profile can be configured. Because Extension Mobility is implemented as an IP Phone service, all phones that should support Extension Mobility must be subscribed to the Extension Mobility phone service to allow a user to log in to the phone. In addition, each device profile has to be subscribed to the Extension Mobility phone service. This subscription is required to allow a user to log out of a phone.

Figure 12-3   *Relationship Between Extension Mobility Configuration Elements*

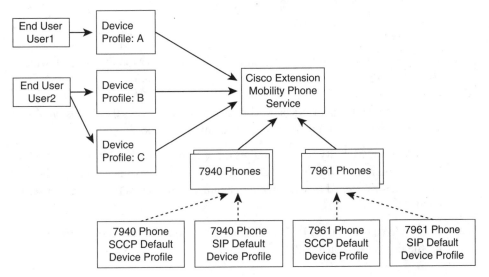

The Cisco IP Phone models 7940 and 7961 are shown as an example in Figure 12-3, but they are not the only Cisco IP Phones supported in CUCM for Extension Mobility.

CUCM Extension Mobility Operation

The following steps, illustrated in Figure 12-4, describe how Extension Mobility works, how phone model mismatches are handled, and how calling search spaces and partitions are updated when CUCM Extension Mobility is used.

Figure 12-4 *Extension Mobility Login Process*

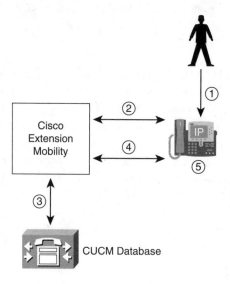

When a phone user wants to log in to a phone with Extension Mobility, the following sequence of events occurs:

1. The user presses the **Services** button on the phone and chooses the Extension Mobility service from the list of phone services available at the phone.

2. The Extension Mobility service requires the user to log in using his or her user ID and PIN. The user enters the required data on the phone by pressing each phone button as many times as needed to select the alphanumeric characters for his or her user ID and PIN.

3. If the entered user ID and PIN are correct, Extension Mobility chooses the device profile that is associated with the user.

NOTE   If a user is associated with more than one device profile, all associated profiles are displayed, and the user has to choose the desired profile, as illustrated for User2 in Figure 12-3. Assigning multiple profiles to a user means that the user is provided with a separate device profile for each site. Doing this is common when the traditional approach is used to implement Calling Search Spaces (CSS). Extension Mobility updates only the line configuration, including the line CSS, but not the device CSS. To allow the choice of a local gateway for outbound PSTN calls, a different line CSS has to be applied for each site. In such a scenario, the user chooses a site-specific device profile that differs from the device profile that is used at other sites in its line CSS. The line CSS of such site-specific profiles gives access to route patterns that route PSTN calls to the appropriate local gateway to minimize toll charges. Extension Mobility also works well if the more modern approach of gateway selection of PSTN at the device (phone) level and blocking the CSS at the line level is implemented.

4.   CUCM updates the phone configuration with the settings of the chosen device profile. User-specific device-level parameters, lines, and other phone buttons are updated with user-specific settings.

5.   The IP Phone is reset and loads the updated configuration.

At this point the phone can be used just as it would be used in the home location. From the user's phone experience, directory numbers, speed dials, and MWI are all correct, as if the user were still on his or her home desk phone, regardless of the location and the IP Phone that is used.

Users can log out of Extension Mobility by pressing the **Services** button and choosing **Logout** in the Extension Mobility service. If users do not log out themselves, the system automatically logs them out after the maximum login time expires. The administrator can configure the CUCM service parameter for the maximum login time. Users can log out only if the Extension Mobility service has been added to their profile.

Users are also automatically logged out of a phone when they log in to another phone and when CUCM is configured for auto-logout on multiple logins. Another option is that the next user of the phone logs out a previous user to be able to log in and have the phone updated with the settings of that new user. After logout, CUCM reconfigures the phone either with the standard configuration of the IP Phone or by using another device profile, as specified in the Phone Configuration window.

Issues in Environments with Different Phone Models

When different IP Phone models are implemented in a CUCM cluster where Extension Mobility is enabled, an end user may log in to an IP Phone that is a different model than the one configured in the user's device profile, as shown in Figure 12-5.

Figure 12-5 *Logging into a Different Phone Model with Extension Mobility*

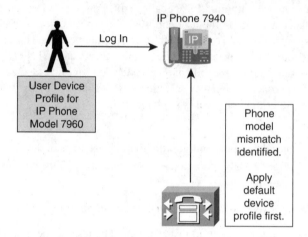

Because different phones support different features, when a user logs in to a phone that supports more features than the model associated with the user, the default device profile is used to apply parameters that are supported by the target phone but that are not included in the user's device profile. The default device profile includes phone configuration parameters such as phone button templates, softkey templates, phone services, and other phone configuration settings, but it does not include line or feature button configurations.

The result is that some phone features available on the user's home desk are unavailable on his remote phone when he logs in with Extension Mobility.

Extension Mobility Solution to Phone Model Differences

After successful authentication, if the phone model of the device profile does not match the phone model of the actually used phone, the following happens:

1. Device-dependent parameters such as the phone button template and softkey template from the default device profile are applied to the phone.

> **NOTE** If the phone button template that is configured in the user's device profile matches the number of buttons on the login device, the system uses the phone button template from the user's device profile. Otherwise, the system uses the phone's default device profile for phone button configuration.

2. The system copies all device-independent configuration settings, such as user hold audio source, user locale, speed dials, and line configuration, from the device profile to the login device. Exceptions are the parameters specified under line settings for this device.

3. The applicable device-dependent parameters of the user's device profile are applied. These parameters include buttons (such as line and feature buttons) based on the phone button template that has been applied from the default device profile.

4. If supported on the login device, phone service subscriptions from the user's device profile are applied to the phone.

5. If the user's device profile does not have phone services configured, the system uses the phone services that are configured in the default device profile of the login device.

For example, the following events occur when a user who has a device profile for a Cisco Unified IP Phone 7960 logs in to a Cisco Unified IP Phone 7905:

1. The personal user hold audio source, user locale, speed dials (if supported by the phone button template configured at the Cisco Unified IP Phone 7905 default device profile), and the user's directory number configuration are applied to the Cisco Unified IP Phone 7905.

2. The user gets the phone button template and the softkey template of the default device profile applied to the Cisco Unified IP Phone 7905.

3. The user has access to the phone services that are configured at the Cisco Unified IP Phone 7905 default device profile.

Extension Mobility and Calling Search Spaces (CSS)

Extension Mobility does not modify the device CSS or the automated alternate routing (AAR) CSS, both of which are configured at the device level. It does replace the line CSS or CSSs configured at the phone with the line CSS or CSSs configured at the device profile of the logged-in user.

Thus, in an implementation that uses the line/device approach, the following applies:

■   The line CSS of the login device is updated with the user's line CSS. This updating is desired to enforce the same CoS settings for the user, independent of the physical device the user logged in on.

■ The device CSS of the login device is not updated, and the same gateways that were initially configured at the phone before the user logged in are used for external route patterns. Because the phone did not physically move, it is desired that the same local gateways are used for PSTN calls, even when a different user is currently logged in to the device.

If the traditional approach is used to implement partitions and CSS, the following applies:

■ If only device CSSs are used, the CSS is not updated, and no user-specific privileges can be applied. The user inherits the privileges configured at the device that is used to log in.

■ If only line CSSs are used, the line CSS configured at the user's device profile replaces the line CSS of the login device. In a multisite environment, this configuration causes problems in terms of gateway choice because the same gateway is always used for external calls.

Alternatives to Mismatching Phone Models and CSS Implementations

To avoid issues with mismatching IP Phone models or with calling privileges (CoS) when the traditional approach toward implementing partitions and calling search spaces is used, multiple device profiles can be configured for each user.

When different phone models are used, issues may arise when the settings of the default device profile are applied, because different users may require different settings. This problem can be solved by creating multiple device profiles for each user. If you configure and associate one device profile per phone model with a username, CUCM displays this list of profiles after successful login, and the user can choose a device profile that matches the phone model of the login device. However, if many users need to be able to use Extension Mobility and many different phone models are used, this solution does not scale well.

The same concept can be used as an alternative to the line/device approach for implementing CSSs. A separate device profile can be created for each site and is configured with the appropriate CSS that allows local gateways to be used for external calls. Again, the user chooses the corresponding device profile after logging in, and the correct CoS and gateway choice are applied without depending on a separate line and device CSS. The recommendation, however, is to use the line/device approach in a multisite environment, because it simplifies the dial plan and scales better.

CUCM Extension Mobility Configuration

The following steps are required to configure Extension Mobility in CUCM. They are explained in detail in the following sections.

Step 1 Activate the Cisco Extension Mobility service in CUCM for the cluster.

Step 2 Set Cisco Extension Mobility service parameters.

Step 3 Add the Cisco Extension Mobility phone service.

Step 4 Create default device profiles for all phone models used.

Step 5 Create device profiles, and subscribe them to the Cisco Extension Mobility phone service.

Step 6 Create end users, and associate them with device profiles.

Step 7 Enable Extension Mobility for phones, and subscribe the phones to the Cisco Extension Mobility service.

Step 1: Activate the Cisco Extension Mobility Feature Service

Activate the Cisco Extension Mobility feature service by choosing **Tools > Service Activation** in CUCM Serviceability, as shown in Figure 12-6. Extension Mobility is disabled by default on a new CUCM Cluster installation.

Figure 12-6 *Step 1: Activate the Cisco Extension Mobility Service*

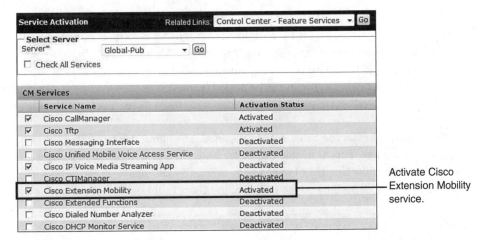

314 Chapter 12: Implementing Extension Mobility

Step 2: Set Cisco Extension Mobility Service Parameters

The Cisco Extension Mobility service has several configurable service parameters. Choose **System > Service Parameters** in CUCM, as shown in Figure 12-7.

Figure 12-7 *Step 2: Set Cisco Extension Mobility Service Parameters*

Choose Server and select Cisco Extension Mobility Service.

| Service Parameter Configuration | Related Links: Parameters for All Servers ▾ Go |

Select Server and Service
Server* Global-Pub (Active)
Service* Cisco Extension Mobility (Active)

All parameters apply only to the current server except parameters that are in the Clusterwide group(s).

Cisco Extension Mobility (Active) Parameters on server Global-Pub (Active)

Parameter Name	Parameter Value	Suggested Value

Clusterwide Parameters (Parameters that apply to all servers)

Enforce Maximum Login Time*	False	False
Maximum Login Time*	8:00	8:00
Multiple Login Behavior*	Multiple Logins Not Allowed	Multiple Logins Not Allowed
Alphanumeric User ID*	True	True
Remember the Last User Logged In*	False	False
Clear Call Log*	False	False

There are hidden parameters in this group. Click on Advanced button to see hidden parameters.

Enable or disable auto-logout after expiration of maximum login time.

Set the multiple login behavior: Allowed, disallowed, or auto-logout.

Enable or disable alphanumeric user IDs, remembering the last logged in user, and clearing the call log on logout.

If the Enforce Maximum Login Time parameter is set to True, the user is automatically logged out after the Maximum Login Time expires. The Multiple Login Behavior parameter specifies how to handle users who log in to a device but are still logged in at another device. Three options exist: Login can be denied, login can be allowed, or the user can be automatically logged out from a phone where he or she logged in earlier and did not log out.

Alphanumeric user IDs can be enabled or disabled. The phone can remember the last logged-in username. This username can be presented as a default on the next login if you set the Remember the Last User Logged In parameter. Finally, call lists can be preserved or cleared at logout, depending on the setting of the Clear Call Log service parameter.

> **NOTE** All of these parameters are clusterwide service parameters of the Cisco Extension Mobility service. You can access them from CUCM Administration by choosing **System > Service Parameters**.

Step 3: Add the Cisco Extension Mobility Phone Service

Add the Cisco Extension Mobility phone service, as shown in Figure 12-8.

Figure 12-8 *Step 3: Add the Cisco Extension Mobility Phone Service*

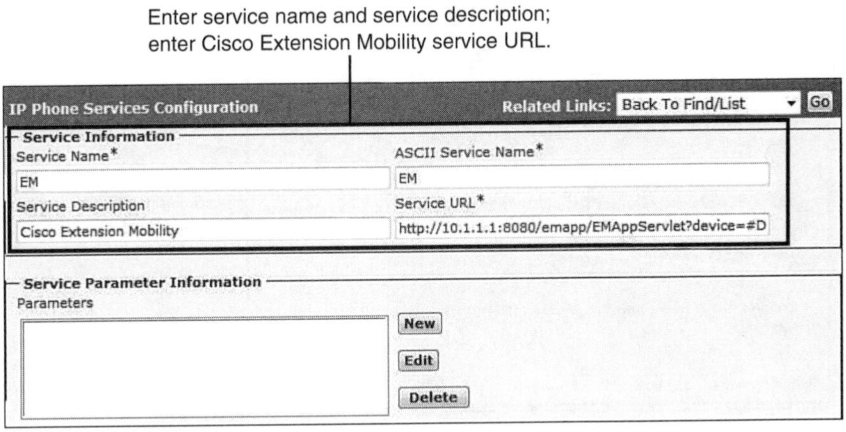

Enter service name and service description;
enter Cisco Extension Mobility service URL.

IP Phone Services Configuration	Related Links: Back To Find/List ▾ Go
Service Information	
Service Name*	ASCII Service Name*
EM	EM
Service Description	Service URL*
Cisco Extension Mobility	http://10.1.1.1:8080/emapp/EMAppServlet?device=#D

Service Parameter Information
Parameters

New
Edit
Delete

Cisco Extension Mobility is implemented as a phone service. Therefore, it needs to be added to the available phone services in CUCM. To add the Cisco Extension Mobility phone service, in CUCM Administration, choose **Device > Device Settings > Phone Services**. Configure the Cisco Extension Mobility service with a service name and description, and then enter the service URL:

> http://*IP address of publisher*:8080/emapp/
> EMAppServlet?device=#DEVICENAME#

NOTE The service URL is case-sensitive and must be entered exactly as worded, except that you replace *IP address of publisher* with the actual IP address of the Publisher CCM server. Be sure not to change anything else when entering this URL.

Step 4: Create Default Device Profiles

If multiple phone models are used for Extension Mobility, default device profiles need to be enabled.

To configure a default device profile, as shown in Figure 12-9, in CUCM Administration, choose **Device > Device Settings > Default Device Profile**. First you must choose the product type, which is the phone model, and the device protocol. Then you can configure the default device profile for the chosen phone model and protocol.

Figure 12-9   *Step 4: Create Default Device Profiles*

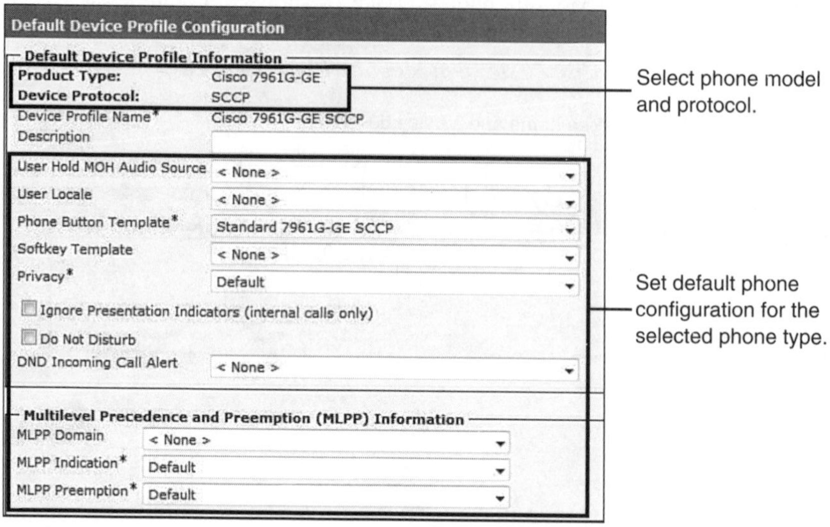

> **NOTE**   The available configuration options depend on the phone model and protocol you choose. The default device profile does not include phone button configuration (for example, lines or features buttons), but it does include the phone button template.

Step 5a: Create Device Profiles

To create and configure device profiles, in CUCM Administration choose **Device > Device Settings > Device Profile**, as shown in Figure 12-10. After choosing the phone model and protocol, you can configure user-specific device configuration parameters. After the phone button template is configured, the appropriate buttons can be configured.

Step 5b: Subscribe the Device Profile to the Extension Mobility Phone Service

Subscribe the configured device profile to the Cisco Extension Mobility phone service, as shown in Figure 12-11.

Figure 12-10   *Step 5a: Create Device Profiles*

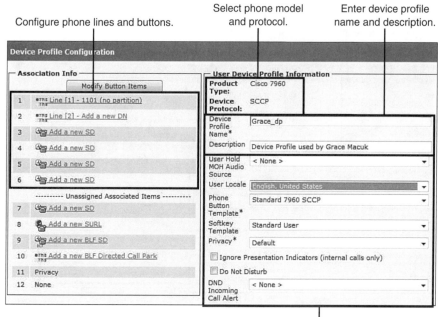

Configure phone lines and buttons.   Select phone model and protocol.   Enter device profile name and description.

Configure user-specific phone parameters.

In the Device Profile Configuration window, choose **Subscribe/Unsubscribe Services** from the Related Links, and click **Go**. Then choose the phone service you added in Step 3, click **Next**, and enter the name with which the phone service should be displayed in the list of phone services at the IP Phone after the **Services** button is pressed. Click **Subscribe**, and then click **Save**. The device profile is now subscribed to the Cisco Extension Mobility service.

CAUTION   If the device profile is not subscribed to the Cisco Extension Mobility service, users do not have access to the Cisco Extension Mobility phone service after they log in and their device profile has been applied. As a result, users can no longer log out of Extension Mobility at the phone. Therefore, make sure that you do not forget to subscribe the phones (see Step 7b) *and the device profiles* that you use for Extension Mobility to the Cisco Extension Mobility phone service.

Figure 12-11   *Step 5b: Subscribe the Device Profile to the Cisco Extension Mobility Phone Service*

1) Choose the Cisco Extension Mobility
   phone service by using the name
   assigned in Step 3. Then click Next.

2) Enter the service name as
   it should appear at the phone.

3) Click Subscribe. Then click Save.

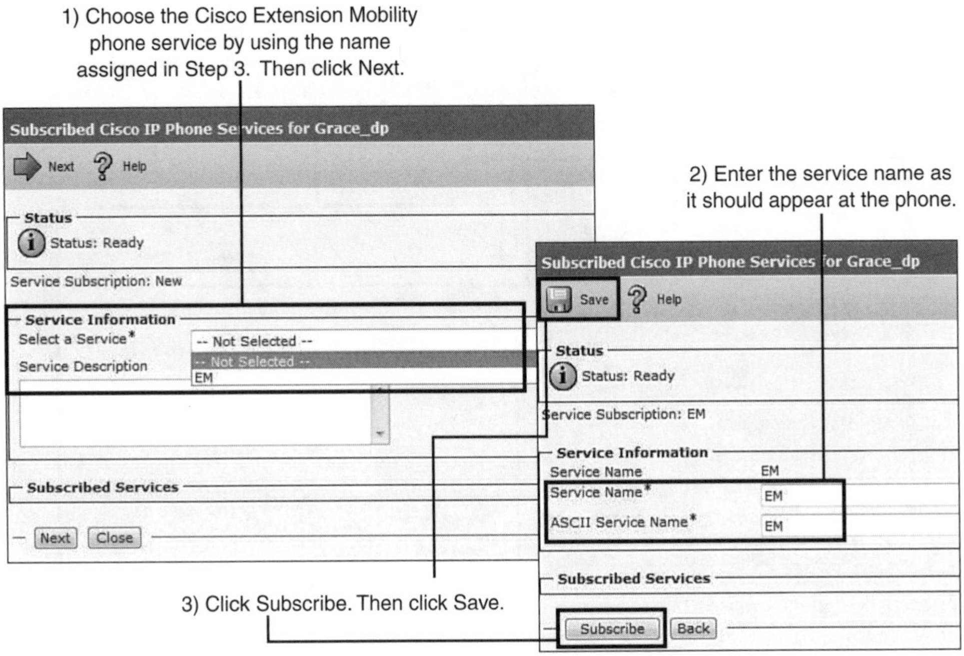

Step 6: Associate Users with Device Profiles

In the End User Configuration window, which you get to by choosing **User Management > End User**, choose the device profile or profiles that you want to associate with the user in the list of Available Profiles. Click the down arrow to add them to the list of Controlled Profiles, as shown in Figure 12-12.

Step 7a: Configure Phones for Cisco Extension Mobility

Next, the phone has to be enabled for Cisco Extension Mobility and subscribed to the Cisco Extension Mobility phone service. Figure 12-13 shows the first part of enabling Cisco Extension Mobility on a phone; choose **Device > Phone**. Check the **Enable Extension Mobility** check box to enable Cisco Extension Mobility. Then choose a specific device profile or the currently configured device settings to be used during the logout state. The recommendation is to use the current device settings.

Figure 12-12   *Step 6: Associate Users with Device Profiles*

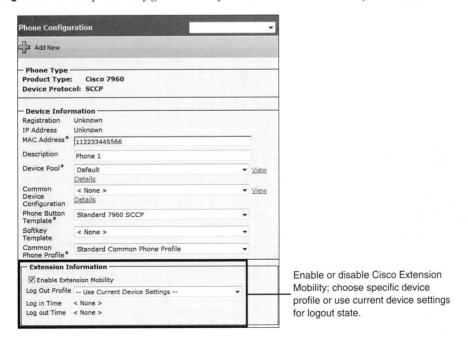

Figure 12-13   *Step 7a: Configure Phones for Cisco Extension Mobility*

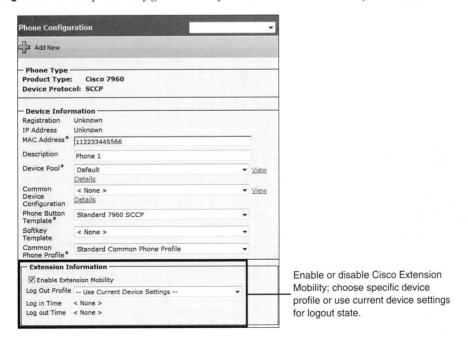

Step 7b: Subscribe the Phone to the Extension Mobility Phone Service

The last step of Cisco Extension Mobility configuration is to subscribe the IP Phone to the Cisco Extension Mobility phone service. This is the same as the process that was explained in Step 5, where the device profile was subscribed to the Cisco Extension Mobility service. In the Phone Configuration window, use the related link **Subscribe/Unsubscribe Services** to open the Subscribed Cisco IP Phone Services window and subscribe to the service, as shown in Figure 12-14.

Figure 12-14   *Step 7b: Subscribe the Phone to the Cisco Extension Mobility Phone Service*

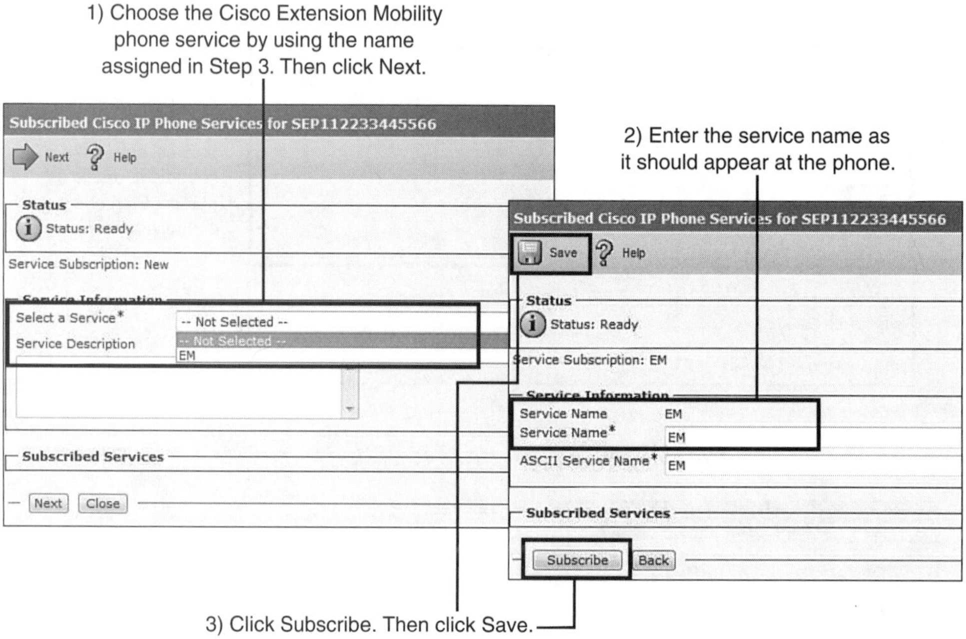

Summary

The following key points were discussed in this chapter:

- The Device Mobility and Extension Mobility features of CUCM allow users to roam between sites.

- Extension Mobility enables users to log in to IP Phones and apply their profiles, including extension number, speed dials, services, message waiting indicator (MWI) status, and calling privileges.

- The user's device profile is used to generate the phone configuration in the login state.

- Seven steps are needed to configure Extension Mobility.

References

For additional information, refer to these resources:

■ Cisco Systems, Inc., Cisco Unified Communications Solution Reference Network Design (SRND), based on Cisco Unified Communications Manager Release 6.x, June 2007

■ Cisco Systems, Inc., *Cisco Unified Communications Manager Administration Guide Release 6.0(1)*

Review Questions

Use these questions to review what you've learned in this chapter. The answers appear in Appendix A, "Answers to Chapter Review Questions."

1. Which of the following is not a problem when users roam between sites and use guest phones in a hoteling office where Extension Mobility is not enabled?

    a. The phone they use uses the wrong location and region settings.

    b. The user gets the wrong extension on that phone.

    c. The user gets the wrong calling privileges from his or her home desk phone.

    d. The user does not have his or her speed dials available.

2. Which two settings cannot be updated when you use Extension Mobility?

    a. Phone Button Template

    b. Softkey Template

    c. Device CSS

    d. Network Locale

    e. Phone Service subscriptions

    f. Phone lines and speed dials

3. Which three of the following are not configuration elements relevant to Extension Mobility configuration?

   a. Location

   b. Phone

   c. End user

   d. Device security profile

   e. Device pool

   f. Device profile

   g. Phone service

4. Which two of the following are Cisco-recommended approaches to implementing calling privileges when using Extension Mobility?

   a. Configure the line(s) of the user's device profile with a CSS that includes blocked route patterns for the destinations the user should not be allowed to dial.

   b. Do not configure a device CSS in this case.

   c. Do not configure a line CSS in this case.

   d. Configure the device with a CSS that includes all PSTN route patterns pointing to the local gateway.

   e. Configure the line(s) of the physical phone with the CSS that includes blocked route patterns for the destinations the user should not be allowed to dial.

5. Which two of the following happen if the user logs into a device but is still logged into another device?

   a. If the multiple login behavior service parameter is set to disallowed, the login fails.

   b. If the multiple login service parameter is set to auto-logout, the user is automatically logged out of the other device.

   c. If the multiple login behavior enterprise parameter is set to allowed, the login succeeds, and the user also remains logged in at the other device.

   d. If the multiple login behavior enterprise parameter is set to prompt, the user is asked whether he or she wants to be logged out at the other device first.

   e. The login fails independent of any CUCM Extension Mobility configuration.

6. Which of the following best describes a user using CUCM Extension Mobility?

    a. An employee travels to a remote site in the same company CUCM cluster and logs in on a Cisco IP Phone to make a PSTN call from the remote location.

    b. An employee travels to a remote site in the same company CUCM cluster and uses IP communicator on his or her laptop to make a PSTN call from the remote location.

    c. An employee travels to a remote site in the same company on a different CUCM cluster and logs in on a Cisco IP Phone to make a PSTN call from the remote location.

    d. An employee travels to a remote site in the same company on a different CUCM cluster and uses IP communicator on his or her laptop to make a PSTN call from the remote location.

7. What role do device profiles play in a CUCM cluster?

    a. It is optimal to configure for users who do not travel but who want to best use their IP Phone Services.

    b. It is optimal to configure for users who travel to other sites but who want to best use their IP Phone Services.

    c. It is optimal to configure for users who do not travel but who want to use the maximum number of their phone features.

    d. It is optimal to configure for users who travel to other sites and who want their home site phone settings to be available remotely.

8. Which statement about configuring Extension Mobility in a CUCM cluster is true?

    a. Extension Mobility is enabled by default on the CUCM cluster but needs to be configured for each user.

    b. Extension Mobility is not enabled by default on the CUCM cluster and must be enabled on a CCM server and configured for each user.

    c. Extension Mobility is not enabled by default on the CUCM cluster and must be enabled on all CUCM servers and configured for each user.

    d. Extension Mobility is enabled by default on the CUCM cluster but needs to be enabled for all CUCM servers and configured for each user.

9. Which implementation example of Extension Mobility would result in the simplest CUCM administrator configuration while maintaining maximum user Cisco IP Phone features for roaming users?

    a. Allow different users to own any Cisco IP Phone model they choose for their homes site and for hoteling.

    b. Standardize on different Cisco IP Phone models for each location to best suit the business models of different sites.

    c. Standardize on the 7961 Cisco IP Phone model to be used for all sites.

    d. Standardize on the 7905 Cisco IP Phone model to be used for different sites.

CHAPTER **13**

Implementing Cisco Unified Mobility

The growing use of mobile devices allows users to enjoy the efficiencies and speed of Cisco Unified Communications. This is true whether users are on a retail floor, at an airport, or at a Wi-Fi hotspot in a local coffee shop. However, as more people own multiple devices, ranging from office phones to home office phones, laptop computers to mobile phones, they spend more time managing their communications across different phone numbers and voice mailboxes. This limits their ability to work efficiently.

Cisco Unified Mobility allows users to be reached at a single number regardless of the device they use. This chapter describes the features of Cisco Unified Mobility, as well as how they work and how to configure them.

Chapter Objectives

Upon completing this chapter, you will be able to configure and implement Cisco Unified Mobility for single number reach and other mobility services. You will be able to meet these objectives:

- Describe the components and features of Cisco Unified Mobility

- Describe the call flows of Cisco Unified Mobility applications

- Describe the requirements for Cisco Unified Mobility

- Configure Cisco Unified Mobility

Cisco Unified Mobility Overview

Cisco Unified Mobility consists of two main components: Mobile Connect and Mobile Voice Access, as shown in Figure 13-1:

- **Mobile Connect:** Allows an *incoming* call to a user's enterprise phone number to be offered to the user's office phone, as well as to up to ten configurable remote destinations. Typically such remote destinations are mobile phones and home office phones.

■ **Mobile Voice Access (MVA):** Built on top of the Mobile Connect feature, Mobile Voice Access provides features similar to those of Mobile Connect for outgoing calls. With Mobile Voice Access enabled, users who are outside the enterprise can make calls as if they were directly connected to CUCM. This functionality is commonly called Direct Inward System Access (DISA) in traditional telephony environments. MVA can benefit the enterprise by limiting toll charges and consolidating phone billing directly to the enterprise rather than billing to each mobile user.

Figure 13-1 *Cisco Unified Mobility*

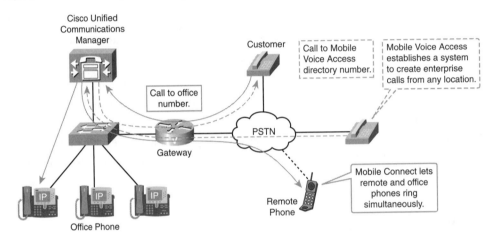

Both allow active calls to be switched between the IP Phone and the remote phone. For example, if a user initiated a call from a mobile phone while traveling to the office, he or she could switch the call to the office phone after arriving at the office.

Mobile Connect and Mobile Voice Access Characteristics

Cisco Mobile Connect enables users to receive business calls at a single phone number, regardless of the device that is used to receive a call. Mobile Connect allows users to answer incoming calls on the office phone or at a remote destination and pick up in-progress calls on the office phone or remote destination without losing the connection. When the call is offered to the desktop and remote destination phone or phones, the user can answer at either of those phones and hand off the call to another phone.

For example, if a user receives a call placed to her business number, the user's office phone and cell phone ring. If the user is traveling to the office, she can accept the call on her cell phone. After arriving at work, she can pick up the in-progress call at her office IP Phone just by pressing a single key on the office IP Phone. The call continues on the office IP Phone without interruption. The person on the other end of the call doesn't notice the handover from the cell phone to the IP Phone.

When Mobile Voice Access is used, users can invoke mid-call features after the call is connected, or pick up the call on their desk phones just like they can with received Mobile Connect calls. This is possible because the call is anchored at the enterprise gateway.

Cisco Unified Mobility Features

Mobile Connect and Mobile Voice Access enable flexible management of enterprise and remote destinations. They provide several features and benefits:

- **Single enterprise number:** Regardless of the device that is used—whether an enterprise phone, cell phone, or home phone—calls can be received at a single enterprise phone number. The caller ID of the enterprise phone is also preserved on outgoing calls, regardless of the phone from which the call is initiated. Having a single enterprise number for incoming calls and always using the same enterprise number for outgoing calls also allows each user to use a single voice mailbox. The enterprise voice mailbox can serve as single, consolidated voice mailbox for all business calls. Incoming callers have a predictable means of contacting employees, and employees do not have to check multiple voice-mail systems.

- **Access lists:** Cisco Unified Mobility users can configure access lists to either permit or deny calling numbers to ring remote destinations. If a permit access list is used, unlisted callers are not allowed to ring remote destinations. If a deny access list is used, only unlisted callers are allowed to ring remote destinations.

- **User interfaces for enabling and disabling Cisco Unified Mobility:** Users can turn Cisco Unified Mobility on and off by using a telephone user interface (TUI) provided by Mobile Voice Access. A GUI for Cisco Unified Mobility user configuration is available on the CUCM user web pages.

- **Access to enterprise features:** CUCM features can be accessed by using dual-tone multifrequency (DTMF) feature access codes: The supported features include hold (the default is *81), exclusive hold (the default is *82), resume (the default is *83), transfer (the default is *84), and conference (the default is *85). The feature codes can be configured as CUCM service parameters.

- **Smart client support:** On phones that have smart clients installed, softkeys can be used to access features such as hold, resume, transfer, and conference. Users can also enable or disable Cisco Unified Mobility from a smart client.

- **Call logging:** Enterprise calls are logged regardless of the device that is used, whether an enterprise phone or a remote phone.

Cisco Unified Mobility Call Flow

Figure 13-2 shows call flows when Cisco Unified Mobility is used for incoming calls to an office phone.

Figure 13-2 *Mobile Connect Call Flow of Incoming Calls to an Office Phone*

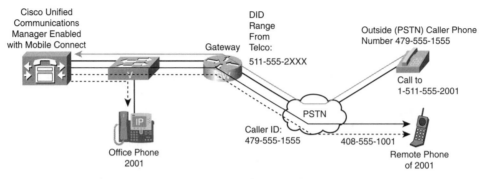

The figure illustrates the call flow when Mobile Connect is used, with an IP Phone at extension 2001 and a mobile phone that belongs to the user of the IP Phone.

A caller using the outside public switched telephone network (PSTN) calls the user's office number, 1 511 555-2001. Because Mobile Connect is enabled on CUCM, both the desktop phone 2001 and the configured remote destination mobile phone number 408 555-1001 ring simultaneously. The call is presented to the remote phone with the original caller ID of 479 555-1555. As soon as the call is accepted on one of the phones, the other phone stops ringing. The user can switch the call between the office phone and the mobile phone and vice versa during the call without losing the connection.

Mobile Connect Call Flow of Internal Calls Placed from a Remote Phone

Mobile Connect influences the calling number presentation. If a call is received from a recognized remote destination, the corresponding internal directory number, not the E.164 number of the remote device, is used for the calling number.

In Figure 13-3, internal extension 2001 has a Mobile Connect remote destination 408-555-1001, which is the cell phone of the user of 2001. If the user places a call from the mobile phone to an enterprise PSTN number of another internal colleague by dialing 1-511-555-2002, the called colleague sees the call coming from the internal directory number 2001 instead of the external mobile phone number.

Figure 13-3 *Mobile Connect Call Flow of Internal Calls Placed from a Remote Phone*

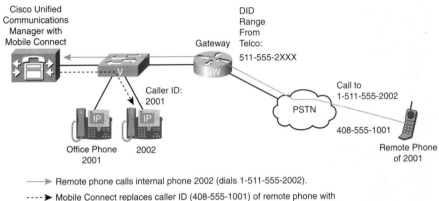

Cisco Unified Communications Manager with Mobile Connect

DID Range From Telco: 511-555-2XXX

Gateway

Caller ID: 2001

Call to 1-511-555-2002

PSTN

408-555-1001

Office Phone 2001   2002

Remote Phone of 2001

──▶ Remote phone calls internal phone 2002 (dials 1-511-555-2002).

----▶ Mobile Connect replaces caller ID (408-555-1001) of remote phone with directory number of associated office phone (2001).

The same process applies to calls placed to other internal destinations, such as voice mail. If the user of extension 2001 places a call to Cisco Unity from the cell phone, Cisco Unity sees directory number 2001 as the source of the call and not the PSTN number of the cell phone, which is 408-555-1001. Cisco Unity can identify the user by the directory number and provide access to the appropriate mailbox instead of playing a generic welcome greeting.

To recognize Mobile Connect remote destinations, the Mobile Connect remote destination number has to match the Automatic Number Identification (ANI) of the incoming call. Typically, Mobile Connect remote destinations include an access code (for example, 9-1 in the number 9-1-408-555-1001). Therefore, access code 9 and the long-distance code 1 have to be prefixed to the incoming ANI 408-555-1001 for the call source to be recognized as a Mobile Connect remote destination. Alternatively, the Cisco CallManager service parameter Matching Caller ID with Remote Destination can be set to Partial Match, and the Number of Digits for Caller ID Partial Match can be specified. This number specifies how many digits of the incoming ANI have to match a configured remote destination number (starting with the least-significant digit).

If the source of the call is not recognized as a Mobile Connect remote destination, the PSTN number of the remote destination is used for the calling number, and it is not changed to the internal directory number.

Mobile Voice Access Call Flow

With Mobile Voice Access, users can place calls to the outside from a remote destination as if they were dialing from the desktop phone. In Figure 13-4, the user of the IP Phone with directory number 2001 uses his cell phone 408-555-1001 to dial the MVA PSTN number of headquarters, extension 2999, by dialing 1-511-555-2999.

Figure 13-4 *MVA Call Flow*

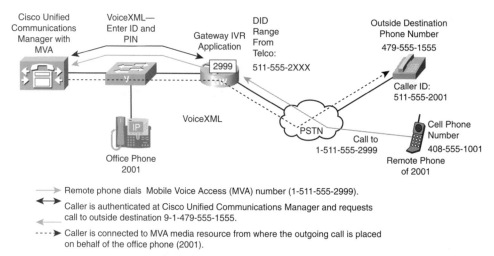

→ Remote phone dials Mobile Voice Access (MVA) number (1-511-555-2999).

↔ Caller is authenticated at Cisco Unified Communications Manager and requests
   call to outside destination 9-1-479-555-1555.

---→ Caller is connected to MVA media resource from where the outgoing call is placed
     on behalf of the office phone (2001).

The gateway is configured to start an interactive voice response (IVR) call application for calls placed to that number. The Voice Extensible Markup Language (VoiceXML)-based call application offers a prompt and asks for the remote destination number and the user's PIN. After login, besides activating and deactivating Mobile Voice Access (MVA), the user can initiate a call from the enterprise network. The call is set up with the E.164 PSTN calling number of directory number 2001 instead of 408-555-1001. This action allows the called party to identify the caller by the user's single office number. It does not matter that the call is actually placed from a mobile phone instead of the office IP Phone; the call appears to come from the office phone.

After the user has initiated a call from a remote destination by using Mobile Voice Access, he or she can switch the call to the office phone during the call without losing the connection and can switch back again as needed.

> **NOTE**   Note that in Figure 13-4 the caller from the cell phone into the gateway, and back out the same gateway to the outside destination phone number that answers, is hairpinned and uses two lines on the gateway.

Cisco Unified Mobility Components

Cisco Unified Mobility requires CUCM Release 6.0 or later. At least one CUCM server in the cluster needs the Mobile Voice Access service to be started. The Mobile Voice Access service interacts with the call application running on a Cisco IOS gateway.

Mobile Voice Access requires an H.323 or SIP gateway to provide a VoiceXML call application to remote callers who are dialing a certain number. The call application actually runs in CUCM and is referenced in the gateway configuration and does not require files in router flash like Tcl scripts use. Media Gateway Control Protocol (MGCP) is not supported, because it does not support call applications.

DTMF has to be sent out-of-band for Mobile Voice Access to work.

The remote destination cannot be an IP Phone within the enterprise. The remote destination has to be an external device, typically a PSTN number. Up to ten remote destinations can be configured. Class of service (CoS) can be configured to limit access to the PSTN.

Cisco Unified Mobility Configuration Elements

Table 13-1 lists the configuration elements of Cisco Unified Mobility and describes their functions.

Table 13-1 *Cisco Unified Mobility Configuration Elements*

Configuration Element	Function
End user	The end user is referenced by the office phone and remote destination profile. Mobile Connect and/or MVA must be enabled. A maximum number of remote destinations can be configured.
Phone	The office phone needs to be configured with an **End User** that is set as an **Owner User ID**.
Remote destination profile	A virtual phone device. A shared line is configured for each office phone number. End user (device), CSSs, and MOH audio sources are specified. One or more remote destinations are added.
Remote destination	Associated with shared line(s) of the remote destination profile. Configured with the destination number. Mobile Phone and Mobile Connect functions are selectively enabled.
Access list	Optional filters used to permit or deny incoming calls placed to the office phone to ring a remote destination. Permitted or denied caller IDs are specified.
MVA media resource	A media resource used to interact with the VoiceXML call application running on a Cisco IOS router. Only required for MVA.

These configuration elements are described in more detail in the following list:

■ **End user:** Each end user must first be created and a PIN configured. Then, three important Cisco Unified Mobility-related settings can be configured for the end user:

  —**Enable Mobility:** Check this option to allow the user to use the Mobile Connect feature. This is required to receive enterprise calls at one or more remote destinations and place calls from a remote phone into the enterprise.

  —**Enable Mobile Voice Access:** Check this option when the user should be allowed to place Mobile Voice Access calls (outgoing enterprise calls from a remote phone that should be placed on behalf of the office phone).

  —**Remote Destination Limit:** This setting is used to limit the number of remote destinations that can be configured. The maximum is ten.

■ **IP Phone:** The office phone of a Cisco Unified Mobility user has to refer to the end-user name. This task is done by setting the owner in the Phone Configuration window to the User ID of the end user.

NOTE   In the End User Configuration window, the end user can be associated with one or more devices, such as IP Phones. Such an association allows the end user to configure the device from the CUCM user web pages, but it is not relevant for Cisco Unified Mobility. The IP Phone must be mapped to the end user by setting the owner in the Phone Configuration window.

■ **Remote destination profile:** This setting creates a virtual phone that is linked to the end user that represents all remote destinations associated with the user. It includes phone device-level configuration settings such as user and network Music On Hold (MOH) audio sources and Calling Search Spaces (CSS). For each office phone that an end user should be able to use for Cisco Unified Mobility, a shared line with the line(s) of the office phone(s) has to be added to the remote destination profile. In addition, the remote destination profile is configured with remote destinations.

■ **Remote destination:** A remote destination is associated with one or more shared lines of a remote destination profile. For each remote destination, the remote destination number has to be specified as dialed from within the enterprise. The rerouting CSS of the specified remote destination profile is used to look up the configured remote destination number.

NOTE   The **Remote Destination Profile Information** has two CSSs that are used for call routing called the **Calling Search Space** (CSS) and the **Rerouting Calling Search Space** (RCSS). The CSS is used for outgoing calls that are initiated by using Mobile Voice Access. The RCSS is then used when a call is placed to the remote destination either when receiving a call to the number of the line shared by the office phone and the remote destination profile or when a call is handed over from the office phone to the remote destination. Therefore, the remote destination number has to be reachable by the RCSS. For Mobile Voice Access calls, the CSS is the CSS configured at the shared line and the CSS of the remote destination profile, with priority given to the CSS of the shared line.

- **Access list:** Access lists can be configured to permit or deny calls to be placed to a remote destination when the shared line is called; the filter is based on the calling number. An access list is configured with one or more numbers that specify the calling number that should be permitted or denied. Access lists are also configured with an owner (end-user ID) and are applied to remote destinations. An allowed access list, a blocked access list, or no access list can be applied. If an allowed access list is applied, all calling numbers that are not listed in the access list are blocked. If a blocked access list is applied, all unlisted numbers are allowed. If no access list is applied, all calling numbers are allowed to ring the remote destination.

- **Mobile Voice Access media resource:** This media resource interacts with the Voice XML call application running on the Cisco IOS gateway. It is required for Mobile Voice Access only. The number at which the Cisco IOS router can reach the media resource has to be specified, a partition can be applied, and one or more locales have to be chosen.

NOTE   The CSS of the gateway that runs the VoiceXML call application has to include the partition that is applied to the number of the Mobile Voice Access media resource.

Shared Line Between the Phone and the Remote Destination Profile

Figure 13-5 illustrates how a remote destination profile shares its line or lines with the associated Cisco IP Phone or phones.

A remote destination profile is associated with one or more IP Phones. Each phone line that an end user should be able to use with Cisco Unified Mobility has to be added to the remote destination profile associated with the end user. The directory number for the user thus is associated with two devices: the IP Phone and the remote destination profile. Such a directory number is also called a shared line. Two shared lines are shown in Figure 13-5. The IP Phone or phones sharing their line with the remote destination profile have to be owned by the end user who is associated with the remote destination profile.

Figure 13-5   *Shared Line Between the Phone and the Remote Destination Profile*

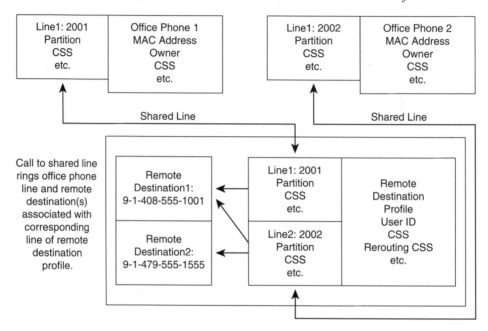

Remote destinations are associated with one or more shared lines that are configured at remote destinations.

As described earlier, the settings of the shared directory number (including the partition and CSS) apply to all associated devices. The remote destination profile is configured with a (standard) CSS that is used for calls placed by a remote phone when it is using MVA and a rerouting CSS that is applicable to calls placed to a remote destination.

In this example, a call is placed to directory number 2002. Line1 at Office Phone 2 and all remote destinations associated with Line2 of the remote destination ring, because the line is a shared line. For the call to the remote destination number, the rerouting CSS is used.

Suppose the remote phone with number 9-1-479-555-1555 (Remote Destination2) calls in to the mobile voice application and requests an outgoing call to be placed. The CSS of Line2 and the CSS of the remote destination profile are used for the outgoing enterprise call initiated by Remote Destination2.

Relationship Between Cisco Unified Mobility Configuration Elements

To use Cisco Unified Mobility, you must activate the Cisco Unified Mobile Voice Access Service if you want Mobile Voice Access in addition to Mobile Connect functionality.

When Cisco Unified Mobility is configured, the end user is the central element associated with IP Phones (at which the user is configured as the owner), access lists (AL), and remote destination profiles. Remote destinations are associated with shared lines of remote destination profiles and access lists. For Mobile Voice Access, the appropriate service has to be activated, and the automatically generated media resource is made available to a router that is running the VoiceXML call application.

Figure 13-6 shows the interaction of these configuration elements.

Figure 13-6 *Relationship of Cisco Unified Mobility Configuration Elements*

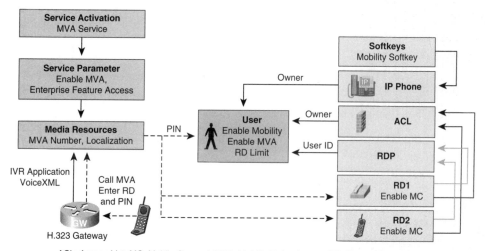

ACL: Access List, MC: Mobile Connect, MVA: Mobility Voice Access, RD: Remote Destination,
RDP: Remote Destination Profile

When the Cisco Unified Mobile Voice Access Service is activated, along with the applied service parameters, a corresponding media resource is automatically added. The media resource has to be configured with the Mobile Voice Access number, a partition, and locales.

The configured number has to be reachable from the Cisco IOS router configured as an H.323 gateway that gives remote phones access to a voiceXML IVR call application.

Incoming Mobile Voice Access callers are authenticated by the remote destination number and the user's PIN.

When Mobile Connect is used and incoming calls are sent to a line shared by an IP Phone and a remote destination profile, access lists applied to remote destinations can be used to control which callers are allowed to ring the remote destination. The access list has to refer to the end user who is configured in the remote destination profile.

To allow an active call to be handed over from an IP Phone to a remote destination, the IP Phone needs to have the Mobility softkey configured for the Connected call state. If the Mobility softkey is also added to the On Hook call state, it can be used to check the status of Cisco Unified Mobility (Mobile Connect on or off).

Cisco Unified Mobility Configuration

The following steps describe how to configure Cisco Unified Mobility by configuring the first piece of Mobile Connect.

Configuring Mobile Connect

Step 1   Add the Mobility softkey to IP Phone softkey templates.

Step 2   Add and configure the end user.

Step 3   Configure the IP Phone.

Step 4   Configure the remote destination profile with a shared line.

Step 5   Add the remote destination or destinations to a remote destination profile.

Step 6   Configure service parameters.

Step 7   (Optional) Implement access lists to specify which caller ID is allowed to ring a remote destination when a call to the office phone is received.

      a.   Configure access lists.

      b.   Apply the access lists to the remote destination.

Step 8   Configure partitions and CSSs to align with the existing dial plan.

Step 1: Configure a Softkey Template

Configure a softkey template that includes the Mobility softkey, as shown in Figure 13-7. In CUCM, choose **Device > Device Settings > Softkey Template**.

Configure a softkey template that includes the Mobility softkey for the call states of On Hook and Connected.

Step 2: Configure the End User

To configure end users, as shown in Figure 13-8, choose **User Management > End User**.

Figure 13-7 *Step 1: Configure a Softkey Template*

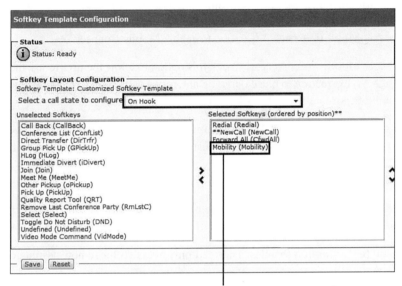

Add the Mobility softkey to On Hook and to Connected call state.

Figure 13-8 *Step 2: Configure the End User*

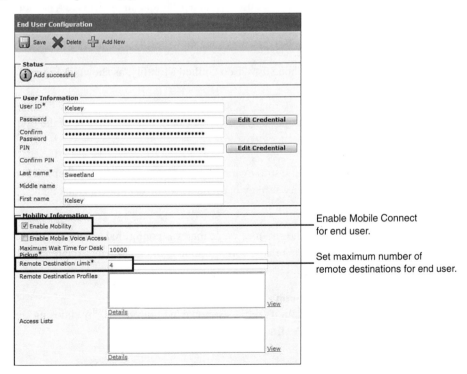

Enable Mobile Connect for end user.

Set maximum number of remote destinations for end user.

Configure the end user for mobility in the **Mobility Information** section of the **End User Configuration** window with the following options:

- **Enable Mobility:** Check this option to enable Mobile Connect.

- **Enable Mobile Voice Access:** Check this option to allow the user to use the Mobile Voice Access feature to place outgoing enterprise calls from a remote phone. The options of Mobile Voice Access will be explained further in later steps.

- **Maximum Wait Time for Desk Pickup:** Enter the maximum time in milliseconds that is permitted to pass before the user must pick up a call that is handed over from the remote phone to the office phone. The range is from 0 to 30,0000 ms, with a default value of 10,000 ms.

- **Remote Destination Limit:** Enter the maximum number of remote destinations the end user is allowed. The range is from 1 to 10; the default value is 4.

- **Remote Destination Profiles:** This read-only field lists the remote destination profiles that have been created for this user.

- **Access Lists:** This read-only field displays the access lists that have been created for this user.

In addition, be sure to associate the end user with the IP Phone in the **Device Associations** pane lower in the **End User Configuration** page.

Step 3: Configure the IP Phone

Configure the user's office IP Phone for Cisco Unified Mobility, as shown in Figure 13-9, by choosing **Device > Phone**.

Two parameters have to be configured in the Phone Configuration window of the user's office IP Phone:

- **Softkey Template:** Apply the softkey template (which was created in Step¬†1) to the IP Phone so that the Mobility softkey is available to the user in On Hook and Connected state.

- **Owner User ID:** Choose the end-user name that was configured in Step 2. This action enables CUCM to locate the related configuration elements, such as the remote destination profile of the end user.

Step 4: Configure the Remote Destination Profile

You configure the remote destination profile, as shown in Figure 13-10, by choosing **Device > Device Settings > Remote Destination Profile**.

Figure 13-9 *Step 3: Configure the IP Phone*

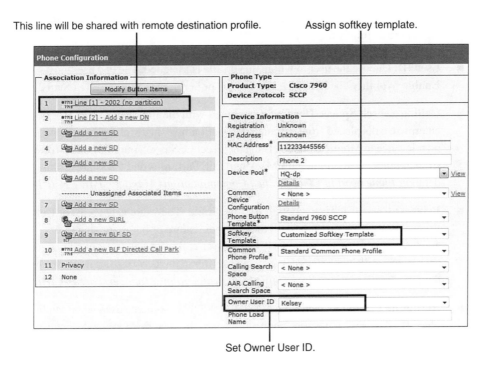

Figure 13-10 *Step 4: Configure the Remote Destination Profile*

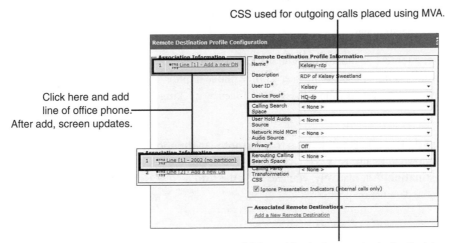

The remote destination profile contains the parameters that apply to all the user's remote destinations. Enter a name, description, device pool, CSS, rerouting CSS, and network and user MOH audio sources for the remote destination profile. The mobility-specific parameters are as follows:

- **User ID:** Choose the user to whom this profile is assigned. The end user must have the **Enable Mobility** check box checked in his or her user profile, as set in Step 2.

- **Calling Search Space:** This CSS (combined with the line CSS) is used for outgoing enterprise calls placed from a remote destination by using Mobile Voice Access. It has no relevance to Mobile Connect. If the incorrect CSS is set, outgoing calls to the PSTN from a remote destination with MVA will fail. Partitions and CSSs are discussed in detail in *Implementing Cisco Unified Communications Manager, Part 1 (CIPT1)*.

- **Privacy:** Choose a privacy option for this profile. The value is On, Off, or Default. Privacy is a setting that relates to the optional feature of barge for shared line appearances. If Privacy is on, CUCM removes call information from all phones that share lines and blocks shared lines from barging in on its calls. Barging is discussed in detail in *Implementing Cisco Unified Communications Manager, Part 1 (CIPT1)*.

- **Rerouting Calling Search Space:** Set the CSS that should be used when sending calls placed to the user's enterprise phone number to the specified remote destinations. This CSS is also used when an active call is handed over from the office phone to a remote phone.

- **Ignore Presentation Indicators:** Check this option to ignore the connected line ID presentation. As shown in Figure 13-10, this is recommended for internal calls. When this is checked, CUCM ignores any presentation restriction that is received for internal calls. Use this configuration in combination with the calling line ID presentation at the translation pattern level.

After a remote destination profile is created, one shared line has to be configured for each directory number used at the user's office phone or phones. To do so, navigate in CUCM to **Device > Phone** and choose the user's phones by clicking **Add a New DN** at the appropriate link.

Step 5: Add Remote Destinations to a Remote Destination Profile

As shown in Figure 13-11, you configure remote destinations by choosing **Device > Remote Destination**. Alternatively, you can click the **Add a New Remote Destination** link in a remote destination profile.

Figure 13-11 *Step 5: Add Remote Destination(s) to a Remote Destination Profile*

Line(s) of remote destination profile are shown only after setting remote destination profile and clicking Save. Once saved, remote destination profile cannot be changed.

Number of remote destination.

Associate remote destination with line(s) of remote destination profile.

Allows calls placed to office phones to also ring the remote destination.

Allows transfers of active calls from office phone to remote destination using the Mobility softkey.

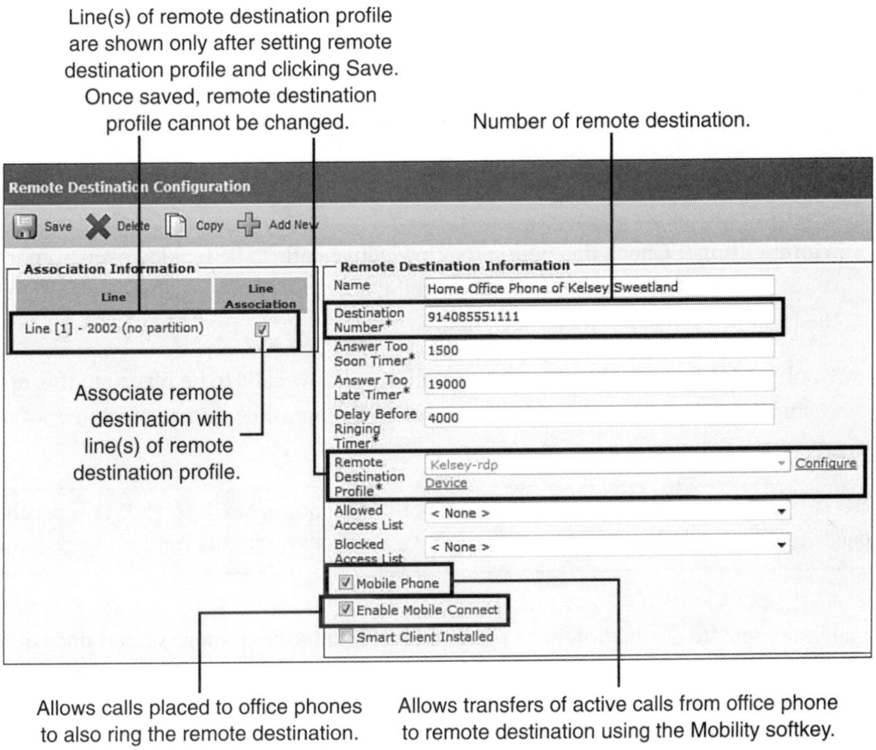

Enter a name for the remote destination, and configure the following parameters:

- **Destination Number:** Enter the telephone number for the remote destination. Include the area code and any additional digits that are required to dial the remote phone from within the enterprise. The maximum field length is 20 characters.

> **NOTE** The destination number must an external number, not an internal directory number. The number has to be entered as though it were being dialed from an IP Phone. Use a full E.164 number that includes the access code so that the number matches a route pattern pointing to the PSTN. The rerouting CSS that is configured in the remote destination profile will be used to look up the specified number in the call-routing table.

- **Remote Destination Profile:** You must choose the remote destination profile if you created a new remote destination after choosing **Device > Remote Destination**. If you open the Remote Destination Configuration window by clicking the **Add a New**

Remote Destination link in the Remote Destination Profile window, or if you are editing an existing remote destination, the remote destination profile is already set up and cannot be changed.

NOTE If you want to associate a remote destination that is already associated with a remote destination profile with another remote destination profile, you have to delete the remote destination and re-create it.

- **Mobile Phone:** Check this option to allow active calls to be handed over from the office phone to this remote-destination cellular or PSTN phone when the user presses the Mobility softkey at the office phone.

- **Enable Mobile Connect:** Check this option to allow calls to be placed to this remote destination when there is an incoming call to a shared-line directory number of an office phone.

NOTE End users can create their own remote destinations on the CUCM user web pages in addition to how the CUCM administrator does so in this step.

Finally, the remote destination has to be associated with one or more shared lines of the specified remote destination profile.

After it is associated, the remote destination rings if a call is placed to the appropriate shared line of an office phone. When a call is placed from a recognized remote destination to an internal destination, the calling number is modified from the remote phone number to the office phone directory number. In most cases the caller ID of that incoming call is a ten-digit number in North America. The remote destination number usually has a PSTN access code (for example, 9) and then an 11-digit number (trunk prefix 1 followed by the ten-digit number). If the incoming calling number is not prefixed with 91, internal phones see the call coming from the E.164 number of the remote phone instead of the associated internal directory number. The next step shows how to resolve such issues.

Step 6: Configure Service Parameters

You can set partial matches so that a calling number can be recognized as a remote destination by configuring Cisco CallManager service parameters, as shown in Figure 13-12.

Figure 13-12 *Step 6: Configure Service Parameters*

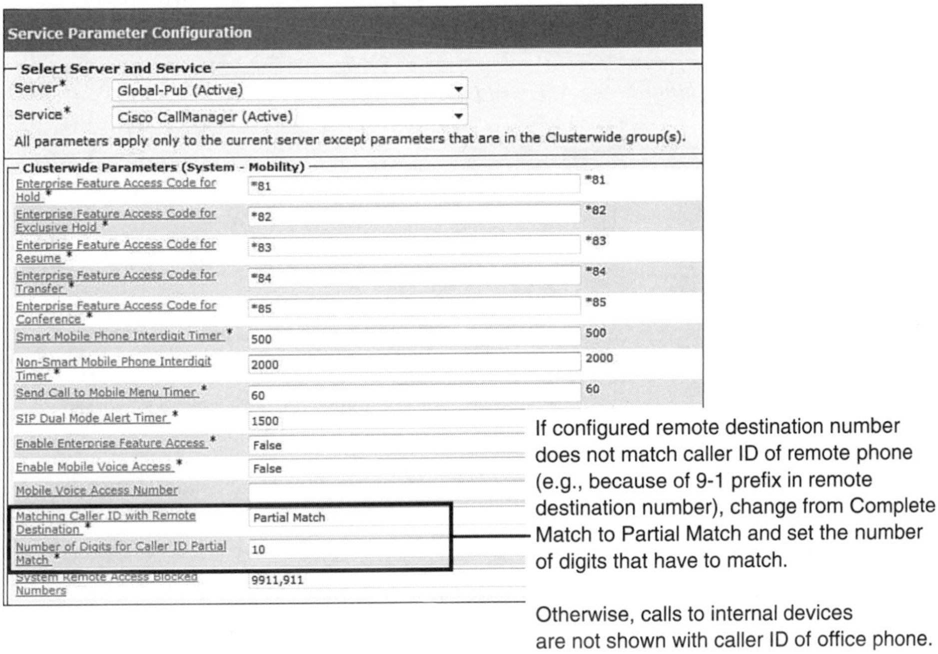

If configured remote destination number does not match caller ID of remote phone (e.g., because of 9-1 prefix in remote destination number), change from Complete Match to Partial Match and set the number of digits that have to match.

Otherwise, calls to internal devices are not shown with caller ID of office phone.

To access CUCM service parameters, choose **System > Service Parameters**, select your CUCM server, and then choose **Cisco CallManager**. To allow incoming caller IDs to be recognized when they do not include the 91 prefix that is used in the remote destination, configure the following parameters:

■ **Matching Caller ID with Remote Destination:** Set this parameter to Partial Match (the default is Complete Match).

■ **Number of Digits for Caller ID Partial Match:** Set this parameter to the number of digits that have to match (beginning with the least-significant digit) when comparing the incoming calling number to the configured remote destination number.

NOTE   Alternatively, you can choose **Call Routing > Transformation Pattern** to configure caller ID transformations. Each pattern can be assigned with a partition. The Calling Party Transformation CSS, which is configured in the remote destination profile, is used to control access to the configured transformation patterns.

Step 7a: Configure the Access List

Access lists can be configured as shown in Figure 13-13 to control which callers are allowed to ring a remote destination.

Figure 13-13   *Step 7a: Configure the Access List*

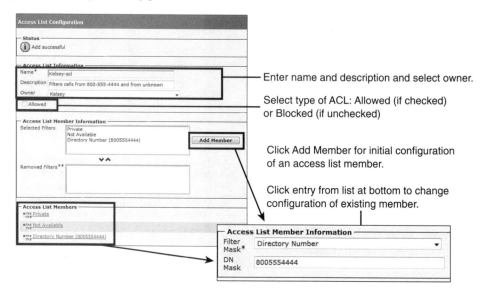

To configure access lists, choose **Device > Device Settings > Access Lists**. Enter a name and description for the access list. Choose the user to whom the access list applies in the **Owner** drop-down list. Then check the **Allowed** option to create a list of phone numbers that should be allowed to ring a certain remote destination when a call is placed to the user's office phone number. To block the numbers listed in the access list from ringing the remote destinations, leave this option unchecked.

After you save the access list, the window reopens to display the **Access List Member Information** area. Click **Add Member** to add a member, and then choose one of the three options from the **Filter Mask** drop-down list. Choose to allow or disallow a specific DN (**Directory Number**), filter calls that do not have caller ID (**Not Available**), or filter calls that do not display their caller ID (**Private**).

You can also change existing members by clicking the appropriate link under **Access List Members**.

In the **Access List Member Information** window, enter a phone number or filter in the **DN Mask** field (only when the filter mask is set to Directory Number). You can use the following wildcards:

- **X:** Matches a single digit.

NOTE The X wildcard has to be entered as uppercase; CUCM displays a syntax error message otherwise.

- **!:** Matches any number of digits.

NOTE # and * are not wildcards but part of the dialed number.

Step 7b: Apply the Access List to the Remote Destination

To apply an access list to a remote destination, open the Remote Destination Configuration window, as shown in Figure 13-14.

Figure 13-14 *Step 7b: Apply the Access List to the Remote Destination*

Either allowed or blocked acess list can be set. If blocked access list is set, all numbers not listed in access list are allowed (and vice versa).

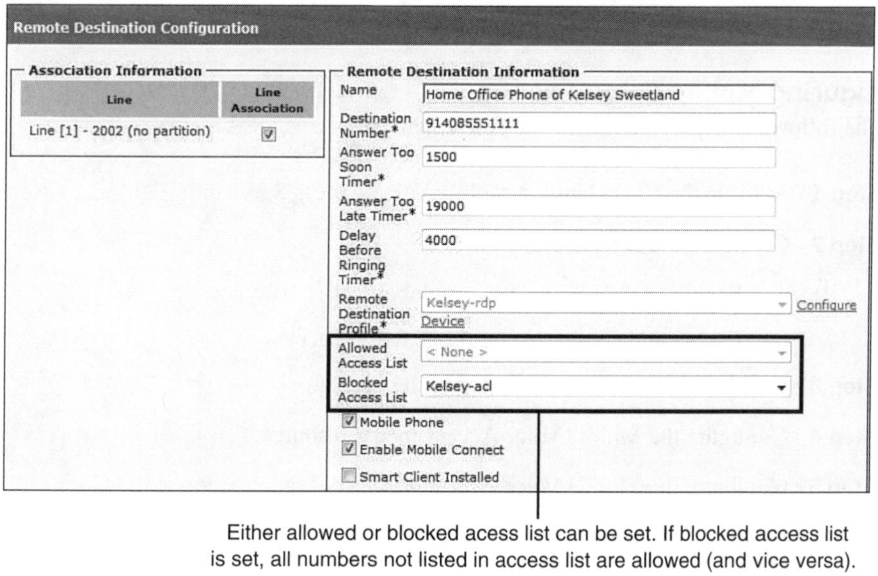

Choose **Device > Remote Destination** or click the appropriate link in the Remote Destination Profile Configuration window. Then choose the access list from the drop-down list under **Allowed Access List** or **Blocked Access List**.

> **NOTE**   You may choose either an allowed access list or a blocked access list, not both. In Figure 13-14, observe that the **Allowed Access List** is automatically dimmed when the **Blocked Access List** is chosen. You may also choose to not have an access list, in which case no calls are blocked and no calls are denied.

Step 8: Configure Partitions and CSSs

The appropriate partitions and CSSs have to be configured and applied to align with the existing dial plan. It is important to note that the shared line directory number can be assigned with a partition. Also note that (standard) CSSs can be configured at the shared directory number (the line CSS) and at the device level (the IP Phone and remote destination profile). In addition, for Mobile Connect calls (that is, calls to a remote destination), a rerouting CSS can be configured in the remote destination profile.

> **NOTE**   Configuring partitions and CSSs is covered in *Implementing Cisco Unified Communications Manager, Part 1 (CIPT1)*.

Configuring Mobile Voice Access

The following steps describe how to implement Mobile Voice Access:

Step 1   Activate the Cisco Unified Mobile Voice Access Service.

Step 2   Configure the service parameters.

    a.   Enable Mobile Voice Access globally.

    b.   Enable and configure enterprise feature access.

Step 3   Enable Mobile Voice Access for each end user.

Step 4   Configure the Mobile Voice Access media resource.

Step 5   Configure the Mobile Voice Access VoiceXML application at the Cisco IOS gateway.

Step 1: Activate the Cisco Unified Mobile Voice Access Service

To activate the Cisco Unified Mobile Voice Access Service, open the **Cisco Unified Serviceability** window. Choose **Tools > Service Activation** to activate the **Cisco Unified Mobile Voice Access Service**, as shown in Figure 13-15. When the service has been activated, verify that it is started by choosing **Tools > Control Center-Feature Services**.

Figure 13-15 *Step 1: Activate the Cisco Unified Mobile Voice Access Service*

CM Services	
Service Name	**Activation Status**
☑ Cisco CallManager	Activated
☑ Cisco Tftp	Activated
☐ Cisco Messaging Interface	Deactivated
☑ Cisco Unified Mobile Voice Access Service	Activated
☑ Cisco IP Voice Media Streaming App	Activated
☐ Cisco CTIManager	Deactivated
☑ Cisco Extension Mobility	Activated
☐ Cisco Extended Functions	Deactivated
☐ Cisco Dialed Number Analyzer	Deactivated
☐ Cisco DHCP Monitor Service	Deactivated

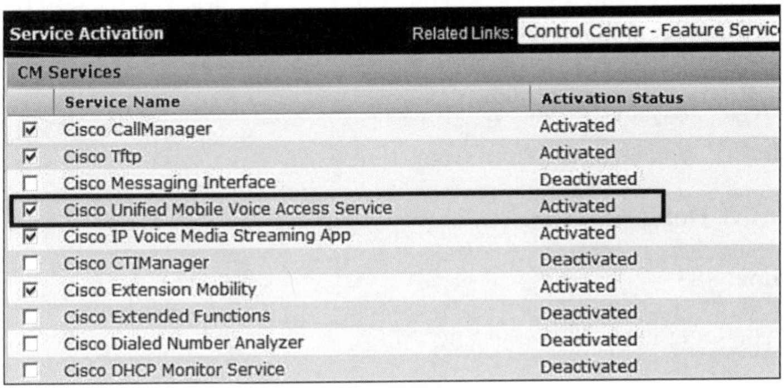

Service Activation — Related Links: Control Center - Feature Servic

Step 2: Configure the Service Parameters

To configure the Cisco Unified Mobility service parameters applicable to Mobile Voice Access, choose **System > Service Parameters** and choose a server, as shown in Figure 13-16. Then choose the **Cisco CallManager** service. The parameters that are shown are clusterwide, which means that they apply to all servers.

Figure 13-16 *Step 2: Configure the Service Parameters*

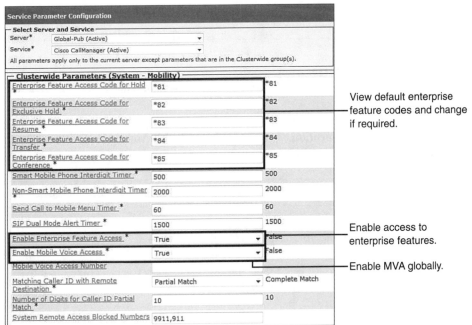

You can enable access to enterprise features by setting the **Enable Enterprise Feature Access** parameter to **True**. In this case, the following features can be used from a remote destination phone, and the corresponding feature access codes can be modified from their default values:

- **Hold:** *81

- **Exclusive Hold:** *82

- **Resume:** *83

- **Transfer:** *84

- **Conference:** *85

These parameters must be unique and two or three characters long. Allowed values are 0 to 9, A to D, and *.

To enable Mobile Voice Access, set the **Enable Mobile Voice Access** parameter to **True** and press **Save**.

NOTE   By setting the Enable Mobile Voice Access parameter to True, you enable MVA on a clusterwide basis. MVA then has to be enabled individually for each end user in the End User Configuration window.

Step 3: Configure the End User

To enable Mobile Voice Access for an end user, as shown in Figure 13-17, choose **User Management > End User**.

In the **End User Configuration** window, check the **Enable Mobile Voice Access** check box to allow the end user to use Mobile Voice Access.

NOTE   All other mobility-related parameters were discussed earlier in this chapter.

Step 4: Configure the Mobile Voice Access Media Resource

The Mobile Voice Access media resource is automatically added when the Cisco Unified Mobile Voice Access Service (see Figure 13-18) is activated. You can configure it by choosing **Media Resources > Mobile Voice Access**.

Figure 13-17 *Step 3: Enable MVA for Each End User*

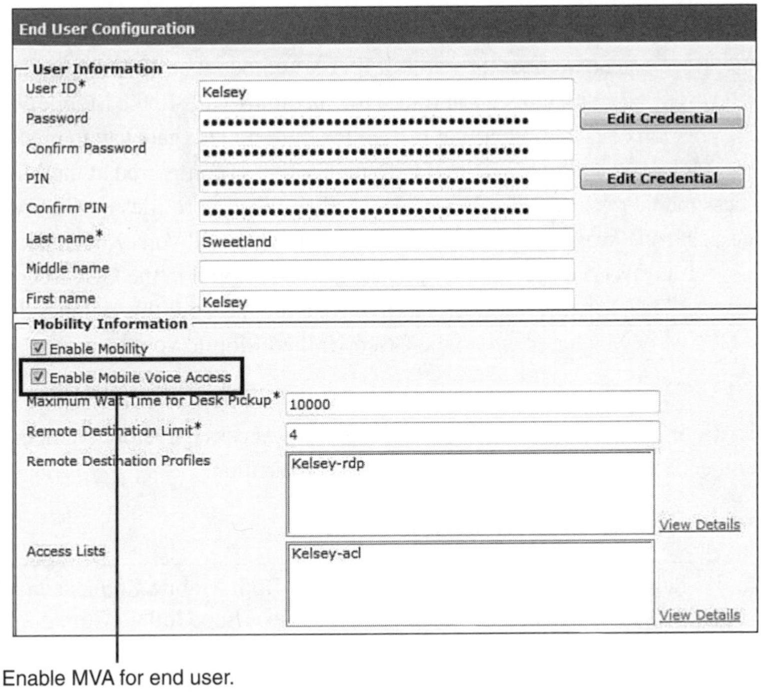

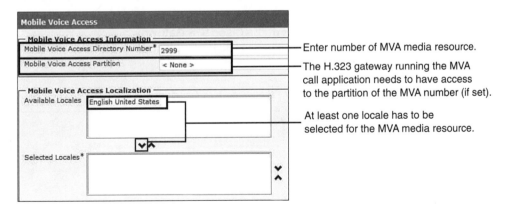

Enable MVA for end user.

Figure 13-18 *Step 4: Configure the MVA Media Resource*

Enter number of MVA media resource.

The H.323 gateway running the MVA
call application needs to have access
to the partition of the MVA number (if set).

At least one locale has to be
selected for the MVA media resource.

The following configuration options exist:

- **Mobile Voice Access Directory Number:** Remote users must dial in to use Mobile Voice Access. The number the call is a PSTN number at an H.323 gateway via a call application. The call application routes the incoming calls to the Mobile Voice Access media resource. The number that is used for this call leg (gateway to media resource) is the Mobile Voice Access Directory Number that is configured at the Mobile Voice Access media resource. The VoiceXML call application resides on CUCM and is accessed from the gateway by HTML. Therefore, the local VoiceXML application code can refer to this configuration parameter, which is stored in the CUCM configuration database. The gateway, however, has to have a dial peer for this number that points to the CUCM or Managers where the Cisco Unified Mobile Voice Access Service has been activated.

- **Partition:** Assign a partition to the Mobile Voice Access Directory Number. Make sure that the CSS of the gateway has access to this partition.

- **Locales:** Choose at least one locale.

> **NOTE** By default, only U.S. English is available. Both Mobile Connect and Mobile Voice Access support a maximum of nine locales, so Cisco Unified Communications Manager Administration blocks you from configuring ten or more locales for Cisco Unified Mobility. In **Mobile Voice Access Localization**, more than nine locales can appear in the **Available Locales** pane if they are installed for Cisco Unified Communications Manager, but you can save only nine locales in the **Selected Locales** pane.

Step 5: Configure Mobile Voice Access at the Cisco IOS Gateway

Example 13-1 shows the configuration of an H.323 gateway that provides access to the Cisco Unified Mobile Voice Access feature.

Example 13-1 *Configure Mobile Access at the Cisco IOS Gateway*

```
application
  service mva http://10.1.1.1:8080/ccmivr/pages/IVRMainpage.vxml
!
voice-port 0/0/0:23
  translation-profile incoming pstn-in
!
voice translation-profile pstn-in
  translate called 1
!
voice translation-rule 1
  rule 1 /.*5552\(...$\)/ /2\1/
```

Example 13-1   *Configure Mobile Access at the Cisco IOS Gateway (Continued)*

```
!
dial-peer voice 29991 pots
  service mva
  incoming called-number 2999
  direct-inward-dial
!
dial-peer voice 29992 voip
  destination-pattern 2999
  session target ipv4:10.1.1.1
  dtmf-relay h245-alphanumeric
  codec g711ulaw
  no vad
!
dial-peer voice 1 pots
  destination-pattern 9T
  incoming called-number 2...
  direct-inward-dial
  port 0/0/0:23
!
dial-peer voice 2 voip
  destination-pattern 2...
  session target ipv4:10.1.1.1
  incoming called-number 9T
  codec g711ulaw
```

This example shows a sample configuration of an H.323 gateway. Note that in the example an incoming translation profile strips the called number to four digits and is applied to the ISDN voice port. Therefore, all other dial peers that are applicable to calls from the PSTN refer to four-digit called numbers only.

Thus, the following happens when a remote user dials the Mobile Voice Access number 1-511-555-2999: The call is routed to the router's voice port, and the PSTN delivers a ten-digit national number that is then stripped to four digits by the translation profile. The called number 2999 matches the incoming plain old telephone system (POTS) dial peer 29991, which is configured with the call application **service mva** command. The service Mobile Voice Access is configured with the URL of the Mobile Voice Access VoiceXML call application. (This is located at the CUCM server where the Cisco Unified Mobile Voice Access Service has been activated.)

When a Cisco IOS release later than 12.3(12) is used, the syntax changes shown in Example 13-2 must be implemented.

Example 13-2 *Syntax Changes at the Cisco IOS Gateway for IOS Release 12.3(12) or Later*

```
application
  service mva http://10.1.1.1:8080/ccmivr/pages/IVRMainpage.vxml
!
dial-peer voice 29991 pots
  service mva
  incoming called-number 2999
  direct-inward-dial
```

When a Cisco IOS release earlier than 12.3(12) is used, the syntax changes shown in Example 13-3 must be implemented.

Example 13-3 *Syntax Changes at the Cisco IOS Gateway for IOS Release 12.3(12) or Earlier*

```
call application voice MVA http:// 10.1.1.1:8080/ccmivr/
  pages/IVRMainpage.vxml
!
dial-peer voice 29991 pots
  application MVA
  incoming called-number 2999
  direct-inward-dial
```

In both examples, replace IP address 10.1.1.1 with the IP address of your CUCM server with MVA activated, and replace the incoming called number 2999 to match your dial plan.

When the call is passed on to the Mobile Voice Access media resource, the number configured at the Mobile Voice Access media resource in the previous step is used. In this case, it is 2999.

> **NOTE**   The number that is used to start the call application on incoming PSTN calls (1-511-555-2999) does not have to match (or partially match) the number used for the call leg from the H.323 gateway to the CUCM Mobile Voice Access media resource. However, it is recommended that you use the same number to avoid confusion.

The outgoing VoIP dial peer that is used for this call leg (dial peer 29992) has to be configured for DTMF relay, and voice activity detection (VAD) has to be disabled.

All other dial peers that are shown in the example apply to incoming PSTN calls to directory numbers other than 2999 (**dial-peer voice 1 pots** and **dial-peer voice 2 voip**) and outgoing PSTN calls. (All received VoIP calls use incoming **dial-peer voice 2 voip** and outgoing **dial-peer voice 1 pots**.) These outgoing PSTN calls include normal calls placed from internal devices as well as calls initiated from remote phones that are using Mobile Voice Access to place enterprise calls to the PSTN.

> **NOTE** More information about incoming and outgoing dial peer matching is provided in *Cisco Voice over IP*.

Summary

The following key points were discussed in this chapter:

■ Mobile Connect enables users to receive calls placed to their enterprise number at the enterprise phone and remote phones such as cell phones. Mobile Voice Access extends the Mobile Connect functionality by allowing enterprise calls placed from a remote phone to first connect to the enterprise and then break back out to the called number using the user's enterprise number as the calling number.

■ Mobile Voice Access requires an H.323 gateway providing an IVR application to Mobile Voice Access users.

■ The Cisco Unified Mobile Voice Access service must be activated in the CUCM cluster for Mobile Voice Access.

■ Implementation of Cisco Unified Mobility includes the configuration of access lists, remote destination profile, and remote destinations.

References

For additional information, refer to these resources:

■ Cisco Systems, Inc., Cisco Unified Communications Solution Reference Network Design (SRND), based on CUCM Release 6.x, June 2007

■ Cisco Systems, Inc., CUCM Administration Guide Release 6.0(1)

Review Questions

Use these questions to review what you've learned in this chapter. The answers appear in Appendix A, "Answers to Chapter Review Questions."

1. Cisco Unified Mobility consists of what two features?

    a. Single-number connect

    b. Mobile Connect

    c. Mobile IVR

    d. Mobile Voice Access

    e. Mobile Voice Connect

2. What is indicated as the calling number for a call placed from a remote destination to an internal directory number?

   a. The MVA number

   b. The number of the remote destination

   c. The directory number of the office phone the remote destination is associated with

   d. The directory number of the called office phone, if it's associated with the calling number of the remote destination

3. What is not a requirement for Cisco Unified Mobility?

   a. Remote destinations must be external numbers.

   b. An H.323 or SIP gateway providing the Mobile Voice Access IVR application

   c. Out-of-band DTMF

   d. A transcoder running at the gateway providing a Mobile Voice Access IVR application

4. What configuration element is not used to implement Cisco Unified Mobility?

   a. Softkey templates

   b. User accounts

   c. Access lists

   d. Remote destination profiles

   e. Remote destinations

   f. Enterprise parameters

5. Which two of the following are requirements to implement Cisco Unified Mobility?

   a. CUCM v6

   b. CUCM v4, 5, or 6

   c. An H.323 or SIP gateway providing Mobile Voice Access IVR application

   d. Extension Mobility enabled for the cluster and users

6. Which of the following statements about Cisco Unified Mobility is the most accurate?

   a. Cisco Unified Mobility is a replacement for CUCM Extension Mobility for traveling users.

   b. Cisco Unified Mobility allows the user to no longer require a cellular phone.

   c. Cisco Unified Mobility allows the user to have a single phone number contact, even if he or she requires several different phones.

   d. Cisco Unified Mobility functions properly only if implemented with Extension Mobility.

7. Which two of the following signaling protocols on the IOS gateway are supported to implement Cisco Unified Mobility?

   a. SCCP

   b. H.323

   c. SIP

   d. MGCP

CHAPTER 14

Understanding Cryptographic Fundamentals and PKI

CUCM supports several security features that are based on cryptographic services. Some of these features use a Public Key Infrastructure (PKI). When implementing security features in CUCM, it is important to understand the underlying security services, algorithms, and concepts. This chapter provides information about cryptographic fundamentals and discusses the concept of a PKI.

Chapter Objectives

Upon completing this chapter, you will be able to describe how cryptographic services are provided and what role a PKI has within a security implementation. You will be able to meet these objectives:

■ Describe cryptographic services

■ Describe symmetric and asymmetric encryption

■ Describe HMAC

■ Describe digital signatures

■ Describe PKI

■ Describe how PKI is used on the Internet with secure web browsing

Cryptographic Services

Internet Protocol is an unsecure protocol by definition. Because Cisco Unified Communications is based entirely on IP, if any network security of audio or signaling is desired, cryptography must be implemented. Cryptography is the science of transforming readable messages into an unintelligible form and the later reversal of that process. The application of cryptography is to send the transformed, unreadable message over an untrusted channel. In the data world, this untrusted channel very often is a public network, such as the Internet.

Cryptography provides four services:

- **Data authenticity:** This service should guarantee that the message comes from the source that it claims to come from. When an application such as e-mail or a protocol such as IP does not have any built-in mechanisms that prevent spoofing of the source, cryptographic methods can be used for proof of sources. Authenticity is analogous to a notary public, who ensures that you really are who you claim to be.

- **Data confidentiality:** This service provides privacy by ensuring that messages can be read only by the receiver.

- **Data integrity:** This service ensures that the messages were not altered in transit. With data integrity, the receiver can verify that the received message is identical to the sent message and that it has not been manipulated.

- **Data nonrepudiation:** This service allows the sender of a message to be uniquely identified. With nonrepudiation services in place, a sender cannot deny having been the source of that message.

All these services are based on encryption and authentication methods. However, different kinds of encryption and authentication techniques are used for different applications. Figure 14-1 illustrates the use of these four security services.

This figure illustrates examples of the four services with participants Alice, Bob, Cal, and Chris:

- **Authenticity:** If Bob receives data expected to come from Alice, how can he be sure that it was really sent by Alice and not by someone else, like Cal? Without any reliable service that ensures authenticity of the source, user Bob will never know.

- **Confidentiality:** On the other hand, even if there are means of guaranteeing the authenticity of the source, Bob might be afraid that somebody else, like Cal, could read the information while it was in transit, resulting in a loss of privacy. This problem could be solved by a service providing confidentiality.

- **Integrity:** If Bob were to receive data, sent in a way that guarantees the authenticity of the source, how could he know that the content was not modified in transit by Cal? A service that ensures the integrity of the message is needed to eliminate this kind of threat.

- **Nonrepudiation:** If Bob receives malicious data from Alice that seems to be authentic, can Bob prove to others such as Chris that the data must have been sent by Alice? A nonrepudiation service is needed in this case.

Figure 14-1   *Services of Cryptography*

It might appear that the authenticity service and the nonrepudiation service fulfill the same function. Although both services address the question of the sender's proven identity, there is a small difference between the two services, which is sometimes quite important:

- When the receiver needs to be sure about the authenticity of the source, the method and the means that are used to achieve the proof of authenticity can be available to both the sender and the receiver. Because the receiver knows that he or she was not the source, it does not matter that sender and receiver both know how to treat a message to provide authenticity of the source.

- However, if the receiver must prove the source of the sender to others, it is unacceptable for the receiver to know how the sender treated this message to prove authenticity, because the receiver could then pretend to be the sender.

An example that contrasts authenticity and nonrepudiation is data exchange between two computers of the same company versus data exchange between a customer and an online store. When the two computers do not have to prove to others which of them sent a message, but just need to make sure that whatever was received by one computer was sent by the other computer, the two computers can *share* the method of transforming their messages.

This practice would be unacceptable in business applications such as an online store. If the online store knew how a customer transforms messages to prove the authenticity of the source, the online store could easily fake orders that would then appear to be authentic. Therefore, in such a scenario, for authenticity to be established (if needed), the sender must be the only party having the knowledge of how to transform messages. In such a case, the online store can prove to others that the order must have been sent by the customer. The customer could not argue that the order was faked by the online store, because the online store does not know how to transform the messages from the customer to make him or her appear authentic.

Symmetric Versus Asymmetric Encryption

The two general approaches to encryption are symmetric and asymmetric. This section addresses how these two types of encryption work, when they are used, and which encryption algorithms are commonly used today.

Symmetric encryption, illustrated in Figure 14-2, has two main characteristics: It is very fast (compared to asymmetric encryption), and it uses the same key for encryption and decryption. As a consequence, the sender and receiver must know the *same key*. To ensure confidentiality, nobody else is allowed to know the key. Such keys are also called *shared secrets* or *shared keys*.

Figure 14-2 *Symmetric Encryption*

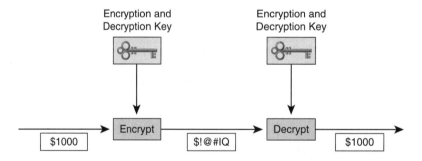

Symmetric encryption has been used for decades in digital computing; several algorithms are commonly used. Among the best-known and most widely trusted symmetric encryption algorithms are Triple Data Encryption Standard (3DES), Advanced Encryption Standard (AES), International Data Encryption Algorithm (IDEA), the RC series (RC2, RC4, RC5, and RC6), Software Encryption Algorithm (SEAL), and Blowfish.

All these encryption algorithms are based on the same concept: They have two types of input (the cleartext and the key) and produce unreadable output (the ciphertext). For decryption, the ciphertext and the key are the input data, and the original cleartext is the output.

> **NOTE** The origin of shared-key or symmetric encryption actually long predates digital computing. Two thousand years ago in Rome, Emperor Julius Caesar used a shared key with his generals in the field to exchange confidential messages. The algorithm they used translated each letter in the message by a numeric quantity represented by the key. Hence, only someone with the key could accurately decipher the original message. This later came to be known as Caesar-cipher.

Symmetric algorithms usually are very simple in their structure and therefore quite fast. As a consequence, they are often used for real-time encryption in data networks. They are, at their essence, based on simple mathematical operations and can be easily hardware-accelerated using specialized encryption circuits called application-specific integrated circuits (ASIC). Typical applications are e-mail, IPsec, Secure Real-Time Transfer Protocol (SRTP), and Secure HTTP (HTTPS).

Keys should be changed frequently, because the longer they're kept, the more likely they are to be discovered. Loss of privacy would be the consequence. The "safe" lifetime of keys depends on the algorithm, the volume of data for which the keys are used, the key length, and how long they are used. The key length is usually 128 to 256 bits.

Because of the limited lifetime of keys (usually hours to days) and the fact that each pair of devices should use a different key, key management is rather difficult.

Algorithm Example: AES

For a number of years, it had been recognized that Data Encryption Standard (DES) would eventually reach the end of its useful life. In 1997, the Advanced Encryption Standard (AES) initiative was announced, and the public was invited to propose encryption schemes, one of which could be chosen as the encryption standard to replace DES.

On October 2, 2000, the U.S. National Institute of Standards and Technology (NIST) announced the selection of the Rijndael cipher as the AES algorithm. The Rijndael cipher, developed by Joan Daemen and Vincent Rijmen, has a variable block length and key length. The algorithm currently specifies how to use keys with lengths of 128, 192, or 256 bits to encrypt blocks with lengths of 128, 192, or 256 bits (all nine combinations of key length and block length are possible). Both block length and key length can be extended very easily to multiples of 32 bits, allowing the algorithm to scale with security requirements of the future.

The U.S. Department of Commerce approved the adoption of AES as an official U.S. government standard, effective May 26, 2002.

AES was chosen to replace DES and 3DES because DES is too weak (in terms of key length) and 3DES is too slow to run on modern efficient hardware. AES is more efficient on the same hardware and is much faster, usually by a factor of about 5 compared to 3DES. It's also more suitable for high-throughput, low-latency environments, especially if pure software encryption is used. However, AES is a relatively young algorithm, and the golden rule of cryptography states that a more mature algorithm is always more trusted. 3DES therefore is a more conservative and more trusted choice in terms of strength, because it has been analyzed for more than 30 years. AES was also thoroughly analyzed during the selection process and is considered mature enough for most applications.

AES is the algorithm used to encrypt both IP Phone to CUCM signaling with Transport Layer Security (TLS) protection and phone to phone and phone to gateway media exchange with SRTP protection.

Asymmetric Encryption

Asymmetric algorithms (sometimes called *public-key algorithms*), shown in Figure 14-3, are used in PKI. They are designed such that the key that is used for encryption is different from the key that is used for decryption. The decryption key cannot (at least in any reasonable amount of time) be calculated from the encryption key, and vice versa.

Figure 14-3 *Asymmetric Encryption*

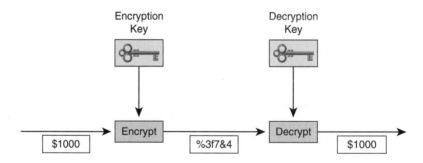

The main feature of asymmetric encryption algorithms is that the encryption key (often called the *public key*) does not have to be secret; it can be published freely, and anyone can use it to encrypt data. However, the corresponding decryption key (often called the *private key*) is known to only a single entity that can decrypt data encrypted with the encryption key. Therefore, when you need to send an encrypted message to someone else, you first obtain the other person's public (encryption) key and transform the message with it. Only the recipient knows the private (decryption) key and therefore can decrypt the message.

Asymmetric algorithms are relatively slow (up to 1000 times slower than symmetric algorithms). Their design is based on computational problems, such as factoring extremely large numbers or computing discrete logarithms of extremely large numbers.

The best-known asymmetric cryptographic algorithms are the Rivest, Shamir, and Adleman (RSA); ElGamal; and elliptic curve algorithms. RSA is recommended because it is widely trusted for its resistance to attacks and because of its well-known internals.

Because of their lack of speed, asymmetric encryption algorithms usually are used to protect small quantities of data (digital signatures, key exchange).

Key management tends to be simpler for asymmetric algorithms than for symmetric algorithms. As stated before, with asymmetric encryption, each device has a pair of keys (public and private). The public key of each device has to be publicly available (known by all other devices) to allow a full mesh of encrypted communication. With symmetric encryption, different symmetric keys have to be safely distributed for each combination of two peers.

Asymmetric keys usually are used for longer periods (months to years).

Algorithm Example: RSA

Ronald L. Rivest, Adi Shamir, and Leonard M. Adleman invented the RSA algorithm in 1977. It was a patented public-key algorithm, and its patent expired in September 2000, putting the algorithm in the public domain. Of all the public-key algorithms proposed over the years, RSA is still the most preferred.

RSA has withstood years of extensive cryptanalysis, and although analysis has neither proven nor disproven the security of the RSA algorithm, it does suggest a justifiable confidence. The security of RSA is based on the difficulty of factoring very large numbers— that is, breaking them into multiplicative factors. If an easy method of factoring these large numbers were discovered, the effectiveness of RSA would be destroyed and, as a side effect, mathematics might take a huge leap.

RSA keys usually are 1024 to 2048 bits long but can be longer.

RSA is used for device authentication for IP Phone to CUCM and vice versa in CUCM. Another example is using your web browser to securely exchange financial information on your bank's website.

Two Ways to Use Asymmetric Encryption

Asymmetric encryption algorithms can be used for the following two purposes:

- **Confidentiality:** The sender encrypts the data with the receiver's public key. Assuming that all senders know the public keys of all the receivers, any sender can generate an encrypted message for any receiver. Because only the receiver knows its private key (which corresponds to the public key that is used to encrypt the message), only the receiver can decrypt the message. This process guarantees that only the receiver can decrypt the data.

- **Authenticity of digital signatures:** The sender uses its private key to sign (encrypt) the data. Because all senders have a private key, each of them can generate a signature that cannot be created by anybody else. Assuming that all receivers know the public keys of all senders, all receivers can verify (decrypt) the signatures of each sender.

Hash-Based Message Authentication Codes

Hash functions are used for several cryptographic applications. They can be used for secure password verification or storage and are also a base component of data authentication.

Hashing is a one-way function of input data that produces fixed-length output data—the digest. The digest uniquely identifies the input data and is cryptographically very strong. In other words, it is impossible to recover input data from its digest, and if the input data changes just a little, the digest (fingerprint) changes substantially (the avalanche effect). Therefore, high-volume data can be identified by its (shorter) digest. For this reason, the digest is called a fingerprint of the data. Given only a digest, it is not computationally feasible to generate data that would result in such a digest.

Figure 14-4 shows how a Hashed Message Authentication Code (HMAC) uses hash functions to provide integrity of packets by adding a secret key as additional input to the hash function. Data of arbitrary length is input to the hash function, and the result of the hash function is the fixed-length hash (digest, fingerprint). Hashing is similar to the calculation of cyclic redundancy check (CRC) checksums, except that it is much stronger from a cryptographic point of view. Given a CRC value, it is easy to generate data with the same CRC. However, with hash functions, generating the data is not computationally feasible for an attacker.

The two best-known hashing functions are Message Digest 5 (MD5) with 128-bit digests and Secure Hash Algorithm 1 (SHA-1) with 160-bit digests.

Figure 14-4 *Hash Functions*

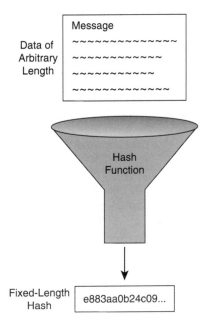

Considerable evidence exists that MD5 may not be as strong as originally envisioned and that collisions (different inputs resulting in the same fingerprint) are more likely to occur than envisioned. Therefore, you should avoid MD5 as an algorithm of choice and use SHA-1 instead.

Algorithm Example: SHA-1

In 1993 the National Institute of Standards and Technology (NIST) developed SHA, the algorithm specified in the Secure Hash Standard. SHA-1 is a revision to SHA that was published in 1994; the revision corrected an unpublished flaw in SHA. Its design is very similar to the MD4 family of hash functions developed by Ron Rivest.

The algorithm takes a message of no less than 264 bits in length and produces a 160-bit message digest. The algorithm is slightly slower than MD5, but the larger message digest makes it more secure against brute-force collision and inversion attacks.

No Integrity Provided by Pure Hashing

Figure 14-5 illustrates that pure hashing cannot guarantee integrity.

Figure 14-5 *Pure Hashing Does Not Provide Integrity*

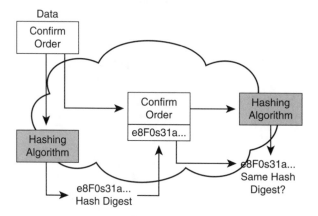

The sender wants to ensure that the message will not be altered on its way to the receiver. The sender uses the message as the input of a hashing algorithm and computes its fixed-length digest, or fingerprint. This fingerprint is then attached to the message (the message and the hash are cleartext) and is sent to the receiver. The receiver removes the fingerprint from the message and uses the message as input to the same hashing algorithm. If the hash computed by the receiver is equal to the one attached to the message, the message has not been altered during transit.

Be aware that no security is added to the message in this example. Why? When the message traverses the network, a potential attacker could intercept the message, change it, recalculate the hash, and append the newly recalculated fingerprint to the message (a man-in-the-middle interception attack). Hashing only prevents the message from being changed accidentally (that is, by a communication error). Nothing is unique to the sender in the hashing procedure. Therefore, anyone can compute a hash for any data, as long as they know the correct hash algorithm.

Thus, hash functions are helpful to ensure that data was not changed accidentally, but they cannot ensure that data was not deliberately changed. To protect data from intentional alteration, you need to employ hash functions in the context of HMAC. This process extends hashes by adding a secure component.

Hash-Based Message Authentication Code, or "Keyed Hash"

HMAC or keyed hashes use existing hash functions. The significant difference is that a secret key is added as additional input to the hash function when calculating the digest, known as the fingerprint, as shown in Figure 14-6.

Figure 14-6 *Hash-Based Message Authentication Code, or "Keyed Hash"*

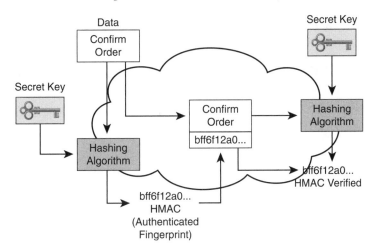

Only the sender and receiver share the secret key, and the output of the hash function now depends on the input data and the secret key. Therefore, only parties who have access to that secret key can compute or verify the digest of an HMAC function. This technique defeats man-in-the-middle attacks and also provides authentication of data origin. If only two parties share a secret HMAC key and use HMAC functions for authentication, the receiver of a properly constructed HMAC digest with a message can be sure that the other party was the originator of the message, because that other party is the only other entity possessing the secret key. However, because both parties know the key, HMAC does not provide nonrepudiation. For nonrepudiation, each entity would need its own secret key, instead of having a secret key shared between two parties.

HMAC functions generally are fast and often are applied in these situations:

- To provide fast proof of message authenticity and integrity among parties sharing the secret key, such as with IPsec packets or routing protocol authentication

- To generate one-time (and one-way) responses to challenges in authentication protocols (such as PPP Challenge Handshake Authentication Protocol [CHAP], Microsoft NT Domain, and Extensible Authentication Protocol-MD5 [EAP-MD5])

- To provide proof of integrity of bulk data, such as with file-integrity checkers (for example, Tripwire) or with document signing (digitally signed contracts, PKI certificates)

Digital Signatures

Digital signatures are verification data that is appended to the data to be signed. They provide three basic security services in secure communications:

- **Authenticity of digitally signed data:** Authenticates the source, proving that a certain party has signed the data in question.

- **Integrity of digitally signed data:** Guarantees that the data has not changed since being signed by the signer.

- **Nonrepudiation of the transaction:** Allows the recipient to take the data to a third party, which will accept the digital signature as a proof that this data exchange really did take place. The signing party cannot repudiate (that is, deny) that it has signed the data.

Digital signatures usually use asymmetric encryption algorithms to generate and verify digital signatures. Compared to using asymmetric encryption for confidentiality, the usage of the keys is reversed when creating digital signatures: The private key is used to create the signature, and the public key is used to verify the signature. The private key is exceptionally "private" and cannot be seen, replaced, copied, or located. If a private key could be stolen, the entire security of PKI would be compromised.

Because digital signatures are based on asymmetric (slow) algorithms, they are not used today to provide real-time authenticity and integrity guarantees to network traffic. In network protocols, they are usually used as proof of endpoint (client, server, and phone) identity when two entities initially connect. Examples include an IP Phone authenticating to CUCM, or a Cisco VPN Client authenticating to a Cisco VPN Concentrator. For real-time protection of authenticity and integrity, which do not require nonrepudiation such as signaling messages between IP Phones and a CUCM, or IPsec packet protection, HMAC methods are used instead.

Relative to shared key encryption, RSA is extremely slow and is not designed for real-time encryption of a large volume of data. Therefore, when it is used to create signatures, the data that is to be signed is first hashed, and only the hash digest is signed by RSA (encrypted with the public key). This practice significantly improves performance, because RSA transforms only the fingerprint of the data, not all the data, as shown in Figure 14-7.

Figure 14-7 *Digital Signatures*

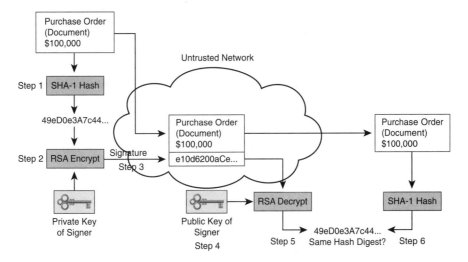

The figure illustrates the following signature process:

1. The signer makes a hash (fingerprint) of the document that uniquely identifies the document and all its contents.

NOTE   A hash of the data is created for two reasons. First, RSA is extremely slow, and it is more efficient to sign only the (shorter) fingerprint than to sign the whole set of the data. Second, if the transferred information should be out-of-band verified, it is simpler to compare the shorter fingerprint than to compare all the transferred information. Out-of-band verification is when the received data is verified over another channel, such as by paper mail or through a phone call.

2. The signer encrypts only the hash with its private key.

3. The encrypted hash (the signature) is appended to the document.

    The verification process works as follows:

4. The verifier obtains the signer's public key.

5. The verifier decrypts the signature with the signer's public key. This process unveils the signer's assumed hash value.

6. The verifier makes a hash of the received document (without its signature) and compares this hash to the decrypted signature hash. If the hashes match, the document is authentic (that is, it has been signed by the assumed signer) and has not been changed since the signer signed it.

Public Key Infrastructure

Achieving scalable and secure key exchange is the main issue in deploying cryptography. Depending on the cryptographic algorithm that is used, varying needs exist.

In symmetric encryption, the keys should be changed frequently. They are shared between two peers. But how can you get the keys safely to the peers? Symmetric keys should be known only by the two peers using them, so *confidentiality* is extremely important to key exchange.

In asymmetric encryption, the public key of a device has to be known by all other devices because it has to be made public. But how can you distribute the public keys safely to your devices? You have to ensure that the public keys that are exchanged over the network are authentic and have not been modified; hence, *authenticity* and *integrity* are extremely important for the key exchange.

Because of scalability issues, manual key exchange or out-of-band verification is not an option for applications such as Cisco Unified Communications.

> **NOTE** Note that with both symmetric and asymmetric encryption, the bigger the key, the better. Key size is described in number of bits, and the larger the key is, the more difficult it is for an unauthorized user to crack using any computational method.

Symmetric Key Distribution Protected by Asymmetric Encryption

Asymmetric encryption can be used to secure the automated exchange of symmetric keys, as shown in Figure 14-8.

Figure 14-8 *Symmetric Key Distribution Protected by Asymmetric Encryption*

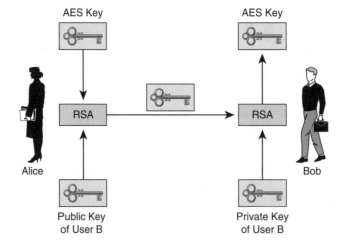

Symmetric keys are encrypted with the receiver's public key and then are sent over the untrusted network. Only the receiver can decrypt the message (the keys), because only the receiver knows the corresponding private key.

In Figure 14-8, user Alice wants to use symmetric encryption with user Bob. For secure key exchange, asymmetric encryption is used as follows:

1. User Alice generates the symmetric key.

2. Alice encrypts the symmetric key with Bob's public key and sends the encrypted key over the untrusted network to Bob.

3. Bob decrypts the key using his private key.

Now both of them know the symmetric key and can start using it for symmetric encryption of packets.

This method solves key distribution issues for symmetric keys but relies on knowledge of the public keys of all possible peers at all the participating devices.

Public Key Distribution in Asymmetric Cryptography

Asymmetric algorithms offer the advantage that one of the keys is public, which simplifies key exchange and distribution, as shown in Figure 14-9.

Figure 14-9 *Public Key Distribution in Asymmetric Cryptography*

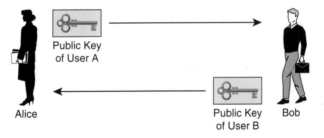

The pitfall of this approach is not obvious at first glance. Obtaining the public key from another person can be tricky. Although it is true that public keys are public information and can be published in a well-known directory, an important issue remains: When you receive a public key from someone, how do you know that it really belongs to that person?

When a public key is requested or is sent over an untrusted network, an attacker could intercept that key and substitute another public key for it. This man-in-the-middle attack would cause the message sender to encrypt all messages with the attacker's public key.

Therefore, you need a mechanism that allows you to verify the relationship between the name of an entity and its public key. The PKI is the solution to this problem. It allows such systems to scale. On a smaller scale, alternative manual solutions can be devised.

PKI as a Trusted Third-Party Protocol

A PKI does not eliminate the need for authenticity when you exchange public keys in an asymmetric encryption environment, but it solves the scalability issues associated with that process.

A PKI uses the concept of a single, trusted introducer. Instead of securely exchanging all public keys among all devices, only the public key of the trusted introducer has to be securely distributed to all devices. This exchange is usually done by downloading the public key and then verifying it out of band.

When all devices know the introducer's authentic key, the introducer can guarantee the authenticity of the public keys of all devices by using a certificate for each device in the topology. The certificate includes information about the identity of a device and its public key. The (publicly trusted) introducer then signs the certificates of the individual devices, and the devices can directly distribute their public keys by sending their certificates. A device receiving such a certificate can verify it by checking the signature of the issuer (the introducer).

PKI: Generating Key Pairs

Figure 14-10 illustrates a network in which each entity has a pair of asymmetric keys—a public key and a private key. User A and user C want to communicate securely, and the trusted introducer is the trusted third party who is unconditionally trusted by all other users.

PKI: Distributing the Public Key of the Trusted Introducer

Every user in the system trusts information provided by the introducer, as shown in Figure 14-11.

In practice, trust is accomplished by digital signatures. Anything that the introducer signs is considered trusted. To verify the signatures of the trusted introducer, each user of this system must first obtain the public key of the trusted introducer, as shown in the figure.

The download of the public key of the trusted introducer has to be out-of-band verified, because an attacker could impersonate the trusted introducer using a man-in-the-middle attack.

Figure 14-10   *PKI: Generating Key Pairs*

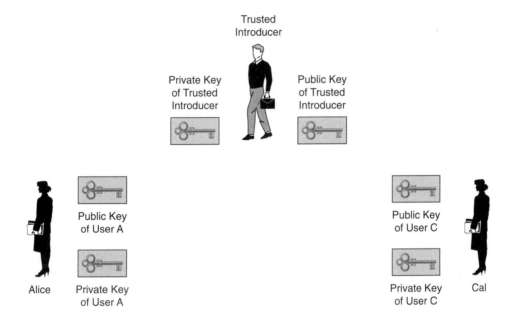

Figure 14-11   *PKI: Distributing the Public Key of the Trusted Introducer*

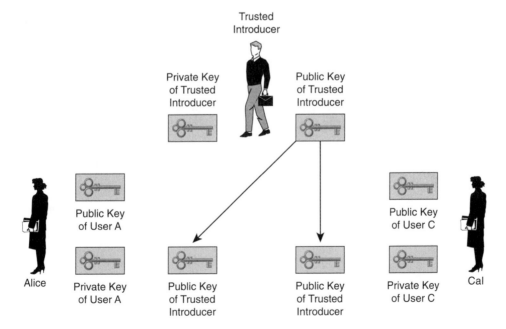

> **NOTE**   A PKI does not eliminate the need for out-of-band verification of public keys, but it solves scalability issues. With a PKI, only the download of the public key of the trusted introducer and the upload of the public key of a new member have to be out-of-band verified. After that, PKI users can safely exchange their public keys on a peer-to-peer basis without any out-of-band verification. Without a PKI, public keys would have to be out-of-band verified every time they are exchanged between any pair of peers.

PKI: Requesting Signed Certificates

To become a part of the trust system, all end users request a signed certificate from the trusted introducer, as shown in Figure 14-12.

Figure 14-12   *PKI: Requesting Signed Certificates*

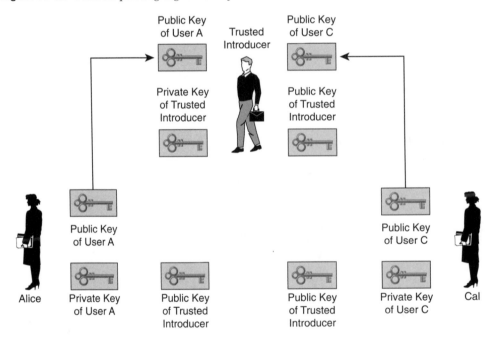

This process is called PKI enrollment. During enrollment, users submit their identity and their public key to the introducer.

PKI: Signing Certificates

Figure 14-13 shows how the trusted introducer verifies the received information and then signs the public keys.

Figure 14-13 *PKI: Signing Certificates*

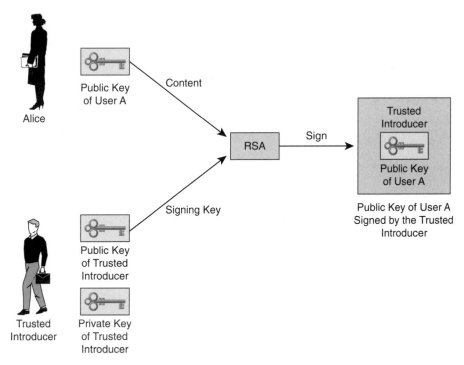

The trusted introducer first verifies the identity and public key of each enrolling user. If they are correct, the trusted introducer digitally signs the submitted public key with the introducer's private key. The result is a kind of "document" for each user that includes the user's identity (name) and public key.

As mentioned, each uploaded public key has to be out-of-band verified, because an attacker could impersonate the trusted introducer using a man-in-the-middle attack.

PKI: Providing Entities with Their Certificates

The trusted introducer provides each user with a signed document. This document contains the user's name and public key, which are bound by the signature of the trusted introducer, as shown in Figure 14-14.

Figure 14-14   *PKI: Providing Entities with Their Certificates*

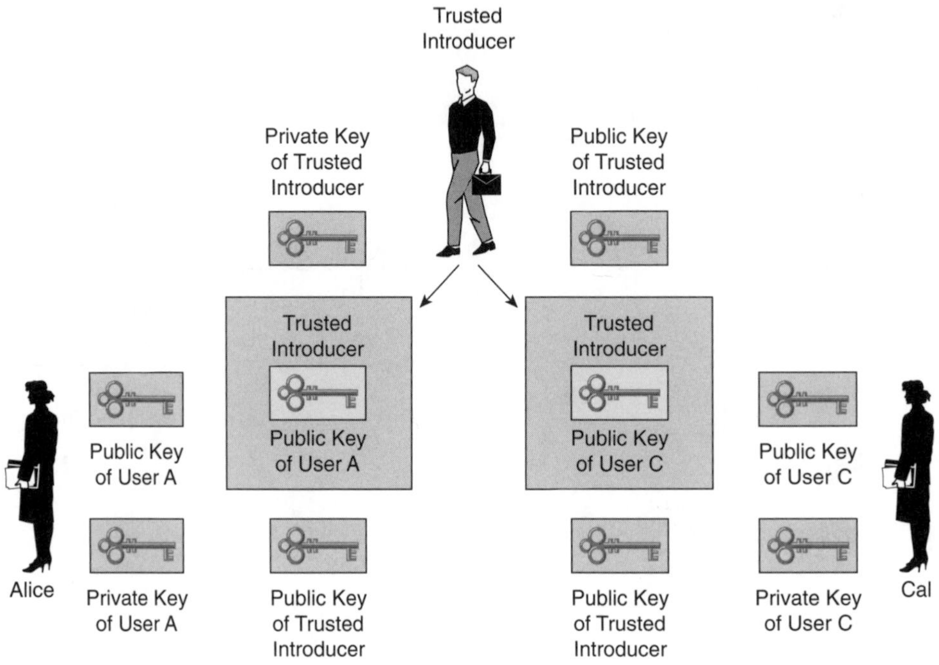

As shown in the figure, each user now possesses a public and private key pair: the public key of the trusted introducer, and a document with the user's identity and public key. This document is signed by the trusted introducer.

PKI: Exchanging Public Keys Between Entities Using Their Signed Certificates

At this point, all entities now can safely exchange their public keys, as shown in Figure 14-15.

Figure 14-15   *PKI: Exchanging Public Keys Between Entities Using Their Signed Certificates*

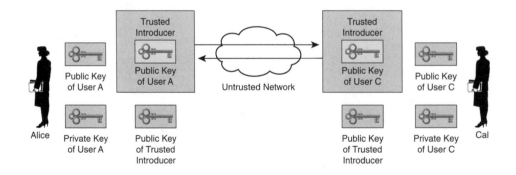

Because all users now have their own documents that contain the correct name and public key, signed by the trusted introducer, as well as the public key of the trusted introducer, they can verify all the data that is signed by the trusted introducer. The entities can now (independently of the trusted introducer) establish point-to-point trusted relationships by exchanging information about themselves in the form of that document.

In practice, end users at this stage can exchange signed public keys over an unsecure medium and use the digital signature of the trusted introducer as the protection mechanism for the exchange. Again, the signature of the trusted introducer is trusted because it can be verified (the entities have the public key of the trusted introducer), and the trusted introducer and its operations are considered secure.

PKI Entities

A PKI is the service framework that is needed to support large-scale public-key-based technologies. It includes several entities, as described in Table 14-1.

Table 14-1 *PKI Entities*

PKI Entity	Relevance
Certification authority (CA)	The trusted introducer signing certificates of PKI entities (PKI users)
PKI users	Devices, users, or applications that want to safely distribute their public keys
Certificates	Digital form (X.509v3), including the identity of a PKI user, its public key, and a signature (created by the CA)
Self-signed certificates	Sometimes entities issue self-signed certificates: • CA, as the root of a PKI • Entities that are not part of a PKI (not associated with a CA) but use PKI-enabled applications • Requires out-of-band verification

The following terms are required for PKI:

■ A *certification authority* (CA) is the trusted third party (the trusted introducer) who signs the public keys of all end entities (PKI users).

■ A *PKI user* is a member of the PKI who has a public and private key pair and a certificate that is issued by the CA.

■ A *certificate* is a document that, in essence, binds the entity's name and public key that has been signed by the CA in such a way that every other entity can trust it.

> **NOTE** Certificates are not secret information and do not need to be encrypted in any way. The idea is not to hide anything but to ensure the authenticity and integrity of the information contained in the certificate.

■ A *self-signed certificate* is a certificate in which the subject (the owner or holder) of the certificate is also the signer of the certificate. Examples of self-signed certificates are certificates of CAs, or certificates of entities that are not part of a PKI but that want to use PKI-enabled (certificate-based) applications. The signature of a self-signed certificate cannot be verified using the standard method (verification by using the signer's public key) because that public key should actually be protected by the signature. Therefore, other methods (such as manual verification) are needed to ensure the authenticity of a self-signed certificate.

X.509v3 Certificates

X.509 is the ubiquitous and well-known standard that defines basic PKI data formats, such as certificates to enable basic interoperability. Table 14-2 shows an example of an X.509v3 certificate.

The X.509 format is already extensively used in the infrastructure of the Internet; it is used for these applications:

■ With secure web servers for website authentication in the Secure Sockets Layer (SSL) protocol

■ With web browsers for services that implement client certificates in the SSL protocol

■ With user mail agents that support mail protection using the Secure/Multipurpose Internet Mail Extensions (S/MIME) protocol

■ In IPsec virtual private networks (VPN) where certificates can be used as a public key distribution mechanism for Internet Key Exchange (IKE) and RSA-based authentication

The most important pieces of information that are contained in the certificate are these:

■ Name of the owner

■ Public key

■ Signature of the CA

Table 14-2 *X.509v3 Certificate*

Certificate Format Version	Version 3
Certificate Serial Number	12457801
Signature Algorithm Identifier for CA	RSA with SHA-1
Issuer X.500 Name	C = U.S. O = Cisco CN = CA
Validity Period	Start = 04/01/04 Expire = 04/01/09
Subject X.500 Name	C = U.S. O = Cisco CN = CCMCluster001
Subject Public Key Information	756ECE0C9ADC7140...
Extension(s) (v3)	—
CA signature	2C086C7FE0B6E90DA396AB...

Other fields give this information:

■ Certificate serial number

■ Certificate validity period

■ Algorithms that are used to generate the CA's signature

PKI Example: SSL on the Internet

If a web server runs sensitive applications, SSL or TLS is used to secure the communication channel between the client and the server.

A company that needs to run a secure web server (a server supporting authenticated and encrypted HTTP sessions) first generates a public and private key on the web server, as shown in Figure 14-16. The public key is then sent to one of the Internet CAs. After verifying the submitter's identity, the CA issues a certificate to the server by signing the public key of the web server with the private key of the CA.

Figure 14-16 *Internet Web Server Certificate*

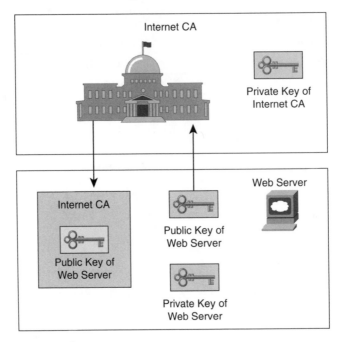

Internet CAs are mainly run by specialized private companies such as VeriSign, telecommunications companies, or governments. The certificates of those CAs are embedded at installation into client operating systems (such as Microsoft Windows) or inside browsers (such as Mozilla). The collection of embedded CA certificates serves as the trust anchor for the user. The user can then verify the validity of signatures of any other certificate signed using the public keys contained in those CA certificates.

Internet Web Browser: Embedded Internet-CA Certificates

An example of embedded Internet-CA certificates can be seen in the Microsoft Internet Explorer web browser, shown in Figure 14-17.

To see the CA certificates installed in your Microsoft computer, open Internet Explorer and choose **Tools > Internet Options.** Choose the **Content** tab, click **Publishers**, and then choose the **Trusted Root Certification Authorities** tab.

Figure 14-17   *Internet Web Browser: Embedded Internet-CA Certificates*

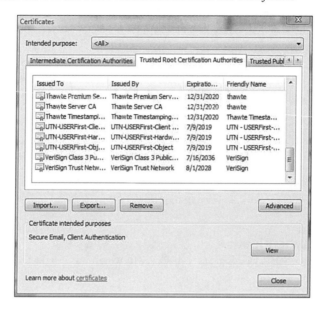

Obtaining the Authentic Public Key of the Web Server

When a browser contacts a secure web server using HTTPS, the first step of the protocol is to authenticate the web server to verify that the browser indeed has connected to the correct web server, as desired by the user. To authenticate the web server, the browser first needs to obtain the public key of the web server, as shown in Figure 14-18.

Figure 14-18   *Obtaining the Authentic Public Key of the Web Server*

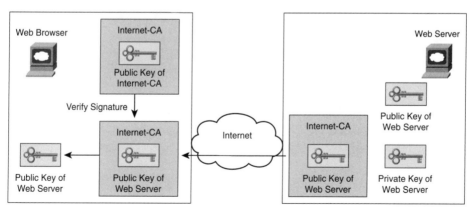

In this example, a user connects to https://www.amazon.com.

Authentication of the web server uses a challenge-response method, with which the server will prove that it possesses the private key of https://www.amazon.com. However, to prove possession of the server's private key, the browser needs the server's public key first. Here is the sequence of events:

1. When the client connects to the https://www.amazon.com web server, the web server sends its certificate, signed by a well-known Internet CA to the client.

2. The client uses one of the local CA certificates (the certificate of the issuer of the server's certificate) to verify its validity. Optionally, it downloads the certificate revocation list (CRL) to verify that the server certificate has not been revoked.

3. If verification is successful, the client now knows that it possesses an authentic public key of the https://www.amazon.com server.

Web Server Authentication

Next, the client checks whether the web server to which it is connected is authentic, as shown in Figure 14-19.

Figure 14-19 *Web Server Authentication*

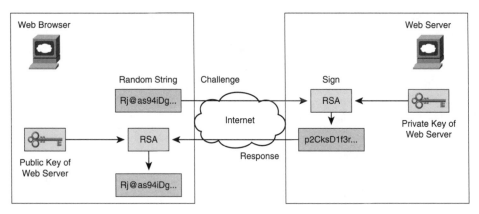

The client challenges the web server to verify that the web server has the private key that belongs to the public key that the client received in the web server's certificate. This private key should be known only to the https://www.amazon.com web server:

1. The client generates random data and sends it to the web server to be encrypted with the private key of the web server (challenge).

2.   The web server signs (RSA-encrypts) the random data using its private key and returns
     the signed random data to the client (response).

3.   The client verifies (RSA-decrypts) the signed random data using the server's public
     key from the verified certificate and compares it to the random data that the client
     generated previously.

4.   If the signature is authentic, the web server really does possess the private key
     corresponding to the public key in the certificate of the web server (https://
     www.amazon.com), and therefore it is authentic.

> **NOTE**   In this example, the web server is authenticated by the client; the web server,
> however, has no idea about the client's identity. Authentication of the client is optional
> in SSL and TLS. If it is used, it uses the reverse procedure to authenticate the client,
> provided that the client also possesses a private and public RSA key pair and a certificate
> recognized by the web server. However, most servers choose to authenticate the client
> using a simple username-and-password mechanism over the secure SSL or TLS session,
> because this method is easier to deploy than client-side certificates.

Exchanging Symmetric Session Keys

Using the web server's authentic certificate, the client can now safely send session keys, as
shown in Figure 14-20. These keys will be required later for SSL or TLS packet encryption
and authentication.

Figure 14-20   *Exchange of Symmetric Session Keys*

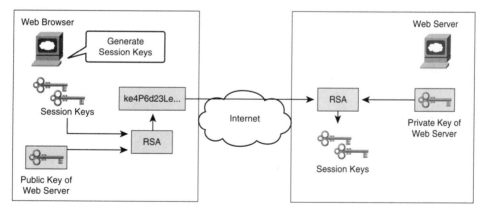

As shown in the figure, session keys are exchanged in the following way:

1. The client generates symmetric session keys for SSL or TLS HMAC and encryption algorithms.

2. The client encrypts these keys using the https://www.amazon.com public key of the web server and sends them to the server.

3. The https://www.amazon.com web server (only) can decrypt the encrypted session keys using its private key.

Session Encryption

Now, because the client and the server share the secret session keys, they can use them to sign and encrypt their packets.

As shown in Figure 14-21, HMAC algorithms (such as keyed MD5 or keyed SHA-1) are used for packet authentication, and symmetric encryption algorithms (such as 3DES, AES, or RC4) are used for packet encryption.

Figure 14-21   *Session Encryption*

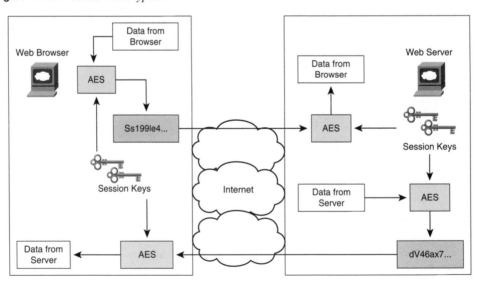

Summary

The following key points were discussed in this chapter:

- Cryptography is the science of transforming cleartext into ciphertext and transforming the ciphertext back into cleartext. It provides four services: authenticity, integrity, confidentiality, and nonrepudiation.

- Symmetric encryption uses the same key for encryption and decryption. Asymmetric encryption uses different keys for encryption and decryption.

- Hashes are one-way functions that can be used to authenticate data if a secret value, shared between the two peers, is added to the input data.

- Digital signatures sign data by using asymmetric encryption to encrypt fingerprints (hashes) of the data.

- PKI uses the concept of a single trusted introducer to eliminate the need for any-to-any authentication.

- SSL is a common example of a PKI-enabled protocol.

References

For additional information, refer to the following book:

- DeLaet, Gert, and Gert Schauwers, *Network Security Fundamentals*, Indianapolis: Cisco Press, 2004 (ISBN-10: 1-58705-167-2; ISBN-13: 978-1-58705-167-8)

Review Questions

Use these questions to review what you've learned in this chapter. The answers appear in Appendix A, "Answers to Chapter Review Questions."

1. Which two of the following are not cryptographic services?

   a. Authenticity

   b. Confidentiality

   c. Integrity

   d. Nonrepudiation

   e. Resistance against DoS

   f. Defense in depth

2. Which two statements about asymmetric encryption are true?

    a. Asymmetric encryption is considerably faster than symmetric encryption.

    b. Asymmetric encryption keys should have about half the lifetime of symmetric encryption keys.

    c. With asymmetric encryption, the private key can only encrypt data, and the public key can only decrypt data.

    d. With asymmetric encryption, either of the two keys can be used for encryption, and the other key has to be used for decryption.

    e. NSA is an example of an asymmetric encryption algorithm.

    f. Asymmetric encryption is often used to create signatures.

3. Which statement about hash functions is true?

    a. A hash digest can practically never be reverted to the hashed data.

    b. It is somewhat computationally difficult to revert a hash digest to the hashed data.

    c. Data can be encrypted if it is hashed with a secret key.

    d. AES can use SHA-1 for data encryption.

4. Which of the following statements is not true of digital signatures?

    a. Digital signatures provide data authenticity.

    b. Digital signatures provide data integrity.

    c. Digital signatures provide nonrepudiation.

    d. Digital signatures do not provide data confidentiality.

    e. Digital signatures are based on asymmetric cryptographic algorithms.

    f. Digital signatures are created by hashing the result of an asymmetric encryption.

5. Which problem does PKI solve?

    a. The lack of a common encryption standard for Internet applications

    b. The problem that asymmetric encryption techniques do not work without a PKI

    c. The fact that Diffie-Hellman is not secure

    d. The problem of scalable, secure distribution of public RSA keys

    e. The problem of manually issuing bulk certificates

    f. The performance problem when using RSA

6. What is the certificate of a web server used for when you are using SSL?

   a. It is used to authenticate the client.

   b. The client uses the server's public key when encrypting the data sent to the server.

   c. The client uses the server's private key when encrypting the data sent to the server.

   d. It is used to authenticate the server and to encrypt the symmetric session keys used for the asymmetric encryption of the data stream.

   e. It is used to authenticate the server and to encrypt the symmetric session keys used for the authentication and encryption of the data stream.

7. Which statement about cryptography is true?

   a. PKI uses symmetric encryption with shared keys.

   b. PKI uses symmetric encryption with public and private keys.

   c. PKI uses asymmetric encryption with shared keys.

   d. PKI uses asymmetric encryption with public and private keys.

CHAPTER 15

Understanding Native CUCM Security Features and CUCM PKI

CUCM supports several security features. Some are natively supported, and others are based on the CUCM public key infrastructure (PKI) discussed in the preceding chapter. PKI does require extra hardware in a CUCM implementation, called Cisco security tokens. The CUCM PKI is standards-based and has some modifications that allow it to be used with Cisco IP Phones. It is important to understand which security features are natively supported, which features rely on the Cisco PKI, and how the CUCM PKI differs from a standard PKI that is used on the Internet. This chapter discusses the natively supported security features of CUCM and provides information about the CUCM PKI.

Chapter Objectives

Upon completing this chapter, you will be able to describe natively supported CUCM security features, and the CUCM PKI implementation, which is used to enable additional CUCM security features. You will be able to meet these objectives:

- List CUCM security features, and state whether they are based on the Cisco PKI or natively supported by CUCM

- Describe how CUCM supports IPsec and when to use IPsec

- Describe how signed phone loads work

- Describe and configure SIP digest authentication

- Describe and configure SIP trunk encryption

- Describe CUCM PKI

- Describe the function of the CTL and how it is created and used

- Describe how secure Cisco Unified SRST works and how it integrates with the PKI used by CUCM

CUCM Security Features Overview

CUCM, voice gateways, and Cisco IP Phones are subject to the same threats as any other network-based application. However, CUCM supports several security features that help protect the application and devices from threats, as shown in Figure 15-1.

Figure 15-1 *CUCM Security Features Overview*

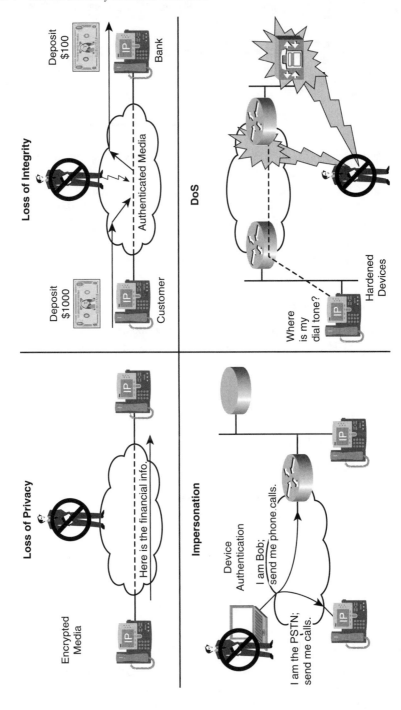

Examples include the following:

- **Loss of privacy:** Can be avoided by encrypted media.

- **Impersonation of phones or gateways:** Can be stopped by device authentication.

- **Loss of integrity:** Can be avoided by authenticated packets.

- **Denial-of-service attacks:** Can be mitigated by device hardening.

CUCM Security Feature Support

Security features supported by CUCM can be categorized into two types: features that are natively supported with CUCM without the need for extra hardware, and features that are based on the CUCM PKI, which requires an extra product called Cisco security tokens to be enabled. Table 15-1 lists the built-in CUCM security features and compares them to the security features that are based on the CUCM PKI.

Table 15-1 *CUCM Security Feature Support*

CUCM Natively Supported Security Features (No Extra Products Required)	CUCM Security Features Based on the Cisco PKI (Requires Cisco Security Tokens)
Hardened CUCM server OS	Signed and encrypted configuration files
Phone hardening	Secure signaling for Cisco IP Phone IP Phones
IPsec support in Unified CM	SRTP between Cisco IP Phones
Signed phone loads	SRTP to MGCP and H.323 Cisco IOS gateways
SIP digest authentication	Secure conferencing
SIP trunk authentication	Secure SRST

For Secure Real-Time Transfer Protocol (SRTP) to Media Gateway Control Protocol (MGCP) and H.323 Cisco IOS gateways, secure conferencing, and secure Survivable Remote Site Telephony (SRST), certain hardware and software requirements have to be met on the router platforms. This is described in the next chapter.

Cisco Unified Communications Security Considerations

A Cisco Unified Communications solution is based on an IP network infrastructure and can involve many products in addition to CUCM.

> **NOTE**   This book covers CUCM security features only. It does not cover legal aspects, the need for written security policies, physical and network infrastructure security, intrusion detection and prevention, audits, logging and log analysis, and other aspects of network security.

For an overall security implementation, all these aspects must be considered. From a security perspective, Cisco Unified Communications should be treated as just another application that uses the network that has to be secured in its entirety. For more information about network security, refer to the current Cisco CCSP books.

It is important to note that securing Cisco Unified Communications against threats might cause the following issues:

- **Signaling application inspection in firewalls:** Firewalls such as the Cisco ASA 5500 Series Adaptive Security Appliance can dynamically permit Real-Time Transport Protocol (RTP) streams based on the information seen in signaling messages. If a call is set up correctly, only those sockets that have been agreed on in signaling messages are permitted. After a call is torn down, the permission is removed, because the firewall has seen the appropriate signaling messages. If encrypted signaling is used, a firewall cannot interpret the signaling messages, and permissions cannot be added and removed dynamically.

- **Features such as contact center call supervision and call monitoring:** Cisco Unified Contact Center includes features such as call monitoring and call supervision. If media streams are encrypted, such features do not work.

- **Performance of servers:** Using Transport Layer Security (TLS) for signaling results in higher CPU load and memory consumption in CUCM servers.

- **Bypassing access lists when IPsec tunnels are used:** When you use IPsec tunnels through firewalls or devices that have IP access lists configured, you cannot filter on the IP packet, which is tunneled through IPsec. IPsec packets can only generally be permitted or denied, independent of their payload (the original IP packet before IPsec tunnel encapsulation).

- **Troubleshooting, packet analysis:** When encrypted signaling is used, troubleshooting is more difficult, because packets that have been sniffed on the wire can no longer be interpreted. You can interpret such packets at CUCM only before they are wrapped into TLS. SRTP can break interoperability with third-party RTP monitoring systems.

CUCM IPsec Support

IPsec is a universal application-independent protocol that can secure any IP packets. It is network layer-based, which means that it is based on IP packets and not on specific application traffic.

IPsec should be used for any sensitive traffic that is not protected by the application. For instance, IPsec should be used for the exchange of Secure RTP (SRTP) session keys in cleartext signaling traffic. This recommendation applies to the following scenarios:

- **Server-to-server intracluster signaling:** When intracluster calls are placed between phones that are registered to different servers in the cluster, server-to-server intracluster signaling is required. If the phones use media encryption, the keys that will be used are sent in cleartext inside server-to-server intracluster signaling messages.

- **Intercluster trunk signaling:** The same requirements that exist for server-to-server intracluster signaling apply to intercluster calls between phones that use media encryption. The SRTP session keys are sent over the intercluster trunk in cleartext signaling messages.

- **Signaling to MGCP and H.323 gateways:** When SRTP is used to signal MGCP or H.323 gateways, the SRTP session keys are exchanged in cleartext between CUCM and the gateways.

CUCM supports IPsec with preshared keys or digital certificates. Authentication Header (AH) is not supported, but Encapsulated Security Payload (ESP) is supported with authentication and encryption.

Because IPsec includes device authentication, it prevents an attacker from impersonating the IPsec peers. IPsec packet authentication prevents falsification of packets (it provides integrity assurance), and IPsec encryption prevents eavesdropping (it provides confidentiality assurance).

IPsec Scenarios in Cisco Unified Communications

CUCM supports SRTP between some IP telephony endpoints where the SRTP session keys are exchanged in cleartext. Such scenarios can be secured by IPsec, as shown in Figure 15-2.

Figure 15-2 *IPsec Scenarios in Cisco Unified Communications*

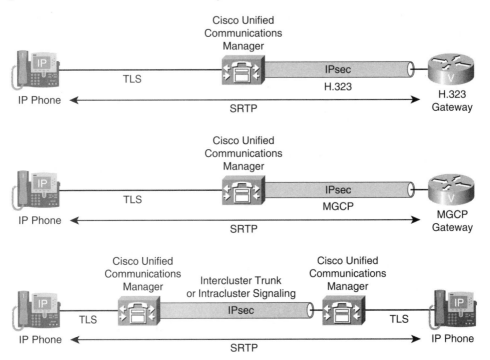

Secure audio can be applied in the following ways:

■ **SRTP to H.323 or MGCP gateways:** In both of these two cases, the session keys are exchanged between CUCM and the gateway in cleartext signaling messages. If you deploy IPsec between CUCM and the gateway, signaling messages can be encrypted, and hence session keys are not exposed.

■ **SRTP between two CUCM servers (intracluster or intercluster):** When SRTP over intercluster trunks or between phones registered to different servers within the same cluster is used, SRTP session keys are again sent in cleartext. If you deploy IPsec between these CUCM servers, signaling messages can be encrypted, and hence session keys are not exposed.

The recommendation, however, is not to enable IPsec in CUCM but to use it between network infrastructure devices only. CUCM servers are not primarily designed to encrypt IP packets, and all encryption and decryption is performed in software. Other network infrastructure devices are specifically designed to perform encryption that is usually performed in hardware, including Cisco ASA, Cisco integrated services routers (ISR), and Cisco virtual private network (VPN) concentrators.

IPsec on Network Infrastructure Devices

For performance reasons, recommended practice dictates running IPsec on network infrastructure devices instead of enabling it on CUCM servers, as illustrated in Figure 15-3.

Figure 15-3   *IPsec on Network Infrastructure Devices*

In most cases, running IPsec on network infrastructure devices is not a problem, because the path between the CUCM server and the next network infrastructure device, such as Cisco ISR, should be trusted anyway. Because servers should be physically secured, it is very unlikely that there would be an attack on that server network between CUCM and the first router. Therefore, no extra protection is required for this segment.

Untrusted networks are usually somewhere else along the path. In most cases, these are WAN links or networks that cannot be physically protected well enough (for example, connections between buildings in a campus environment). These untrusted networks should be protected by IPsec (not only for Cisco Unified Communications traffic, but also for other network traffic). This means that the routers that face these insecure links are the optimal endpoints of IPsec tunnels.

Careful evaluation of trusted and untrusted network segments is important when IPsec is deployed on the infrastructure instead of on the actual endpoints of CUCM servers.

Signed Phone Loads

Signed phone loads are supported on all Cisco IP Phone models. With signed phone loads, the images are signed by Cisco manufacturing (by using a private key), and the signature is appended to the actual firmware. Figure 15-4 shows a Cisco IP Phone, with images from a TFTP server, protected from falsification.

Signed phone loads were introduced with Cisco CallManager Release 3.3(3). In this and later releases, phone images include the public key that corresponds to the private key that is used by Cisco manufacturing to sign phone images. In addition, the firmware accepts new images only if the signature is authentic.

Figure 15-4   *Signed Phone Loads*

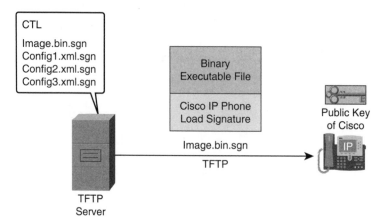

Signed phone loads do not need any additional configuration and are totally independent of the CUCM PKI that is used for other features.

The phone also checks the image device type so that incorrect images (those for other phone models) are not loaded.

> **NOTE**   If you need to downgrade to an IP Phone image that does not yet support IP Phone image authentication (earlier than Cisco CallManager Release 3.3[3]), a special "breakout" image can be obtained from the Cisco Technical Assistance Center (TAC). Simply trying to load an older image will not work, because the current image will accept only signed images.

SIP Digest Authentication

Session Initiation Protocol (SIP) digest authentication can be used when Transport Layer Security (TLS) is not supported. Third-party SIP phones and Cisco Unified IP Phone 7905, 7940, and 7960 models using SIP instead of Skinny Client Control Protocol (SCCP) do not support TLS; thus, SIP digest authentication can provide security for such devices.

SIP digest authentication provides signaling protection by authenticating components of SIP signaling messages. SIP digest authentication uses Hashed Message Authentication Code (HMAC).

SIP digest authentication is based on a client/server model in which the server sends challenges to the client and the client responds to these challenges.

CUCM supports SIP digest authentication for SIP phones and on SIP trunks. CUCM can act as a server toward SIP phones and supports both functions (client and server) on SIP trunks.

It is important to note that SIP digest authentication is authentication only, whereas messages are not encrypted.

When SIP digest authentication with Cisco IP Phones is used, the HMAC key is downloaded to the IP Phone inside the IP Phone configuration file. So that you do not expose the SIP digest HMAC key, it is recommended that you use encrypted configuration files in this case.

SIP digest authentication prevents falsification of SIP signaling messages.

SIP Digest Authentication Configuration Procedure

SIP digest authentication configuration involves phone configuration, SIP phone security profile configuration, and end-user configuration. The configuration steps are as follows:

Step 1 Check the Enable Digest Authentication check box in a SIP phone security profile.

Step 2 Apply the SIP phone security profile to the phone.

Step 3 Configure the digest credentials in the End User Configuration window.

Step 4 Choose the digest user in the Phone Configuration window.

SIP Digest Authentication Configuration Example

Figure 15-5 shows Steps 1 and 2 of the configuration procedure.

In Step 1, check the **Enable Digest Authentication** check box in the SIP phone security profile that you intend to use on the phone. In Step 2, apply the SIP phone security profile you created in Step 1 to the SIP phone.

Figure 15-6 shows Steps 3 and 4 of the configuration procedure. In Step 3, add the end user if that user does not already exist, and enter the digest credentials. The digest credentials consist of a string of alphanumeric characters. In Step 4, from the **Digest User** drop-down list in the Phone Configuration window, choose the digest user you created in Step 3.

Figure 15-5 *SIP Digest Authentication Configuration*

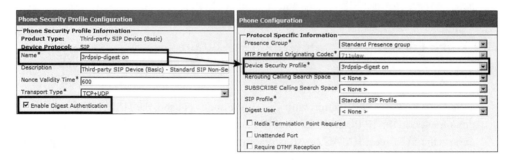

Figure 15-6 *SIP Digest Authentication Configuration, Continued*

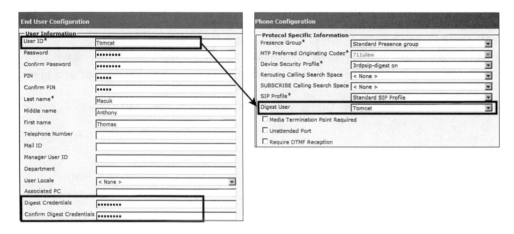

SIP Trunk Encryption

SIP digest authentication is not considered to be very secure. It also lacks confidentiality because it hashes only a username, password, and some message components, such as the SIP uniform resource identifier (URI).

For increased security, SIP trunks also support encryption.

SIP trunk encryption protects SIP signaling messages by using TLS with packet authentication (HMAC) and encryption (AES). SIP trunk encryption uses mutual certificate-based TLS device authentication. Therefore, CUCM must trust the issuer of the certificate for the peer. The certificate can be self-signed or signed by a certification authority (CA). The subject that will be used in the certificate has to be configured when SIP trunk encryption is enabled so that CUCM knows what certificate should be used on the trunk.

SIP trunk encryption protects SIP signaling messages by using TLS only. It does not support SRTP for the media channels.

SIP Trunk Encryption Configuration Procedure

SIP trunk encryption involves SIP trunk security profile configuration, SIP trunk configuration, and certificate management. The configuration steps are as follows:

Step 1   Set the Device Security Mode to Encrypted in a SIP trunk security profile.

Step 2   Set the X.509v3 certificate subject in the SIP trunk security profile.

Step 3   Apply the SIP trunk security profile to the trunk.

Step 4   Add the certificate of the issuer of the peer's certificate to CUCM.

SIP Trunk Encryption Configuration

Figure 15-7 shows Steps 1 to 3 of the configuration procedure.

In Step 1, set the **Device Security Mode** to **Encrypted**. In Step 2, enter the subject of the certificate that the peer will use. In Step 3, apply the SIP trunk security profile to the SIP trunk. Step 4 is performed in the third party or another Cisco SIP peer and is not shown in the figure.

Figure 15-7   *SIP Trunk Encryption Configuration*

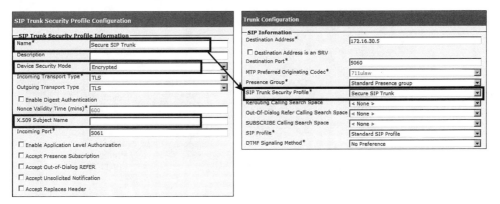

CUCM PKI

Unlike classic enterprise PKI deployments, the PKI topology in CUCM is not a single PKI system. Instead of having a single certification authority (CA) that issues all certificates, different types of certificates are issued by different entities:

- **Self-signed certificates:** CUCM services (Cisco CallManager, TFTP, and CAPF) issue their certificates on their own.

- **Certificates signed by the Cisco manufacturing CA:** Some Cisco IP Phone models (including Cisco IP Phone 797x, 794[125], and 796[125] and 7911 models) have manufacturing installed certificates (MIC).

- **Certificates signed by CUCM Certificate Authority Proxy Function (CAPF) or by an external CA:** Locally significant certificates (LSC) can be assigned to Cisco IP Phones that have MICs and to Cisco IP Phone 7940 and 7960 models. LSCs are issued either by the CUCM CAPF acting as a CA or from an external CA. If LSCs are issued by an external CA, CAPF acts as a proxy for the CA toward the IP Phones.

NOTE   External CAs are supported in Cisco Unified CallManager Release 4.0 or later, Cisco Unified CallManager Release 5.1 or later, and CUCM 6.0 or later. Cisco Unified CallManager Release 5.0 does not support external CAs.

Self-Signed Certificates

Figure 15-8 illustrates several IP telephony services with self-signed certificates.

Figure 15-8   *Self-Signed Certificates*

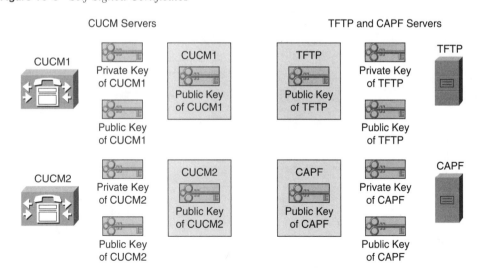

The self-signed certificates shown in the figure are as follows:

■ Each CUCM server running the Cisco CallManager service has a self-signed certificate.

■ CUCM TFTP servers have self-signed certificates.

■ If the CAPF is used (needed for LSC), it has a self-signed certificate.

All these services act as their own PKI root.

Manufacturing Installed Certificates

Figure 15-9 shows the PKI that is used for MICs.

The PKI that is used for MICs has the following characteristics:

■ Cisco IP Phones with MICs have a public and private key pair, a MIC for their own public key, and a Cisco manufacturing CA certificate, all of which are installed during production.

■ The IP Phone certificate (MIC) is signed by the Cisco manufacturing CA.

The Cisco manufacturing CA is the PKI root for all MICs. Cisco IP Phones that have MICs include the 7911, 7941/5, 7961/5, 7970, and 7971 models.

Figure 15-9   *Manufacturing Installed Certificates (MIC)*

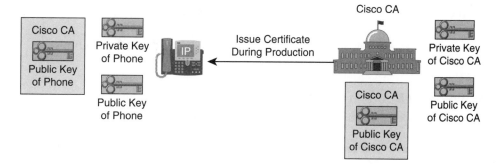

Locally Significant Certificates

Figure 15-10 shows LSCs being issued to Cisco IP Phones.

Figure 15-10 *Locally Significant Certificates (LSC)*

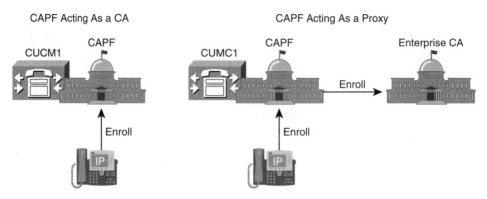

Cisco IP Phone 7940 and 7960 models do not have a MIC installed. They have to request an LSC from the CAPF, which is signed in one of two ways:

■ The CAPF can issue the certificate on its own (acting as a CA).

■ The CAPF can issue proxy enrollment requests to an external CA, and the external CA issues the certificate.

Cisco IP Phones that have MICs can also request an LSC from the CAPF. If a phone has a MIC and an LSC, the LSC has higher priority.

The CAPF or an external CA is the root for all LSCs.

NOTE   External CAs currently are not supported with CUCM Release 5.0.

Multiple PKI Roots in CUCM Deployments

As illustrated in Figure 15-11, several PKI topologies may coexist in CUCM deployments.

Note how there is no single root. Instead, there are multiple independent PKI topologies. All of them have to be trusted by an IP Phone. Like the built-in root certificate store in a web browser, IP Phones require a list of PKI roots they should trust. The Cisco Certificate Trust List (CTL) is used for that purpose.

Figure 15-11 *Multiple PKI Roots in CUCM Deployments*

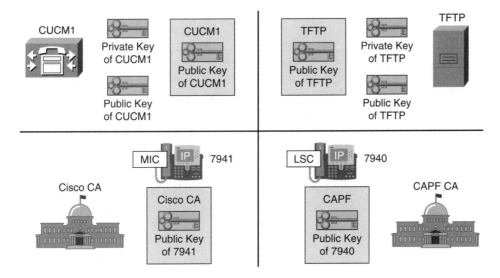

Cisco Certificate Trust List

The Cisco CTL is a list of certificate issuers (PKI roots) that a Cisco IP Phone needs to trust. It is created by an application, the Cisco CTL client, as shown in Figure 15-12.

Figure 15-12 *Cisco CTL*

The Cisco CTL client collects certificates of PKI roots (including the certificates of the Cisco CTL client, which are its security tokens), builds the Cisco CTL, and then signs the list by using a security token.

> **NOTE** A security token is like a "mini computer" that acts like a CA. It has a public and private key, and a certificate, and it can sign data by using its private key. The private key never leaves the token. An application such as the Cisco CTL client, which has data (the Cisco CTL) that needs to be signed, first passes the data to the security token. Inside the security token, the data is signed. Then the data, along with its signature, is returned to the application.

The Cisco CTL needs to be updated (and signed again) only if there are any changes to one of the PKI roots: the CallManager, TFTP, or CAPF services or Cisco CTL client (security tokens).

The Cisco CTL also acts as an authorization list that specifies what certificate can be used for what purpose.

Cisco CTL Client Function

Figure 15-13 shows how the Cisco CTL client creates and signs the Cisco CTL:

Step 1 The Cisco CTL client obtains the certificates of all entities that issue certificates (self-signed certificates only or certificates for other devices).

Step 2 The certificates of the Cisco CTL client itself have to be added to the list. They are stored on security tokens (together with a public and private key pair). A Cisco CTL must include at least two different security tokens (for backup reasons). The recommendation is to have one security token per administrator plus one spare security token.

Step 3 The certificates of the security tokens are added to the list one by one.

Step 4 The Cisco CTL client signs the list of these certificates, the Cisco CTL, by using one of its security tokens that were added to the Cisco CTL.

Step 5 Finally, there is a single, trusted introducer in the system again: The Cisco CTL client "introduces" trusted devices such as the TFTP or CUCM servers. It does this not by signing their certificates, but by signing a list of these trusted devices—all PKI roots that exist in the system.

Figure 15-13 *Cisco CTL Client Function*

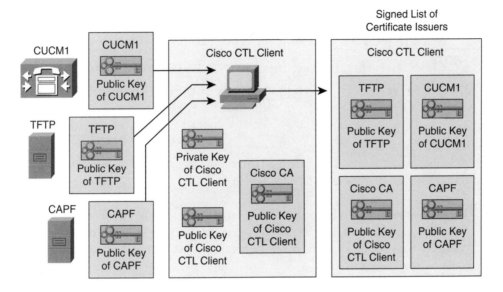

> **NOTE** The Cisco CTL can be compared to the root certificate store of a web browser. Both are a list of trusted certificate-issuing entities.

The Cisco CTL usually includes these certificates:

- **Cisco Unified Communications Manager CallManager certificates:** Each Cisco CallManager service has a self-signed certificate. It allows IP Phones to verify the authenticity of the Cisco CallManager service during registration.

- **TFTP server certificate:** The TFTP server that provides the IP Phone with files, such as the IP Phone image or the IP Phone configuration file, is trusted by the IP Phone only if the TFTP server is listed in the Cisco CTL.

- **CAPF certificate:** When you are using LSCs, the CAPF issues certificates to the IP Phones. The certificate of the CAPF allows the CAPF to authenticate to an IP Phone during the enrollment. The IP Phone verifies that certificate by comparing it to the one in the Cisco CTL.

- **Cisco manufacturing certificate:** MICs and the certificate of the security tokens (storing the keys that are used by the Cisco CTL client) are issued by the Cisco manufacturing CA. To allow the phone to verify certificates issued by this Cisco CA, the phone needs the certificate of the Cisco manufacturing CA.

- **Cisco CTL client certificate:** The Cisco CTL client signs the CTL by using one of its security tokens. The IP Phone must know the certificates of the Cisco CTL client (one per security token) to allow the CTL's signature to be verified.

Initial CTL Download

After the Cisco CTL client has been used to create a Cisco CTL, IP Phones obtain the Cisco CTL during the next boot, as shown in Figure 15-14.

The first download of a CTL to an IP Phone is not secure. The IP Phone accepts any Cisco CTL. The reason for this is that the IP Phone cannot verify the signature of the Cisco CTL because it does not yet know the public key of the Cisco CTL client (it does not know any of the security tokens).

This problem occurs only at initial deployment, when the phone does not yet have a local Cisco CTL. In this case, any security token could pretend to be a valid security token of the Cisco CTL client. An attacker could either replace the Cisco CTL file on the TFTP server with a falsified file or change the Cisco CTL file in the path between the IP Phone and the TFTP server.

Figure 15-14 *Initial CTL Download*

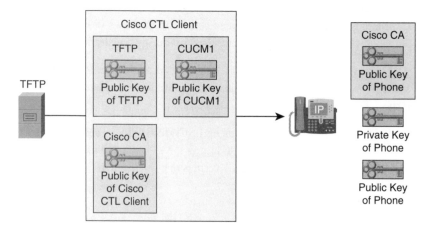

The problem can be solved by downloading the initial Cisco CTL over a trusted network to ensure that no falsified initial Cisco CTL is loaded to the phone. When the phone has a valid

Cisco CTL, it trusts new Cisco CTLs only if they are signed using a security token that is already known to the IP Phone.

If the Cisco CTL file in the IP Phone is erased, the same problem occurs. Again, you must ensure that the next Cisco CTL download is done over a trusted network path, because the IP Phone will blindly accept any Cisco CTL.

After the IP Phone is deployed, it is usually difficult to trust the network path between the phone and CUCM. Therefore, a user should not be able to erase the initially installed Cisco CTL. There are two ways to remove a CTL from an IP Phone: a factory reset or by using the IP Phone Settings menu. A factory reset is not simple, but using the Settings menu is rather easy. To prevent users from using the Settings menu to remove the CTL, you should disable settings access at the phone.

> **NOTE**   When you use authentication strings as the authentication method during CAPF phone certificate operations, you have to enable settings access during the enrollment. After successful enrollment, you should disable settings access again. This process is explained in detail in the next section.

IP Phone Verification of a New Cisco CTL

Every time an IP Phone receives a new Cisco CTL, the new Cisco CTL is verified, as shown in Figure 15-15. The new Cisco CTL is accepted by the IP Phone only if it was signed by the Cisco CTL client with one of its security tokens.

Figure 15-15   *IP Phone Verification of a New Cisco CTL*

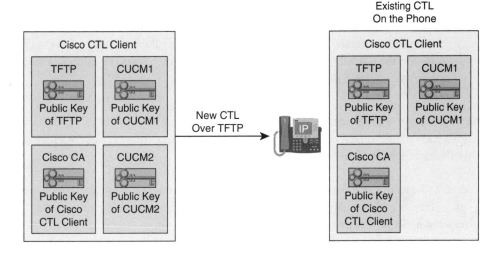

The phone can verify the signature by using the public key (the certificate) of the Cisco CTL client (the certificate of the appropriate administrator token), which must be included in the currently installed ("old") Cisco CTL.

This certificate of the security token is signed by the Cisco manufacturing CA. This signature is also validated by using the certificate of the Cisco manufacturing CA, which also must be included in the currently installed Cisco CTL.

This process works well after an initial Cisco CTL has been deployed to the Cisco IP Phones.

IP Phone Usage of the CTL

The Cisco CTL inside a Cisco IP Phone is used in the following situations:

- **Encrypted signaling:** When SCCP or SIP over TLS is used, two-way certificate-based authentication is performed. The Cisco IP Phone verifies the received, self-signed certificate of the Cisco CallManager service against its Cisco CTL.

- **LSC enrollment:** When a Cisco IP Phone requests an LSC (enrolls with the CAPF by using TLS), CAPF-to-IP phone authentication in TLS is certificate-based. The Cisco IP Phone verifies the received, self-signed certificate of the CAPF against its Cisco CTL.

- **Signed IP phone configuration files:** When signed configuration files are used, the IP Phone configuration file is signed with the private key of the TFTP server. The Cisco IP Phone needs to know the corresponding public key to be able to decrypt the configuration file.

- **Signed Cisco CTL file:** As stated earlier, Cisco CTL files are signed by the Cisco CTL client. The Cisco IP Phone only accepts a new Cisco CTL file if it was signed by one of the security tokens of the Cisco CTL client. To check whether the new Cisco CTL file has been signed by an authorized token and to verify the signature of the new Cisco CTL file, the Cisco IP Phone needs to know the trusted Cisco CTL client certificates (certificates of the Cisco CTL client security tokens).

PKI Topology with Secure SRST

Figure 15-16 illustrates a portion of the PKI topology that is used by secure SRST when an IP Phone has a conversation through a voice gateway.

An SRST gateway at a remote site can provide call control services in the event of central site failure. If cryptography is used with CUCM, the same security services are often required in SRST mode as well.

Secure SRST allows Cisco IP Phones to continue using TLS for signaling and SRTP for media exchange when in SRST failover mode. Secure SRST therefore prevents impersonation of the SRST gateway and IP Phones, as well as falsification and eavesdropping of signaling and media packets.

Figure 15-16 *IP Secure SRST Overview*

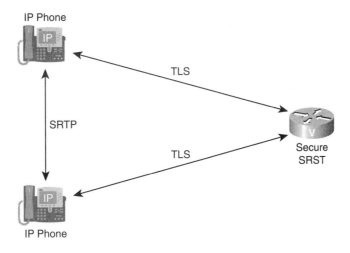

The SRST gateway acts like a Cisco CallManager service when in failover mode, because it provides signaling to the IP Phones. Therefore, it needs its own certificate, as shown in Figure 15-17. It will use this certificate to authenticate itself to the phone in a TLS protected signaling session. The SRST gateway obtains this certificate from a CA, either via Simple Certificate Enrollment Protocol (SCEP) or via manual cut-and-paste enrollment performed by the administrator.

Figure 15-17 *PKI Topology with Secure SRST*

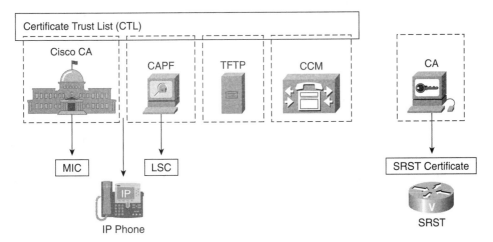

The SRST gateway cannot generate a self-signed certificate or enroll with the CAPF. Instead, it has to obtain a certificate from a proper CA. This CA can be a Cisco IOS CA, which can even run on the same router.

Trust Requirements with Secure SRST

IP Phones and the secure SRST gateway need to trust each other when in SRST mode.

When the IP Phone registers with the secure SRST gateway, the secure SRST gateway presents its certificate to the IP Phone. This certificate was issued by an external CA, which the IP Phone does not know about. The IP Phone does not verify the certificate of the secure SRST gateway by its signature. Instead, CUCM obtains the certificate of the secure SRST gateway during configuration time and then adds it to the phone configuration file. After CUCM receives the certificate of the SRST gateway, the certificate has to be out-of-band verified.

The IP Phone can now check the certificate received from the secure SRST gateway against the one found in its configuration file.

On the other hand, the IP Phone has to authenticate to the secure SRST gateway. IP Phone certificates are issued either by CAPF (in case of LSCs) or by a Cisco manufacturing CA (in case of MICs). Therefore, the secure SRST gateway must know CAPF and Cisco manufacturing CAs. These certificates are added manually to the secure SRST gateway.

The IP Phone can now check the signature of received IP Phone certificates by using the public key of the issuer.

This process is illustrated further in the next chapter.

Secure SRST: Certificate Import: CUCM

When the secure SRST gateway is configured, CUCM pulls the SRST gateway certificate from the credentials service over the network. The authenticity of the certificate is verified out-of-band. CUCM presents the fingerprint (Secure Hash Algorithm 1 [SHA-1] hash) of the received certificate. As a result of adding the SRST Reference, as shown in Figure 15-18, the administrator sees an Internet Explorer (IE) popup and must manually compare the entries with the known authentic fingerprint of this certificate.

Alternatively, this initial contact between CUCM and the SRST router could be performed over a trusted network. Then no out-of-band verification is needed.

Figure 15-18 *Secure SRST: Certificate Import: CUCM*

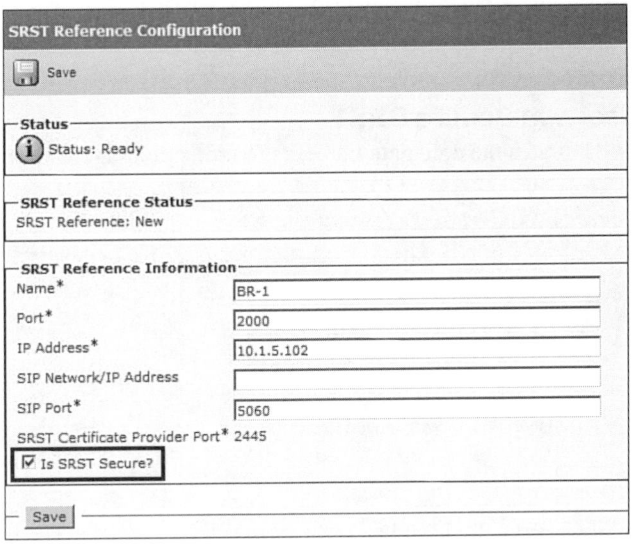

Secure SRST: Certificate Import: Secure SRST Gateway

Example 15-1 shows how the certificates of phone certificate issuers are added to the secure SRST gateway.

Example 15-1 *Certificate Import: Secure SRST Gateway*

```
srst(config)#crypto pki trustpoint CAPF
  srst(ca-trustpoint)#enrollment terminal
  srst(ca-trustpoint)#revocation-check none
  srst(ca-trustpoint)#exit
srst(config)#crypto pki authenticate CAPF
Enter the base 64 encoded CA certificate.
End with a blank line or the word "quit" on a line by itself
(Paste the certificate)
                  :
quit
Certificate has the following attributes:
Fingerprint MD5: F7E150EA 5E6E3AC5 615FC696 66415C9F
Fingerprint SHA1: 1BE2B503 DC72EE28 0C0F6B18 798236D8 D3B18BE6
% Do you accept this certificate? [yes/no]: y
Trustpoint CA certificate accepted.
% Certificate successfully imported
```

On the SRST router, the Cisco manufacturing certificates and the CAPF certificate have to be pasted into the configuration of the gateway. The certificates are copied from CUCM manually into the SRST gateway configuration and therefore do not need to be out-of-band verified.

Certificate Usage in Secure SRST

Figure 15-19 illustrates the complete process of certificate usage with secure SRST.

Figure 15-19   *Secure SRST Certificate Usage*

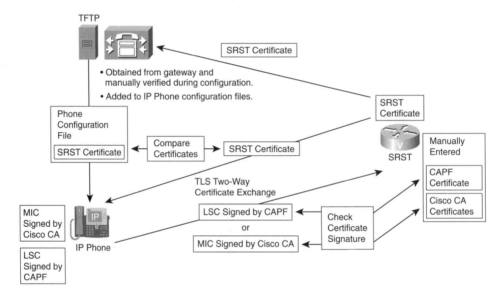

Certificate usage in secure SRST consists of the following steps:

■ The scenario begins with a secure CUCM deployment that includes IP Phones with certificates issued by either Cisco manufacturing or the CAPF.

■ The secure SRST gateway enrolls with a CA.

At this point, the IP Phones and the secure SRST gateway have certificates.

■ When the secure SRST gateway into the CUCM configuration is added, CUCM obtains the certificate of the secure SRST gateway from the gateway and manually verifies it out-of-band.

■ If the verification is okay (and the administrator accepts the certificate), CUCM adds the certificate to IP Phone configuration files.

- The Cisco manufacturing and CAPF certificates are manually copied into the secure SRST gateway configuration.

Now both sides have the means to verify each other:

- When an IP Phone registers with the secure SRST gateway by using TLS, the secure SRST gateway sends its certificate to the IP Phone.

- The IP Phone does not verify the signature of that certificate. Instead, it compares the certificate itself against the one in the phone configuration file. If the thumbprints of these two are identical, the received certificate is considered to be authentic.

- The IP Phone presents its certificate to the secure SRST gateway.

- The SRST gateway has the certificate of the issuer of the received phone certificate (either CAPF or Cisco manufacturing) in its configuration. It can now verify the signature of the certificate of the IP Phone. If the signature is valid, the received certificate is considered to be authentic.

The IP Phone and secure SRST can now establish the TLS session that is used for authenticated and encrypted signaling. The result is a secure communication between the IP Phone and the SRST gateway.

Summary

The following key points were discussed in this chapter:

- CUCM natively supports security features and provides additional security features based on the Cisco PKI, which can be enabled by Cisco security tokens.

- IPsec can be used if no application-layer protection is supported.

- Cisco IP Phone loads have been signed since Cisco CallManager Release 3.3(3).

- Digest authentication can be used on SIP trunks and IP Phones that do not support TLS.

- SIP trunk encryption allows TLS to be used for signaling across SIP trunks.

- The Cisco PKI in CUCM consists of multiple PKI topologies with different roots.

- The Cisco CTL includes certificates of all certificate issuers that a Cisco IP Phone has to trust.

- SRST gateways support TLS, which provides secure calls in cases where CUCM is not reachable and Cisco IP Phones register with SRST gateways instead.

References

For additional information, refer to these resources:

- Cisco Systems, Inc., Cisco Unified Communications Solution Reference Network Design (SRND), based on CUCM Release 6.x, June 2007

- Cisco Systems, Inc., *CUCM Administration Guide Release 6.0(1)*

- Cisco Systems, Inc., *Communications Manager Security Guide*

Review Questions

Use these questions to review what you've learned in this chapter. The answers appear in Appendix A, "Answers to Chapter Review Questions."

1. Which two of the following are not security threats to an IP telephony system?

   a. Loss of privacy

   b. Impersonation

   c. Integrity

   d. Loss of integrity

   e. Loss of control

2. Which statement about IPsec in CUCM is true?

   a. CUCM supports IPsec with preshared keys only.

   b. CUCM supports IPsec with certificates only.

   c. CUCM supports IPsec with preshared keys or certificates.

   d. CUCM does not support IPsec. It can be done only on network devices.

3. Which statement about SIP digest authentication is false?

   a. It provides authentication only using HMAC.

   b. It is based on a client/server model (the server challenges the client).

   c. CUCM supports only the server function to IP Phones (it sends challenges only).

   d. If used with third-party SIP phones, an HMAC key is downloaded in the TFTP configuration file.

   e. Some phones have a built-in conference bridge supporting G.729.

4. SIP trunk encryption provides TLS protection for SIP signaling but does not support SRTP.

   a. True

   b. False

5. Which statement about enrollment in the CUCM PKI is true?

   a. MICs are issued by CAPF.

   b. LSCs are issued by the Cisco CTL client or by CAPF.

   c. CAPF enrollment supports the use of authentication strings.

   d. CAPF itself has to enroll with the Cisco CTL client.

   e. Enrollment of IP Phones occurs automatically if the cluster is in secure-only mode.

   f. LSCs can be issued by an external CA when using the CTL client as a proxy.

6. Which of the following entities uses a smart token for key storage?

   a. CTL

   b. CTL client

   c. CAPF in proxy mode

   d. CAPF in CA mode

   e. Cisco IP Phone 7940 and 7960

   f. Cisco IP Phone 7970

7. Which statement about secure SRST is true?

   a. You have to manually enter the certificates of CAs that issue phone certificates to the gateway.

   b. You have to manually enter the gateway's certificate into CUCM.

   c. You do not have to enter any certificates manually.

   d. In a fallback event, the gateway requests all phone certificates from CUCM.

CHAPTER 16

Implementing Security in CUCM

Cisco Unified Communications implementations and CUCM, like anything on the network, are subject to several threats, including eavesdropping, identity spoofing, and denial of service (DoS) attacks. CUCM can be secured against these threats by enabling authentication and encryption features that are based on the CUCM public key infrastructure (PKI).

This chapter explains how to enable the Cisco PKI and how to implement PKI-enabled cryptographic features.

Chapter Objectives

Upon completing this chapter, you will be able to configure a CUCM cluster for secure operation. You will be able to meet these objectives:

- Describe how to change CUCM clusters to mixed mode to support Cisco PKI-enabled security features

- Describe how Cisco IP Phones can obtain certificates from CAPF

- Describe and enable signed and encrypted configuration files

- Describe and enable secure signaling

- Describe and enable secure media transmission

- Describe and enable secure media transmission to H.323 and MGCP gateways

- Describe and enable secure conferencing

Enabling PKI-Based Security Features in CUCM

CUCM supports PKI-based authentication and encryption features, as illustrated in Figure 16-1.

Figure 16-1 *PKI-Based CUCM Security Features*

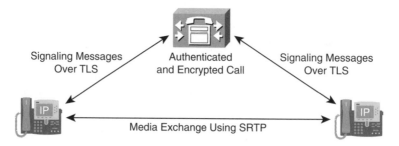

By using these features, you can secure the following communications:

- **Signaling messages between Cisco IP Phones and CUCM or secure Survivable Remote Site Telephony (SRST) gateways:** Cisco Unified IP Phone 7906, 7911, 794[0125], 796[0125], and 797[015] models can be configured to use Transport Layer Security (TLS) for authenticated and encrypted signaling when Skinny Client Control Protocol (SCCP) is used. Cisco Unified IP Phone 7906, 7911, 794[125], 796[125], and 797[015] models can be configured to use TLS for authenticated and encrypted signaling when session initiation protocol (SIP) is used. Secure SRST currently supports only SCCP phones.

- **Media exchange between IP Phones within a CUCM cluster or between CUCM clusters that are interconnected with an intercluster trunk:** Cisco Unified IP Phone 7906, 7911, 794[0125], 796[0125], and 797[015] models can be configured to use Secure Real-Time Transport Protocol (SRTP) for authenticated and encrypted media exchange if they support secure signaling. Secure media exchange is also possible between IP Phones that use secure signaling when they are registered to a secure SRST gateway during fallback. Secure media with SRTP prevents playback of captured audio frames.

NOTE CUCM-to-CUCM intracluster and intercluster communication is not encrypted. If two Cisco IP Phones are configured to use SRTP and are registered to different CUCM servers within the cluster or to CUCM servers in different clusters, there is a security risk, because the SRTP session keys need to be exchanged between the CUCM nodes (in cleartext). Therefore, if the communication paths between CUCM nodes within a cluster or the intercluster trunk between two clusters are not trusted, the recommendation is to use IPsec between the CUCM nodes.

■ **Media exchange between Cisco IP Phones and MGCP or H.323 gateways:** Cisco Unified IP Phone 7906, 7911, 794[0125], 796[0125], and 797[015] models and Cisco IOS MGCP gateways (running Cisco IOS Software Release 12.3(11)T2 or later) or Cisco IOS H.323 gateways (running Cisco IOS Software Release 12.4(6)T or later) can be configured to use SRTP for authenticated and encrypted media exchange if they support secure signaling.

> **NOTE** When SRTP with an MGCP or H.323 gateway is used, the SRTP session keys are exchanged in cleartext between CUCM and the MGCP or H.323 gateway. Therefore, if the communication path between CUCM and the MGCP or H.323 gateway is not trusted, the recommendation is to use IPsec between CUCM and the MGCP or H.323 gateway.

■ **Signaling messages between CUCM and secure conference bridges:** A secure conference bridge can use SCCP over TLS.

■ **Media exchange between Cisco IP Phones and secure conference bridges:** A secure conference bridge can exchange audio with conference members by using SRTP.

■ **Cisco IP Phone configuration file content:** The CUCM TFTP server supports signed and encrypted configuration files.

With the current release of CUCM, authenticated and encrypted calls are not possible in any situation other than those listed here. This includes calls that are connected to media resources other than secure conferences, including transcoders, Media Termination Points (MTP), and Music On Hold (MOH).

> **NOTE** Resource Reservation Protocol (RSVP) streams that use pass-through MTPs (such as when RSVP agents for RSVP-based call admission control [CAC]) are used) do support SRTP.

Configuration Procedure for PKI-Based CUCM Security Features

The following are the high-level configuration steps for enabling PKI-based security features in CUCM:

Step 1 Enable security services: The Cisco Certificate Trust List (CTL) Provider service and the Cisco Certificate Authority Proxy Function (CAPF) service must be enabled if locally significant certificates (LSC) are issued.

Step 2   Use the Cisco CTL client to activate security options: The cluster must be configured for mixed mode, and a signed CTL must be created.

Step 3   Configure devices for security: IP Phones must have certificates (either manufacturing installed certificates [MIC] or LSCs), IP Phones must be configured for a security mode (authenticated or encrypted), and the CAPF parameters must be set for deployment of LSCs. If configuration files should be encrypted for supported devices, the TFTP Encrypted Configuration parameter has to be enabled in enterprise parameter configuration.

Enabling Services Required for Security

Activate the required CUCM services for secure cluster operation from the CUCM Serviceability Service Activation window, as shown in Figure 16-2.

Figure 16-2   *Enabling Services Required for Security*

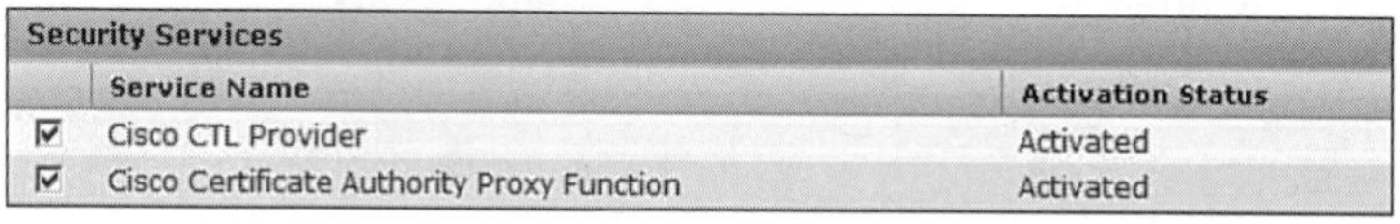

When security in a CUCM cluster is enabled, the following services must be activated:

■   **Cisco CTL Provider:** This service has to be activated on all CUCM servers and Cisco TFTP servers of the cluster.

■   **Cisco Certificate Authority Proxy Function:** This service has to be activated on the publisher server if LSCs are deployed.

Installing the Cisco CTL Client

The Cisco CTL client application is installed from the CUCM Administration Install Plugins window, as shown in Figure 16-3.

During installation, a prompt for the destination folder appears. You can set any directory, or you can accept the default.

The Cisco CTL client application can be installed on any PC running Microsoft Windows 2000 or later, as long as that PC has at least one Universal Serial Bus (USB) port.

Figure 16-3 *Installing the Cisco CTL Client*

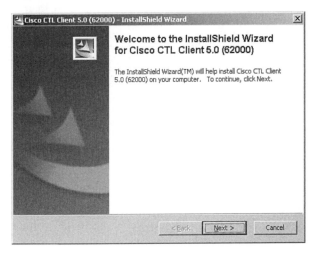

The Smart Card service has to be activated on the PC. To activate the Smart Card service under Microsoft Windows 2000, choose **Start > Settings > Control Panel > Administrative Tools > Services** to launch the Microsoft services administration tool. Then use the tool to verify the status of the Smart Card service. Set the startup type to **Automatic** and the current Status to **Running**.

Cisco CTL Client Usage

The Cisco CTL client is needed in the following situations:

■ For the initial activation of security in a cluster by setting the cluster security mode to mixed mode

■ For the deactivation or reactivation of security in a cluster

■ After modifying CUCM or Cisco TFTP server configuration, which includes adding, removing, renaming, or restoring a server or changing its IP address, hostname, or certificate

■ After adding or removing a security token

NOTE   Reasons to remove a security token include loss or theft of the security token.

■ After replacing or restoring a CUCM or Cisco TFTP server

In all the situations listed, the Cisco CTL client creates a new CTL and signs it by using a security token. The Cisco IP Phones load the new CTL and are then aware of the changes to the IP telephony system. Any changes that are not reflected in the CTL cause the Cisco IP Phones to treat the corresponding device as untrusted (for instance, if the IP address of a server is changed but a new CTL that uses the Cisco CTL client application was not created). From this perspective, the CTL can be seen as the certificate root store of a browser (listing all trusted certificate-issuing entities). If any device that was previously trusted is not trustworthy anymore (for instance, when a security token is lost), there is no need for a certificate revocation list (CRL). Instead, the Cisco CTL client is used to update the CRL by removing the untrusted entry (such as a lost security token) from the list.

Setting the Cluster Security Mode

When starting the Cisco CTL client for the first time, either the cluster security mode can be set, or the CTL file is updated. A CUCM cluster supports two security mode options:

- **Mixed mode:** This mode allows secure calls between two security-enabled devices and allows insecure calls between devices where at least one of the devices is not security-enabled.

- **Nonsecure mode:** This is the default configuration, in which all calls are insecure.

Figure 16-4 shows how to use the CTL client to enable mixed mode in a CUCM cluster.

Figure 16-4 *Setting the Cluster Security Mode*

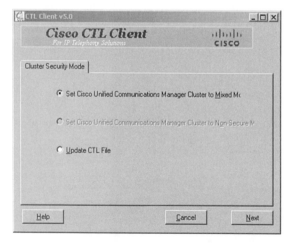

> **NOTE**   The third option, **Update CTL File**, lets you create a CTL before enabling mixed mode in the cluster for preloading IP Phones with CTLs or lets you modify CTL files, regardless of the cluster security mode.
>
> If no CTL file has been created and the cluster is set to mixed mode, creating the CTL file is an integrated part of the procedure to set the cluster security mode.

Updating the CTL

In addition to setting the cluster security mode, the Cisco CTL client is used to create or update the CTL file, along with a physical security token, as shown in Figure 16-5.

Figure 16-5   *Updating the CTL*

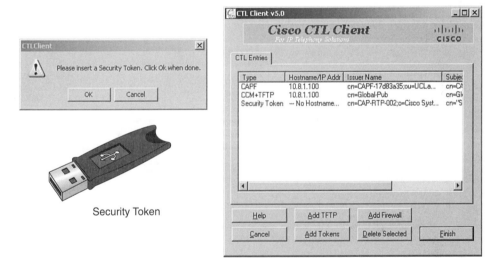

Security Token

This update is needed after you add or remove components, such as servers or security tokens. After you change the list of CTL entries, the new CTL needs to be signed using a security token, as shown in the figure.

CAPF Configuration and LSC Enrollment

Cisco Unified IP Phone 7940 and 7960 models do not have MICs, and they work only with LSCs. The Cisco Unified IP Phone 797[015], 796[125], 794[125], 7911, and 7906 models can use either MICs or LSCs. If an LSC is installed in such a Cisco IP Phone, the LSC has higher priority than the MIC.

CAPF is used to issue LSCs. CAPF can act as a certification authority (CA) itself, signing the LSCs, or it can act as a proxy to an external CA, having the external CA signing the LSCs.

> **NOTE**   CAPF cannot proxy to an external CA in CUCM Release 5.0 and 6.0. All versions of 4.x, Release 5.1, and later versions of the 5.x release train support proxying to external CAs.

CAPF Service Configuration Parameter

CAPF is configured in the CAPF Service Parameter Configuration window, as shown in Figure 16-6. In CUCM, choose **Cisco Unified Communications Administration > System > Service Parameter > Cisco Certificate Authority Proxy Function**.

Figure 16-6   *CAPF Service Configuration Parameter*

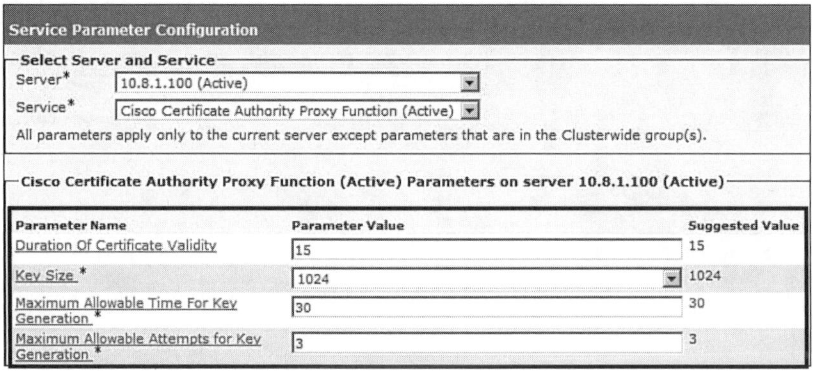

The certificate issuer—whether the CAPF itself or an external CA and IP address of the external CA—can be set if doing so is supported by the CUCM software release. Some default values, such as the Rivest, Shamir, and Adleman (RSA) key size, or the certificate lifetime, can also be modified.

CAPF Phone Configuration Options

Two main settings must be configured in the Phone Configuration window when you install or upgrade LSCs for Cisco IP Phones, as shown in Figure 16-7.

The first setting is Certificate Operation, which lets you manage LSCs. This setting is used to delete, install, or upgrade certificates.

The second setting is Authentication Mode, which specifies how the phone should authenticate to CAPF during enrollment.

Figure 16-7 *CAPF Phone Configuration Options*

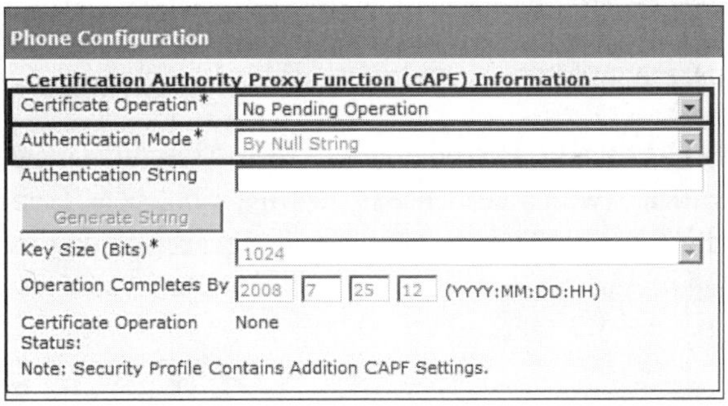

For the Certificate Operation setting, one of these four options can be configured:

■ **Install/Upgrade:** This operation lets you install an LSC if the IP Phone does not have one. It also lets you upgrade or replace an existing LSC if the IP Phone already has one.

■ **Delete:** This operation removes an LSC from a Cisco IP Phone.

■ **Troubleshoot:** This operation retrieves all existing IP Phone certificates from the IP Phone and stores them in CAPF trace files. MICs and LSCs have separate CAPF trace files. The CAPF trace files are located on the external computer where traces are configured in the Real-Time Monitoring Tool (RTMT) to be stored.

■ **No Pending Operation:** This is the default value. Change back to this value when you cancel a previously configured operation that has not yet been executed.

For the Authentication Mode setting, you can choose one of four options:

■ **By Authentication String:** This authentication mode is the default. It requires the Cisco IP Phone user to manually initiate the installation of an LSC. The user must authenticate to CUCM using the authentication string that has been set by the administrator in the Authentication String field. To enable the user to enter the correct authentication string, the administrator must communicate the configured authentication string to the user.

■ **By Null String:** This authentication mode disables Cisco IP Phone authentication for the download of IP Phone certificate enrollment. The IP Phone should be enrolled only over a trusted network when this setting is used. Because no user intervention is needed, the enrollment is done automatically when the Cisco IP Phone boots or is reset.

- **By Existing Certificate (Precedence to LSC):** This authentication mode uses an existing certificate (with precedence to the LSC if both a MIC and an LSC are present in the IP Phone) for IP Phone authentication. Because no user intervention is needed, the enrollment occurs automatically when the IP Phone boots or is reset.

- **By Existing Certificate (Precedence to MIC):** This authentication mode uses an existing certificate (with precedence to the MIC if both a MIC and an LSC are present in the IP Phone) for IP Phone authentication. Because no user intervention is needed, the enrollment occurs automatically when the IP Phone boots or is reset.

First-Time Installation of a Certificate with a Manually Entered Authentication String

For a first-time installation of a certificate with a manually entered authentication string, as shown in Figure 16-8, set the **Certificate Operation** field to **Install/Upgrade** and the **Authentication Mode** to **By Authentication String**.

Figure 16-8   *First-Time Installation of a Certificate with a Manually Entered Authentication String*

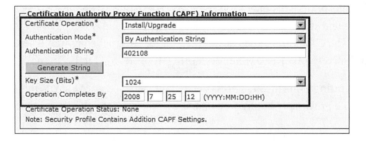

You can enter a string of four to ten digits. Or you can click **Generate String** to create an authentication string that then populates the Authentication String field. After the IP Phone reset, the IP Phone is ready for enrollment. However, enrollment is not automatically triggered; the user must initiate it from the Settings menu of the Cisco IP Phone.

> **NOTE**   The Settings menu can also be used to gain information about the IP telephony system or to remove the CTL. Usually, IP Phone users should not have access to such options. Therefore, access to the settings on the IP Phone is often restricted or disabled. LSC enrollment with authentication by authentication string is not possible if settings access is not fully enabled. If access to settings is restricted or disabled, it has to be enabled for the enrollment and then returned to its previous value.

A user or an administrator must enter the authentication string at the beginning of the enrollment procedure. If the process is successful, the certificate is issued to the IP Phone.

For example, on a Cisco Unified IP Phone 7940, the user would complete these steps:

Step 1   Press the **Settings** button to access the Settings menu.

Step 2   Scroll to the **Security Configuration** option and press the **Select** softkey to display the **Security Configuration** menu.

Step 3   Press ****#** to unlock the IP Phone configuration.

Step 4   Scroll to **LSC** and press the **Update** softkey to start the enrollment.

Step 5   Enter the authentication string and press the **Submit** softkey to authenticate the IP Phone to the CAPF when prompted to do so.

Step 6   The IP Phone generates its RSA keys and requests a certificate signed by the CAPF. When the signed certificate is installed, the message "Success" appears in the lower-left corner of the Cisco IP Phone display.

Certificate Upgrade Using an Existing MIC

Figure 16-9 shows an example of a certificate upgrade that uses an existing LSC.

Figure 16-9   *Certificate Upgrade Using an Existing MIC*

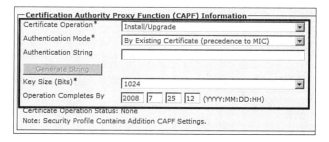

Upgrades may be required when, for example, an LSC will soon reach its expiration date. If a new LSC is issued shortly before the existing LSC expires, the existing LSC can still be used for the upgrade.

For this scenario, set the **Certificate Operation** to **Install/Upgrade** and the **Authentication Mode** to **By Existing Certificate (Precedence to LSC)**.

After reset, the IP Phone automatically contacts the CAPF for the download of the new certificate. The existing certificate is used to authenticate the new enrollment, and there is no need for a manually entered authentication string.

Generating a CAPF Report to Verify LSC Enrollment

CUCM lets you create CAPF reports in comma-separated values (CSV) file format, as shown in Figure 16-10.

Figure 16-10 *Generating a CAPF Report to Verify LSC Enrollment*

To generate a CAPF report, follow these steps:

Step 1   In CUCM Administration, choose **Device > Phone** to open the Find and List Phones window.

Step 2   In the Find and List Phones window, choose the **CAPF Report in File** option from the **Related Links** menu and click **Go**.

> **NOTE**   For you to see the CAPF Report in File option, phones must be listed in the Find and List Phones window. If no phones are listed, perform a search by clicking **Find** and choosing search criteria.

Step 3   CUCM generates the report file, and a file download dialog box opens. Click **Save** to save the report file to the PC's hard disk.

Step 4   Open the file from the hard disk. Figure 16-11 shows a CAPF report opened in Microsoft Excel.

Figure 16-11 *CAPF Report*

	A	B	C	D	E
1	Device Name	Device Desc	Partition	Directory Number	Security Profile
2	SEP002155531360	Phone 3-1		2203	Digest Authentication SIP Phone Security Profile
3	SEP002155531460	Phone 1-1		2204	Authenticated SCCP Profile auth by String
4	SEP002155531560	Phone 4-1		2205	Digest Authentication SIP Phone Security Profile
5	SEP002155531660	Phone 5-1		2206	Encrypted SCCP Profile auth by String
6	SEP002155531760	Phone 6-1		2207	Non Secure SCCP Profile auth by null String

	F	G	H	I	J
1	Security Mode	LSC Status	Owner	Authentication Mode	Authentication String
2	Non Secure	None		By Null String	
3	Authenticated	None		By Authentication String	
4	Non Secure	None		By Null String	
5	Encrypted	None		By Authentication String	1234
6	Non Secure	None		By Null String	

Finding Phones by Their LSC Status

Find IP Phones with security features from CUCM Administration by using the **Find and List Phones** window, as shown in Figure 16-12.

Figure 16-12 *Finding Phones by Their LSC Status*

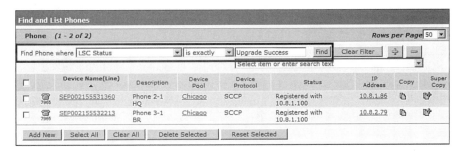

You can search for the following security-oriented criteria:

■ LSC status

■ Authentication string

■ Security profile

Signed and Encrypted Configuration Files

An IP Phone loading a new configuration verifies the configuration file before applying it. The IP Phone needs the public key of the TFTP server to do so. Because the public key of the TFTP server is different for every installation, it cannot be embedded in the firmware of the IP Phone. Therefore, phones require a CTL to use this feature.

The configuration files are signed by the Cisco TFTP server with its private key, as shown in Figure 16-13.

Figure 16-13 *Signed IP Phone Configuration Files*

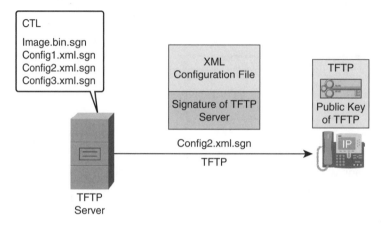

Signed IP Phone configuration files prevent tampering with the files on the TFTP server or in transit.

> **NOTE** When the cluster is enabled for security, phone configuration files are automatically signed for all IP Phones that have a certificate. Cisco Unified IP Phones 7940 and 7960 that run SIP receive signed configuration files. However, these phones do *not* verify the signature of the configuration file.

Encrypted Configuration Files

Encryption of phone configuration files is a CUCM feature that protects privileged information in the configuration file in transit from the CUCM TFTP server to the phone. The configuration file contains information that many organizations might deem sensitive, such as SIP digest authentication credentials, username and password, and the IP addresses for the CUCM, TFTP server, Domain Name System (DNS) server, and so on.

Encrypted configuration files are available on all Cisco PKI-enabled SIP phones, Cisco Unified IP Phone 7905 and Cisco Unified IP 7912 SIP phones, and the following SCCP phones: Cisco Unified IP Phone 797[015], 796[125], 794[125], 7931, 7911, and 7906 models.

> **NOTE** The Cisco Unified IP Phone 7931 model does not support SIP. Also, the 7905 and 7912 phones have reached end-of-sale status.

Obtaining Phone Encrypted Configuration Files

The manner in which phones obtain encrypted configuration files depends on whether the phone has a certificate.

First, the CUCM TFTP server uses a symmetric encryption algorithm to encrypt the configuration file.

If the receiving IP Phone has a certificate, the CUCM TFTP server encrypts the key that it used for the symmetric encryption of the configuration file content with the public key of the IP Phone. This asymmetrically encrypted key is appended to the configuration file that now contains both the symmetrically encrypted phone configuration and the asymmetrically encrypted key that was used to encrypt the phone configuration. The receiving phone uses its private key and decrypts the symmetrically encrypted key that was attached to the configuration file. Now the phone can decrypt its configuration, because it knows the symmetric key that was used for the encryption.

If the receiving IP Phone does not have a certificate, the CUCM TFTP server makes the symmetrically encrypted configuration file available for download. The receiving phone needs to know the key that was used for the encryption. Because it cannot be appended to the configuration file in a secure way (it cannot be asymmetrically encrypted because the phone does not have a certificate), the administrator must enter the key into the phone manually.

Cisco Unified IP Phone 7940 and 7960 models do not support the Cisco PKI in SIP mode, and Cisco Unified IP Phone 7905 and 7912 models do not support the Cisco PKI at all. All four models support encrypted configuration files only in SIP mode but not when they are being used with SCCP.

When these phones are used with SIP and enable encrypted configuration files, the phone configuration file encryption key must be manually entered into each phone.

The Cisco Unified IP Phone 7905 and 7912 models have a writable web server, so the phone configuration file encryption key that the CUCM TFTP server uses can be copied and pasted to the phone over a web interface.

The Cisco Unified IP Phone 7040 and 7960 models have a read-only web server, so using the web interface is not an option. The keys have to be entered manually using the phone keypad.

Configuring Encrypted Configuration Files

To encrypt phone configuration files, follow these steps:

Step 1 Verify that the cluster security mode is set to Secure.

Step 2 Create a new Phone Security Profile, and check the TFTP Encrypted Config check box.

Step 3 Apply the phone security profile to the phone(s). For phones that do not have certificates, set a symmetric configuration file encryption key in the Phone Configuration window.

Step 4 Enter the symmetric configuration file encryption key into phones that do not have certificates. Use the key that you configured in the Phone configuration window of the corresponding phone.

The encrypted phone configuration file uses the following format, depending on the phone model:

- Cisco Unified IP Phone 7905 and 7912 (SIP): LD*MAC*.x

- Cisco Unified IP Phone 7940 and 7960 (SIP): SIP*MAC*.cnf.enc.sgn

- Cisco Unified IP Phone 797[015], 796[125], 794[125], and 7911 (SIP): SIP*MAC*.cnf.xml.enc.sgn

- Cisco Unified IP Phone 797[015], 796[0125], 794[0125], 7931 (SCCP only), and 7911: SEP*MAC*.cnf.xml.enc.sgn

Phone Security Profiles

Phone security profiles are used to apply common security settings to one or more phones. To configure phone security profiles, choose **Cisco Unified CM Administration > System > Security Profile > Phone Security Profile**, as shown in Figure 16-14.

You can configure the following security features in a phone security profile:

- **Encrypted configuration files:** This feature can be enabled only in a phone security profile; it cannot be enabled individually in the Phone Configuration window.

- **Device Security Mode:** This feature (which is discussed later) can be enabled only in a phone security profile; it cannot be enabled individually in the Phone Configuration window.

- **CAPF Authentication Mode and CAPF Key Size:** These two settings can be configured in the phone security profile as well as in the Phone Configuration window. The setting of the phone configuration has higher priority.

> **NOTE** CAPF settings also can be configured directly in the IP Phone Configuration window.

Figure 16-14 *Phone Security Profiles*

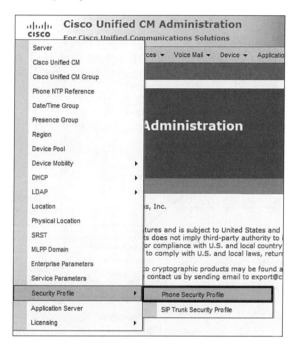

Default SCCP Phone Security Profiles

CUCM has a number of default phone security profiles with nonsecure configurations, as shown in Figure 16-15.

Figure 16-15 *Default Phone Security Profiles*

	Name ▲	Description	Copy
Find and List Phone Security Profiles			
☐	Analog Phone - Standard SCCP Non-Secure Profile	Analog Phone - Standard SCCP Non-Secure Profile	📋
	Cisco 12 S - Standard SCCP Non-Secure Profile	Cisco 12 S - Standard SCCP Non-Secure Profile	📋
	Cisco 12 SP - Standard SCCP Non-Secure Profile	Cisco 12 SP - Standard SCCP Non-Secure Profile	📋
	Cisco 12 SP PLUS - Standard SCCP Non-Secure Profile	Cisco 12 SP+ - Standard SCCP Non-Secure Profile	📋
	Cisco 30 SP PLUS - Standard SCCP Non-Secure Profile	Cisco 30 SP+ - Standard SCCP Non-Secure Profile	📋
	Cisco 30 VIP - Standard SCCP Non-Secure Profile	Cisco 30 VIP - Standard SCCP Non-Secure Profile	📋
	Cisco 3911 - Standard SIP Non-Secure Profile	Cisco 3911 - Standard SIP Non-Secure Profile	📋
	Cisco 3951 - Standard SIP Non-Secure Profile	Cisco 3951 - Standard SIP Non-Secure Profile	📋
	Cisco 7902 - Standard SCCP Non-Secure Profile	Cisco 7902 - Standard SCCP Non-Secure Profile	📋
	Cisco 7905 - Standard SCCP Non-Secure Profile	Cisco 7905 - Standard SCCP Non-Secure Profile	📋
	Cisco 7905 - Standard SIP Non-Secure Profile	Cisco 7905 - Standard SIP Non-Secure Profile	📋
	Cisco 7906 - Standard SCCP Non-Secure Profile	Cisco 7906 - Standard SCCP Non-Secure Profile	📋
	Cisco 7906 - Standard SIP Non-Secure Profile	Cisco 7906 - Standard SIP Non-Secure Profile	📋

The figure shows a list of default SCCP security phone profiles. One profile exists per phone model and supported protocol. Default security profiles have the name *Device - Standard Protocol: SIP or SCCP* Non-Secure Profile. These profiles cannot be modified or deleted. If nondefault settings are required, new security profiles must be created. You can create them from scratch or by copying and modifying a standard security profile.

Configuring TFTP Encrypted Configuration Files

To enable configuration file encryption for a phone, as shown in Figure 16-16, check the TFTP Encrypted Config check box in a phone security profile, and apply this phone security profile to the phone.

Figure 16-16 *Configuring TFTP Encrypted Configuration Files*

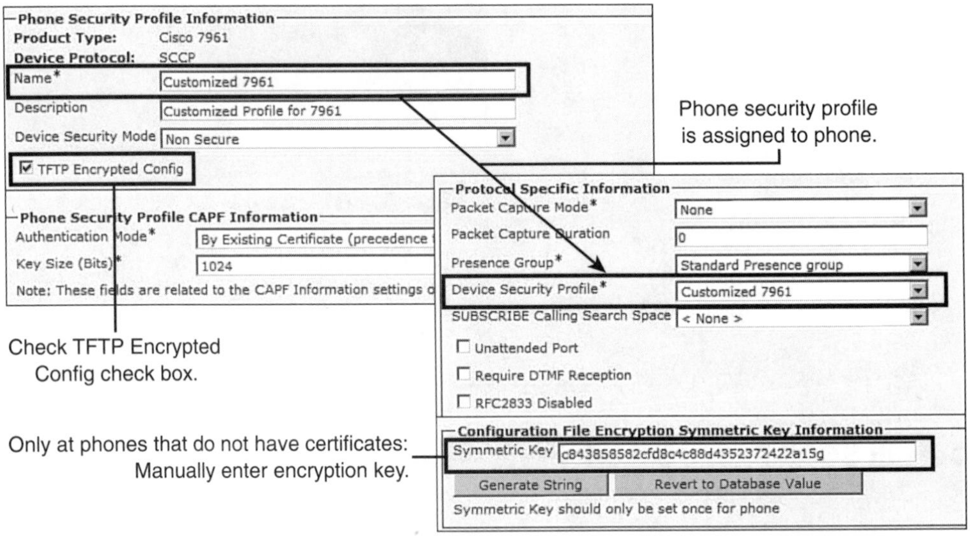

For phones that do not have a certificate (the Cisco Unified IP Phones 7905, 7912, 7940 [SIP], and 7960 [SIP]), a symmetric key, which is used to encrypt the configuration file, has to be entered as shown in the bottom right of Figure 16-16. On these IP Phones, the same key has to be manually entered into the phone.

Secure Signaling

Secure signaling in CUCM provides authentication and authorization of communicating devices of Cisco IP Phones and CUCM and authentication of the signaling messages exchanged between them. It can also provide encryption of the signaling messages.

Secure signaling is supported for SCCP and SIP phones. Only type B phones support encrypted signaling; type A phones are limited to authenticated signaling messages.

Figure 16-17 illustrates how secure signaling is implemented in CUCM when two Cisco IP Phones on the same cluster call each other.

Figure 16-17 *Secure Signaling Overview*

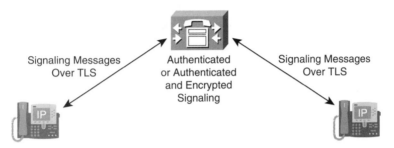

TLS is used to protect signaling messages by two-way certificate-based device authentication and Secure Hash Algorithm 1 (SHA-1) Hashed Message Authentication Code (HMAC) for packet authentication, and Advanced Encryption Standard (AES) for packet encryption.

To ensure the authenticity of encrypted packets in CUCM, packet encryption is supported only if it is combined with packet authentication.

> **NOTE**   It is a general rule in cryptography to always complement packet encryption with packet authentication. If encryption is used without authentication, the receiver of an encrypted packet has no guarantee that the packet comes from the expected source. If an attacker does not know the key that is to be used for the encryption, the attacker might not be able to send valid data but could send arbitrary data to keep the receiver busy decrypting the packets. Because decryption performed at the receiver can cause considerable processing overhead, an attacker could launch a DoS attack just by flooding a system with packets that the receiver will decrypt. In some situations, the attacker could even inject incorrect data into the application. This is possible when the sent data does not have any special format but when any bit patterns are considered to be valid data and are accepted by the receiver, such as encrypted digitized voice samples. The receiver can detect invalid data, such as in the transfer of an encrypted Microsoft Word file. In this case, after decrypting the received arbitrary data (or a valid file that has been encrypted with an incorrect key), the receiver would not recognize the file as a valid Word document.

Certificate Exchange in TLS

Figure 16-18 illustrates the certificate exchange that occurs at the beginning of a TLS session.

Figure 16-18 *Certificate Exchange in TLS*

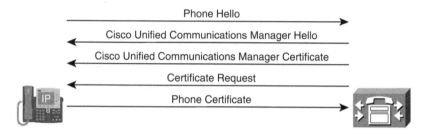

The CUCM server and the IP Phone first exchange certificates by using the following messages:

1. The IP Phone and the CUCM server negotiate the cryptographic algorithms in the IP Phone Hello and CUCM Hello messages.

2. The server sends its self-signed certificate to the IP Phone.

3. The server requests a certificate from the IP Phone.

4. The IP Phone sends its certificate to the server.

At this point, both the IP Phone and the server validate the certificates they just received over the network:

- The IP Phone simply looks up the certificate of the server in its local certificate store. The received certificate must be found locally because it must have been sent in the CTL. If it is not included in the CTL, the session is dropped. If it is found, the server's public key is extracted from the certificate.

- The server looks up the IP Phone in the local device database to see whether this IP Phone is known and authorized to connect via TLS. Then the certificate of the IP Phone is validated by using the locally available CAPF public key from the CAPF certificate. If the certificate is valid, the public key of the IP Phone is extracted from the IP Phone certificate.

Server-to-Phone Authentication

The next stage of the TLS "handshake," as shown in Figure 16-19, is when the IP Phone authenticates the server.

Figure 16-19 *Server-to-Phone Authentication*

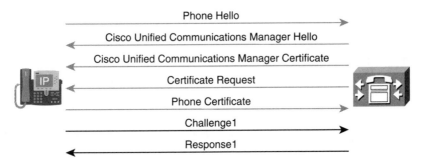

Here's a simplified version of the authentication steps shown in the figure:

1. The IP Phone generates a random challenge string and sends it to the server. This is a request for the server to sign the message with the server's private RSA key.

2. The server signs the message with its private RSA key and returns the result (response) to the IP Phone.

3. The IP Phone verifies the signature by using the server's public key.

Phone-to-Server Authentication

After the server has authenticated to the IP Phone, the IP Phone needs to authenticate to the server, as shown in Figure 16-20.

Figure 16-20 *Phone-to-Server Authentication*

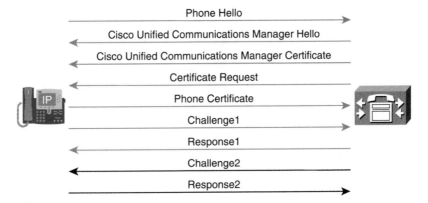

Here's a simplified version of the authentication steps shown in the figure:

1.   The server generates a random challenge string and sends it to the IP Phone. This is a request for the IP Phone to sign the message with the private RSA key of the IP Phone.

2.   The IP Phone signs the message with its private RSA key and returns the result (response) to the server.

3.   The server verifies the signature with the public key of the IP Phone.

NOTE   In the certificate of the IP Phone, the public key of the IP Phone is tied to the IP Phone's identity. Because CUCM identifies an IP Phone by MAC address and not by IP address or name, the phone's MAC address is used as the identifier in the certificate of the IP Phone.

TLS Session Key Exchange

Figure 16-21 shows the session key exchange that occurs after the bidirectional authentication.

Figure 16-21   *TLS Session Key Exchange*

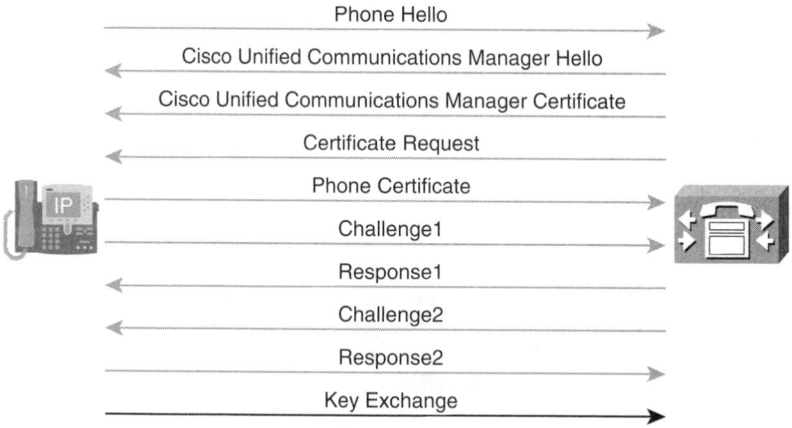

Session key exchange involves these steps:

1.   The IP Phone generates session keys for SHA-1 HMAC packet authentication and AES packet encryption.

2.   The IP Phone encrypts the message by using the server's public RSA key and sends the keys to the server.

3.   The server decrypts the message and thus also knows which keys to use to protect the TLS packets.

Secure Signaling Using TLS

The IP Phone and the server can now exchange SCCP or SIP signaling messages in a secure way by using TLS packet authentication and encryption, as shown in Figure 16-22.

Figure 16-22 *Authenticated Signaling Using TLS*

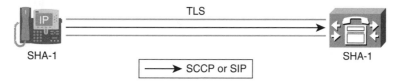

The authenticated and encrypted TLS session ensures the integrity and authenticity of each signaling message that is exchanged between the two devices.

NOTE   TLS encrypts SCCP or SIP signaling on Layers 5 through 7. The headers on Layers 2, 3, and 4 are not encrypted. This allows routers between the phone and CUCM to route the signaling packets without being involved in the encryption process.

Secure Media Transmission Between Cisco IP Phones

Cisco IP Phones can be configured to use secure media exchange in a CUCM deployment. As shown in Figure 16-23, SRTP is used to encrypt the Real-Time Transport Protocol (RTP) payload and to authenticate the complete RTP packet. The payload contains the actual digital content of the audio voice. By these means, SRTP provides integrity, authenticity, and confidentiality of the RTP packet so that the packets cannot be modified while they are in transit or listened to.

Figure 16-23 *Secure Media Exchange Overview*

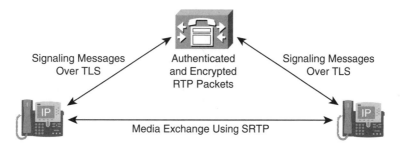

If an attacker modifies, removes, or adds SRTP packets, the receiver detects this manipulation because of the missing or incorrect authentication data. If an attacker captures SRTP packets for later or immediate playback, the encrypted payload ensures that the extracted voice stream will just be noise.

SRTP is standards-based (RFC 3711, *The Secure Real-Time Transport Protocol*) and is an application-layer encryption method that performs inside-payload encryption in which the protocol headers do not change. Because the headers in RTP and SRTP are the same, an attacker who sniffs the conversation does not know whether the RTP stream has been encrypted when examining the packet header only. Only further analysis of the sniffed packets and an attempt to play them back can let the attacker know whether the audio has been encrypted.

SRTP cannot be used for packet authentication alone. It supports authentication and encryption only.

SRTP Protection

As previously mentioned, media streams are encrypted by using SRTP. CUCM generates the SRTP session keys for media authentication and media encryption and sends them to the IP Phones inside signaling messages.

If signaling messages carrying SRTP session keys are not protected, an attacker could easily learn the SRTP keys just by sniffing the signaling messages. To ensure protection of the key distribution, CUCM requires authenticated *and encrypted* signaling to be used with SRTP. Therefore, SRTP cannot be used with IP Phones that are not configured or that do not support the use of authenticated and encrypted signaling.

As stated earlier, encrypted packets in CUCM always have to be signed to ensure the authenticity of the source and the content of the packets.

In fact, CUCM supports only two device security modes (except for the nonsecure device security mode):

■ **Authenticated:** This mode provides authenticated signaling only (TLS SHA-1).

■ **Encrypted:** This mode provides authenticated and encrypted signaling (TLS SHA-1 and TLS AES) and authenticated and encrypted media transfer (SRTP SHA-1 and SRTP AES).

SRTP Packet Format

As shown in Figure 16-24, the SRTP packet header is nearly identical to the RTP packet header.

Figure 16-24 *SRTP Packet Format*

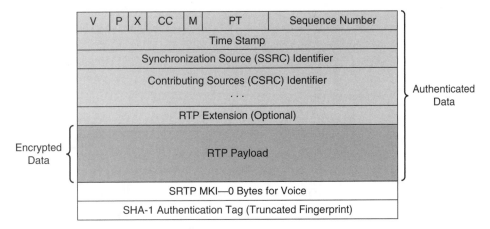

The RTP payload differs only in the sense that it is not cleartext voice but encrypted voice. In addition to the encrypted payload, a 32-bit SHA-1 authentication tag is added to the packet, which adds a few bytes to its size. The authentication tag holds the first 32 bits of the 160-bit SHA-1 hash digest that was computed from the RTP header and the encrypted voice payload ("truncated fingerprint").

As shown in the figure, the RTP packet header and the RTP payload of encrypted voice are authenticated. Therefore, RTP encryption is performed before RTP authentication.

NOTE The SRTP Master Key Index (MKI) shown in the figure is optional and is not used in secure IP telephony.

SRTP Encryption

Figure 16-25 illustrates the process of SRTP encryption.

Figure 16-25 *SRTP Encryption*

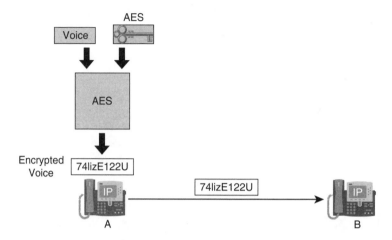

The sender encrypts the RTP payload by using the AES algorithm and the AES key that it received from CUCM when the call was set up. The receiver then uses the same AES key also received from CUCM to decrypt the RTP payload.

> **NOTE** If a packet capture of an SRTP audio stream is taken with a protocol analyzer such as Wireshark, the content can actually be saved as an .avi file and played back in an audio player such as Windows Media Player. However, the sound plays back as randomized white noise, completely unrecognizable.

SRTP Authentication

Figure 16-26 illustrates the process of SRTP authentication.

The sender hashes the RTP header and the RTP payload together with the SHA-1 key it received from CUCM when the call was set up. Then the first 32 bits of the hash digest are added to the RTP packet, and the packet is then sent to the receiver.

Finally, the receiver uses the same SHA-1 key, also received from CUCM, to verify the hash digest.

> **NOTE** Cisco IP telephony endpoints always encrypt and authenticate RTP packets. These two processes of encryption and authentication have been illustrated separately only for purposes of explanation.

Figure 16-26 *SRTP Authentication*

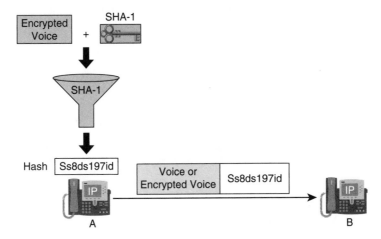

Secure Call Flow Summary

When encryption is enabled, the following sequence occurs when a call is placed between two IP Phones creating a secure call flow:

1. The IP Phones and CUCM exchange certificates.

2. The IP Phones and CUCM authenticate each other by requesting some random data to be signed. When this process is finished, CUCM and the IP Phones know that the other devices are authentic.

3. Each IP Phone creates TLS session keys. One key will be used for TLS SHA-1 authentication; the other key will be used for TLS AES encryption.

4. Each IP Phone encrypts the generated keys with the public key of CUCM and sends the encrypted keys to CUCM.

5. Each IP Phone now shares its session keys with CUCM. At this stage, each phone can exchange signaling messages with CUCM over an authenticated and encrypted TLS session.

6. When the call is established between the two SCCP IP Phones, CUCM creates SRTP session keys. One key is used for SRTP SHA-1 authentication, and the other key is used for SRTP AES encryption. Different keys are used for each direction. In the case of SIP phones, the phones generate session keys. However, they are again exchanged via CUCM because no direct signaling connection exists between the phones.

7. CUCM sends the generated SRTP session keys to both IP Phones over the secured TLS session.

The IP Phones now share the session keys for authenticating and encrypting their RTP packets. At this stage, the two IP Phones can start secure media exchange.

Configuring IP Phones to Use Secure Signaling and Media Exchange

To configure Cisco IP Phones to support authenticated or encrypted calls, in CUCM choose **Device > Phones** and select a phone, as shown in Figure 16-27.

Figure 16-27 *Configuring IP Phones to Use Secure Signaling and Media Exchange*

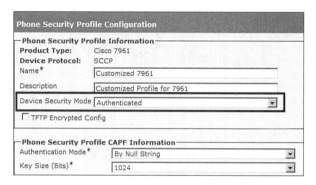

After CUCM is configured for mixed mode and the Cisco IP Phones have certificates, configure the IP Phones to support authenticated or encrypted calls. The device security mode is used to configure a Cisco IP Phone for one of three security modes:

■ **Non-secure:** The IP Phone does not support authenticated or encrypted calls.

■ **Authenticated:** The IP Phone supports authenticated calls.

■ **Encrypted:** The IP Phone supports encrypted calls.

The default device security mode is configured by using phone security profiles, as shown in the figure.

> **CAUTION**   In several situations, cryptographic services for Cisco IP Phones should not be used. With some Cisco Unified Contact Center applications, for instance, cleartext signaling messages or media packets have to be seen by other devices such as attached PCs. Another example is the use of Network Address Translation (NAT) or Port Address Translation (PAT). Because the translating device has to see cleartext signaling messages to be able to dynamically allow the negotiated UDP ports that will be used for RTP, encryption cannot be used.

The Actual Security Mode Depends on the Configuration of Both Phones

The actual security mode that is used for a call depends on the configuration of both IP Phones participating in the call, as shown in Table 16-1.

Table 16-1 *Actual Security Mode Depends on the Configuration of Both Phones*

		Phone 2		
		Non-secure	**Authenticated**	**Encrypted**
	Non-secure	Non-secure	Non-secure	Non-secure
Phone 1	**Authenticated**	Non-secure	Authenticated	Authenticated
	Encrypted	Non-secure	Authenticated	Encrypted

As shown in the table, these rules apply:

- If one device is set to Non-secure, an insecure call without authentication and without encryption is placed. This is the same level of nonsecurity in CUCM without PKI.

- If both devices are set to Encrypted, an encrypted call with both authentication and encryption is placed.

- In all other situations, if both IP Phones are set to Authenticated or if one is set to Authenticated and the other is set to Encrypted, an authenticated call with authentication only is placed.

NOTE If one phone is set to Authenticated and the other is set to Non-secure, the end-to-end call is not considered to be authenticated, because only one phone uses authenticated signaling to CUCM.

Secure Media Transmission to H.323 and MGCP Gateways

SRTP to H.323 gateways is supported by CUCM Release 5 and later and has the following characteristics:

- The H.323 devices generate encryption keys and send them to CUCM through the signaling path.

- This key exchange is not protected. The keys are sent in cleartext. Therefore, if the network between CUCM and the H.323 device is not trusted, IPsec should be used to encrypt H.323 signaling traffic.

SRTP support for H.323 gateways or trunks is not enabled by default. It must be enabled by checking the SRTP Allowed check box in the Device Configuration window in CUCM Administration. In the H.323 Gateway, this is performed in the H.225 Trunk (Gatekeeper Controlled) or Inter-Cluster Trunk (Gatekeeper Controlled) configuration window. If this option is not checked, CUCM uses RTP to communicate with the device. If the option is checked, CUCM allows secure and insecure calls to occur, depending on whether SRTP is configured at both endpoints.

H.323 SRTP CUCM

To implement SRTP support for an H.323 gateway in CUCM, select the **SRTP Allowed** check box, as shown in Figure 16-28. Choose **Device > Gateway** and select an existing H.323 gateway.

Figure 16-28 *H.323 SRTP CUCM Configuration*

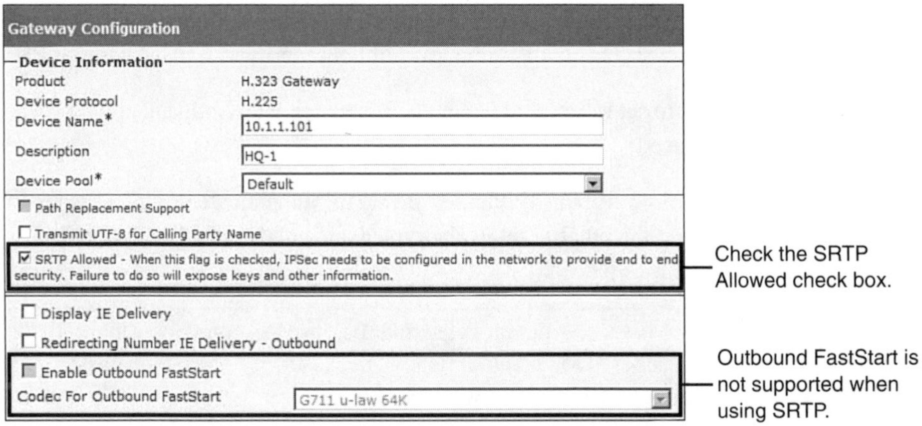

Note that if SRTP for an H.323 gateway is enabled, the outbound FastStart feature cannot be chosen and is dimmed, because these two features cannot be combined.

Example 16-1 shows how to implement SRTP support for a Cisco IOS H.323 gateway.

Example 16-1 *H.323 SRTP Gateway Configuration*

```
voice service voip
  srtp fallback
!
dial-peer voice 1 voip
  incoming called-number 9T
  no srtp
!
dial-peer voice 2 voip
```

Example 16-1 *H.323 SRTP Gateway Configuration (Continued)*

```
  incoming called-number 915125552001
  srtp
!
dial-peer voice 3 voip
  incoming called-number 91552.......
  srtp system
```

The example shows an H.323 gateway that is configured for SRTP with three dial peers:

- Dial peer 1 is not configured with the command **srtp**. The default is **no srtp**, which is shown in the configuration as an example. This means that calls that use this dial peer do not use SRTP.

- Dial peer 2 is configured with the **srtp** command. This means that calls that use this dial peer use SRTP. Because the fallback keyword is not specified, a fallback to non-secure calls is not permitted. In other words, the use of SRTP is mandatory for this dial peer.

- Dial peer 3 is configured with the **srtp system** command. This means that calls use the system setting for SRTP. The system setting (**no srtp**, **srtp**, or **srtp fallback**) is configured under **voice service voip**.

Cisco IOS Release 12.4(6)T or later is required for H.323 SRTP. SRTP can be used with any of the following modules:

- PVDM2

- AIM-VOICE-30

- AIM-ATM-VOICE-30

- NM-HDV2 (all types)

- NM-HDV (all types)

- NM-HD-1V/2V/2VE

When Digital Signal Processor (DSP) 549 or 5421-based modules are used, the following command is required to support SRTP:

```
  voice-card card-number
    codec complexity secure
```

SRTP to MGCP Gateways

SRTP to H.323 gateways is supported in CUCM Release 4 and later, and has the following characteristics:

- When SRTP to an MGCP gateway is used, CUCM generates the SRTP session keys and sends them to the MGCP gateway in signaling messages.

- This key exchange is not protected; the keys are sent in cleartext. Therefore, if the network between CUCM and the MGCP gateway is not trusted, IPsec should be used to encrypt MGCP signaling traffic.

To support SRTP to an MGCP gateway, the gateway has to support the SRTP MGCP package. The security capabilities of the gateway and the other device such as a Cisco IP Phone are exchanged in signaling messages. The security mode that is best supported by both devices is then automatically used. The result can be a nonsecure call, an authenticated call (if the device security mode of the IP Phone is set to authenticated), or an encrypted call if the gateway supports the SRTP package and the device security mode of the IP Phone is set to encrypted. No further configuration is required.

NOTE   If the gateway does not support the SRTP package and the device security mode of the IP Phone is set to authenticated or encrypted, only the signaling messages between the IP Phone and CUCM are authenticated (TLS SHA-1), and no SRTP is used. Nevertheless, the call is considered to be an authenticated call at the IP Phone. On the IP Phone, the shield symbol is displayed.

Secure Conferencing

Secure conferencing is a new feature introduced with CUCM 6.0. Secure conferencing requires a secure conference bridge media resource, which is provided by a Cisco IOS DSP farm. The secure conference media resource needs a certificate, which can be issued by any CA (including a Cisco IOS CA that runs on the same Cisco IOS router).

The secure conference bridge media resource registers with CUCM by using SCCP over TLS. CUCM PKI-based two-way certificate exchange is used for TLS device authentication. AES and SHA-1 are used for TLS packet authentication and encryption.

To verify the certificates exchanged in TLS, the following are required:

- CUCM systems have to recognize the certificate of the issuer of the certificate that is used by the secure conference media resource. In this way, the CUCM server that the secure conference bridge registers can verify the signature of the certificate presented by the secure conference bridge.

■ The Cisco IOS router that provides the secure conference media resource needs to recognize the certificate of all the CUCM systems with which the secure conference bridge can register. This information allows the Cisco IOS router to compare the certificate presented by the CUCM with which the secure conference bridge registers against the locally stored certificate.

Secure conferences are supported on the following Cisco Unified IP Phones:

■ 7940 and 7960 only when SCCP is used and only for authenticated conferences

■ 7906, 7911, and 7931, only when SCCP is used

■ 794[125], 796[125], and 797[015]

A secure conference can be authenticated (all members use authenticated signaling), thus ensuring that the member devices are authentic and not spoofed. Or a secure conference can be encrypted (all members use authenticated and encrypted signaling and SRTP), thus also providing confidentiality—not only for signaling, but also for the RTP streams.

Secure Conferencing Considerations

To successfully set up a secure conference, an IP Phone that invokes a conference must be allowed to allocate a secure conference by its media resource list configuration. This action, however, is no guarantee that the conference will be secure.

The conference starts at the corresponding security level only if a secure conference media resource is allocated for the conference and the device security mode of the IP Phone is authenticated or encrypted.

This security level changes as members join or drop out of the conference, and it always uses the maximum possible level that is supported by all conference members. The levels can be nonsecure, authenticated, or encrypted.

For Meet-Me conferences, a minimum level can be configured for secure conferences in the Meet-Me Conference Configuration window. Devices that do not support the configured minimum level do not gain access to the secure Meet-Me conference in this case.

The minimum Cisco IOS release that is required for secure conferencing is 12.4(11)XW1.

Secure Conferencing Configuration Procedure

The following steps are required to implement secure conferences:

Step 1   Obtain a certificate for the secure conference media resource from any CA.

Step 2   Configure a secure conference bridge media resource in Cisco IOS.

Step 3   Export the certificate that is used by CUCM (to be done on each server).

Step 4   Add the CUCM certificate or certificates to the Cisco IOS router.

Step 5   Export the certificate of the CA that issued the certificate to the secure conference media resource (see Step 1).

Step 6   Add the CA certificate to CUCM (to be done on each server).

Step 7   Add and configure the secure conference bridge in CUCM.

Step 8   Optionally, configure a minimum level for Meet-Me conferences, if desired (the default is nonsecure).

Unless all media resources should be available to all users, media resource groups and media resource group lists are implemented. When you are adding one or more secure conference media resources, media resource groups and media resource group lists have to be updated appropriately. If they are not updated, all phones support signaling over TLS and SRTP for media. If secure conference bridges and nonsecure conference bridges are available, media resource groups (MRG) and media resource group lists (MRGL) should be implemented in such a way that phones not supporting security should always prefer nonsecure conference media resources over secure conference media resources. This configuration prevents valuable secure conference media resources from being hooked up for insecure conferences that could also be provided by other (nonsecure) conference media resources.

NOTE   Media resource group and media resource group list configuration is covered in detail in *Implementing Cisco Unified Communications Manager, Part 1 (CIPT1)*.

TIP   It is extremely important to keep in mind that all devices that receive certificates must have correct date and time information. If they do not have the correct date and time, certificates might not be accepted if their validity period is out of the range of the receiving device. Running NTP in the network is strongly recommended when certificates are used.

Step 1: Obtain a Certificate for the Secure Conference Media Resource

The first step in implementing a secure conference bridge is to obtain a certificate for the secure conference media resource at the Cisco IOS router, as shown in Example 16-2.

Example 16-2 *Step 1: Obtain a Certificate for the Secure Conference Media Resource*

```
!
crypto pki trustpoint secure-cfb-tp
  enrollment url (URL of CA)
  serial-number none
  fqdn none
  ip-address none
  subject-name cn=HQ-1_Secure-CFB, ou=Pod-1, o=Lab
  revocation-check none
!
crypto pki authenticate secure-cfb-tp
crypto pki enroll secure-cfb-tp
```

Example 16-2 shows the Cisco IOS configuration that is required to obtain a certificate from a CA. After you enter the **crypto pki authenticate** command, the certificate of the CA specified in the enrollment URL is downloaded. The fingerprint of the received certificate is displayed and should be out-of-band verified. If correct, the certificate must be accepted to get stored in the router's NVRAM. After the CA's certificate has been downloaded, it can be requested from the CA. Enter the **crypto pki enroll** command to start the enrollment with the CA that is specified in the enrollment URL. After the certificate is received, you see a message that shows the fingerprint of the received certificate. This should be out-of-band verified.

The specified CA has to support Simple Certificate Enrollment Protocol (SCEP), which is used for the enrollment. Any CA can be used. Therefore, the required configuration steps at the CA vary. Example 16-3 shows the configuration of a Cisco IOS router that acts as a CA.

Example 16-3 *Cisco IOS Router Configuration Acting as a CA*

```
ip http server
crypto pki server ios-ca
  grant auto
  no shutdown
```

NOTE   The enrollment URL for a Cisco IOS CA is http://*IP of Cisco IOS router*:80.

The Cisco IOS CA can run on the same router that is configured with the secure conference media resource.

Step 2: Configure a Secure Conference Media Resource at the Cisco IOS Router

Example 16-4 shows the configuration of a secure conference media resource at the Cisco IOS router.

Example 16-4   *Step 2: Configure a Secure Conference Media Resource at the Cisco IOS Router*

```
!
voice-card 0
  dspfarm
  dsp services dspfarm
!
sccp local Loopback0
sccp ccm 10.1.1.1 identifier 1 version 6.0
sccp
!
sccp ccm group 1
  associate ccm 1 priority 1
  associate profile 1 register secure-cfb
!
dspfarm profile 1 conference security
  trustpoint secure-cfb-tp
  codec g711ulaw
  maximum sessions 2
  associate application SCCP
  no shutdown
```

This step differs from configuring a nonsecure conference bridge only in that you have to add the keyword **security** to the **dspfarm profile** command. You also must refer to the obtained certificate by specifying the corresponding name in the **trustpoint** command, which is entered under the **dspfarm profile** command.

The remaining configuration is identical to the configuration of a nonsecure conference media resource.

Step 3: Export the CUCM Certificate

To export the CUCM certificate, as shown in Figure 16-29, in CUCM Operating System Administration choose **Security > Certificate Management** and click **Find**.

From the list of certificates, download the Cisco CallManager certificate in .pem format by clicking the Cisco CallManager .pem link. A download window opens; save the certificate file on your PC.

> **NOTE**   This procedure must be performed for each Cisco Unified Communications server with which the secure conference bridge can register. These servers are specified in the **associate ccm** command under the **sccp ccm group** command. For each server, a different trustpoint name has to be used.

Figure 16-29 *Step 3: Export CUCM Certificate(s)*

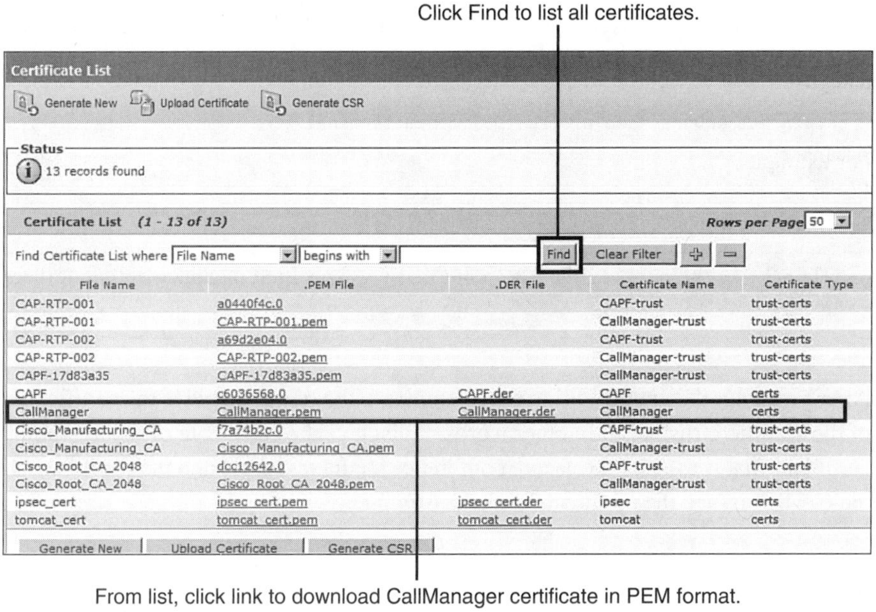

Click Find to list all certificates.

From list, click link to download CallManager certificate in PEM format.

Step 4: Add CUCM Certificates to a Cisco IOS Router

Next you add the previously exported certificate to the Cisco IOS router, as shown in Example 16-5.

Example 16-5 *Step 4: Add the CUCM Certificate(s) to a Cisco IOS Router*

```
!
crypto pki trustpoint CUCM1-1
  enrollment terminal
  revocation-check none
!
crypto pki authenticate CUCM1-1
```

At the Cisco IOS router where you set up the secure conference media resource, in global configuration mode, enter the commands shown in Figure 16-29. You are prompted to paste the certificate by using the CLI. You can do this by opening the previously downloaded file (see Step 3) in a text editor, copying its content, and then pasting it into the router.

> **NOTE** This procedure has to be performed for each Cisco Unified Communications server with which the secure conference bridge can register. These servers are specified in the **associate ccm** command under the **sccp ccm group** command. For each server, a different trustpoint name must be used.

Step 5: Export the CA Certificate

Next you export the certificate of the CA that issued the certificate to the secure conference media resource at the Cisco IOS router that will provide the conference media resource. Enter the following command in global configuration mode:

```
crypto pki export name-of-trustpoint pem terminal
```

For example:

```
crypto pki export secure-cfb-tp pem terminal
```

> **NOTE**   Enter the name of the trustpoint that was specified during enrollment (see Step 1).

After you enter the **crypto pki export** command, the router displays the certificate chain of the specified trustpoint. In other words, it displays the certificate of the trustpoint (the certificate that is used by the secure conference media resource) and the certificate chain of the CA that issued the certificate of the trustpoint.

The .pem-formatted certificate is displayed in text format (and therefore is unreadable). Select the text of the displayed certificate of the CA, and copy it into a text editor. Then save it as a file.

Step 6: Add the CA Certificate to CUCM(s)

In this step, you upload the previously exported CA certificate to the CUCM(s). As shown in Figure 16-30, in Cisco Unified Operating System Administration choose **Security > Certificate Management**.

In **Cisco Unified OS Administration**, choose **Security > Certificate Management** and click **Upload Certificate**.

Choose **CallManager-trust** for the Certificate Name to indicate that the certificate that will be uploaded is a certificate that the **Cisco CallManager** service should trust.

Click **Browse** and specify the location of the previously saved file that contains the certificate of the CA that issued the certificate to the secure conference media resource.

Click **Upload File** to upload the file to the CUCM server.

> **NOTE**   This procedure has to be performed for each Cisco Unified Communications server with which the secure conference bridge can register. These servers are specified in the **associate ccm** command under the **sccp ccm group** command. For each server, a different trustpoint name must be used.

Figure 16-30 *Step 6: Add the CA Certificate to CUCM(s)*

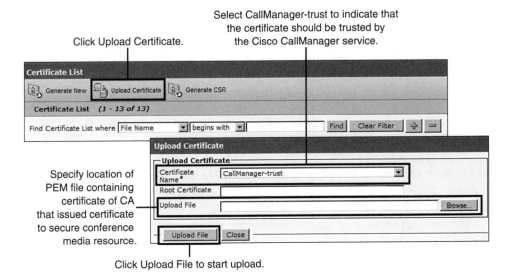

Click Upload Certificate.

Select CallManager-trust to indicate that the certificate should be trusted by the Cisco CallManager service.

Specify location of PEM file containing certificate of CA that issued certificate to secure conference media resource.

Click Upload File to start upload.

Step 7: Configure a Secure Conference in CUCM

To configure the secure conference media resource in CUCM Administration, as shown in Figure 16-31, choose **Media Resources > Conference Bridge** and click **Add New**.

Figure 16-31 *Step 7: Configure a Secure Conference in CUCM*

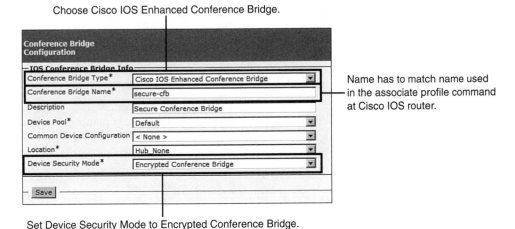

Choose Cisco IOS Enhanced Conference Bridge.

Name has to match name used in the associate profile command at Cisco IOS router.

Set Device Security Mode to Encrypted Conference Bridge.

Choose **Cisco IOS Enhanced Conference Bridge** for the **Conference Bridge Type**. Enter the name that was specified for the secure conference media resource at the Cisco IOS router in the **associate profile** command under the **sccp ccm group** command (see Step 2).

> **NOTE**   The Conference Bridge Name is case-sensitive.

Enter a description, and assign the appropriate device pool and location.

For the **Device Security Mode**, choose **Encrypted Conference Bridge** and click **Save**.

Step 8: Set the Minimum Security Level for Meet-Me Conferences

Figure 16-32 shows how to configure a minimum security level for Meet-Me conferences in CUCM Administration. Choose **Call Routing > Meet-Me Number/Pattern** and click **Add New**, or choose an existing Meet-Me.

Figure 16-32   *Step 8: Set the Minimum Security Level for Meet-Me Conferences*

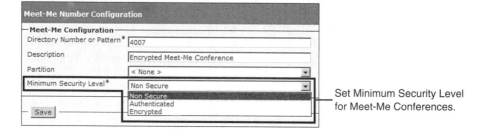

In the Meet-Me Number Configuration window, you set the minimum level that is enforced for the Meet-Me conference using the Minimum Security Level parameter. The three possible values are Non-Secure, Authenticated, and Encrypted.

> **NOTE**   Because the minimum security level is set for each Meet-Me number, you can configure Meet-Me numbers for each security level. Inform users which Meet-Me number they have to use to get a certain minimum security level.

Summary

The following key points were discussed in this chapter:

- The first steps in enabling security for a CUCM cluster are starting services and running the CTL client.

- LSC can be assigned to all IP Phones that support PKI-enabled security features.

- CUCM TFTP server automatically signs configuration files for IP Phones that have a CTL. CUCM can encrypt configuration files based on certificates or on manually entered keys.

- TLS is used for secure signaling between IP Phones and CUCM.

- SRTP is used for secure media exchange.

- Cisco IOS MGCP and H.323 gateways support SRTP for secure media exchange. Signaling is not protected and should be secured using IPsec.

- Cisco IOS conference media resources can be configured as secure conference bridges. The security level of the conference depends on the capabilities of its members.

References

For additional information, refer to these resources:

- Cisco Systems Inc., Cisco Unified Communications Solution Reference Network Design (SRND), based on CUCM Release 6.x, June 2007

- Cisco Systems Inc., *CUCM Administration Guide Release 6.0(1)*

- Cisco Systems Inc., *CUCM Security Guide Release 6.0(1)*

- Cisco Systems Inc., Media and Signaling Encryption (SRTP/TLS) on DSP Conferencing Farm

Review Questions

Use these questions to review what you've learned in this chapter. The answers appear in Appendix A, "Answers to Chapter Review Questions."

1. Which of the following is the most accurate list of tasks required to configure a CUCM cluster for security?

   a. Enable services, set the cluster to mixed mode, create a signed CTL, and deploy certificates to the IP Phones.

   b. Enable services, set the cluster to secure-only mode, create a signed CTL, and deploy certificates to the IP Phones.

   c. Enable extended services, set the cluster to authenticated or encrypted mode, create a signed CTL, and deploy certificates to the IP Phones.

   d. Enable services, set the cluster to secure mode, create a signed CTL, deploy certificates to the IP Phones, and set the device security mode.

   e. Run the auto-secure feature.

2. Which two statements about LSCs are true?

   a. On a Cisco IP Phone 7970, an LSC has priority over a MIC.

   b. On a Cisco IP Phone 7960, a MIC has priority over an LSC.

   c. The CAPF certificate operation can be set to Install/Upgrade, Delete, or Troubleshoot.

   d. The CAPF certificate operation can be set to Install, Upgrade, or Delete.

   e. CAPF authentication can be configured to be done by authentication string, null string, or existing certificates.

3. Which task is not required to get an encrypted configuration file into a phone?

   a. Set the cluster security mode to secure.

   b. Manually enter a key into the phone if the phone does not have a certificate.

   c. Manually enter a key for the phone at the phone configuration page of CUCM if the phone does not have a certificate.

   d. Activate configuration file encryption in the phone's security profile.

   e. Set the TFTP Encrypted Configuration enterprise parameter to True.

4. What are the two options for secure signaling between Cisco IP Phones and CUCM?

   a. Signaling over authenticated TLS

   b. Signaling over encrypted TLS

   c. Signaling over authenticated and encrypted TLS

   d. Signaling over encrypted IPsec

   e. Signaling over authenticated and encrypted IPsec

5. During an encrypted call between two IP Phones, which two of the following do not happen?

   a. Mutual certificate exchange between CUCM and each IP Phone

   b. Mutual certificate exchange between the IP Phones

   c. SRTP packet authentication and encryption

   d. Encrypted transmission of SRTP session keys between the IP Phones

   e. TLS packet authentication and encryption

   f. Encrypted transmission of TLS session keys between CUCM and the IP Phones

6. Which statement about H.323 and MGCP gateways is true?

    a. SIP gateways support TLS and SRTP.

    b. Key exchange between CUCM and H.323 and MGCP gateways is secure.

    c. H.323 gateways support only TLS, not SRTP.

    d. Even when using SRTP, signaling messages between CUCM and MGCP and H.323 gateways are sent in cleartext.

7. Which two events happen to an encrypted conference when a phone attempts to join the conference, which is configured for authentication only?

    a. If it is an ad hoc conference, the phone can join, and the conference turns into an authenticated conference.

    b. If it is a Meet-Me conference, the phone can join if the minimum security level of the conference is not set to encrypted.

    c. The phone cannot join the conference.

    d. If it is an ad hoc conference, the phone can join if the minimum security level of the conference is not set to encrypted.

    e. The phone can join the conference.

8. When enabling the Cisco CTL Client, which is a valid option for client security?

    a. Enabling secure mode, ensuring that every call is required to be secure in a cluster

    b. Enabling secure mode, ensuring that every call is secure in the cluster and that nonsecure calls will not be allowed

    c. Enabling mixed mode, allowing secure calls in a cluster if both clients support security or allowing calls nonsecurely if one of the clients is not secure

    d. Enabling secure mode between all calls in all CUCM clusters in an enterprise

9. Which two signaling protocols are supported between CUCM v6 and Cisco IP Phones for secure signaling?

    a. MGCP

    b. H.323

    c. SIP

    d. SCCP

10. Which statement most accurately describes media encryption between two secure Cisco IP Phones in a CUCM v6 cluster?

    a. The entire RTP audio frame is encrypted.

    b. The entire SRTP audio frame is encrypted.

    c. The RTP payload in the audio frame is encrypted.

    d. The RTP payload and the RTP header in the audio frame are encrypted.

11. If one IP Phone set to Non-secure calls another IP Phone set to Encrypted in a CUCM cluster, what is the resulting security?

    a. The call is not permitted.

    b. The call defaults to the more secure setting and is encrypted.

    c. The call goes through but is nonsecure.

    d. The call is permitted to route through the PSTN, which is nonsecure.

Answers to Chapter Review Questions

Chapter 1

1. D
2. C
3. C
4. E
5. A, C
6. B
7. A
8. C
9. C

Chapter 2

1. D
2. B, C
3. B, C
4. D, E
5. A
6. A
7. B, C
8. C
9. C

Chapter 3
1. B
2. C, D
3. B
4. C
5. B
6. B, C
7. A
8. C
9. C

Chapter 4
1. C
2. A
3. D, E
4. A, C
5. B
6. C
7. B
8. C

Chapter 5
1. C
2. B, C
3. C, D
4. D
5. C, D
6. B
7. B
8. A

Chapter 6

1. B

2. B

3. D

4. D

5. A

6. D

7. C

8. B

9. D

10. D

Chapter 7

1. B, C

2. A, B

3. B, C

4. A

5. D

6. D

7. C

8. B

Chapter 8

1. D
2. A
3. B
4. C
5. D
6. B
7. B
8. B
9. B
10. B, C

Chapter 9

1. B
2. A
3. C
4. B, E
5. A
6. A
7. B
8. C
9. B
10. B
11. A
12. C
13. B

Chapter 10

1. A, C
2. D
3. A
4. C
5. B, C
6. C
7. B
8. C
9. B

Chapter 11

1. B
2. A, C
3. C
4. B
5. A, D
6. C
7. B
8. B
9. A, C, D

Chapter 12

1. A
2. C, D
3. A, D, E
4. A, D
5. A, B
6. A
7. D
8. B
9. C

Chapter 13

1. B, D
2. C
3. D
4. F
5. A, C
6. C
7. B, C

Chapter 14

1. E, F
2. D, F
3. A
4. F
5. D
6. E
7. D

Chapter 15

1. C, E
2. C
3. D
4. A
5. C
6. C
7. A

Chapter 16

1. D

2. A, C

3. E

4. A, C

5. B, D

6. D

7. A, B

8. C

9. C, D

10. C

11. C

Index

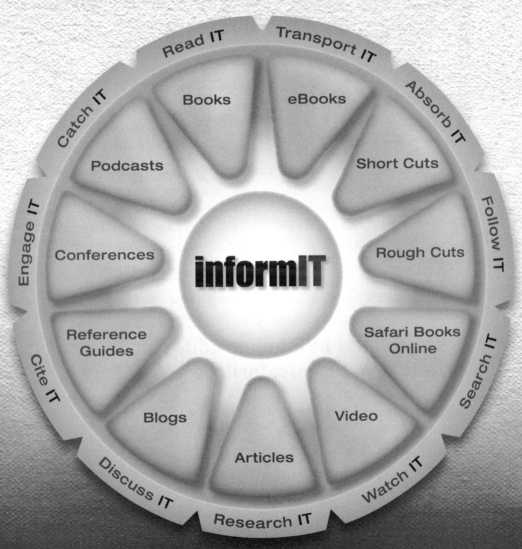

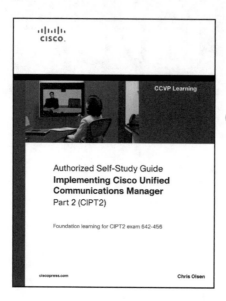

FREE Online Edition

Your purchase of **Implementing Cisco Unified Communications Manager** includes access to a free online edition for 45 days through the Safari Books Online subscription service. Nearly every Cisco Press book is available online through Safari Books Online, along with over 5,000 other technical books and videos from publishers such as Addison-Wesley Professional, Exam Cram, IBM Press, O'Reilly, Prentice Hall, Que, and Sams.

SAFARI BOOKS ONLINE allows you to search for a specific answer, cut and paste code, download chapters, and stay current with emerging technologies.

Activate your FREE Online Edition at www.informit.com/safarifree

> **STEP 1:** Enter the coupon code: TVZRYCB.

> **STEP 2:** New Safari users, complete the brief registration form.
> Safari subscribers, just login.

If you have difficulty registering on Safari or accessing the online edition, please e-mail customer-service@safaribooksonline.com